# Beyond the Tragic Vision

*The Quest for Identity*

# Beyond
# the Tragic Vision

*in the Nineteenth Century*

*by* Morse Peckham

GEORGE BRAZILLER · NEW YORK · 1962

*To the memory of my parents*

*"...rejoice in the midst of tragedy."*

W. B. YEATS

# Contents

INTRODUCTION: *The Problems of the Historian*    11

*PART ONE* / THE END OF ANCIENT
                 THINKING    33

    I   *Orientation and Culture*    35
   I I   *Paradise and Eternity*    46
  I I I   *Enlightenment*    61

*PART TWO* / THE ALIENATED VISION    85

  I V   *The Discovery of the Self*    87
         GOETHE—KANT
    V   *Explorers: 1.*    100
         BYRON—STENDHAL
  V I   *Explorers: 2.*    112
         WORDSWORTH—GOETHE
  V I I   *Explorers: 3.*    129
         FRIEDRICH—CONSTABLE
V I I I   *Explorers: 4.*    146
         SCHOPENHAUER—BEETHOVEN

*PART THREE* / THE HEROIC REDEEMER   161

  I X   *The World without Value*    163
         BEETHOVEN—KANT—HEGEL—SCHOPENHAUER
    X   *Transcendental Authority*    177
         CARLYLE—BALZAC—SCOTT

x i *The Transcendental Ear* 196
TENNYSON—BALZAC—BERLIOZ—SCHUMANN
—HOFFMANN

x i i *The Transcendental Eye* 215
BAUDELAIRE—DELACROIX—TURNER

PART FOUR / ILLUSION AND REALITY 227

x i i i *Transcendentalism in Difficulty* 229
DISRAELI—CARLYLE—BALZAC

x i v *The Hero Frustrated* 240
*1. Wagner's Dramas* 244
*2. Wagner's Music* 263

x v *Self and Object* 271
RUSKIN—BROWNING—FLAUBERT—BAUDELAIRE—
HANSLICK—BRUCKNER

x v i *The Crisis of Style* 285
SCHUMANN—FLAUBERT—RUSKIN—BROWNING
—BAUDELAIRE—TENNYSON—ZOLA—DARWIN—
COURBET—MANET

PART FIVE / STYLE AND VALUE 305

x v i i *Identity and Personality* 307
WAGNER—SWINBURNE—WILDE—MOREAU

x v i i i *Identity and Style* 326
BRAHMS—MALLARMÉ

x i x *Style and Freedom* 343
SEURAT—CÉZANNE—GAUGUIN—DEBUSSY

x x *Beyond Tragedy* 364
NIETZSCHE

INDEX 373

# Introduction

# The Problem
# of the Historian

"**D**ESCENT INTO HELL." Thus Thomas Mann names the prelude to his great tetralogy, his summation of the nineteenth-century vision, *Joseph and His Brothers;* and he begins in his legendary, ironic tone, "Very deep is the well of the past. Should we not call it bottomless? Bottomless indeed, if—and perhaps only if—the past we mean is the past merely of the life of mankind, that riddling essence of which our own normally unsatisfied and quite abnormally wretched existences form a part; whose mystery, of course, includes our own and is the alpha and omega of all our questions, lending burning immediacy to all we say, and significance to all our striving. For the deeper we sound, the further down into the lower world of the past we probe and press, the more do we find that the earliest foundations of humanity, its history and culture, reveal themselves unfathomable. No matter to what hazardous lengths we let our line . . ."

And he continues to tell us how the past opens out, offers us no answers, always suggests beyond each beginning a further beginning, farther back, deeper down, endlessly, so that whenever we begin we begin arbitrarily, whether now or at some distant time. From whatever point we choose, there always stretches backward into the bitterness, the waste, the appalling desert of the past, a desire of the mind to plunge into the vacuum of the unknown, where time shifts, and twists, and condenses, and expands, and our vision of history becomes more abstract, and thinner, and fades; where each event is separated by a thousand years, or ten, or a hundred thousand, and we scarcely can tell the one period of time from another, nor can we maintain our concern, for the mind is disoriented into mysterious depths.

But we, in this book, are engaged in a cozier exploration. Less than two hundred years ago is our beginning point, and its place is not the mysterious hither Orient, now a desert but once a paradise of green grassy plains and forested hills, not the strange evocative name of Arabia over which are scattered innumerable ruins of ancient cities. No, the place of our beginning is Europe, in the sunny eighteenth century of our own resplendent Revolution when Williamsburg was not restored but alive and busy and illuminated by the radiant mind, clear, clean, and enlightened, of Thomas Jefferson. A sunny world, for it sometimes seems that in 1800 it started to rain, and rained for a century and more. Surely if we begin so recently and move toward the present up to 1914, when the rain turned into snow and the skies into lead, surely we will encounter no distortions of the mind such as Thomas Mann had to feel when he plunged back beyond Joseph toward the mysterious legend of Eden?

"Very deep is the well of the past." It is a tricky metaphor, for in Mann's hands the well changes into the abyss of the sea, and the line with which he plumbs changes into a ship, feeling its way along an unknown coast. Even in Mann's hands the metaphor becomes slippery and deceiving. The reason is that the past is not a well, nor any of these other things. The past does not exist at all. We cannot start at some arbitrary point in the past—neither at the birth of Joseph nor at the Versailles of Benjamin Franklin —and work forward and backward as we choose. We can only start at this moment, when I write and you read, and as we read and write the moment slips inexorably away, neither backward nor forward, nor up nor down, nor sideways; the present does not slide back into the past; it simply disappears.

I write this page; it is late at night; I go to bed, confidently predicting that when I return to my study tomorrow morning the page will still be here in the typewriter, waiting for me. By the analogies built into my memory, into the circuits of my brain cells, I know now that tomorrow I can, if I wish, resume; for the study and the paper and the typewriter will be here. I know this about the future. What do I know about the past? Nothing—only I know that tomorrow morning I must assume, on the evidence of the typewritten document before me, that there was a past. Every morning, unconsciously and consciously I create myself a past, and every morning, indeed every second, or that fraction of a second which is the span of mental activity, I recreate the past. And it is always different.

If your past and mine is thus always changing, always shifting, impermanent, evanescent, inaccessible, what shall we say of the past which Clio, the Muse of History, that benign and instructive goddess, reveals to us. Charming, smiling, and armed today in the flashing steel of science, she comes to us, a dear teacher who tells us in her entrancing accents All About What Really Happened. Is it unkind to ask of so delicious a goddess, "What is your authority? How do you know? Why should we believe you?" Unkind or not, it is dangerous; upon such questions she disappears, leaving neither a ghost of a rainbow nor a faint smell of gunpowder, leaving only the paper in the typewriter, leaving only the document, the artifact, the ruined city and the inscribed tablet, and behind them, the plains and the mountains, which, if we lived at a faster rate and longer, would melt together and vanish.

Looked at down such a skeptical and melancholy perspective, the historian seems a man compounded of deceit, whom nobody in his right mind would trust for a moment. And if we look at his works, if we arrange, say, the histories of the French Revolution in the order of time which the dates on their title pages appear to justify, we find not one French Revolution but a hundred. If we accuse the historian of being untrustworthy, of not telling us the truth, he is not, oddly enough, distressed or hurt. "The truth? Of course not. As everyone knows, truth is the province of the scientists. I am an artist. The scientist predicts, and by predicting successfully he verifies his statements; he shows to all the world that he is right. To be sure, I too use scientific methods. And consequently when I tell you something happened, you can be sure that my statement is true. Only, since it happened in the past, I cannot verify it as the scientist does. My trustworthiness lies in my methods, which are as sound as sound can be, and as scientific as the physicist's methods. My reliability rises from my methods, not my results. Because my methods are dependable, you can believe in what I tell you. This is what happened, and it happened this way. The scientist can demonstrate by exploding a bomb. I can't. That's all the difference there is, and it is quite trifling. There's really nothing to worry about, and no occasion for melancholy and skepticism. I am an artist *and* a scientist." Is this satisfying? And if not, where is the trickery? And if there is trickery, where is the truth about the past?

The difficulty seems clear enough. Either the historian ranges himself beside the scientist, and carries out the complete scientific process, whatever it is, or he ranges himself beside the artist and has the artist's latitude and license, and objectives. To be sure, the artist and the scientist, when they are not quite certain of what they are doing, will, to relieve their anxieties, claim the prestige of each other. The artist, jealous of the scientist's immense value in the public eye and fearful, especially in the United States, that his own work is underestimated, will claim that his art is really a science, and that in fact he is doing what the scientist is clumsily fumbling to do, only better. The public is aware of this; and, faced with extreme forms of modern art, will sometimes demand that the artist subject his work to scientific test and tell us in his painting what the world is really like.

But is the public aware of how often the scientist, equally unsure, equally uncertain of his own value, equally ridden with anxiety, and jealous of how the public pursues the artist, will make a counterclaim, will insist that he is really the artist, that he more than the artist exhibits the glories of the imaginative and creative temperament and genius?

In this situation the fortunate historian plays off one role against the other and claims the virtues and prestige of both contestants. But we, who wish to do the impossible, to understand and penetrate the vanished and inaccessible past, cannot allow him thus so lightly to escape us. Yet if we wish to trap him we must have a clearer understanding of what the scientist and the artist are up to. If we can clearly separate these two functions of the human mind, we can back the historian into one stall or another.

In any situation in which our senses give our minds messages about the world, two elements are present. On the one hand is the real world, the public world, which we all agree is there: the mountain, the tree, the table, the contents of the test tube, the pointer on the measuring scale. On the other is the pattern in the mind, the Gestalt, the neural path, the orientation, with which we organize these public data. This orientation (for this is the most general and least demanding word we can use, and therefore I shall use it throughout this book) is made up of a thousand elements, about which we know not very much; except that we are sure that even for the scientist there are not only neural patterns and systems of interrelations among the brain cells, but at another level emotions, feelings, childhood traumas, anxieties, and traces of former gratifications and frustrations.

On the one hand we wish to find our way about the public world where we encounter real objects and other people. We wish to be able to predict what is going to happen next, so that we may be prepared to deal with it, to manipulate it for our benefit, to maintain ourselves as on-going organic processes. From the proto-man who gave greater weight and force to his hand and arm and body by closing his fingers around a stone, to the astronomer who sends messages to the stars by delicately manipulating inconceivably elaborate electronic equipment, the human mind has been engaged for eons in improving its predictions, in refining its predictive behavior. But side by side with this activity the artistic effort has been at work. From the early man who carved his image of the generous and fertile woman, with great breasts and enormous thighs, ready to receive him like a graciously enveloping cloud and equally prepared to produce his children, to the painter of today who throws paint at a canvas, and dribbles paint on it, and walks on it, and exploits accidental relationships to symbolize his most subtle and rationally inaccessible feelings and desires—the artist has been engaged in realizing in words, in stone, in buildings, in music, in dances, those attitudes, Gestalten, orientations, which organize his world by selecting, from the blizzard of sensory data in which he gaspingly manages to survive, information which he can use.

Man as scientist uses his orientations to explore the public world and predict its behavior. Man as artist uses the sensory data from the public world to disengage his orientations from his whole complex and unanalyzable personality, to symbolize what cannot be talked about. And man as philosopher, in his queasy way, forever strives to distinguish between the two activities, to separate what, in the act of perception, is inseparable—the data perceived and the pattern in the mind which controls the perceiving.

With these notions, perhaps we have a net to catch the historian, who, we are determined, shall no longer elude us. He is concerned, he tells us, with events of the past; but since the past is inaccessible, what reliance can we place on his statements? "Does anyone doubt," he counters, "that Booth shot Lincoln, and when and where this unfortunate event happened?" We find it hard to say that we do doubt it. Yet somehow our consent makes us uneasy. The reason is that he cannot predict that Booth will shoot Lincoln, or that, affirming a law of regular recurrence, some patriot or madman will shoot our next president. It is nervewracking to be in a state of neither doubting nor assenting. Consequently we find it hard to stop him when he proceeds from this one fact to others, and from them creates a pattern of meaning in history, of the inevitability of the struggle of North and South, or of tyranny and freedom—though whether Booth or

Lincoln was being tyrannical depends on one's orientation—or of economic determinism, or of the nature of the conflicts within the culture of the American past. But since he is proceeding on the basis of real though inaccessible events, surely the patterns he discovers have the same reliability as those events which together go to form the patterns. It is a matter of personal taste as to whether he wishes to concentrate on the unique event (and how does one separate from the blizzard of data a unique event?) or, like Arnold Toynbee, to concentrate on the patterns he discerns, which in Toynbee's case most gratifyingly confirm what his own persuasion, the Anglican Church, has already told us. Events and patterns are equally reliable and equally unreliable. The poor philosopher, trying to distinguish between the two, is baffled; the orientation and the data melt together; and the historian, with mocking sympathy, once again eludes us. He is neither artist nor scientist, but somehow or other, both.

Is history bunk, after all? Such a notion we cannot accept, for if public history is bunk, so is our own private history; and if we try to live as if nothing had ever happened before this present moment of consciousness, and if at every such moment we should attempt to do so and succeed, our world would collapse and we should be unable to function. Perhaps amoebae can live in such a way, though it is doubtful, but we human beings cannot. Somehow or other we must have some kind of knowledge about the prior existence and behavior of the things and beings we find around us; we cannot let the historian claim to be an artist. The artist tells us, in his symbols, about those patterns with which we organize the real world and which we can never know but only experience; but we need to know, we must know, about the past, to survive; and somehow or other we must force the historian to classify himself with the scientist. And, indeed, by understanding a little better what the scientist does, we can succeed.

We begin by considering the statement, "A flow of water striking the paddles of a mill wheel causes the mill wheel to revolve." If this sentence means something, we ought to be able to translate it into predictive terms; and indeed, it gives us no trouble. "If I divert the flow of water so that it does not strike the paddles, the mill wheel will cease to revolve." If I do these things, and if the wheel acts as I predict, I have begun with a reliable sentence. Now in the second form of the sentence, a very puzzling word has disappeared. The new sentence works perfectly well by giving us directions what to do, but it omits the word "causes." It is convenient that we can get along, at least in this situation, without this word, for "cause" has been the occasion of more trouble than almost any word in the language. If, instead of translating the sentence as I did, I said, "What makes the mill wheel revolve is a cause," or still worse, "What makes the wheel revolve is the law of cause and effect," I would be in very grave trouble indeed. For I should get farther and farther away from the real world, which the original sentence was designed to manipulate, and into the labyrinths of language and eventually of the mind from which I should never get out.

At least, no one who has pursued this word has ever escaped from the labyrinth, or, for that matter, penetrated to its heart and slain the minotaur, that unnatural paradox. I should end up by appealing to the "First Cause," or to "God," or to "Nature," or to some other handy capitalized word.

"Cause," it seems, is part of an orientation; it may be regarded as a word that does not refer to anything outside of itself but rather acts as a giver of directions. It merely tells us what to do with what, if we wish to get certain results. And if we really understand the word we comprehend that it tells us, "If you don't get the results you anticipate, make up another sentence. If the wheel continues to revolve after the water is diverted, something else is causing it to revolve. Don't look for the 'cause'; look for the something else." "Cause," then, is something in the orientation with which we relate ourselves to and control the data our senses give us, not something in the data. It is in our minds, not in the public and objective world. We created first a theory about the relation of water and wheel; then we translated that theory into a recipe or set of directions; and then finally we performed an operation—we manipulated the world. Thus "cause" turns out to be a very handy word, because it is useful in selecting from our sensory data something we can manipulate and use to our benefit.

If we carefully observe the historian, we will see that he is actually doing the same thing. And in such an effort, just as with the mill wheel, we must try to keep our eye on the pea and make sure it is under the right walnut shell. We must try to see exactly what constitutes the data from the public world which he is manipulating, and what constitutes his orientational pattern. A couple of examples will clarify the matter, one taken from artifacts and one from documents.

An archaeologist is an historian who is concerned primarily with artifacts, things made by man and still surviving in the world the archaeologist lives in. A Greek archaeologist, to invent a case, has observed that the ancient Greeks apparently liked to build temples to Apollo at the ends of capes extending eastward into the Aegean sea. Selecting such a cape, more or less at random, from the innumerable capes that project eastward from Greece, he journeys to it, he digs, he discovers the base of a temple, a few broken column feet still intact, and nearby, buried in the ground, sizable fragments of temple drums, cornices, pediments, as well as pieces of pottery scratched with Apollo's name, and fragments of a statue which, when assembled, has all the characteristics of early fifth-century B.C. statues of Apollo. He therefore concludes: "About 490 B.C. the Greeks erected on this cape a temple to Apollo, which was in use until about 300 A.D."

This looks like a statement about an event or series of events of the past. But a little analysis shows that it is no such thing. The data from the real world consists of a cape, ruins, statue fragments, and potsherds. The orientational pattern is made up of "The Greeks," "Apollo," "temple," "votive offerings," "as a general rule were accustomed to erect." The final sentence, which he writes in his report to his home museum, is a theoretical sentence which he could have written before he started digging. Certainly it was formulated in his mind before he set out to the unexplored cape. He translated it into a recipe which gave him directions about how to select a promising archaeological site, how to get there, and what to do when he got there, including how to categorize the material he hoped to discover. But now, after the excavation, he can add, "I know this is true, because I went to the cape and dug, and you can repeat what I did; indeed you will find traces of my excavations which will make it all the easier for you." He may be an archaeologist, concerned with old things and peoples, but he proceeds by making theoretical statements, translating them into operational statements, or recipes, and manipulating the real world. His statement is not about the past but about the future. He is no different from the scientist. He is not concerned with events of the past but with presently existing artifacts, and his statements about them are predictive.

The historian who works with documents is in an exactly similar position. Consider the case of an historian who is writing a biography of a minor political figure of nineteenth-century England. From various existing documents, newspaper articles, papers of the House of Commons, references in the memoirs of other figures of the time, he constructs a theory that from 1872 to 1879 his man was in retirement from political life, and that after he returned to the House of Commons his knowledge of India evident in his Parliamentary speeches indicates that he traveled privately there during those years about which the historian has no information. Knowing that English families of note are very careful about keeping old family papers, he traces, with the aid of genealogical dictionaries, correspondence with other scholars, and so on, a descendant now living in South Africa. To this man he writes. Yes, there are documents. Yes, he may see them; microfilms will be sent forthwith. Yes, there is a family tradition that Grandfather traveled in India sometime or other. Perhaps the papers will help. The films arrive; they are projected. Ah, a series of letters dated 1873–78, and dated from India! The minor politician had indeed gone there, at his own expense, to get information with which to attack the government's India policy. Our historian can now let his original statement stand and can add to it information taken from the letters. Further, he can now relate the speeches in Parliament after 1879 to the letters from India.

But observe—the passage in the complete biography only appears to refer to the past, just as the original sentence about the mill wheel only appeared to refer to "cause." Actually the historian has proceeded by making theoretical statements based not on a gap in the life but upon a gap in the documents, recasting those statements in predictive or recipe form, and performing certain operations. He has proceeded by predicting where he will find the documents and what they will say. As in the case of the archaeologist and the scientist, upon analysis it is revealed that he is not talking about the past but about the future. Earlier, we found the historian denying that he predicted; but he was wrong. And it turns out that the pea under the shell is really there, that it can be detected, and that it consists not of events of the past, but of documents existing in the present; and that the historian builds up systems of relations among these documents—orientative systems —by making predictions about the future, and by confirming them or by proving that they are not to be relied upon. The first kind of prediction he keeps by translating his operational statements back into theoretical form. The second kind, the unconfirmed predictions, he rejects, or would if he knew what it is he is doing. If he imagines he is talking about events of the past, he is both artist and historian, but satisfactory as neither. If he realizes that he is in fact talking about documents and artifacts existing in the present, that is, at the time of his operations, we have him where he cannot escape, and where he should be content to stay. He is a scientist, and we can demand of him what we demand of the scientist. That does not mean that his science is as mature as that of the physicist—far from it; but we can demand of him, and he can demand of himself, the same kind of activity. Thus our melancholy skepticism is dissipated. We can now be skeptical without being melancholy.

For we must remain skeptical. We have a hundred histories, it will be remembered, of the French Revolution. Is there not therefore an instability about historical knowledge which does not characterize the scientist's work? After all, what in the modern world is so solid, so reliable, as science? The scientist is our contemporary saint, when he is not our contemporary devil. Not that there is much difference between the two when we observe how we use saints and devils. Either is a means to symbolize and to make firm and lasting a particular orientation; saint or devil, each is a kind of shorthand for referring briefly to certain states of mind, and for evoking such states. It must be confessed that some scientists do not resist this role. But not the better scientists. They have discovered the secret of modern science, which is the acceptance of the instability of knowledge. If an orientation is useful, it is capable of being changed as the world changes, and the world changes as the way we look at it changes. "Nature," Oscar Wilde said, "imitates art." As our artists change the way they paint sunsets, so we see sunsets in a different way.

But it is also true that nature imitates science. As our science changes, we see new things and old things in a different way. The relation between orientation and perception, then, is not static but dynamic. The orientation controls our perception, but the perception, if we can manage to observe a disparity between the two, changes our orientation. This is the great task of the philosopher, to point out the difference, to separate the inseparable, and thus enable us to correct our orientation or modes of perception. So long as the scientist thought he was accumulating final truths about the laws governing the natural or public world, he moved slowly and he tended to collect isolated bits of data rather than to create theories. But about fifty years ago, as soon as he realized that what he thought was knowledge was actually a theoretical construct made up of orientation and data, as soon as he brought his assumptions out into the open, science exploded, and the inconceivably rapid metamorphosis of science in the twentieth century was upon us. When the historian recognizes that he is doing the same thing, that his solid volumes of history are not narratives about the events of the past but theoretical constructs about the existing documents and artifacts, constructs which have, as a firm base, operational constructs or statements and actual manipulations or operations—the equivalents of the scientists' experiments—when he comes to this realization, then our knowledge of the past will also change into something infinitely more solid and reliable than it is now. We should preserve our skepticism; for, generally speaking, the historian does not yet know these things. He is living in terms of a worn-out intellectual tradition.

But we need not be melancholy; there is already much in history upon which we can rely, so long as we always remember that we are talking about documents and not events. Such a theoretical construct is this book. Its subject is the cultural history of the nineteenth century in Europe and America, from the beginning of a great change in the human mind to the breakthrough of that new orientation into the modern vision and its release from the exhausted past. But not all the cultural history of the nineteenth century—only a fraction of it; only what may appear a thin film on its surface, at least in the beginning. I shall attempt to isolate one strand of nineteenth-century culture, the one I consider the most important. Why I think it is the most important will emerge in the course of the book. But its importance is not the sole reason why I isolate it from the many other strands. Related to it are other and special circumstances which make the nineteenth century a unique problem for the historian, baffling and perplexing—a situation which he has only begun to understand and which as yet he knows not how to handle. And to that novel situation I must turn before plunging into the story I have to tell.

One of the most striking facts about the nineteenth century, perhaps time will show it to be the most important, is the population expansion in the area of Western European culture. In England at the end of the century there were four times as many people as at the beginning, while in the United States the ratio was sixteen to one. Other countries followed suit, as they were affected by the industrial revolution. To clothe this new population would have been impossible—that is, the population increase itself would have been impossible—had it not been for the perfection, in the county of Lancaster in England, of cotton spinning and weaving machinery, shortly followed in the 1790's by the invention in America of the cotton gin. For the first time the perennial textile shortage of Europe was relieved. Perhaps the industrial revolution itself was made possible, or at least speeded up; for a scarcity of cloth would have meant that immense sums would have had to be diverted, through wages, to clothing. As it was, these sums could be used for capital reinvestment, while the cotton textile industry employed and supported large numbers of people and enabled the European masses to live according to steadily rising standards of hygiene—though this was not true of the American Negro slaves from whose sweating muscles the whole structure resulted.

Another consequence of cotton production was just as striking and in the long run perhaps even more important. A by-product of cotton was, naturally, an immense increase in worn-out clothes, or rags. Rags were the raw material of the paper-making industry which, so long as linen was the only source for rags, perennially suffered a shortage of raw materials. There had been a consequent shortage of paper itself in Europe ever since its innovation in the late Middle Ages, which prevented the expansion of the printing and publishing industries. Books, which for economic reasons could command only part of the available paper supply, were luxury goods, printed in editions of but a few hundred. The coming of cotton meant that the shortage of raw material for paper disappeared. It is no surprise to learn, therefore, that in the first decade of the nineteenth century, England perfected a paper-making machine, named after the men whose fortunes went to develop it, the Fourdrinier brothers. The machine, their monument, still bears their name. It was as important as the invention of the printing press, and I emphasize it because historians invariably neglect it. For the most part they seem to be wholly ignorant of it.

This invention involved a whole chain of reactions. First, paper making could move from a hand process to a machine process, run by the newly exploited energies of water and steam. Paper became cheap and plentiful. The next step was to apply water and steam power to printing, for there had been no point in improving the original fifteenth-century model of the printing press so long as there was not enough paper to keep the presses from standing idle. Now there was enough, and printing also became part of the industrial revolution. Bookbinding also could now profitably be taken out of the stage of handwork and made a machine process. The huge quantities of books manufactured could be profitably distributed because of the new energies available for transportation.

By 1830, publishing had been revolutionized. Printed matter was now cheap; for the first time in human history literacy could be massively extended through all levels of the population. In England the population grew by a ratio of one to four; but the literate population grew by a ratio of one to thirty-two. Not merely book manufacture was affected, but every type of communications and record keeping involving paper—magazines, newspapers, letters; business, government, and military correspondence and orders. Every imaginable area of human interaction was revolutionized by the dovetailing of the efforts of Eli Whitney and the Fourdrinier brothers. The final steps came in the last third of the century when a method was perfected to make paper out of wood pulp and when the linotype was introduced. The nineteenth century experienced a communications revolution which, though a part of the industrial revolution, may very well have been the most important of its results.

Certainly for the historian the consequences have been terrifying. The historian's technique was developed centuries before the communications revolution. It was a product of the fact that documents were limited in number. A single human mind could master them. All the surviving documents of ancient Greece can be intimately studied within a few years, including inscriptions cut into stone. Consequently we have a clear picture of the history of ancient Greece. That clarity is a consequence, not of our understanding, but solely of the fact that there is so little to understand. When the historian attempts to grapple with any period after the communications revolution had begun, he is lost in a chaos of documents. His technique no longer serves him. There is, however, a consolation. He is forced to recognize the fact that history is a construct; he can no longer delude himself into thinking that what happened was identical with what was recorded in a very small number of surviving documents; he cannot escape—at least so one would think—the conclusions that his construct is an instrument which he uses to organize the documents and that it is successful to the degree it is unstable. To be sure, many historians have so far managed to evade noticing what has happened; but historians who devote themselves to the nineteenth and twentieth centuries, the age affected by the communications revolution, are beginning to show a very healthy despair, to realize that in any traditional sense of "history" the history of the nineteenth century cannot be written.

The problem of the cultural historian, in one way identical with that of the political or economic historian, is in another way quite different. Theirs is solely a problem of quantity; his is a qualitative and a quantitative problem.

The mass of mankind wants its existing orientations reinforced, no matter how outworn and false they may be; for new ideas are uncomfortable and disturbing. The market for the exhausted and dead is limitless; the market for the new and the real is tiny, and profitless. Only a fraction of mankind can endure either novelty or a little more reality than they are adapted to. No matter what he would like to do, the publisher's economic existence depends upon the mass market. Books from and for the high cultural level can usually only be published at a loss; the money comes from profits in mass publishing or from subsidy, and the author usually cannot live on what he makes from his writing. As we shall see, the nineteenth-century author was culturally alienated from his society; at the same time he was being progressively forced out of the immensely expansive market by the consequences of the revolution in paper making. The cheaper publishing became, as it was harnessed into the industrial age, the more profit depended on exploitation of the mass market, and the more high-level cultural writing became economically marginal. A kind of cultural Gresham's law took over: inferior culture drives out superior. In the early eighteenth century Alexander Pope made a small fortune and achieved financial independence by writing poetry; in the early twentieth Wallace Stevens, as great a poet, perhaps greater, was a lawyer on the staff of an insurance company.

The revolution in publishing automatically forces the cultural historian into an extraordinarily difficult position. Before the nineteenth century the cultural tradition of the majority of mankind was orally transmitted; little of it found its way into print. Works in print—and before printing, manuscripts—were almost entirely devoted to high-level culture, whether classics from the past or important and novel writings that exhibited the advancing edge of cultural development. For such eras cultural history is, by comparison with the nineteenth century, fairly straightforward; the cultural historian's construct can absorb most of the documents with comparative ease; chronological arrangement of published books tends to be approximately identical with the cultural development.

In the nineteenth century, however, vast and steadily increasing masses of printed matter were issued for a market composed of that great majority of men who never before had had a written culture. Culturally, they did not live in the nineteenth century at all. The publisher's profit was increasingly to be derived from reinforcing orientations established not only long before the nineteenth century but even before the beginning of recorded history, about five thousand years ago.

The problem of the cultural historian is to cut away this fatty deposit from the vital nerve which is embedded in it, that writing which continues the expression of the advancing edge of human consciousness. To perform this delicate operation he must have an instrument, which can only be an historical construct; to create such an instrument is the purpose of this book.

Yet to attempt to write a history of even the major monuments of truly nineteenth-century European and American culture —science, philosophy, the major and minor arts—would be merely to compile a chronologically arranged annotated list of books, paintings, music, buildings. The nineteenth century is a jungle through which hardly more than a few trails have ever been hacked, and they are grown over again almost as fast as they are opened. The output of the Fourdrinier machines, although it steadily reduced the proportion of culturally advanced work published, at the same time increased the quantity. To examine every-thing is beyond the reach of human powers. Even to discuss what is important is impossible. I said earlier that I shall attempt to isolate a strand of nineteenth-century culture, but it is clear that I do so not merely because I want to or because I think it a good idea, or because this is not a twenty-volume work, but really because I have no choice.

The purpose of the construct presented here, then, is to select one aspect of nineteenth-century culture, to show its origins, its major stages of development and metamorphosis, and its cul-mination and climax of self-realization in the final twenty years of the century. I have taken my title from two works by the man whose thinking marked most completely that culmination and climax, Friedrich Nietzsche's *The Birth of Tragedy* and *Beyond Good and Evil*. To explain my title, *Beyond the Tragic Vision*, is the final purpose of the book itself.

Since even to select the major works of just this one strand would be impossible, I shall take up in detail only a few works, which I shall select because each presents an important further development or metamorphosis or aspect of the orientational revo-lution I am concerned with, as I at present understand it. My construct will not be complete, detailed, with every corner filled in, and every nail driven home. Some of the boards will be very loose indeed, and the whole thing must be walked through with caution; the reader must always be prepared to avoid falling tim-bers and to watch out for holes in the floor and boards that give way. But this does not worry me. It is only a way of saying that I shall be as solid and consistent as I possibly can, knowing all along, and wishing you to know, that like all structures of knowledge, it is an unstable interim report. What I really shall try to do is to give you a skeleton frame which you can fill in with the results of your own explorations into this fascinating era, and which you can dismantle at your pleasure.

However, before it is possible to undertake even such a construct, it will be necessary to sketch in its historical background, to show with large and sweeping strokes of the brush how it came about that the advanced man of this century found himself in an unprecedented historical and cultural situation, inescapably facing human problems which required original solutions. Before we can even begin dealing with nineteenth-century material, it is essential to have a conception of previous cultural history that will enable us to see as sharply as possible the cultural situation at the beginning of that century. This will be the job of the next three chapters. With such an instrumental construct we can proceed to run up the framework which is all I promise and all I can hope to offer. However, in order to relate what happened before the nineteenth century to that century itself, I need certain assumptions about cultural behavior; before we can think historically we must think humanly, psychologically, socially. To put those assumptions to work I need a kit of tools, a specialized vocabulary. With the presentation and illustration in use of that basic vocabulary, therefore, I shall begin.

# Part One

# The End of Ancient Thinking

# CHAPTER I

# Orientation and Culture

THE LONG INTELLECTUAL STRUGGLE to define a culture, to circumscribe a society by definition, to set up rules to govern the use of such phrases as "socio-cultural entity," has produced no widely accepted result. We appear to mean something when we talk about European culture, or Hindu or Buddhistic culture, or the culture of the Australian Bushman, but it is hard to get very many people to agree on what is meant. That struggle began in the eighteenth century, and it emerged in a distinguishable form with the writings of Johann Gottfried von Herder (1744-1803), who pretty well established the notion of a society or a culture as an organism; his conception was modeled on the image of a plant or an animal, an on-going self-contained process with its own unique character.

For some centuries travelers and traders had been bringing back to Europe not only new plants and animals but also information about new varieties of human beings and hitherto unknown organized societies, primitive, barbarian, and civilized or very near it. It occurred to Herder, who was not the first to conceive the idea, however cloudily, that such groups of human beings, related to each other by similar beliefs and patterns of living, could be classified biologically. He was probably influenced by the great botanist Linnaeus, who devised the system by which we still structure and classify the biological world. Societies, it seemed to Herder, could be classified and studied in the same way; for he

35

looked at society as a natural product, not something divinely instituted. It shares the characteristics of the natural world. Each society is an organism.

Given the intellectual atmosphere Herder was breathing, such a notion almost had to be arrived at by someone, sooner or later. We shall see further on how it was that the idea caught on and became so common in Europe and America that today it is often an unspoken and indeed unconscious assumption in our thinking. The vastness of its influence on political thinking and action cannot be exaggerated. For our modern conception of a nation is not that of a group of people who have agreed to live together in harmony, but rather of a social organism, with its own unique culture and its own life. From this perspective, the duty of national morality is plain: it is to preserve that uniqueness, to foster it, to keep it from being invaded and destroyed by different and therefore inimical cultures. Such a notion is the root idea of Wilson's notion of the self-determination of peoples, just as it lies behind the decision of a Texan school board that no history but Texan history, not even the history of the United States, should be taught in the public schools. The preservation of that organic entity justifies, in the minds of myriads of people, war itself. And we all know the terrible fascination of the idea when it is fused with the notion of race and racial purity, in the name of which any enormity is justified, including wholesale slaughter.

To call a society an "organism," then, is a very dangerous thing, and for that reason we tend today to resist the idea, preferring, if necessary, to dissolve human societies into random assemblages of individuals, rather than entertain a notion which, harmless as it originally appeared, has had such frightful results. Nevertheless, there do seem to be "socio-cultural entities" in human history. But how can we tell one from the other? How can we define the "natural borders" or frontiers between one culture and the next? Today we can scarcely do so, except with recently discovered primitive societies which have maintained their isolation from the rest of the world over long periods of time. Unfortunately, as soon as they are discovered, they begin to lose their individuality; cultural invasion and fertilization take place. Indeed, it works both ways, as we have seen in the instance of Herder himself. The discovery of the mere existence of other modes of living transformed European culture and created new and still unresolved problems.

Again we are faced with the problem of a theoretical construct, and in wrestling with this problem men have used any number of ideas which, they thought, would settle the matter. One of these has been race; and though it has possibilities, it takes a brave and learned man—or an extremely stupid one—to use it today. Another has been language; others have been religious beliefs, economic patterns, geographical environments, dietary laws, systems of thinking about kinship. Everything possible has been tried, it would seem; but we may be sure that others will be thought of.

The problem is perhaps incapable of solution. No matter what criterion is set up to define a culture, someone can come along and show its weakness. The truth seems to be that all these ideas work up to a point. The difficulty is that no surviving culture, however primitive and however isolated, has been completely untouched and unaffected by another culture. Every existent culture is synthetic, in the sense that the human mind has incorporated new and once foreign elements into every on-going "organic" cultural entity.

Indeed, if we look back to Herder and how he used his idea, we can understand a little better its function in his personality as typical of its function in all personalities. He used it to define what he conceived to be the true nature of European cultural organisms, and he found its roots in ancient Scandinavian and Germanic epics, legends, and myths. He was eager to define his own culture; that is, he was endeavoring to define himself in natural terms, for he was of a generation that had come to see eighteenth-century culture as artificial and therefore wrong and vicious. To get back to, to recover, the pure idea of being a German would be to discover the pure idea of himself.

If a man has to search for a conception of himself, something has happened to the cultural tradition in which he is living; for normally our cultural tradition teaches us quite unconsciously how to conceive of ourselves, how to define our own limits. What had happened to Herder's cultural tradition is one of the problems of the first part of this book. For the moment it is sufficient to close in on the notion of a culture and its tradition of self-definition. If we reflect a moment we can perceive that in our cultural tradition there are many modes of self-definition. A human being thinks, "I am a man, or a woman; a child, an adolescent, or an adult; a businessman, an artist, a ditch digger; a Jew, a Christian, an atheist; a Texan, a New Englander; an American, an Englishman; a European, an Asiatic"—and so on, though for no man *ad infinitum*. If all of these fail, a man can do one of two things: he can retreat to a single definition, becoming psychotic if he has to; or he can cast about, partly at random, partly actively, searching for a special kind of new knowledge, until he finds a means of self-definition that will serve him at least for a time. We have seen what Herder did; he returned in his imagination to the primitive life of the geographical area where he was born and where he matured—and in doing so, he shook Europe.

What the orientational life of primitive man was really like, and what were his modes of self-definition, or when that bit of human behavior we call self-definition emerged into human history, we can scarcely know. Nevertheless, from their surviving myths and tales we can deduce with some certainty that early peoples too were concerned with self-definition, for they thought of themselves as the "People of the River," or the "People of the Dog," thus separating themselves from other human "socio-cultural" entities they were in contact with. Can it be that what defines a culture is that the people in it have a common mode of self-definition? Let us consider this possibility a bit.

One early form of artistic activity is tattooing. Certain cultures universally practice it; in others only the men tattoo themselves; in others the custom is confined to a certain category of men, warriors, for example, if the society has progressed to the point where the warrior role has been distinguished. In the last in-

stance, obviously the tattooing functions as a means of differentiating one particular role, just as a military uniform does today.
But in the other examples, especially the first, though individual
designs may distinguish various socially-structured roles, the
world-wide incidence of the practice suggests that another psychological function may be served, the function of self-identification. We may, perhaps justifiably, distinguish between self-
definition and self-identification. The first serves to say, "I know
*who* I am; I am one of the People of the Dog." The second, to
say, "I know *that* I am." Tattooing that serves this second function is a means of asserting one's own existence. Thus a woman
buys a new hat, or a man a new tie, after a distressing, disturbing,
and disorienting experience, as a means of reconfirming, reinforcing the sense of identity.

Perhaps, at an even profounder psychological level, more
subtly, tattooing and its modern equivalents serve to establish
and settle the body-image by identifying the body-image with
the actual physical surface of the body. At any rate we know
that people in a state of emotional disturbance will frequently have
an image of themselves as either bigger or smaller than they actually
are. "I felt nine feet tall," is not entirely a joke or a rhetorical
device. In terms of its psychic roots it is a strict statement of
truth. To relate one's sense of identity to the surface of the body
by tattooing appears to be a basic orientative activity, for the body,
to one's conscious and unconscious sensory perception, is part
of the psychic environment.

At this point it is useful to think of another characteristic
of tattooing. It is invariably patterned. It introduces order into a
random world, frequently by emphasizing the symmetry of the
human body. We call any situation or perceptual field ordered if
among its various elements we can observe relations with a minimum expenditure of energy and time. Almost any American home
exhibits at least some degree of more than random order. Sometimes it is very obvious: all the furniture is arranged at right
angles. Sometimes it is more complex: every fabric has a different
floral design, but they all have designs and all the designs are

floral. Or the furniture and its placing may be selected to emphasize unbroken horizontal planes.

A very clear example of orientative behavior is something
everyone experiences in Venice. After wandering through the
narrow twisting streets of Venice, closed in by high buildings with
only a thin strip of sky far above, so that one constantly feels lost
or on the verge of it, one comes suddenly to the great Piazza of
San Marco. At once the wanderer feels an enormous sense of relief, for he can relate himself easily to this vast rectangular space,
with the glorious vision of San Marco so placed across one end
that the whole square seems like an immense axis organized to
throw the church into the most splendid spatial climax. Yet, most
interestingly, the piazza is not rectangular, but irregular, with
only one right angle, while the axis of the church, projected, strikes
not the middle of the short side of the piazza which it faces but
two-thirds of the way up one side. Nor should one neglect to
mention the buildings around three sides. They are arcaded, with
open loggias below and windows above. So powerfully does the
space appear to be perfectly oriented that at first it is hard to believe—it is disturbing—to observe that far from being the same
on all sides, each side is made up of a separate building, each with
its unique façade and architectural style.

From these considerations it seems clear that the sense
of order, the sense of orientation, and the sense of identity are
strongly related. But, to return to the example of tattooing, another factor is also at work. Not only is tattooing invariably patterned; the cultural tradition which determines the patterns usually
permits a certain amount of individual latitude in pattern, as it
must if it is to continue to serve for self-identification as well as
self-definition. This point is clear if we consider a uniform which
serves only for self-definition in terms of a role; at first almost
everyone feels anonymous and offended when he puts on a uniform, especially in a society where individuality is prized. (Some
people, to be sure, feel better, not worse.) It is no pleasure to be
even unconsciously aware of oneself only as an actor and not as
a separate human entity. Perhaps this is the source of the popular-

ity of tattooing among sailors. Permitted to wear only uniforms off duty as well as on, and living usually in an abnormal situation— for a sea voyage must be conducted in an atmosphere of crisis which requires each individual to submerge his identity into that of a highly organized group—the sailor has himself tattooed to confirm the fact that his identity survives underneath the role, that the body-image is there, and the self is there, although both are hidden by an unvarying and externally imposed uniform. The tattooed sailor is thus asserting his value as a unique human entity, as something quite separate from his value as a sailor.

Putting all this together we find a group of psychic experiences, or at least of terms, which seem properly to be associated: identity, order, value—and orientation. To be psychically oriented is to experience identity, order, and value; to be disoriented is to experience their attrition or loss. Perhaps identity, order, and value, as words, refer to the same psychic experience or datum. Perhaps they are merely three different ways of referring to the same thing, and we have three words only because different situations and different kinds of material require separate terms. They are perhaps three aspects of the sense of orientation, looked at not from the point of view of the observer but from the point of view of the environment. That is, they may select different kinds of relation between the psychic self-awareness and the world that self-awareness must relate itself to. Certainly it would seem that the basic sense or feeling of being oriented is a mechanism developed by a self-conscious animal as a means of adapting himself psychically to his environment. Without it he cannot function; we have only to study our friends in mental institutions to observe what ravages the loss of psychic orientation can produce and what fantastic efforts the human mind will make to create an oriented world if for some reason it can no longer use the culture's traditional orientative devices, whether psychically existing or external and public. A man who cannot bear to be tattooed in a society where everybody is tattooed is out of luck; in the country of the blind, the one-eyed man must put out his remaining eye to stay alive.

Whether all this is anthropologically and psychologically

verifiable or not—that is, whether it is "true" or not—it has at least served to define and use certain basic terms I shall use throughout this book. The trouble with these abstractions, however, is that in actual fact we are never completely oriented, except perhaps in those peculiar states sometimes called "mystic," and only rarely are we so disoriented that all automatic body functions are interrupted and we die, though it must be remembered that a sudden disorientation in persons of weak heart can cause death, and that their doctors advise such unfortunates to avoid all emotional disturbance. Our normal way of living is to move up and down, as it were, along a scale. The bottom point marks a psychophysical situation in which the sympathetic nervous system, that segment of the autonomic nervous system which rouses us to unusual efforts when we encounter a disorienting stimulus, is so out of control that we die from internal stress; the top point marks a situation in which the sympathetic nervous system is so totally subjected to the parasympathetic nervous system, which keeps the normal rhythms of the body going, that we are unable to respond defensively to any kind of threatening stimulus—and we die from external invasion. If you insist on meditating yourself into a mystic state, it is best to do so in a clean safe monastery cell, or under a bo tree, protected by devoted disciples. "Hell is the shadow of a soul on fire," said Edward Fitzgerald in his *Variations on Themes by Omar Khayyám*. More precisely, it is the psychic projection of an unbearably stimulated sympathetic nervous system.

And heaven is, of course, a symbol of perfect orientation, a place where identity is never threatened, where everything, including oneself, is radiant with value, and where the world is totally ordered, a place where a complete system of relations is immediately apprehensible, with no loss of time and no expenditure of energy.

Thus man is forever forced in opposing psychological directions by opposing drives. Since he cannot deal with his environment unless he experiences sufficient internal equilibrium to observe what goes on around him, one drive is toward perfect orientation; but if he devotes himself too whole-heartedly to orientative activity, he will neglect the genuinely threatening aspects of the external world. And there is another factor, perception. At the extremes of the orientation-disorientation scale, in heaven or in hell, his perception is narrowed as he approaches the top or bottom, to a smaller and smaller area of the world his sensory perceptions bring to him. Indeed, as is well known, he can approach such states by concentrating on only one object and gradually blocking out every other sensory message the mind receives, until that too is blocked out, and his mind receives no sensory percept. On the other hand one of the devices of black psychiatry is to place the individual in a room in which the shapes and colors of differentiated areas of walls and ceiling are continuously changing in so random a way that the mind cannot grasp the principle which controls the metamorphoses. The result is so extreme a disorientation that the personality disintegrates. Yet another device is sensory deprivation, for from recent experiments we know that a human body submerged in water at body temperature, with only a breathing tube, will experience hallucinations and a partial—and presumably in time complete—personality disintegration. Any orientation offered to an individual suffering from sensory deprivation is eagerly received and believed.

The human mind needs, therefore, a flow of external stimuli. If it has too much or too little it will lose contact with reality. But it is a mistake to think that the primary drive is toward perfect equilibrium, if by this is meant that there is no counterdrive of equal importance, to be conceived not so much as a drive toward disturbance, though that is its effect, but rather as a drive toward sensory stimulation.

The drive toward perception is the foundation of science; the drive toward orientation, toward peace of mind, is the foundation of religion. But in this highly schematic way of looking at the matter, another drive may be perceived, which is the foundation for another profoundly important human activity. Any given orientation, or psychic "set," or Gestalt, works in two ways. It screens our minds from receiving everything, so that we may act on what we do observe; it also prevents our minds and our nervous

systems from breaking down under the strain of excessive stimulation, including stimulation from within the mind itself. But at the
same time, whether the stimulation comes from the external world
or from within the mind, a psychic set prevents us from responding
to those stimuli which it screens out. Thus there is always a disparity between an orientative set and the data of the real world.
On the one hand the drive toward equilibrium preserves the set;
on the other, the drive to engage the mind with the real world must
break the set down, show up its weaknesses, reorganize it, introduce new material. The drive toward sensory stimulation, toward
perception, toward getting around and through the set, is the predictive drive, the foundation of science. But the drive to break
down the set, to permit oneself to experience enough emotional
disturbance to open holes in it, to rend it so that new knowledge
may enter, whether from within the mind or from the outside
world—that drive is the foundation of art.

With the aid of this scheme, then, this construct, one can
see that religion and art are allied by their common concern with
orientative sets; that art and science are allied by their common
desire to disturb an orientation; that, on the other hand, the aims of
religion and art are also diametrically opposed, each trying to exploit the other; and that likewise art and science are in conflict, each
constantly claiming the other's territory, each under the impression
that it has a rival.

It is therefore the disparity between any given orientation
and the random and as yet unorganized and unrelated information
from the real world or from within the mind, which disturbs the
orientation. But any disturbance is disorienting and threatening,
because every disturbing datum, no matter how rapidly we relate
it to ourselves, by threatening the internal consistency of the orientation, threatens our sense of order, our sense of value, our sense
of identity. Is there any reason to be astonished, then, that as far
back as we look—and for the vast majority of human beings today,
most of whom are threatened constantly by hunger—man should
value orientation above disturbance, and heaven above the real
world?

"Heaven is the vision of fulfilled Desire," to quote Fitzgerald again. Heaven is a symbol of total orientation, a state in which identity is never threatened and never insecure. Hence if there is any truth in the notion that what defines a culture is that the people in it have a common mode of self-definition, then it is also true that what defines a culture and holds it together is a common mode of conceiving heaven, a common way of symbolizing self-identification. For if our cultural fellows agree with our conception of heaven they offer no threat to our mode of self-identification, and thus no threat to our very sense of identity, which keeps us functioning as self-aware on-going biological processes.

Certainly as each of the civilizations about which we know anything emerges from the primitive world and enters history, a history of hardly more than fifty-five hundred years, each has a separate image of heaven, common to all its members. When Arabia emerged in the form of the Mohammedan armies thirteen hundred years ago, the organizing symbol was Mohammed's new vision of heaven. It was their commonly believed-in symbol of perfect orientation that gave the Mohammedans the self-possession and the psychic energy to create an empire and found a new civilization. But nineteen hundred years ago, half a millennium before Mohammed, another Near Eastern symbol of heaven, in the form of a vision of the end of the world and immediate though selective salvation, had erupted from Palestine and had swept the West. It still dominates most of its population, even though its original promise that Christ would return when those who witnessed his death were still living was not fulfilled. Behind the Palestinian vision, however, lay an older orientation, one with which it is proper for any student of Western culture to begin, for that great myth of paradise and paradise lost was to be its great organizing symbol for centuries, and still is.

# CHAPTER II

# Paradise and Eternity

THERE IS THE THEOLOGICAL WAY of looking at the story
of the fall from paradise as we find it in the opening chapters of
*Genesis;* and there is the literary way. The two methods yield
shockingly disparate results, for the one shows how theology drives
toward orientation, and the other how art, by complex ironies,
drives to break orientations down. I shall begin with the second and
look at the story as if it were a work of art.

It is as curious as it is extraordinary that innumerable explanations have been offered for the expulsion of Adam and Eve
from paradise, just as one is always surprised to discover that not
one but two trees were involved, the tree of the knowledge of good
and evil and the tree of life. In the infinite pictorial and literary accounts of the story, it is exceedingly rare for more than one tree to
appear, and in the popular Christian mind, it would seem, the two
trees are identified. Nor is it often observed that though God says
that if Adam eat of the tree of good and evil, he will die, the serpent
denies it, and the serpent turns out to be right. Did God start things
off by lying to man? And the serpent by telling man the truth? Further, God tells Adam that he is being expelled because he has dis-
obeyed; but he tells others (Who can they be?), "Behold, the man
is become as one of us, to know good and evil: and now, lest he put
forth his hand, and take also of the tree of life, and eat, and live for
ever." The sentence remains unfinished, and the text continues,
"Therefore the Lord God sent him forth from the garden of Eden"

and "he drove out the man." The motive he presented to Adam was one of just punishment; the motive he presented to the mysterious others was fear.

If this were an ordinary story, and not a sacred text, we would undoubtedly say that one of the principal protagonists, God, deceived man not once but twice, that his practice was deception and his motive fear that man become like "us," knowing both good and evil, and fear lest man become immortal, like "us." Surely a polytheism is lurking somewhere in the background. And in truth, the story as we have it is not terribly old. Yet it is significant that the aspect of the story which the Western world has chosen to re-member and has enshrined in the center of its mythology is punish-ment, not God's fear, while endless ingenuity has been expended by learned theologians in trying to reconcile the various conflicting aspects of the story and to explain that mysterious "us." Not that explanations are lacking. They are endless, but without exception they are logically unsatisfactory.

The essence of the story is this: Adam and Eve are placed in a paradise on the unspoken and concealed condition that they accept unquestioningly what is in fact a lie. It may be objected that they *do* eat of the tree which they are informed is death-bear-ing, and that they *are* driven forth from the garden and *do* die. But since it was the other tree that granted immortality, presumably they would have died anyway. In that case the serpent is telling the truth—they will not die—and is lying—they do die; and God is telling the truth—they will die—and is lying—they are going to die anyway. From such a tangle of self-contradictory statements what are we to deduce? Simply this: It is impossible for Adam and Eve to comprehend why they were created, placed in the garden of Eden, and then expelled into a world of sweating toil and painful parturition.

Were this an ordinary story, we would say that it was writ-ten by a very wise and witty and diabolically subtle man who was trying to dramatize something tremendously important about human experience, some foul and comic secret. The reason for the expulsion being incomprehensible, the mind is forced to contemplate and consider the contrast between the garden and the world outside of it. What in fact is the garden like? It is a place of perfect beauty and order, where Adam has a perfect mate, and where he even knows the right names for all the animals. But it is also a place which contains opportunities to learn divine secrets, which are forbidden him, a place filled with lies and deceptions. Again, as Fitzgerald puts it, God, "e'en with Paradise did devise the snake," another impossible difficulty which Christian theologians have spent centuries trying to rationalize away. Outside lies a land of suffering and pain; nor is there any mention whatever of the beauty and charm which man did indeed find there. It is as if our cruel and clever author had divided the world right down the middle, splitting it into a half of deceptive beauty and a half of real ugliness. Were this an ordinary story, it would be impossible to imagine anything more cruel and bitter. For in the world of real ugliness, man continues to worship the power that created the beauty and the deceit, the reality and the ugliness. And he is required to worship, in spite of the fact that if he does he is, like Abel, permitted to be killed, and if he does not he is, like Cain, permitted to live under divine protection, to have wife and descendants, among whom is the inventor of music. One is tempted to think that it must all be historically true, for nothing made up could make so little sense.

Or, perhaps, if we press a little harder, it will yield some meaning. God is responsible for everything, good and evil, and the knowledge of good and evil. God has placed man in a world of perfect good, has permitted him to learn of the distinction between good and evil, and has plunged him into a world of evil. Had God simply plunged man into a world of evil directly, man, without having had the prior experience, would not have known that world as evil. He had to be told it was evil, and God so informs him, at considerable and even wearisome length. Man, therefore, knows of a world radiant with order and value, and is ignorant of its deceptiveness; he lives in a world of hunger, toil, and sin. It is the contrast between the two worlds that gives him his awareness of the character of the world he lives in. It is his consciousness of his fate, his ability to remember, to experience in his imagination, an infinitely better world that makes this one so bitter and cruel. Man is the victim of a cosmic joke the point of which he can never see—and consequently he can respond only to its cruelty but never to its humor.

This is what literary interpretation can do to this famous revelation, to this notorious myth. What a literary orientation sees is a subtle attack on the psychological validity of an orientative symbol. The contrast between what man can imagine and what he must experience, and the realization that what he can imagine is a deception—all this corresponds with great exactness to the contrast between the drive toward creating a fixed orientation or set which assures the individual of the existence of order, value, and identity, and the actual experience of a continuous flow of disturbing stimuli. But the experience is valued above the orientation, in this interpretation, because a fixed orientation is presented as a source of deception and danger.

But if this is what literary criticism does, or can do, with the opening of *Genesis*, it is not what theology does with it, nor the popular mind. I know of no interpretation of the story like the one I have presented here. Quite the contrary; it is always discussed as if it were quite unambiguous, except by learned theologians, who devote themselves to draining the ambiguity and irony away. Its meaning is simple: God intended that man live in paradise; man sinned; he was expelled; he suffers in consequence of his sin; but God promised to restore him; and God sent his Son to earth to make that restoration possible, at least for a few, or, according to more sanguine interpreters, for everyone. The ironies, the deceptiveness, the malice, the lies, all have been drained from the story. It has been subjected to the blind and self-deceiving power of the orientative drive. The illusory character of the garden has been ignored, and the imaginary, and deceiving, paradise of order, value, and identity, has been converted into a reality. And perhaps rightly; for what I have presented as an astoundingly bitter and ironic dramatization of the human condition may only be the result of bad writing, of a clumsy and botched effort to unite two or more inconsistent versions of the same myth; or it may be a late work, like *Job*, in which man bows down before the incomprehensible, and is as mysteriously rewarded as he was pointlessly punished.

Whichever the version in *Genesis* may be—and who can tell?—the myth in its origins and in all its subsequent interpretations was and is a symbolization of the human drive to live according to a perfectly gratifying orientation which corresponds in every point, with no data excluded, to a real world. It states in no equivocal terms that it is an historical fact that heaven was once on this earth, and since man was excluded from it it is in the realm of possibility that he may return to it. And in the human mind a desired possibility is automatically translated into a certainty. From this point of view, it is possible to see that Christianity inevitably had to emerge from Hebraism, just as we cannot sleep until we hear the other shoe hit the floor. It is the drive toward completion, toward fulfilling the logical and emotional potentials of a pattern. Even chimpanzees suffer from this drive; given an uncompleted circle and a piece of chalk, they will finish the circle. Christianity completed the Hebraic circle. And then it received a powerful reinforcement from Greece, from Plato.

The striking, the almost unique element in the Hebraic vision of a world of perfect order and value is its historical character. As far as the Western world is concerned, it was the Hebrews who introduced History into history. In other cultures the realms of the gods, heaven, paradise, were outside of time. Time was the essential character of the disordered world we live in; timelessness that of the ordered world we imagine, and believe to be existent outside of time. Perhaps because the Hebrews were originally a wandering desert tribe, they imagined a world of value as a garden, existent in historical time, from which they had been driven forth. Their drive was away from the inimical desert and toward a land flowing with milk and honey, as Palestine was when they first came to it. The notion that they had been excluded from such a world and had received a divine promise that they would return to it seems to have been one of the great motivating forces of their historical experience. And from the pattern of experience and fantasy emerged the chiliastic or millennial idea that is so adverse to one aspect of European orientative patterns and so acceptable and tempting to another.

The chiliastic or millenial dream is that paradise will be regained upon this earth, in time; that its coming will be heralded by apocalyptic events in which all the kingdoms of the earth will crumble, and Israel, "the son of man," the people chosen by God for this great task, will establish the kingdom of God in which man will be at once perfectly good and perfectly happy.

As the Jewish kingdoms became more and more subject to external pressures and to foreign domination in the last centuries before the birth of Christ, side by side with the ironic and skeptical orientation we have seen in *Job* and perhaps in *Genesis*, an attitude necessarily confined to a sophisticated few, there developed a more exciting and more comforting millennial tradition. This was the popular tradition, of which the Bible and various non-Biblical Jewish works contained numerous traces; the tradition from which Jesus emerged, identifying himself as the true Israel, the true Son of Man and of God, who prophesied, or was believed to have prophesied—in these matters it makes no difference—that he would "come in the glory of his Father with his angels; and then he shall reward every man according to his works. Verily I say unto you, there be some standing here, which shall not taste of death, till they see the Son of Man coming in his kingdom." That the early Christians, nourished in the same apocalyptic and millennial tradition as Jesus, believed that he would return shortly from heaven and establish the perfect kingdom on earth in their own lifetimes is unquestionable.

This certainly was the good news that the early Christian proselytizers carried to the Mediterranean world. Less than a century had passed after Christ's death when John of Patmos wrote and placed in circulation his *Revelation*, a work of almost irresistible emotional power, which, once it had been accepted into the canon of the Holy Book, remained forever the chief source of apocalyptic millennialism for Western civilization. It is and remains the foundation for every Utopian dream and revolutionary effort Europe has undergone, including the Communist. Yet by the fourth century the church, now established and successful, its leaders enjoying the good things of this earth, began its efforts to control the millenial dream and to expel paradise from time. The struggle—and the alliance—between Judaism and Platonism began. Indeed, it may have already begun with the *Gospel According to St. John*, written, it now appears, much earlier than the late second century, in which the nineteenth-century Biblical scholars had placed it. There certainly seems to be a Platonic character about *John*, a Greek influence through which is transmitted an entirely different notion of a world of perfection from that created by the Jews.

Of the Platonic dialogues an infinitude has been written. It is only a blessing that less has been written than said and thought. Everything, it would seem, is to be found in them, just as everything is to be found in the Bible. They comprise Europe's other Bible. The reasons for this plenitude are several: the richness of the thought, the inconsistency of the conclusions at which they arrive, and sometimes the failure to conclude. Perhaps the best explanation of their literary and philosophic character is that they are not supposed to be consistent, either within themselves or with one another. Rather, we should think of them as novellas, short novels of ideas; we should not ask "What did Plato *really* mean?" but read them as exercises in philosophical imagination. Such a notion may be useful; certainly it could not have been entertained before forty or fifty years ago. Advanced thinkers in the nineteenth century sought to resolve the problem by arranging the dialogues in order of composition and extracting from this order the line of Plato's intellectual development. Since not merely the notion of such a development but also what line that development took necessarily had to be arrived at before the chronology could be arranged, such an effort of course proved to be unsatisfactory, though this conception has by no means been abandoned.

Before the nineteenth century, however, all the way back to Plato's immediate successors, the effort had always been to make a consistent intellectual structure out of Plato's notions, for the drive of the human mind toward orientation irresistibly leads it to make sense out of the confused and order out of the inconsistent.

Surely—such was the assumption—surely the thinking of so abominably clever a mind as the divine Plato's must have been dictated and controlled by a single dominating and regnant principle. Our task is to discover that principle, to show how it governs everything in the dialogues, and to assert its beauty and truth. Who knows? Perhaps Plato's mind was so governed. At any rate, by the time the Neoplatonists were finished with the poor man, Plato's thinking was perfectly consistent, though it made little sense. The task of the philosopher, so the Neoplatonists postulated, is to discover the principle of order in the world; Plato was a great philosopher; therefore he discovered a principle of order; hence our only task is to discover what it was; since we too are great philosophers, we can discover it—and here it is: reality is to be found in the world of ideas, not in the world of sensory experience.

The drive of the human mind toward perfect orientation exposes it to a temptation at best very hard to resist, the identification of the orientation with the world it purports to organize, whether that world is the interior world of the mind or the public world which everybody experiences. The orientation is projected on the world, but since it is so difficult to distinguish a set or Gestalt from the data to which it is applied, the irresistible tendency of the mind is to believe that it has discovered the orientation in the public world, not that it has projected it upon it. In the first chapter I suggested how the word "cause" is the source of endless difficulty because it is thought of not as a verbal directive of an advisory nature but because it is believed to refer to a characteristic inherent in external reality, in the public world. (If the use of the word "because" in this sentence does not amuse the reader, it ought to.) An equally splendid example of this failure of the mind is to be found in the word "is." One contemporary student of such matters has distinguished eight different functions for the various forms of the word "be," yet philosophers have written, and continue to write, enormous tomes on "being." Our libraries are full of such books, most of them quite dusty. If we assume an attitude of skepticism toward the concept of "being," if we entertain doubts about whether such an entity exists, we can find good reasons in language and linguistic behavior why men should think that such a thing as "being" should really be.

Our suspicions are aroused if we examine the following sentence: " 'Being' is an 'entity.' " Now "entity" means simply "that which has *ens*," the Latin noun for "being." "Being," then, is that which has being. This seems to be getting nowhere. The difficulty lies in two common assumptions which everybody makes and which are rarely examined: first, that there is a common meaning to all words derived from the same root word, to all words which are, in the history and structure of language, related; second, that if a word exists it must have a meaning, that is, it must refer to something outside of the realm of language.

As for the first assumption, consider the word "royal." "Edward VII had a royal bearing." The way he stood and walked conformed to our culture's notion of the way a king ought to stand and walk. But "Royal Baking Powder" does not mean either the kind of baking powder kings use when they bake, or the kind cooks use when they bake for kings. It simply means, "baking powder which we, the manufacturers, want you to think of so highly that you will buy it in preference to other baking powders." "Royal" bathes "baking powder" in an aura of superior value in the hope that the customer will unconsciously respond to that aura and buy.

When it comes to the second assumption, it is not difficult to see that though some words do refer to things outside language, many others do not. What, for example, is the meaning of the word "the"? Put in that form, and with the common assumption that a word necessarily refers to something outside of itself, the question is almost unanswerable, although the dictionary gives an elaborate answer which I defy anyone to understand. If I restate the question, however, and ask "What information does 'the' give?" the answer is obvious: It tells us that we are about to get a noun. The dictionary definition assumes that if a word does not refer to something in the world of our senses, it must refer to something in our minds; that is, to a concept. But the only way we can experience a concept is to hear or see it in the form of a statement in words, and this holds for our own concepts as well as concepts communicated to us. However, the further assumption is then made that the concept existing in our mind is, in some strange way nobody has ever been able to fathom, an entity.

Yet we have already seen that the notion of "being" derives from certain assumptions we have about language: that all similar words have a root meaning and that all words have meaning, or reference. Obviously it is far better to think about the functions of words, what they do in the sentence, or by themselves, what directions they give us, what connections and relations they set up between other words, than to think of meaning in this very puzzling and ultimately circular way. With some words, in short, as with "the" and "being," it is impossible to get out of the closed world of language; they simply refer to other words or give us directions as to how other words should be interpreted.

Now this, to put it in a simplified way, is what Plato observed. Certain rules govern the use of language, rules which we all learn more or less well, and unconsciously. When we are uncertain about the rules we look up the word in a dictionary, which does not give us the "meaning" of the word but rather tells us under what circumstances it was considered proper, at the time the dictionary went to press, to use it. But Plato, since he did not have centuries of written words to call upon nor a vast organization of meaning-functions and rules set down in dictionaries, assumed that the rules for the use of words were fixed, permanent, unchanging, and that the misuse of a word was a consequence of ignorance of the rules or an unintelligent failure to determine the rules. The fact is, however, that the rules are constantly changing; and indeed some modern students of the matter go so far as to say that *every* time a word is used it has a slightly different function. On Plato's assumption, however, the task of the thinker is to make an absolutely consistent, airtight, and perfectly ordered structure of language. Having done so, he would then have "truth."

Since it is perfectly obvious that such a structure of meanings does not correspond to the random nature of reality as we indeed experience it, it follows that since the world of perfectly organized words—or better yet, of mathematics—is "true," the world of our sensory experiences, the public world we share with other people, is "false." But since even Plato knew that the worlds of words and mathematics are not real, the real and true world must exist in the only place that is left—the mind, that world of ideas to which all the words "really" refer and from which, tidily enough, they are derived. However, the mind of a given individual, who lives in the imperfect world, the false world, the world of shadows, cannot have the qualities of perfection, truth, and reality. There must, therefore, be another world where the ideas "really" exist, a divine world, a world of pure truth, order, and real reality—and goodness. For if perfection, truth, and reality are not good—and beautiful—what on earth is? The answer is that nothing on earth is, for everything on earth is imperfect, false, unreal, evil, ugly—and changing. Therefore the last attribute to be assigned to the superior and divine world of the ideas is unchangingness or eternity.

After all, not until the middle of the twentieth century was it discovered that no mathematical system or language system of meaning-functions can be absolutely consistent, that the foundation of every such system is therefore necessarily an unresolved and unresolvable contradiction. Surely we should not blame Plato for not knowing something so recently discovered. Even Bertrand Russell, only sixty years ago, studied mathematics because he thought that mathematics had as its reference an ideal world of perfect order. Yet perhaps it would not have taken so long to discover this fundamental weakness of all intellectual constructs if Plato's work had not acquired, partly because of the way his thought fused with Christianity, such enormous prestige. Certainly no great philosopher has had such a powerful drive—which came to him from Greek religion and the early quasi-religious philosophers—toward orientation, or has been so determined to identify orientation and value. Yet his great achievement, the thing that makes all Western philosophy a footnote to Plato, is that he was the first to demonstrate beyond the point of refutation that a perfect orientation does not correspond with the data it organizes, that there is always a disparity. However, his irresistible emotional tendency, and that of his followers, since their minds had been cast in a religious foundry, was to say, "In that case, so much the worse for the data. What I care about is the orientation." Thus although there was a Platonic skepticism and a Platonic skeptical tradition, throughout European cultural history his force has preeminently been exerted in favor of the drive toward orientation. That is why he preferred the authoritarian Sparta to the democratic Athens; and that is why he excluded poets from his ideal commonwealth, for the poet's primary task is to disturb orientations, which Plato wished to establish permanently and impose on mankind through force.

When Christianity erupted westward from Palestine into the rest of the Mediterranean basin, it was no mere historical accident that it fused so rapidly with Platonism. The Jewish-Christian vision was, as we have seen, an historical one; its path was from the lost paradise to the abiding millenary Zion, to the earth redeemed by the chosen people. But when it became apparent that Christ was not going to return, or at least that he hadn't, it became necessary to reinterpret his promises (or the promises made in his name), to turn them into symbols. At some future time, then, heaven would come to earth; earth would be another heaven; the divine and the human would be forever joined and never again sundered. When, however, we introduce words like "forever" and "never" we extrude ourselves from time, and in consequence the relation of the perfect world and the fallen world is not conceived historically, or temporally, with order preceding and following disorder, but spatially: order is in the divine realm, which is above the human and disordered world we live in.

Indeed, this is the character of virtually all religious orientations, including Plato's, except the Jewish. The religious theater was now set for the fusion, accomplished in Alexandria as well as a good many other places, of Christianity and Platonism into that strange and fantastic system called Neoplatonism. The result though superficially incredibly elaborate, was fundamentally very simple. The unreal world of the Platonists was identified with the fallen world of the Judeo-Christian tradition, and the restored world of the latter was identified with the radiant world of the ideas of the former. Time was contained in eternity. To go to heaven was to leave time and enter eternity. Man's soul originated in heaven, it emanated from God, a spark of the divine fire, it descended to earth, it suffered temporal unreality, and then, having achieved salvation, it returned to heaven and was reabsorbed in God.

Augustine completed the Christianization of this scheme and the subordination of Plato to Christ, by founding his philosophy on Paul and perfecting the doctrine of grace. Not through an automatic cosmic process does all this happen but by the will of God, who chooses, with a terrible final justice, which men should enter heaven and escape from time, which men should live in the City of God. In the meantime it is God's will—and man's punishment through inherited sin—that man should live out his life in an imperfect world, disordered and drained almost entirely of value. The difference between this and the original Platonic conception lay precisely here. To Plato, as he was subsequently interpreted, the world of appearances, the world of sensory experience, was entirely without value; but to Augustine such a position was untenable, for God had created this world.

Our world, then, is a world of partial, of deteriorated, of half-destroyed value, as the consequence of the fall from paradise; its temptation is to persuade us that its original full value is still structured within it, and it is the duty of Satan so to tempt us. Our moral task is to resist that temptation, to fight the world, the flesh, and the devil, and to devote our lives entirely to winning salvation so that we may enter a world of pure order and unsullied value, where identity will never be threatened. Or rather, as entirely as we can, because, made of flesh as we are, pure devotion to God and salvation is almost impossible; only saints can achieve it. The power of the martyrs was proof, both to the pagans and to other Christians, that an orientational drive into which all the energies of the personality are poured can sustain an individual's personality in the midst of the most frightful suffering. To make a good death became the mark of the believing Christian. As a corollary, to endure any threatening or even mildly frustrating aspect of human experience became equally the sign of the good Christian. Not to kick against the pricks, not to commit suicide, was a sign to oneself that a believing orientation had been fully accepted; to accept the suffering and randomness of this world was to accept the will of God, was the mark of grace, as strong a proof as one could have that one would indeed achieve salvation.

This vision of human life was inherently both stable and unstable. Its stability is shown in its survival, virtually unchanged, in spite of all kinds of superficial differences, in the minds of the vast majority of human beings now living in Europe and America and their economic-religious colonies. Its instability is indicated by the fact that the history of Christianity is the history of heresy. Its lasting power arises primarily from the fact that it contains in a single vision both order and disorder, both structure and randomness, both value and the failure of value. It corresponds to the texture of human experience, of which it is a perfect symbolization. Further, its validity is automatically reinforced every time an individual maintains it in the face of experiences which threaten it. It recognizes and *almost* fully explains the disparity between orientation and data.

However, a touch of skepticism, and its instability becomes immediately apparent. If God knew in advance—as He must have, since He was God and thus knew what He was doing —that He was creating a man who would plunge himself from a paradise into a world of sin and suffering, why did He do so? It is all very well to say, "I cannot answer this question, but since it is a question that appears in the fallen world, it is obviously another of those temptations which serve, if I rightly respond to them, to make my faith stronger. Therefore I conclude that it is God's incomprehensible will that I find His will incomprehensible. *Credo quia impossibile est.* I believe because it is impossible." But if one says, "If I can receive a comprehensible answer to this question, I will believe in God and this whole system," obviously the whole orientation shatters. Hence to read the opening chapters of *Genesis* as I have read them, to give them the simplest and most obvious interpretation, was never done, and intense intellectual efforts were devoted to avoiding such an interpretation.

Another source of instability lay in the very union of Platonism and Judeo-Christianity, which on one level matched so perfectly. The Palestinian tradition was essentially historical; it was a pattern of paradise-exile-restoration, all taking place on this earth. But the Platonic was one of a simple contrast between a perfect eternity and a shadowy temporality, between reality and unreality, value and non-value. This conflict in turn led to two further kinds of instability.

One was the disparity between the belief that restoration was to be outside of time, in heaven, and the belief that restoration would take place on this earth. Politically and economically, the first belief was conservative and reactionary; whatever is wrong on earth must be accepted. But the second was chiliastic and revolutionary; whatever is wrong on earth must be totally corrected. Christianity contained within it, therefore, the seeds of violent political, class, and economic explosions, and such explosions have occurred not infrequently in the past two thousand years.

The other instability inherent in this union was this: Since God created everything, there are two real worlds, the divine and the earthly, man partaking of both. Opposed to this belief is the Platonic notion that the divine is real and the earthly unreal. One consequence is that Christianity both produces and rejects mystics who experience the direct knowledge of God, or at best regards them with suspicion. The ascetic is in the same ambivalent position. No religion is so fruitful in producing heretics nor so violent in suppressing them. Indeed, the first real break within the Christian structure of belief came with the re-emergence of the half-buried Platonic element.

# CHAPTER III

# *Enlightenment*

THE ENLIGHTENMENT—MAGICAL NAME! To us it means the world of Benjamin Franklin and Thomas Jefferson. Philadelphia of two hundred years ago, the green town with its ordered park-like squares and its neat rows of brick houses with white wooden trim. Williamsburg, now so charmingly and perhaps a little absurdly restored, eagerly visited by Americans from every part of the country, the perfectly ordered dream-world of American sub-urbia, the scene today of the desired honeymoon, the new Niagara Falls where it seems infinitely appropriate to begin one's married life. Williamsburg, with its great stretches of shaded streets, its noble open spaces, a university at one end of the town, the seat of the government at the other, and to one side, facing its own green, the palace of the governor, the very image of beneficent and benevolent authority, in which it seems impossible that a tyrannical and capricious governor could have held court. And at the point where the palace axis and the university-state house axis intersect, the simple and tasteful church, where man worships in comfort and good form a benevolent deity who wishes us only well, all of us.

It can scarcely be accidental that these two towns, among the wealthiest and loveliest of the eighteenth-century British Empire, should be the setting of resistance against the disorder and unpredictable tyranny of king and parliament. When we think of Philadelphia and Williamsburg, the beauty of the eighteenth century still dominates our minds, still forms our ideal of an adequate human setting. Not so ravishing as Venice nor so crushingly grand as Rome, they were in their simplicity, their taste, their humanity, their relation to nature, the loveliest towns European civilization has yet produced. They were Enlightened cities, and our Revolution was an Enlightened revolution.

The orientation which brought about our eighteenth-century townscapes and our Revolution was not an eighteenth-century phenomenon. Indeed, the first use of the English word "enlightened" to mean "free from superstition and prejudice" is said to have been in 1663, and this meaning gives us some idea of the complex of attitudes that it referred to even then, although the term "Enlightenment" itself was not used in England until the 1860's. The French "*Éclaircissement*" and the German "*Aufklärung*" are older. In all three words is to be found the root metaphor of "light." "Light," of course, has traditionally been opposed to "dark" to symbolize the opposition between intellectual understanding and emotional confusion, between good and bad, between value and the absence of value, between order and disorder, between the conscious and unconscious divisions of the mind. Our 1663 usage shows us clearly what was meant; to be enlightened was to be free from the superstitious, illogical, and unrealistic prejudices of medieval Christianity, of the "Dark" Ages. It is only too easy to see why this meaning became current in the 1660's in England: the twenty-odd years before the restoration in 1660 of Charles II to the English throne had been filled with a terrible and bloody struggle over religious issues; and that struggle itself was only part of the religious wars which had swept back and forth across Europe for over a hundred years and was to continue for another fifty.

However, it would be too simple to say that the religious wars revealed the dangerous inadequacy of the Christian vision. After all, the vast majority of Europeans believed that the struggle between the two forms of Christianity was over a problem of inconceivable importance: How shall we be saved and redeemed to paradise? Indeed, it may be said, or at least has been said, that in this country the religious wars continue in the enmity between the Christian South and the secular North, precipitated by the Scopes monkey trial in Tennessee in 1925, as well as, in an older form, in the defeat of Al Smith and the somewhat surprising election of John Kennedy to the presidency. The second is a continuation of the religious wars of the sixteenth and seventeenth centuries; the first, of that struggle between Enlightenment and Christianity which was the crux of so much eighteenth-, nineteenth-, and twentieth-century intellectual and political effort.

No, the realization that the religious wars showed up the failure of medieval Christianity was not due to the wars themselves, but to an attitude already existing in the minds of a few people that made that realization possible. Only to the tiny minority of the European population who already entertained a new vision of human experience was this perception of the meaning of the religious wars possible, and this consequent judgment of Christianity. Voltaire's great cry, "*Écrasez l'infâme*," "Annihilate the church" —not Christianity but organized and socially institutionalized political Christianity—did not spring from his knowledge of the religious wars. It sprang from an orientation which preceded both perceptually and historically the bloodshed which Europe wallowed in to enforce by military authority those theological convictions which to the new Enlightened vision already appeared arbitrarily chosen and illogically affirmed. To the Enlightened mind it was no longer a glory to sacrifice oneself or others to an impossibility.

We may see, however, in a less strident form than religious wars, the consequences of the new vision. In quieter parts of cultural history than war and political manipulation can be better seen the true significance and importance of a cultural redirection. For instance, in the seventeenth century a new attitude toward mountains puts in a brilliant light what it meant to be free from priestcraft, tyranny, superstition, and prejudice.

By the sixteenth century the Middle Ages had richly developed the basic notion of a fallen world. The common assumption was now that the earth, being one of God's creatures, had its own soul, the *anima mundi*, as well as the body that we observe and on which we live. And just as man had been excluded from paradise, so the earth had, as a consequence of man's sinful disobedience of God, been excluded from its celestial company. In *Paradise Lost* Milton puts it thus:

> ... [Eve's] rash hand in evil hour
> Forth reaching to the Fruit, she pluck'd, she eat:
> Earth felt the wound, and Nature from her seat
> Sighing through all her Works gave signs of woe,
> That all was lost.

And when Adam also bit into the fruit,

> Earth trembl'd from her entrails, as again
> In pangs, and Nature gave a second groan,
> Skie lowr'd, and muttering Thunder, som sad drops
> Wept at compleating of the mortal Sin
> Original;

Before this all the earth had been fair and ordered, but now at God's orders the angels let loose winds, and intolerable cold and heat, required the moon to exert a noxious influence on earth, twisted the axis of the earth so that the equatorial plane was no longer identical with the plane of the planets, and set the animals, who had hitherto lived in peace one with the other, into flight and ravening pursuit. So wrote Milton, in the middle of the seventeenth century, after the new vision had been formulated; in such passages he still belongs to the Middle Ages.

Earth, now suffering from disorder and discord, also shows, in its body, the signs of age and death. It was a commonly held notion that before the fall there had been no mountains, that the surface of the earth had been smooth, a perfect sphere, for the most perfect thing conceivable is a sphere. By analogy with the human body, it was concluded that the mountains are earth's wrinkles. What is excluded from perfection and exposed to disharmony and decay must age, and what ages must, in the course of nature, die. Luther, indeed, expected that the world was growing older even more rapidly than John's *Revelation* was thought to indicate, that it would hardly outlast the sixteenth century. Edmund Spenser, meditating on the mutability of earthly things and the changeless eternity of the divine, longed for the coming of the Sabbaoth, the death of the world and the creation of a new world that should be changeless and eternal. "O that great Sabbaoth God, grant me that Sabbaoth's sight," are perhaps the last words he wrote of his great fragment *The Faerie Queene*, before his death in 1599, and we must not regard it as a fanciful notion. He meant it; he hoped to live to the end of the world, to see the Great Sabbaoth.

Mountains, then, are ugly, signs of the disorder from which man and earth suffer as a consequence of man's sin. When, therefore, toward the end of the seventeenth century, a few people suddenly, and with a sense of great daring, of entering into a new vision of the world, with a sense of religious fear and awe, began to see mountains as beautiful, as symbols of the power and beauty and majesty of God, as emblems of the divine, as evidence not of the disorder of the earth but of the order of the entire natural universe, clearly a profound reorientation had taken place. Order and value are seen not as something outside of time, or as something that existed before history and will again exist after it is finished, but as qualities inherent in the very universe, inherent here and now. Order and value are not something to be longed for in a future life but something which can be enjoyed in the present. To worship God is not to regard the beauty of the natural world as something that Satan uses to tempt us but as a quality which symbolizes the divine attributes. Our moral task is not to turn our backs upon the visible universe, but to turn toward it, to relate ourselves to it. The drive toward orientation does not find its goal in the divine mind or in the lost paradise revealed by religion, but discovers its gratification in the world itself. An orientational construct is projected upon the world. The vision of order that the human mind creates is identified with the structure of the world, and the structure of the mind and the structure of the world our senses give us are seen as identical. Reason, with its demand for consistency and simplicity, is the source of our knowledge of the character of reality, and deductive logic is the method by which we confirm in nature the intellectual structure our reason creates. And our reason shows us that nature is not evil but good.

We are living after this reorientation, and so we are confused by Shakespeare's *King Lear*. When Edmund appears in the first scene as a modest young man, we incline to be indulgent toward him, not in spite of the fact that he is illegitimate, a "natural" son, but because he is. If he suffers from certain social disadvantages, he is not at fault; he is the sufferer, to be pitied. And when he appears alone in the second scene and begins, "Thou, Nature, art my goddess; to thy law My services are bound," we feel at one with him. We have as yet no clue that he is going to turn out to be the villain of the piece. But the Elizabethan audience knew at once, in the very first scene, that he is to be regarded with suspicion, for he is the consequence of a natural relation, the most terrible and irresistibly delicious temptation of Satan, a relation unhallowed and unredeemed into the world of order and value by the divine ceremony of marriage within the church. And when he addresses nature with worship and passion, the Elizabethans knew at once, as Shakespeare intended they know, that here was an absolutely unscrupulous, vicious, and evil man.

It is difficult to comprehend how this extraordinary reorientation came about. It is not enough to say that it was the tendency of European culture so to develop. To say that is to say nothing. Nor is it sufficient to say that it was the necessary consequence of the mind's ability to perceive the disparity between the orientation and the data. On the contrary, to get ourselves, let alone anyone else, to perceive that disparity is fearfully difficult in any situation. The very fact that the inadequacy of orientation is revealed only in small-scale situations, and in extremely practical and pragmatic circumstances in which we are forced, for survival, to observe the disparity, militates against any general reorganization of our constructs. The emotional advantages of a fixed orientation are so tremendous, the explanations it offers are so universal, so all-embracing, its pragmatic value in maintaining a sense of continuity of identity is so well-nigh irresistible, that the disadvantages it may show in dealing with a fleeting and tiny segment of experience are as nothing.

For centuries upon centuries, it would appear, certain Indians of the southwestern United States have performed dances which they conceive as responsible for forcing the gods to send rain. When the rain fails to come, do they conclude that there are no gods, or that the rain ordinarily comes within a certain seasonal range, but sometimes comes outside of that range, that the coming of the rain is inherently, as far as we can see in a limited state of knowledge, irregular and somewhat random and not certain? Not at all; they save the orientation by concluding that they made an error in the dance ritual. Consequently, a vast amount of their time is spent in rehearsal, so that in actual performance no mistake will be made. "Millions for the orientation; not one cent for the reality," is the great human motto. Man can bear little reality; he prefers to live inside the screens which protect him from its onslaught.

Hence we cannot say that the old orientation had to be abandoned. Indeed, as I have suggested, for the majority of members of the Western cultural community, it never has been. No, we cannot say that there is something inherent in the human mind which forces him to abandon his fantasies, or at least in most minds. We must observe that the Enlightenment vision originally affected only a few hundred of the millions of Europeans who lived during the centuries of its formation, and that even today probably the majority of Europeans and Americans live in pre-Enlightenment terms, at least most of the time. Indeed, the coming of the Enlightenment was almost unique in human experience. Only Europe has, in historic times, experienced such a profound reorientation, let alone, as we shall see, another one on top of it. There must be some unique condition in European culture to account for this.

It is a tall order to attempt to account for what happened, yet I think it may be possible to find the reason in the extraordinary union of the Greek and the Hebraic visions accomplished in the early centuries of Christianity. As we have seen, the Hebrew and the Greek patterns matched, in one sense, perfectly, but in another they were in violent opposition. Both were emotionally satisfying in that they symbolized the drive for orientation and the drive toward reality, and both had a similar hierarchy: value lies in the divine order, and the failure of value in the world we live in. Yet the one was static, non-historical, regarding this world as unreal, while the other was dynamic, historical, regarding this world as not a non-world, but as a fallen world, of partial and damaged value, capable of redemption. In the one, order and value are eternally outside of time; in the other they will be restored to the world in time. The two visions were held together by the notions of creation and incarnation.

Yet if the divine world created the human world, knowing that the human world would be a failure, why did it do so? And how can the divine world, the sole realm of reality, be responsible for the human world, which is unreal? And why did the divine world create a human world that would have to be redeemed by the incarnation? So that it would have the pleasure of redemption? A rather selfish pleasure, considering the suffering involved. The questions are endless and the answers incredibly voluminous. But the more the questions were asked, the more the impossible paradox was revealed. Perhaps every religious orientation contains a terrible puzzle, an impossible paradox at its heart, a paradox which attempts to resolve the opposing drives of the human mind; but the unique experience of Europe was that its synthesis of two different cultural traditions meant that it had two solutions for the paradox, and that is one too many.

The consequence was that the higher cultural levels of religious behavior in Europe began to be characterized by an intellectual effort rather than by a worshipful cult. The rational strain inherited from sophisticated Jewish wit and Platonic analysis began at this level to come to the fore, to separate itself from the general confusion of a theology becoming progressively wilder and more dependent on political force to sustain itself. If the church, which was supposed to transmit order and value, to be the very model of order and value, which was supposed to exhibit the qualities of something instituted by the divine will and fiat, to calm the confusions of the human mind through the divine revelation which emanated through it to mankind—if this church was in fact the very source of orientative confusion, what was the individual to do, if he was aware of this? There was only one thing he could do—strip his mind of its medieval and ecclesiastical inheritance and let it face the world with its native powers.

Such an effort cannot in fact succeed, yet the attempt was magnificent and the consequences incalculable—and terrifying.

We are still, and more profoundly than ever, involved with the results. It is no wonder that thousands of men since then have looked back to the medieval world as itself a kind of paradise lost, a world when men were united in a common belief and protected from intellectual suffering by faith in a single sheltering church. But that is a dream. The Middle Ages were not like that. Ignorant armies clashed by night then also. Men did not leave the medieval vision because they were vicious, infected with the pride of Satan, any more than Adam and Eve left paradise because they had sinned. They left because of the conditions of paradise: it included a snake, and so did the medieval vision. They left paradise because it was impossible, Adam and Eve and the men of the Enlightenment alike.

Three doors out of the Middle Ages were discovered, from which three paths led, three ways of life, different yet uneasily alike. Each attempted to solve the same problem, and each used basically the same means to an answer, the power of the individual mind to create, on its own, a vision of order, to discover by itself a true ground for the sense of value, its own source for identity. And they were alike in that all three were primitivistic; each re-created the past in order to find strength for the present and the future. Each rewrote history.

The most conservative was the Protestant way, and it was perhaps the oldest, although it did not become a successful movement until the sixteenth century. The Protestants created a vision of the primitive church, before the coming of the Fathers who created the Catholic, the Roman, church. In its essence Protestant-ism says that the church is a social institution, a human conven-ience, an expression of charity, that it is not a necessary intermediary between man and God, that man, by cherishing the divine spark and soul within himself, can know God and expe-rience the divine within himself, can feel the loving presence of Christ the Redeemer by his own efforts and his own devotion, by opening his heart in privacy or with his fellows in congregations to the divine influence. Sustained as he is by such a vision, it is not surprising that the Protestant is enormously successful in economic and political activity, or in any area of human activity where he can enjoy the illusion that what he achieves he achieves by his own efforts.

More radical, but also more primitivistic, was the Platonic way. In this, Christianity was either dispensed with entirely, or, less drastically, beside it was structured another religion, which was used as a kind of model to reorganize Christianity. Platonic rationalism was revived, sometimes in a pure form, and the cultural elements of the ancient world were reorganized to symbolize the rationalistic vision, the power of the Platonized man to create a symbol of the divine, which would be quite separate and apart from the traditional Christian symbols. Florence was the great center of this activity, and Brunelleschi, Leonardo, Raphael, and Michelangelo were the aesthetic heroes, the men who created the new symbols, all four of them ravished by the Platonic vision. But the important thing about the Platonic way is that just as the Protestant way made it possible to achieve the Christian vision outside of the Roman church, so the new Platonists made it possible for the human mind to achieve the vision of order and value outside of Christianity. It gave men a new freedom and power and independence, though it also exposed them to the temptation of the most terrible orientative fantasy of all, short of the fantasies of schizophrenia, the notion that the world of the senses is unreal and only the consistent constructs of the mind are truly real. The seventeenth-century emotional intoxication with pure mathematics was one of the consequences; it too survives to the present.

The third way may be called the empirical way. Although he had his predecessors and learned much from the skeptical side of Plato, here the great culture hero was Francis Bacon. He was even more primitivistic than the Platonists, for he turned back, or fancied he had, to the pre-Platonic philosophers and separated with the utmost rigor natural philosophy from theology. To this tradition more than to any other is due the appearance in the seventeenth and eighteenth centuries of the symbol of the noble savage, the natural man, whose mind perceives reality directly—whose eye is innocent, uncorrupted by the sophistications of civilization, the idols, as Bacon called them, of the tribe, the cave, the market place, and the theater: that is, the illusions that man suffers from because he is a human being, because he is a unique cultural product, because he uses unanalyzed language, and because he has been intellectually amused and deceived by all preceding philosophies. Bacon was aware that the eye can never be absolutely innocent, that the mind can never be completely free from its limitations, yet he insisted—and he was of course right—that it can be infinitely freer than it normally is, so much freer that it might as well (and here he went too far) for practical purposes be regarded as capable of directly apprehending the structure of reality. For the empirical way is the way, as we now call it, of physical science, known until the middle of the nineteenth century as natural philosophy. And "nature" is the essence of the empirical way.

If all preceding thought has resulted in nothing but confusion, there is but one thing to do: examine the world as we find it. By painfully, laboriously, and patiently comparing things in the world with each other, by studying with all the instruments and intelligence under our control what we can see, feel, taste, and touch, we can build up a picture of what that world is really like, discover its laws and causes. Indeed, had not Copernicus, by putting the sun in the center of the solar system, and Galileo, by discovering a new planet, shown what could be done? Milton made himself believe in the medieval picture, but he was excited by Galileo. These initial successes confirmed what Bacon and his predecessors were sure of. The world is essentially simple, organized by a few laws and principles which the human mind can grasp. All we have to do is to go out and find them. Even if, as this tradition shortly began to show, and Bacon dimly came to perceive, we can never have a final and absolute knowledge of the structure of reality, we can always be moving toward it. It is there, for it was created by God, whose divine and orderly mind lies behind it. What is the world really like? It is like the mind of God, and for very good reasons.

Thus the empirical way was not so innocent as it believed. It proceeded on the basis of certain assumptions about what it was going to discover. That being the case, it is not surprising that very shortly it found what it had preconceived. But above all it asserted that order is inherent in the visible world, and it followed therefore that value was there also. Consequently disorder, the absence of value, the unreality of the sensory world, are all illusions and are the source of our ignorance. Mountains are beautiful, for they are the consequence of natural laws which rule the universe because God willed that they should. Thus the great medieval paradox of time and eternity, of history and non-history, of unreality and partial value, of illusion and disorder is resolved. Order and value exist here and now in the visible world, and our identity is to be derived from the observation, study, and comprehension of that visible world. Is it any wonder that modern science is founded on the intellectual achievements of the seventeenth century, which has been called the great century, the century of escape from the medieval fantasy?

All three ways—the Protestant, the Platonic, and the empirical—were united by and culminated in a single discovery, a single tremendous reorientation. We are ill at ease in our world not because of sin but because of ignorance. To the Protestant a power-mad church keeps us from the true knowledge of God and the real nature of the Christian inheritance. Freed from ignorance, we find that grace, as John Bunyan said, abounds even to the chief of sinners. To the Platonist, ignorance of the powers of the human reason is the great inhibitor of the mind's freedom. To the empiricist, ignorance of the structure of the world prevents us from knowing our place in that world, in which we are properly at home, for we too are natural products, and the natural laws govern us as well as the stars. For all their many and unending quarrels with each other, there are always men who try, with some success, to draw them together, and the three ways can fall into an alliance against the medieval church. "*Écrasez l'infâme*," cried Voltaire, and he meant it. In place of the ignorant conviction of sin, they prayed for intellectual light. They were new men, these men of the Enlightenment, and they were sure of it.

If we look at man as a biological organism with an environment to which he must adapt himself, as a few men of the later seventeenth century began to, the substitution of ignorance for sin meant that man's failure to relate himself to his environment, to establish what we now would call a perfect ecology, was a consequence not of his failure to obey certain absolute moral laws but of his failure to understand the laws of nature. His moral task, as Bacon insisted, was to comprehend those natural laws and to act accordingly. So far so good. The men of the Enlightenment saw their task clearly, but beneath this apparent clarity was a terrible tangle; though it was some time before the difficulties began to appear, it is useful for us to be aware of them before we examine the stages in the development of the Enlightenment.

We live, thus runs the argument, in an ordered universe; even though we do not and never can understand fully the nature of that structure, the fact of that order assures us that value is structured into reality. Part of that ordered universe is the natural world, the earth on which we live. If laws govern the universe, laws govern our immediate natural environment. Now men, since they are part of that environment and historically subsequent to it, must have developed out of that environment. Since man is primarily a social animal (both reason and revelation—Adam was lonely—tell us that), society must be a natural product, the basic social unit being the family. It follows that man is truly human only when his life is socially structured, that is, when he is playing a role sanctioned by tradition and function. Man's identity, then— and this is the most important point if we are to understand nineteenth century culture—is derived from society. Up to this point there appear to be no particular difficulties. However, there is a snake in this garden too. If value is structured into the universe, and if this value takes the form of universal laws of nature, then whatever is natural is good. In Pope's famous statement, "Whatever is, is right." Whatever exists, exists in the way it ought to exist. Yet obviously there is evil in the world, or at least something that looks like evil from the human point of view. Thus the Enlightenment was faced with the same old problem it set out to resolve. The terms are different but the pattern is the same. If God created man out of love, why did He plunge him into a world of sin? If nature produced man by natural, that is by "good," processes, how is it that he lives in a world to which he is not perfectly adapted?

Pope's solution is instructive. It has always been a puzzle

that, after having created in his *Essay on Man* of the 1720's a vision of perfect natural order in which everything is as it ought to be, he then spent the next fifteen years writing the most powerful satires in the English language, culminating in his great second version of *The Dunciad*, which foresees imaginatively the return of chaos. How could he have justifiably attacked man after having demonstrated that man cannot act other than he does, and, looked at within the entire scheme of nature, other than he ought? This appears so gross an inconsistency that even the silliest optimism could not have have missed it. Pope was far from being a silly man. The answer lies in man's ignorance. Dullness, not merely stupidity but intellectual perversity, is the goddess of *The Dunciad*, his epic attack on the intellectually corrupt. As we have seen, to the mind of the Enlightenment ignorance assumes the function of sin in the Christian scheme. Pride is not rebellion against God, that is, the fantasy that a man can live without the moral governance of God; pride is the fantasy that man understands the world perfectly and can live without the corrective agency of knowledge and the scientific comprehension of his environment.

For a time and at first glance this seems to be fully satisfying, but it is only to push the problem one step back in what is in fact an infinite regress. That is, it is unsolvable. For if man is the product of nature, man's mind must be the product of nature. How, then, are we to account for his ignorance, for the gap between mind and nature? It is not enough to say with Pope that man has only to know his limitations in order to act correctly; the very scheme in which the problem is set up demands that we ask why man has limitations.

Nor is this the only unsolvable problem the Enlightenment encountered. There was the question of moral choice. Once men refused to accept the inherited scheme of moral judgments sanctified by the church and began to subject moral decisions to rational analysis, it was necessary to decide on what grounds a moral decision should be made. Clearly, according to the new scheme of thinking the right decision is the natural decision. But since man's actions are a product of natural laws, it is as natural to commit murder as it is to give alms. Three solutions were developed to this problem, all of them inherently unsatisfactory.

The first was what has been rightly called cosmic toryism. According to this solution, society being a natural product, the customs that society has legalized and institutionalized are natural. Thus it is wrong to commit murder, but right to hang a murderer. The moral task is to adapt ourselves to things as they actually are. The weakness of this position is that no society has a consistent structure of customs and laws, and that various societies have various customs.

A second solution was to identify the statistically most frequent with the normal, the normal with the natural, and the natural with the good. The most common custom, the consensus, is the good. But here again, there is a weakness. What is statistically most frequent at one time and in one social area may be abnormal in another. If you had been brought up in the company of thieves, what is abnormal, unnatural, and evil about conforming to the statistically most frequent behavior of your neighbors? Among thieves, the honest man is abnormal. One had best lead such a man to a thieves' psychiatrist.

The third dominating solution, and the most dangerous, was to create a hierarchy of the natural. There is no evil; true. But some actions are better than others. Intelligence and knowledge can tell us which action conforms better to the laws of nature. Since man is a social animal, it is less natural to murder than to cherish. It is likewise more natural to live in social harmony than under the domination of political tyranny, which plays upon men's ignorance and maintains itself by keeping men ignorant. Education is the solution of all ills. Man, therefore, is perfectible. But to make him perfect, whatever impedes his perfection, his perfect adaptation to his environment, the way he ought to live, must be destroyed. And since your ends are natural, therefore good, your means to achieve those ends are by definition good. If the French aristocracy stands in the way of creating a perfect society, slaughter them. Or to put it in modern terms, if the Communist theory of history is scientifically true, therefore the aims of the Communist state are natural. It follows that the rulers of the Communist state are justified in doing anything they think advisable, that is, what their theory of history tells them is advisable, in bringing about Communist ends. The temptations—and possibilities—of such a moral theory for the self-righteous man are breath-taking. He is exposed, without correction, to the self-indulgence of the puritan, the fantasy that he is invariably right. And there was no puritan so puritanical as Robespierre, who, had he not been stopped, would no doubt have ended up by sending everybody to the guillotine— and then have married Alice's Queen of Hearts and started a new human race.

Today it is not difficult to see the value problem and the moral problem of the Enlightenment. It turned out that these men had no orientation which firmly structured value into the universe, for the whole orientation was so mutually interdependent in all its parts—the cosmos, the natural environment, society, and the individual—that the uncovering of an inconsistency in any part brought the whole thing to the ground. The unsolvable moral problems which were the consequence of Enlightenment thinking, once it was realized that there was no natural or empirical basis for morality, threatened and eventually ruined the entire construct. Yet we must always remember that just as millions of people in Europe and America have never truly entered the Enlightenment, so millions of people have never truly left it, have never seen its weaknesses. When the American capitalist insists that what is good for his industry is good for the nation, that is, what is good for him is good for mankind, he is thinking in Adam Smith's terms: If the individual follows scrupulously his own self-interest, the invisible hand—that is, natural laws or the God who decrees the natural laws —will insure that all mankind will be benefited, automatically. And how many times have we not heard, how many times have we not ourselves said, in defending ourselves against one who accuses us of immoral behavior, "What are you complaining about? It's legal, isn't it?" or "Everybody's doin' it, aren't they?" or "It's natural, isn't it?" How rarely we get beyond these replies! Yet the Enlightenment must not be denigrated. Man is young, and the men of the

Enlightenment made a mighty step forward. They turned the attention of men to their environment. They created a few more chinks in the screens with which we surround ourselves. Though they knew less about the character of the natural world than they thought they did, at least they said, "Study nature, and master it."

Turning to the historical development of the Enlightenment, we can discern three stages, though it is necessary to remember that not everybody went through these stages—some did not live long enough—and that while the last stage was being experienced by a few, others were still discovering the second, or the first, or passionately resisting even the first. Nevertheless, each of these three stages emerged in an historical order, and each subsequent one developed from the preceding and led to the next. But always, in this and in what follows, it must be remembered that it is intolerably difficult for any individual to transcend an old general orientation and create a new one. But once he has done that, it is ordinarily even more difficult to proceed to another. Any individual who had arrived at one of these stages, therefore, was exceedingly prone to resist the next one, and to struggle against the revelation of any inconsistency in his current one. Not infrequently, a more advanced stage of development is distorted to conform to a previous one. Thus many Enlightenment ideas were distorted to fit into some kind of Christian scheme; and for obvious reasons the Protestants were particularly eager to make this kind of confusion, though there were plenty of Catholics who attempted these awkward syntheses.

The first stage was the development of rationalism, which is the particular character of the first half or so of the seventeenth century. The assumption of rationalism is that the structure of the mind is identical with the structure of non-mental reality. Thus, if I decide that by examining the laws of the mind I perceive a system of functional interrelations of ideas which has the character, let us say, of a mathematical system, I will conclude that the world can be completely described in mathematical terms. Or if this mental structure has the character of a machine, the world likewise can be exhaustively described in mechanistic terms. Or if this mental structure has, looking at it in terms of its history, the character of an organism, the world can be so described, because it really is an organism. The source of rationalism is not difficult to locate, given the terms I have so far used, and indeed I have already suggested how it came about. It is a selection of the two logically matching parts of the four elements of the Judeo-Platonic synthesis. Value and reality are in the world; order is the embodiment (or incarnation) of value and reality. Since God created both mind and the world, order, value, and reality are in both. It follows that order is the character of the real world, and that value is derived from that real world, that is, from nature. Since, then, the mind by observing its own operations arrives at order, it follows that that order is identical with the order in the real world. The individual, then, without the aid of a revelation transmitted by an institutionalized church, can arrive at value. In short, the unaided reason deduces the existence of order, and thus of value.

Descartes' apparently clear, straightforward, and irresistibly self-evident remark is the central specimen of seventeenth-century rationalism. *"Cogito, ergo sum."* "I think, therefore I am." He does not mean, "I as a biological organism am characterized by certain behavioral brain patterns." Not at all. His assumption is, that since his mind performs certain self-consistent logical, mathematical, and deductive operations, it has the characteristic of order. Therefore, a real entity—since that which has order is an entity— must be performing these operations. Put this way, his famous statement appears to be a bit of orientative mythology, a hocus-pocus. And indeed, I am afraid that it is. Further, the proud rejection of revelation contained seeds of further trouble, difficulties which Descartes himself felt.

To reject revelation as a basis for truth means that the individual is thrown forward on experience itself, and Descartes quickly came to the realization that the mind could deduce all kinds of structural patterns which are not to be found in nature at all. It became necessary, therefore, to test the mental construct of order. Hence it is no accident that the seventeenth century saw the birth of modern science and of the experimental method, though there is still, even today, considerable argument about precisely what the experimental method amounts to, and what degree of solidity can be ascribed to its results. In any event, empiricism, as distinguished from what I earlier called the empirical way, was the next stage in the development of the Enlightenment. But it must always be remembered that it was by no means a raw empiricism. No, it was an empiricism based upon a rationalistic principle, that is, the principle that order and value are structured into the universe, and that our moral task is to discover them.

This stage occurred toward the end of the seventeenth century, aided by the mental empiricism of Locke and the apparent demonstration by Newton that the world is indeed a perfectly structured mechanism. (I say "apparent" because Newton himself did not believe that he had done anything of the sort. The general cultural interpretation put on his work, however, was that he had.) Now once it has been admitted that the mind can make mistakes, even though those mistakes are perfectly consistent with the established principles from which they are deduced, and that every proposition must be tested by examination, two things irresistibly follow: first, that there are degrees of error; second, that every accepted notion must be re-examined. Further, as we have already seen, the test of a proposition is how well it conforms to natural law—any proposition, including moral propositions. For example, are the institutions of monarchy and aristocracy the consequence of man's ignorance or of man's wisdom?

The great myth of the Enlightenment was written at this point, and published in 1719: *Robinson Crusoe*, by Daniel Defoe. Here we have an ordinary man, isolated on a desert island with nothing but his tools who proceeds to adapt himself perfectly to that environment, and to create an ordered society by becoming the master, savior, and employer of a natural inferior, the black man, Friday. The importance of the Protestant way in this solution is scarcely to be missed, but even more significant is the adequacy of the individual to get along in the world without the support of a traditional social order. It was a revolutionary book. Now Defoe was perfectly aware of the intellectual developments of the preceding century, and he was particularly aware of the power of science to correct our ignorance. In an odd way, *Crusoe* is a kind of symbolic autobiography, for Defoe himself toured all England, taking an inventory of the country's resources, and informing his fellow businessmen of what he had found and suggesting how his findings might be used. He also was one of the projectors of the time, those men who wished to use the new knowledge by conquering nature and creating new industries. Such was the scientific ignorance of the time that most of the projectors were wild and spectacular failures, but those who were not laid the foundation for the industrial revolution of the eighteenth and nineteenth centuries.

Yet shortly thereafter, less than a decade, Pope published his *Essay on Man*, and we have seen what difficulties it involved and what further difficulties it led to. Why is it natural to be unnatural? Why does man have limitations? To keep ourselves firm in the terribly confusing decades that followed, let us have the scheme of things perfectly clearly before us: Value is structured into the cosmos; the natural world is part of the cosmos; society is part of the natural world; man is a member of society. His own value and his own identity, therefore, are dependent upon his ability to maintain a faith in the structure of the cosmos. Yet if a radical imperfection is discovered in that cosmos, or if a radical defect is discovered in nature, or if society is, by its nature, necessarily unjust, then the whole structure collapses. The next stage of the Enlightenment, then, was characterized by an attempt to hold the Enlightenment vision together by enthusiasm, that is, by emotional rather than rational affirmation, or to do just the opposite, to disengage oneself from the problem by a total skepticism.

For in fact these radical defects in the universe, in nature, in society, in the moral character of man and in his very mind, were being discovered. It seems astonishing to us now, but the Lisbon earthquake and tidal wave of 1755 sent a thrill of emotional horror through the Enlightened minds of Europe. Since we have lived long after this event, our attitude tends to be, "There are volcanoes; why whimper?" Yet it was not an intellectual shock; it was a shock to the orientation that had led men to affirm a continuity of interest and purpose between man and the natural world. The realization that nature is utterly indifferent to man has always caused a convulsion of feeling ever since the source of value was transferred from outside the world to inside the world. When people ask, "What is the purpose of human existence?" they assume they are asking a question that can be answered. If what happened to Lisbon can happen to any city, it is hard to believe that God is working through nature to benefit mankind. It really makes God seem a kind of sublime jester; or like the Marquis de Sade, one concludes that God is cruel, that He has arranged the world so that He can enjoy the spectacle of human suffering. So far as anyone could see, except belated medievalists who interpreted it as God's punishment to a wicked city, the Lisbon earthquake was simply pointless.

Voltaire drew the conclusion quickly, in *Candide*. Reason gives us a false picture of the world; experience reveals our inability to organize empirical data into meaningful patterns, whether natural or moral. The only thing to do is to work in our gardens. And in truth, we know now that the optimism of the Enlightenment began to fade at this point, that many of the great Enlightenment figures, sometimes secretly, sometimes for circulation in manuscript, only rarely for publication, began to show a pessimistic strain. It was not dominating, any more than skepticism was dominating, but it was there, and it heralded profound changes.

In the meantime, the dominating mode was enthusiasm and sentimentality. In particular, imagination assumed the function of reason. Since neither reason nor direct, natural experience could demonstrate that value was structured into the world, the Enlightenment fell back on a profounder level of personality, the poetic power to penetrate intuitively and imaginatively into the structure of the world, and to affirm its order and value in noble and exciting language. We can understand what was going on if we observe the sentimental strategy to dissipate a threat to an orientation.

In 1790, a year after the French Revolution had begun, in the Champ de Mars, on the western outskirts of Paris, was built a vast circular assembly place. The citizens of Paris, aided by the king himself, constructed a great shallow bowl, and in the center they built a round altar, raised on circles of steps, with a hearth at the middle. This was the Altar of the Fatherland, and hither came, a year after the taking and destruction of the Bastille, representatives from every department in France, carrying their local banners. Here they assembled, filling the sides of the bowl and its floor, gathered within the very symbol of perfection and order, a circle, and swore an oath to devote their lives to King and to Country; those there assembled, the whole city of Paris looking on, took on themselves the magic name of Patriot. This was the regeneration of France, this was a moment of incredible enthusiasm and joy and good feeling. Here every tension aroused by the whirlwind of political and social and economic events that had struck France, was resolved. Here, indeed, the problem of society was resolved, for the social contract was sworn anew.

All public events of this sort, including the swearing-in of a new president on the steps of the United States Capitol, have a silly and sentimental aura about them. They do nothing; they accomplish nothing; but they make everyone feel good and subtly convinced that now his problems will be solved. But of all such events, probably this ceremony on the Champ de Mars was the silliest and the most sentimental. If a tension cannot be discharged by comprehending a situation, if the situation is so complex and obscure that there is no understanding it, we ascribe value to any stimulus able to discharge that tension in emotional release, in tears and enthusiasm, and simultaneously we use the threatened orientation to suppress any data or information that is inconsistent with it. Clearly, it was apparent to the intelligent observers of France in 1790 that the worst was yet to come, that a process of social disintegration had begun which no ceremony in the Champ de Mars could possibly halt. Anyone with half an eye could see it.

This event was typical of the cultural tone of the third stage of the Enlightenment. Those who could not face the skepticism, those who could not endure the pessimism, turned to the imagination. The imagination perceived nature in such a way that nature, through the imagination, redeemed man. The Boy Scout movement was one of the odder results, but it is an orientation which certainly is one of the most common today, in the middle of the twentieth century. To go out into nature, to camp, to visit famous gardens, to feel this élan, is to experience a flowing into the personality of a kind of virtue in the old sense—strength, dignity, value. It is a kind of ritual of rebirth, and it is fascinating to see how in so many modern churches, there has been a synthesis of Christianity and late Enlightenment nature worship. Innumerable modern churches are set not only on landscaped grounds, but even on grounds left in their natural state. In the architectural magazines of today and in certain popular magazines that report on architectural fashions, one finds example after example of a church in which the wall behind the altar and the crucifix have been replaced by great sheets of glass which permit the congregation to see a beautiful landscape. It would be impossible to find a better symbolization of the Christianized Enlightenment, nor a better way to understand the shock to Enlightenment enthusiasm when it is suggested that nature is indifferent and cares nothing for mankind.

Yet there are always people for whom the sentimental solution to a problem is impossible. The development, half-concealed, of pessimism and skepticism indicates this. But they did no more than doubt, and they cannot be taken too seriously. They were superficial. The skeptics and the pessimists were not thoroughgoing. Like Voltaire they said, "Let us turn our backs upon the problem and work for the betterment of men." Thus Diderot, one of the most passionate workers for political betterment, was also, in a work he did not publish in his lifetime, one of the most despairing of the late eighteenth-century *philosophes,* as they were called. This orientative schizophrenia could endure no better than the kind which emerges from deeper levels of the personality, perhaps from the biochemistry of the human organism itself. It could be maintained by men who had behind them the drive of a lifetime of progressive Enlightened effort to clear away ignorance, but it was of no use to those born later, men born in the last decades of the century, who grew up in the shrill enthusiasm of those decades, who felt the moral impossibilities which the Enlightenment mode of thought led to. There were a few such, scattered here and there throughout Europe, thinking for the most part in isolation, and to them the French Revolution was the ultimate test. Here was a vast political endeavor in which an enormous effort was made to put the Enlightenment faith into practice, in a situation supported by the enthusiasm—not yet perceived as sentimental—of millions of people, both in France and in other countries. What was its lesson? It released social, emotional and moral forces of which the Enlightenment tradition had been totally ignorant, which the vaunted nature and reason, and enthusiasm, and empiricism had never discovered. And it showed that those forces could be controlled only by a brutal and repressive tyranny which—and here was the real horror—was in itself perfectly justifiable on Enlightenment principles.

The logical possibilities had been exhausted. Value is not to be found in a divine world into which we shall enter in the future, or into which we can now penetrate by pure thought or mystic rapture; nor is value structured into the world we know. The universe is a chaos, a meaningless chaos; nor is society any different. But if order is lost, and value is lost, then identity is lost. And man—or man as a few men see him—truly enters the waste land. This had happened before, that a man had lost his orientation, but before, he could always find his way back to what he had left. Now a few men saw clearly that return was impossible. Culture was in an unparalleled historical crisis; and the man who felt it became a wanderer on the face of the earth, rooted out of his social context, and lost in a meaningless cosmic chaos.

At this point the truly modern age begins. To understand it, or to understand the construct which I shall present as an instrument to organize its multifarious data, it is necessary to change focus. So far I have discussed the history of orientation and culture abstractly, generally, at a great distance from the documents themselves. Now, after looking at things from afar so that detail disappears in general contours and patterns, we shall swoop down on individual men and individual works. Let us see how fundamental orientative patterns, and metamorphoses of patterns, are to be perceived in unique, individual, self-contained works of art and thought.

# Part Two

# The Alienated Vision

# CHAPTER IV

## *The Discovery of the Self*

W HEN THAT CHAOS first appeared we can scarcely
know. Who were the first men who could no longer maintain
enthusiastic sentimentalism by suppressing their perceptions of
disorder? Who first passed through pessimism and saw that to say
that this is the worst of all possible worlds is no more satisfactory
than to say it is the best? Who first perceived that the skepticism
which placed pessimism and sentimentalism in ironic juxtaposition
left the individual no place to go, no role to play in society, and not
merely no basis for making moral choices but—and this was the
most devastating blow to the sense of identity—no reason to go to
the trouble to make any? All we have to go on, it must be remembered, is documents, and the first document that reveals the breakdown of the Enlightenment orientation and its failure to solve the
profoundest problems of existence is *The Sorrows of Young Werther* by Johann Wolfgang von Goethe, first published in 1774
and reissued in a revised edition in 1787.

Indeed the very structure of that novel indicates the failure
of eighteenth-century forms. It begins as an epistolary novel, a
story told in a series of imaginary letters, but before the end
Werther is so distraught that we begin to get fragments of diaries,
jottings on odd slips of paper, and finally direct narration. The
novel in letters had been established by Samuel Richardson thirty
years before; it had been widely imitated; and it was related to
such things as Montesquieu's *Persian Letters* and Goldsmith's

*The Citizen of the World*, both purporting to be written by Asiatics visiting Europe. Further, the ability to write a good letter was a requirement for the eighteenth-century gentleman or gentlewoman, and not a few individuals, men like Horace Walpole, Lord Chesterfield, Alexander Pope, wrote their personal letters with a side glance toward publication, or revised them for the press. The importance of letter writing for the men of the Enlightenment can scarcely be exaggerated. The exchange of information and ideas, many of them unorthodox and objectionable to political and religious authorities who were for the most part still living in the medieval world, had to depend on letter writing, to avoid both censorship and the delays of printing and publication.

In a sense, the Enlightened consisted of a vast secret society extending throughout Europe and the settlements of America. The Masons were but one of a number of these secret or semi-secret groups which specifically recognized that if the Enlightenment was to succeed, it must remain, at least in part, under cover. All kinds of correspondence societies were the heart of Enlightenment activity, and behind each of the revolutions of the time, American, French, Polish, Irish, and the rest of them, lay a web of internationally organized letter-writing organizations. Letters were semi-public documents, and good, important letters were passed from member to member, copied, preserved, and often eventually printed.

Any letter, even the most casual, even the semi-literate, is a work of art. It exists not merely to exchange information, but to project an attitude, a social role, an orientation. By innumerable touches, most of them unconscious, any letter writer tries to inform his correspondent of the attitude from which the interpretation of the statements in the letter is to be developed. And in the letters of the Enlightenment, it is hard to say which was the more important, the information or the orientation. The letter, then, was considered to be adequate to say anything, to project any kind of attitude. And in the Enlightenment, as always in human affairs, the private letter existed to reinforce the configuration of the role in which the writer wished his correspondent to cast him. But most important, since to the Enlightenment the sense of identity existed only in terms of a social role derived ultimately from society's adaptation to nature, the letter existed to reinforce to writer and to reader the social role in which the writer perceived himself.

Thus when Goethe permitted the epistolary structure of his novel to break down, he was not merely wrestling with the problem of how to present a suicide in letters written by the man who commits it. That was a minor technical problem, capable of a dozen solutions. Indeed, had he wished, a solution was at hand, for a brief headnote suggested that the book had been put together by an editor. A similar note at the end could have told us of the suicide. But in fact, long before the end, the epistolary structure is partially abandoned, and the editor assumes the role of narrator and commentator, of one who had known Werther and had conducted an investigation to discover the circumstances of his fearful death and his burial in unconsecrated ground. Something else, then, is at work besides a mere technical difficulty. That new element is the breakdown of socially structured role-playing itself. The violence of Werther's feelings sunders him from both traditional and late Enlightenment roles, and his suicide is symbolic of the failure of his sense of value and the extinction of his sense of identity.

When we first meet him he is a typical late Enlightenment enthusiast, determined to be good-humored in every situation (ill-humor he regards as the worst of vices), glowing in the goodness of simple men, rhapsodizing over nature and the wisdom and benevolence of God as displayed in the natural world. To be sure, he has turned his back on the great world, and his effort to find a satisfactory career in the train of an ill-tempered ambassador turns out disastrously; but he resigns his position solely because he has created a scandal by lingering at a nobleman's house and mingling with the aristocratic guests, who alone were to be received that evening. But this incident is given to indicate that he has rejected artificial distinctions and has arrived at the democratic vision of Burns' "A man's a man for a' that." It is the new conception of a truly natural society that he is interested in. He is not alienated from society, but only from outworn social structures.

It is perfectly consistent, then, that at his first sight of Lotte, his beloved, she is slicing bread for her younger brothers and sisters, whose social mother she has become on the death of their biological mother. Poor Werther falls desperately in love, and the degree of his desperation is indicated by his sudden vision that the world is as full of meaningless destruction as it is of beautiful creation. He plunges, that is, from sentimentalism into its equally illusory opposite, pessimism. For Lotte is engaged to another. He respects her, he respects Albert, her betrothed, and thinks of him, after a bit of initial bridling, as a dear friend. Yet he feels it wise to get out of the situation, takes his position as the ambassador's assistant, and as result of his *faux pas* experiments with skepticism. He is now beyond and above the world, but in fact he is nowhere. The gates of the waste land are beginning to open.

Now it is that his passions, the deep, irrational forces of human nature which even Christianity makes better orientative sense out of than the Enlightenment, really begin to invade his life. In spite of himself, he is pulled back to Lotte, and when he returns to the countryside where she lives, he finds that a happy mother has been crushed by the pointless death of a child, that a trusting father has been cheated by his relatives and reduced to penury, that a vicious and stupid clergyman's wife has cruelly cut down some linden trees that everyone loved, that a good quiet boy had gone insane for no reason at all and after partial recovery looks back to his period of total and confined insanity as his only time of happiness, that a charming young man, in love with a woman for whom he worked but whose social position did not make marriage with him impossible, had been dismissed when he revealed his love and soon after had murdered the man hired in his place. It is no wonder that Werther writes, "Alas! The void—the fearful void within me! Sometimes I think, if I could once—only once—press her to my heart, this void would all be filled." Lotte has become his sole source of value.

And what of Lotte, the radiant Lotte, now the bride of the

dear friend Albert? One wonders. As Werther's passion grows he begins to hate Albert, the husband; he begins to use all kinds of subterfuges to see Lotte when Albert, the busy, correct, and dull court official, is not around. Taking her cue from Werther's earlier state, Lotte attempts to maintain the sentimental design for living with two men, one her husband, one her dear *Hausfreund*, as the Germans say. Her behavior reveals sharply the weaknesses of sentimental enthusiasm, for she is attempting to do the impossible, to control profound and irrational passions, a thousand times more powerful because they now have only Lotte herself as their focus and source of gratification. She alone, in Werther's waste land, retains radiance. She is the symbol of all the affirmative power left to him. Uncontrollably, he breaks the shimmering sentimental bubble in which she has attempted to contain all three of them. Like all sentimentalists, she wants her tune without paying the piper. Werther counters by seizing her in his arms; she repulses him, but not before responding. She flees, refuses to see him. He goes home and prepares for suicide.

And now comes Goethe's most subtle and powerful touch. To do the job, he sends his servant to borrow Albert's pistols under the pretext that he needs them for a journey he is about to take. Albert is not at home. Lotte, fearful and trembling, gives the weapons to the servant—and omits to tell her husband what she has done. Poor Werther! He bungles this job too, and lingers for hours with his brains half shot out. But when Lotte hears the bell rung by the servant who has rushed to fetch his master's dear friends, she shudders even before she knows who is ringing, and when she hears what has happened, she falls senseless. Lotte, in short, knows what has happened, just as she knew why the pistols were borrowed. Werther has aroused in her those very powers which he could not control in himself. Does her cooperation in Werther's suicide mean that she sees this as the only way out? Or does she too wish to surrender to frightful forces which sentimentalism mistakenly thought it could control? Goethe does not tell us, nor can we with certainty deduce an explanation; for in Lotte's act he wishes to symbolize that vision—of pointless, purposeless chaos—which destroys Werther.

Goethe himself—for the story is, except for the conclusion, autobiographical—got away from his Lotte, fled from a situation which was driving him, perhaps, to suicide, but which certainly had revealed to him the failure of the terminal Enlightenment solutions. Thus the symbolic significance of Werther's act is the destruction of identity, consequent upon the failure of the vision of an ordered cosmos and of a meaningful society, either traditional or sentimental. Candide could find redemption by growing cabbages, by adjusting himself to the demands of the environment at the simplest and most "natural" level. But to Werther—and to Goethe—such a solution was no longer possible. Order, meaning, value, and identity were lost; and for the first time the problem of nineteenth-century man is revealed. He cannot begin building his world from a lost paradise, from an attainable heaven, or even an attainable hell, or from a perfectly structured world in which he lives. He must begin in the waste land, which is worse than hell, for hell at least has order and meaning; its absence of value implies the existence of value—with God; it is not a place of non-value; and though identity may be a torment, it is still identity. Guilt implies the existence of virtue, but the waste land has neither virtue nor guilt.

Total disorientation has appeared. Neither within the personality nor without, in the empirical world, can be discovered any but the most trivial and transitory gratifications for the orientative drive. And life without profound orientative gratifications is not worth the trouble. Such a life is almost unendurable; insanity, suicide, or wild destruction seem to be the only sensible ways to act. The individual is sustained, more and more feebly, by behavior at the automatic level, but the relentless knife of self-probing strikes deeper and deeper; and more and more of civilization and acquired culture is cut out. Or the individual can sustain himself by forcing upon himself a purely external discipline accepted and self-imposed solely as a means to keep going the processes of life at their basic biological levels.

But a sensitive and cultivated and intelligent person can live this way only a certain amount of time. Either there is a despairing and self-deceiving return, blind and unquestioning, to an orientation such as religion which has already been rejected as inadequate, or the individual must break through into an entirely new orientation. The problem was: Where should he begin: and how?

For a moment Werther himself touched lightly the nerve that was, for a few, to release the orientative drive in a new direction. Total disorientation is emotionally—and physiologically—unbearable; the orientative drive must have gratification; for that drive is a consequence of biological adaptation and is built into the brain and the nervous system. In a flash of momentary insight Werther says that he has lost the power to make the world beautiful and orderly. Yet he could do nothing with that sudden burst, and in the final words of his last letter to Lotte he mindlessly reiterates a conventional piety and belief in immortality which all his actions deny and which it is impossible to take seriously. Goethe himself, we can guess, could do nothing with this notion of "making" the world beautiful and orderly instead of "seeing" it as orderly. For a second a European man sees the source of beauty and order in himself and yet does not deny the reality, in a Platonizing manner, of the experienced world.

While Goethe was writing *Werther* in Frankfurt, far to the east in Königsberg in East Prussia an extraordinary mind was at work on a book which has been called the most important in the history of modern thinking, the most important work of philosophy since Plato. Whether it was or not, it certainly appeared to offer, and in a sense did offer, the solution to Werther's and Goethe's orientative dilemma; and when Immanuel Kant's *The Critique of Pure Reason*, i.e., "The Critical Analysis of those Mental Activities which Operate Independently of Sensory Data," appeared in 1781, although Goethe hesitated to plunge into its labyrinths, he was at least prepared for Kant's 1790 book, *The Critique of Judgment*, which he did read and admire.

For Goethe saw in Kant a man, twenty years older than himself, who was arriving by a somewhat different course of thinking at results similar to his own in the years after *Werther;* and since these conclusions were so strange, so profoundly aberrant in the light of Christian and Enlightenment thinking, Goethe took comfort in the thought that he was not alone. And indeed, all over Europe, here and there, in one way or another, various personalities who had had the experience of Werther were turning in the same direction, the only way, it appeared, out of the Wertherian waste land. So similar were their ideas to Kant's that over and over again scholars have attempted to demonstrate or have simply assumed that these ideas were derived from Kant. And yet I think that it was not so. It was the very force of the cultural situation, of the orientative collapse at the end of the eighteenth century—a collapse which became apparent to different individuals in a variety of circumstances and in endlessly different phenomena—that channeled separate individuals in the same direction. What we have to deal with here is the peculiar phenomenon of cultural convergence, of the strange fact that individuals quite unknown to each other, and with no possible means of communication, simultaneously invent machines or instruments, or create ideas or artistic styles, which are astoundingly similar, or even almost precisely the same. It is a phenomenon which we shall meet frequently in this book; in a way it is both my subject and my justification.

In any event Kant's new vision, which in its incredible richness, prolixity, and even inconsistency (one source of its difficulty) may for our purposes be reduced to something not perhaps precisely simple but at least statable in not very many words. Reacting against the total skepticism of the Scotsman, David Hume, who had dissolved the mind, Kant first demonstrated that since pure reason because of the very way it operates invariably arrives at antinomies, at pairs of concepts—such as the finite and the infinite character of the universe—both of which cannot be true, and that therefore the mind can operate independently of sensory data, he proceeds to establish a series of important notions: that order is a characteristic of the mind; that order, since it is a consequent of the way the mind works, is not, in the Platonic sense, a reflection of a divine or transcendent order—one that is above, beyond, outside of, other than, the mind and the real world; that the forms with which we organize experience (that is, the data which the senses feed to the mind) are derived from the mind and not from nature; that therefore whether nature has structure or not, we cannot possibly know it. And the same goes for any possibility of knowledge of God. Perhaps we are right in thinking there is a God, but reason cannot assure us of it nor tell us anything about him.

No wonder the King of Prussia ordered Kant into silence, a silence which, as an old, frail, and weary man of seventy, he observed. From our point of view the orientative drive was freed from the divine, and it was freed from nature. The rage for order was, it appeared, only a human rage. Or, should we say, being human, for the first time its real importance could be grasped? For Kant turned the world inside out. The human mind was no longer seen either as a degenerate emanation from the divine or as the ignorant offspring of the cosmic order of nature, but the very creator of the cosmos and of the divine—the reality of which was saved *because* the mind cannot know that they exist. Here the mind boggles, and Kantian metaphysics suddenly appears to be very desperate indeed.

But not so desperate as would first appear. A metaphysics may be, I think properly, regarded as a conscious and "logical" verbal organization of an orientation. Kant's great contribution was to demonstrate that such systems cannot be "constitutive"; that is, they cannot describe the way the empirical world is really organized. They can only regulate the forms with which we organize the data the senses bring to the mind. They are, to use the terminology of this book, orientations of orientations, and they arise from the deepest layer of the mind by a process of interaction between the mind and the real world.

For our purposes, two aspects of metaphysical systems are of the highest importance. First, the mind can create a variety of metaphysical systems, each of which is to be regarded as a kind of model of the real world. Like Hume, Kant saw that it was just as possible to conceive the world on the model of an organism as on that of a machine, the most common Enlightenment metaphor. These models or metaphysical hypotheses control the behavior of the subsidiary orientations and tell them what to look for *in the real world*. Here was a really new cultural redirection, for, unlike the ideas of the Judeo-Platonic-Christian tradition, it subordinated the drive toward orientation to the drive toward reality, even though the structure of that reality could not be known.

The second important notion was this: Since this more profound or archetypal level of the mind exhibits a purposive drive toward organization, although any specific organization it arrives at cannot be constitutive and only regulative, it seems reasonable and indeed necessary to assume—though it can never be proved—that because the mind is after all a product of reality, reality itself is informed by a purposeful organizing drive. Not in its structure but in its drive toward structure, is the mind analogous to reality. Nor is it forbidden to make a further guess and postulate that behind the drive lies a power responsible for it, a power which—and who can stop us?—we might as well call God. And corresponding to God there may be assumed or hypothesized a force within the mind which can be called the self. Thus the personality exhibits two selves, the phenomenal self, which corresponds to the forms at the front of the mind which organize data, and the noumenal self, analogous to God, which directs the archetypal powers which organize the superficial mental forms.

Thus the great and difficult ideas Kant gave to the nineteenth century were two: we are properly occupied in engaging with sensory or empirical reality, not in constructing metaphysical systems which we dogmatically assert to be true; and there is a deep or true self which controls and directs the various lesser orientations—or, socially speaking, roles—with which we confront and engage the real world. To this may be added a third, almost as important. When we study temporally the formation and organization of the archetypal powers, we perceive that the organism is a better model for understanding how they come into existence and are developed than is the machine. Consequently the closest approximation we can attain to the purposive drive of nature is to conceive of it as an organism; and thus organicism, an Enlightenment idea in its origin, became a dominating mode of nineteenth-century thinking.

The efforts of subsequent philosophers to wrestle with the problems left by Kant, as terrifying and baffling as any he resolved, we shall encounter farther on; here the cultural—that is, the emotional—impact and significance of his ideas must engage our attention, for the real power of Kant in the nineteenth century lay in the fact that people could, with only a very vague notion of approximately what he was saying, use his ideas to furnish for themselves a supporting superstructure for a state of feeling that they had arrived at by different routes. How a superstructure can support anything may be difficult to perceive, but that, for some decades, is precisely what happened. In short, the same old wearisomely entertaining human impudence occurred once more: a rationalization was perceived as an explanation and justification and proof for an emotional necessity.

That emotional necessity—a solution to the Wertherian negation—was this: If the sense of identity, perhaps after all a purely illusory sense—which men had variously called the soul, or the spirit, or the ego, and were beginning to call the noumenal self—is derived neither from God nor from nature (Werther frequently felt in his emotional storms that the very belief in his own existence was vanishing), and if it is impossible to exist, to relate, to orient oneself to inner or outer experience without such a sense and thus have the sense of value, then the only thing to do is to make a pure assertion of the self—to feel the sense of identity without any rational justification at all, and to perceive, to feel consciously, that the world and the divine, order and meaning and value, all emerge from this inner necessity, from the self. Perhaps it was illusion, but at the time it was the only illusion that could possibly work. There was no other direction to go, nothing else to do but perform a logical inversion of the orientative patterns that had dominated the European mind from the remotest eons.

In 1814, in inscribing verses in young Arthur Schopenhauer's album, Goethe stated the whole problem in a baker's dozen of words. *"Willst du dich deines Wertes freuen, So musst der Welt du Wert verleihen."* "If you have a driving necessity to experience and celebrate your own value, you must loan value to the world," you must project upon the world a value derived from yourself.

With Goethe's words before us, we can glance once again at Kant's thinking and perceive that he too, like Werther, like Goethe, was escaping from the waste land into which Hume's corrosive and dissolvent skepticism had led him. For Hume, he said, awoke him from a "dream of dogma"; after Hume the traditional ways of redeeming the world could no longer be accepted. Neither God nor nature redeemed man; rather, man's task was to redeem nature, and even God; for man cannot live without redemption, without the experience of value. And this realization in turn led to what was perhaps Kant's—and Goethe's—most signal achievement: the realization that the noblest, the most complete, the fullest and profoundest means to achieve and to symbolize redemption is the work of art, for art creates from the archetypal patterns, from the redeemed noumenal self, a world—whole, complete, self-consistent, and self-supporting—which is the only world that can be set over against nature, and which in terms of value is nature's equal. For religion is not a source of knowledge, and formalized religious thinking (theology) can only result in paralogisms, fallacies of which the thinker is unconscious. Art and not religion, then, is the source of value; and the artist—not the priest, not the metaphysician—introduces value into the world.

One question remained. Since it was too early in the development of this new orientation to do without some of the supports the mind was accustomed to, too early to think that "self" is merely a name for the feeling of identity, a source had to be found for the self. I have mentioned earlier our almost inescapable tendency to think that because there is a word, there must be an entity, some kind of a "thing," to which that word refers. Since there was the word "self" there must be an entity within the personality to which that word refers. And since all entities have a point of origin and circumstances of creation, where did the self come from? It was no longer possible to believe that it descended from God or entered into the personality from nature. But fortunately there was a handy word hanging around which had not been used much, a word filled with significance for the future. If the self comes neither from above nor from outside, it must come from below, from the unconscious. This poor little philosophic pawn suddenly gets to the back row and becomes queen—and sweeps the board. With what astonishing results, we shall see. But first it will be good, I think, to look at a group of superb dramatizations of the reduction of the world to disorder and, from the rubble, the emergence of the self.

# CHAPTER V

# Explorers: 1

"THE WANDERING OUTLAW of his own dark mind"; self-alienated from his society and his culture; self-isolated within a meaningless universe plunging toward a meaningless extinction; a volcano lit, in the eyes of his contemporaries, by hellfire; compulsive, uncontrollable; incestuous, homosexual, heterosexual enough to inspire any man's envy; the most fascinating of friends, and at times the most indifferent; incredibly handsome, sometimes sunk in fat; convinced of man's helplessness, dying in an effort to further Greek political liberty; a mind of dazzling power, mentally undisciplined and indeed, in the Goethean sense, uneducated; but always incredibly productive of torrents of poetry and avalanches of the most inspiriting letters in English—such was Byron, whom Arthur Schopenhauer, in Venice, in 1819, refused to meet for fear that the English lord would steal his mistress.

I have seen attributed to Byron pornographic poetry of such technically low order that he would not have read it, let alone have written it, verses which have apparently circulated for generations in manuscript and in typescript. He is one of the few writers to have become an international myth, a kind of god or at least saint of the world-defiers. The pornographic poetry may be dull, but its attribution to Byron is of the highest interest. The only kind of social transgression the ordinary sensual man is interested in—or even, poor soul, can imagine—is sexual; and it is proper that such poetry should claim Byron as its creator; just as travelers put their automobiles under the protection of St. Christopher; just as modern secularists, needing a saint, canonize Albert Schweitzer. In the popular mind Byron has survived as the one who dared to do what others only dream of doing, and to ascribe a sexual transgression to Byron is to give it a value which the mores of the culture deny it. Nowadays, at a higher cultural level, his saintly place and dignity have been usurped by D. H. Lawrence. For both of them, like the Marquis de Sade, show the symbolic connection between sexual transgression and moral freedom.

For a dozen years, from the appearance of *Childe Harold* in 1812 to the publication of the last cantos of *Don Juan* in 1824 and his terrible and sacrificial death in the same year, he dominated the European imagination, even that of Goethe, who gave him a high place in the second part of *Faust*. The amount of work he turned out was prodigious; his greatest work was unpopular, and its superiority to his earlier poetry was not begun to be generally realized until the 1870's; for *Don Juan*, published in installments from 1819 to 1824 and left unfinished, destroyed the image his earlier work and his life had created.

His earlier achievements—*Childe Harold, The Bride of Abydos, The Giaour, Manfred* (and these are only a few)—must not be minimized. In their day they were flashes of lightning, illuminating a cultural situation briefly but with unbearable brilliance; later eras, accustomed to the landscape thus shatteringly revealed, can no longer experience their original power but feel for the most part the rawness, the aesthetic crudeness, the undisciplined violence. Even at the time their affinity with the negation of *Werther* was perceived; it was Byron's signal achievement—and this is why Goethe admired him so—to dramatize, to symbolize, in extension and depth what had been but adumbrated in Goethe's youthful work.

By the time Byron started growing up (he was born in 1788) in the first decade of the new century, the collapse of the Christian and Enlightenment orientations had been felt by enough people and recorded by enough men of talent and genius to make it possible for him to grasp utterly the implications of total negation, of total loss of value. His two greatest figures are Childe Harold and Manfred, the one symbolizing alienation from nature and society, the other alienation from the self. Harold is the wanderer, Manfred the criminal, although both themes are present in each, for each is, metaphorically, an outlaw, self-outlawed.

Henceforth the primary symbolic figure of the post-Enlightenment negation is the wanderer; whether he is called the Wandering Jew, or Melmoth, or Paracelsus, or Ishmael, or Ahab, the rest of the century is full of Harold-descended wanderers. They survive even today in Ralph Ellison's *Invisible Man* or Jack Kerouac's *On the Road*. The imagination of the last century and a half has found in Harold, through his inability to establish permanent relations, to stay anywhere, even to fall in love, an enduring symbol of the man no longer comfortable in the web of social circumstances, no longer able to play a socially structured role. But since, before the Wertherian negation, identity was maintained only in terms of such a role, for Harold and his brothers identity has become a burden. Yet—and this is a step forward from Werther—they do not commit suicide; they endure.

Here is the enormous power of the Harold figure, the capacity to survive in the waste land. Werther could not. Nevertheless, identity is a burden, and Harold thus displays two attitudes toward nature. In the earlier phase, still dominated by the Enlightenment orientation, nature appears to him a source of redemption—but not in the Enlightenment way, which confirmed, through the power of the imagination, human identity. On the contrary, over and over again Harold wishes to become a portion of the tempest, of the sea, of the mountains. He wishes to experience completely what Werther had but mentioned in passing, the loss of his identity by merging it into the natural world. It is Byron's symbolization of the feelings that led Werther to suicide. But a symbolization is a step forward from a self-destructive act. Werther does return to nature; he wishes to be buried in some remote valley by the wayside. Harold only imagines it. Yet later, and in other circumstances, Harold and his successors Manfred and Cain stand appalled before the blind destructiveness of the natural world, and the feeling that Werther also briefly entertained, that this is no world for the miserable spirit of man, becomes powerfully dominant. Thus he is driven back upon himself.

In *Manfred* another theme only lightly touched upon by Goethe becomes dominant, as it already had in *The Giaour* and *Lara:* the theme of guilt. A terrible crime, a frightful transgression, lies in the background and the past of these figures; but what it was we are never told, or at best are given only hints of. And these hints suggest a violation and destruction of another personality, or at least an attempt at it. It is not simple murder that appears to haunt these men but the murder of a soul. The sense of chaos and wild deformation within is acted out by involving another human being, as if that sense could be justified or made real by drawing another into it. By the capacity of Manfred to involve another, the reality of that self-alienation is proved, demonstrated, made sane, and given an extraordinary power. And its power must be recognized and admitted; the aesthetic crudeness and rawness of *Manfred* cannot be reduced to mere melodrama, any more than William Faulkner's novels can. Byron's work of this period may have the badness that only sincerity can give a poem, but that sincerity cannot be denied, nor its force critically argued away. Alienation from man and nature, guilt before man and the universe, are the problems Byron had to resolve; and resolve them he did, in of all things a comic, ironic epic, the unfinished *Don Juan*.

Mozart's *Don Giovanni* was first presented in Prague in October 1787, only a few months before Byron was born in the following January. It was already an old theme, this myth of the eternal seducer who is finally brought to justice by the ghost of the murdered father of an outraged woman; of the eternal pursuer, willing to risk anything to get another woman, insatiable. But thirty-one years after Mozart's great success with an image of Don Giovanni which dominated the operatic stages of all Europe for more than a generation, Byron turned the whole thing topsy-turvy. His hero is not the pursuer, but the pursued; he does not seduce women: women seduce him. In the ritual of seduction and betrayal Don Juan is the victim, not the aggressive sacrificer. But it is not merely Mozart's pattern which is inverted; it is Byron's. Manfred had been guilty before man and nature; but in *Don Juan* the guilt is shifted to society and the world.

All of Europe was—or was to be, had Byron finished the work—the stage of Don Juan's adventures, from Spain to St. Petersburg and from the Isles of Greece to London. At the end he planned to have him appear in the following of Anacharsis Clootz, when that extraordinary Prussian revolutionary brought representatives of all the nations of the world before the Assembly of the French Revolution. Unfortunately, Clootz's noble gesture was a bit fraudulent, for he had simply dressed up bums from the Parisian streets in national costumes rented from the theaters of Paris. What did Byron intend by Juan's straight-faced participation in this farce? And would Juan have known it to be a farce? As least one can say this much. Clootz's early travesty on the United Nations was a masquerade, and Juan's conscious participation in that masquerade would have been consistent with what he had been learning, that social roles are masks, that beneath each mask is a self forever inaccessible to socially conditioned perception, a self which the individual can be aware of only when he has been alienated from society and can see through its self-deceptions. The guilt of society lies in its forcing the individual to wear a mask and betray himself. To see through society a man must have had experiences which force him to discover the self and its difference from the role. Such experiences formed the adventures of Juan.

*Don Juan* is, in short, a farce—of the most serious sort imaginable. Born in Spain, early left fatherless, brought up by a bluestocking mother, young Juan is seduced by an enchanting woman older than himself and married. The husband's discovery of the intrigue creates a scandal. Juan's mother thinks it best to send Juan on his travels, accompanied by his tutor, Don Pedro. Their ship is wrecked; only a few survivors drift across the

Mediterranean, waterless, foodless, and in due course cannibalistic. (Byron was careful to document the cannibalism from accounts of shipwrecks.) Poor Don Pedro is devoured, following his pet spaniel down the gullets of the starving. Juan refrains from sampling this meal, and at least avoids madness. Another storm wrecks the boat; all are drowned save Juan, who is cast ashore on an island in the Aegean. He is stripped of clothing and money and almost dead. Now he enters paradise, for he is found by Haidée, the lovely daughter of a Greek pirate, who warms him, feeds him, clothes him, and loves him. It is important that Haidée offers no resistance, nor does Juan, that neither seduces the other. Their love is as unconscious and irresistible as a star. Now paradise, I have suggested, is a symbol of a state of being in which the individual experiences pure value and pure identity. With this in mind we can see what Byron is talking about.

Juan is born to position and wealth in the corrupt and complacent late eighteenth-century society; his mother is the typical late Enlightenment emancipated woman. But in this society the innocence of the self is destroyed, and one is cast out not because one has sinned but because one has been caught. The pretensions of this society are shown up by the shipwreck, when the moral structure of Europe breaks down under the brutal onslaught of natural forces and human demands. Shipwreck and cannibalism are more than adequate symbols for the total disorientation experienced by Manfred and Harold. Everything in the earlier works is present by implication in these scenes, including the violation of one personality by another in the fate of Don Pedro. But that violation is not presented as one man's guilt; it is the universal guilt of all men toward each other's selfhood. Yet in their island paradise of pure identity Juan, the naked self stripped of its social superstructure, and Haidée, the uncontaminated innocent, do not violate one another. Now we can see what Byron is really after.

Juan's and Haidée's idyll is interrupted by the return of Lambro, the lovely creature's pirate father, who behaves according to type. Haidée goes mad and dies; Juan is sold into slavery at

Constantinople. Bought for her pleasure by the favorite wife of the sultan of Turkey, disguised as a woman, escaping—who knows how?—to the Russian army, forced into battle, sent to Catherine the Great who promptly makes him her lover, posted, when she has worn him out, to England as ambassador, Juan enters the society of English aristocracy. Women, married and unmarried, begin to struggle for him; and as the poem breaks off, one, the Duchess of Fitz-Fulke, masquerading as the ghost of an abbot, has captured him—at least temporarily.

If we divest the poem of its comic style—for even the shipwreck and the cannibalism are funny, though grimly so—the pattern emerges; the theme is violation. In shifting from the orientation of *Manfred* to that of *Don Juan*, Byron has perceived that the guilt of violation was mistakenly taken by Manfred upon himself. Manfred had displaced to himself the guilt that permeates the condition of things. Byron's new perception is Blake's superb cry, "The mind-forged manacles." The narrator of *Don Juan* is like Shelley's Prometheus, whose release from the rock to which he is chained begins when he understands that the Jupiter who has chained him there was his own creation, that the source of his punishment for creating human culture was his own feeling of guilt for defying Jupiter. He had chained himself to the rock. And so had Byron.

From this perspective the comic style is comprehensible. It is the armor Byron puts on to defend himself from his own self-accusations, and it also enables him to encounter the ridiculousness, the horror, and the beauty of human experience, without surrendering to a traditional orientation which would select one aspect of that experience and provide a pseudo-explanation and a paralogistic justification. The irony of his fantastic juxtapositions gives him exactly the perspective which enables him to see through the pretensions and rationalizations of the social structure and to maintain his identity independently of it. For if Juan is violated, he is never destroyed. Here emerges the armored self; it is a step forward from Werther. The self may be indifferent—Juan doesn't want to do anything—but at least it is now inviolate. The self is alienated from society, true; perhaps it can never return. We shall see how the men of the nineteenth century faced that problem. But certainly, following without knowing it the Kantian lead, Byron has perceived that the role of comic and ironic indifference enables the self to control the orientative drive and to encounter reality. For *Don Juan* is the first great work in one of the nineteenth century's most notable and uncompromising modes—realism.

A French book published in 1830, six years after Byron's death, carries forward his latest perceptions as well as his realistic technique and his ironic detachment, and develops a theme implicit in *Don Juan* beyond the point Byron had. *Le Rouge et le Noir—The Scarlet and the Black*—was published under the pseudonym of Stendhal by Marie Henri Beyle at the age of forty-seven. Born in 1783, five years older than Byron, he matured more slowly and was strongly influenced by the great Englishman. As who was not, in those years? Julien Sorel is a child of Harold. Stendhal has left a record of his encounter with Byron in Milan in October 1816. Byron had finished Part III of *Childe Harold*, which Stendhal thought he was then writing, and had begun *Manfred*. Stendhal tells us he was then "mad" about *Lara*; but *Harold* in its first two parts he of course knew, and he read the other works including *Don Juan* as they came out, since he could read English. Stendhal had been writing for years before he undertook his life of Julien Sorel, but *The Scarlet and the Black* was his first novel and his first important publication. Julien is to Stendhal as Manfred and Juan are to Harold; they are abstractions from the total personalities of these complex men, selections from their experiences and their orientations which reveal most sharply the cultural pressures, rifts, and faults. To Stendhal Byron was a volcano; and in Julien he is concerned with that interaction of social forces and brilliant genius which causes an explosion; in Julien's case the explosion is the attempted murder, in a church, of the one women he loves.

Julien is born into a family peasant by origin but moving up to the bourgeois level. Yet he is in physiological type, in

character, and in native talent utterly different from his parents
and his brothers. He is a natural aristocrat, and it is hinted that
he is really the son of a French nobleman. But the possibility of
illegitimacy plays little part in the story and in Julien's sufferings.
He is actually a kind of biologic sport. In the device of unknown
parentage Stendhal uses a myth constantly in force in this period
and throughout the century. It is the equivalent of the mysterious
past of Lara and Manfred. The orphan, the illegitimate child, the
foundling, are literary figures used again and again to symbolize
social alienation when the author is after the uniqueness of the
self and its opposition to the social role. And this sundering of
self from role is the theme of *The Scarlet and the Black*.

The title indicates the two possibilities for a career in
France in the 1830's to a man of genius born in a lower social
level: the clergy or the army. To the young Julien, whose first
step upward is his employment as tutor to the children of a
wealthy bourgeois married to an aristocrat, Napoleon is the inspiring model. In reality Napoleon was probably the tool of
counterrevolutionary forces; but to Julien, who was only a
child when Napoleon fell and the Bourbons were restored, he
was the great defier, the great uprooter. Carlyle put this notion of
Napoleon perfectly when he compared him to the American
pioneer who must cut down an ancient forest before the land can
be cultivated. It is a Napoleon partly recast in the Byronic image.
But Napoleonism is not quite Byronism, for Napoleonism involves
violating as well as setting free; and Napoleonism is a social perception. Consequently his adulation of Napoleon leads Julien in two
directions.

In the paradisiacal garden of Madame de Rênal's country
estate, he forces himself to seduce his employer's wife. But this
act is not only a violation of Madame de Rênal; it is a violation of
himself. For he is not naturally the conquering Napoleonic rapist;
he is charming, irresistible, wonderfully distinguished in intelligence and personality. Madame de Rênal falls in love with him,
and once he has forced himself into her bed, he falls in love with
her. On the one hand, then, his forcing of himself leads to a

self-discovery; but on the other hand, success gives him a reliance upon role-playing and seduction and emotional violation of himself and others which leads to fatal consequences. What is he really? He does not know; but like Don Juan on Haidée's isle, he has experienced paradise, his true self. Yet he does not know what he has experienced. Henceforth, he is torn between a desire to return to that lost paradise and the desire to go forward in his role-playing—as he does, first in his training to be a priest, then as secretary to a Parisian aristocrat whose daughter he seduces, then as an army officer with a brilliant career opening before him and with his marriage to the aristocratic girl in immediate prospect.

At this point, Madame de Rênal writes to his future father-in-law. Under the influence of black priests, she has repented her sin and thinks it her social duty to present Julien as a moral monster. The marriage is broken off; Julien rushes back to Verrières and attempts to murder Madame de Rênal in church but only wounds her; he is arrested, tried, found guilty of attempted murder, condemned to death, and, refusing to appeal, is executed. Madame de Rênal, who has forgiven him and is his one consolation in prison, shortly thereafter dies, for she has not forgiven herself; but his betrothed, Mathilde, who like Madame de Rênal has defied society by openly defending and visiting Julien, has the cave in which at his request he is buried "adorned with marbles sculptured at great cost in Italy." Mathilde has never truly seen Julien; her panoply of grief tells us that she has seen him only as the natural Napoleonic aristocrat. But Madame de Rênal has seen Julien as he really is; and so has Julien. For he has perceived that his role-playing led him inevitably to the destruction of the one creature he loved, to his symbol of value, to, therefore, the destruction of himself. Consequently he dies happy; his prison, he says, is a paradise. Like Goethe, he has learned to lend value to the world. Value comes from himself, not from acting out social dishonesty. He is his own source of orientation. He has arrived at a sense of identity independent of social structure and in contradiction to it.

And there lies the problem that Stendhal has dramatically

analyzed. He has made clear one conception of sovereign importance. It has been wearisomely reiterated that the nineteenth-century tradition values emotional disturbance for its own sake, and that this judgment marks it as adolescent, immature, and absurd to the mature man. But generally this accusation has been made by academic scholar-critics who have settled comfortably into their socially approved roles, who have surrendered complacently to the great temptation of academic life, moral pomposity. From the Stendhalian point of view they have sold their birthright for a mess of pottage, and got it. They have happily put on the chains which Stendhal is trying to strike off. For the advancing men of the nineteenth century did not in truth value emotional disturbance for its own sake. They perceived, rather, that emotional equilibrium and stasis can come only at the price of subjecting the drive toward reality to the drive toward orientation. Emotional disturbance, then, is to be valued not for itself but because it is the only way to break through the culturally inherited orientations which screen us from reality. Thus at the head of his novel Stendhal placed a marvelous quotation from Danton: "Truth—Truth in all her rugged harshness."

And hence the paradox of his novel. Role-playing and self-violation are essential to self-discovery; they are the direction-finders for the explorer which lead him to a continent he did not know existed. Thus Don Juan in his Greek island paradise experiences his self in its innocence, but Julien in his garden paradise experiences only a superficial outward layer of the real thing. Paradise given by the accident of circumstance is not the same thing as a paradise self-generated and self-created—in a prison, in total social opposition. Thus it is only after Madame de Rênal has violated him that both of them can arrive at a true social alienation. But a further paradox remains, now more sharply revealed than by Byron. How is the individual to live? A man who has penetrated to the deepest levels of existence cannot live in society, but no man can live in total social alienation. It is no accident that Stendhal buries Julien in the cave in which he had once hidden for a day, for caves are frequently from now on, and

even before, symbols of the self-in-hiding. Stendhal's solution was
a kind of controlled schizophrenia. He lived publicly and in his
later years even held a government job as consul in Civitavecchia
in his beloved Italy, though he did not particularly care for the
town. He became the buried man, the man-in-hiding, one, as he
put it, of the happy few who know how to live the double life.
Yet such a solution is not satisfactory; it leaves too much out of
one's life. Julien's death indicates that in truth Stendhal had not
found a satisfactory answer to the problem of how the new man,
who derives value from the self and thus can engage with
reality, is to live in a society dependent for its existence on orientative illusions, and do so without compromising his vision.

   To find what is perhaps the first answer, though it was to
work for only a couple of generations, I shall turn back in time
to a work written between 1797 and 1805, William Wordsworth's
*The Prelude.*

# CHAPTER VI

# *Explorers: 2*

WORDSWORTH IS USUALLY CALLED a nature poet; but that is an error, and a particularly unfortunate one, for so to categorize him is to identify him with the nature poets of the eighteenth century, who selected from the natural world in order to confirm their conviction that by the activity of the imagination man derives value from nature through the imaginative perception of the meaningful order of the world. But Wordsworth saw in nature not merely the source of "moods of calmness" but equally a source of emotional disturbance; and it was the interaction of the two which led to genius and the stimulation and growth of the poetic imagination. The mind was not merely reflective and imitative; it was not a mere mirror; it was a lamp. The capacity of the individual to profit from the order and disorder of the natural world was a function of the strength and health of his "imagination." Therefore the climax of *The Prelude* is called "The Imagination and Taste, How Impaired and Restored." Clearly, the old meaning of "imagination" has been discarded for a new one.

The pre-Enlightenment meaning, for which Coleridge and Wordsworth used the word "fancy," a lesser power of the mind, was the mental ability to create something unreal out of elements found in reality, like a unicorn or a chimera. It was regarded as a dangerous power, closely allied with madness. Shakespeare put in the same category the lunatic, the lover, and the poet. During the Enlightenment "imagination" was not regarded with such suspicion. On the contrary, the poet's imaginative power allied him not with the madman but with the philosopher and the scientist. It was the power to see beyond the superficial confusion of phenomena to the laws of order and of cause which governed the world. The notion of Wordsworth and Coleridge was profoundly different. The one poet speaks of "What we half create and half perceive," while the other insists that "we receive but what we give." But both statements are virtually the same, and to attempt to say what he meant Coleridge coined the word "esemplastic," from Greek "into" plus "one" plus "make." The imagination now becomes radically creative. The forms with which it organizes the world are derived from within, not reasoned, or perceived, or intuited from the outer world.

The power of the new perception is that it can see both order and disorder in experience without claiming that one or the other is the true character of reality. This is the orientation Coleridge symbolizes in "Kubla Khan," in which Kubla's paradisiacal garden includes both beauty and terror, both sun and ice. To Coleridge the imagination was the power to experience the reconciliation of opposites without emptying them of their contradictions and disparities. And Keats, learning from both Wordsworth and Coleridge, saw the poetic power as the power of "negative capability," the power not to make up your mind in the face of logical contradictions but to maintain those contradictions. Such notions clearly make it possible for the poet to engage his mind with reality in all its contradictory and confusing concreteness; like Wordsworth, he felt that here is our home, not in some lost paradise or future heaven. To Wordsworth the imagination is an adaptive power, and his theme is how that imaginative power grows, how it is destroyed, and how it is restored. His subject is not nature but psychology.

*The Prelude* has a peculiar history. In 1797, encouraged by Coleridge, Wordsworth set out to write a long poem on his views of man, nature, and society; it was to be named *The Recluse*. From the beginning, the idea of withdrawal from society, an act which he had indeed performed, was at the front of his mind. It was to be a contemplative poem on what a man sees who has sufficiently disengaged himself from society. Yet he was never able to write it. According to Coleridge's notion it was to be the work of a man who had made up his mind about things. But if the character of a poet is imagination, and if the character of the imagination is to grow, clearly a man who has made up his mind has impaired his growth. All he can do, really, is write about the process which has brought him to the point he now occupies. Naturally enough, Wordsworth decided first to write a poem about how he got where he was. It took him years; he was not finished until 1805, and even then it had no title. He was dissatisfied; he could not bring himself to publish it; but he could not let it alone.

As a result we have two *Preludes*, the one copied out in 1805 and sent to Coleridge, a reasonable enough act, since the form of the poem is that of thirteen verse epistles to his friend; the other published in 1850 after his death in that year, a very considerably revised and even rewritten version, in some ways a stylistic improvement but in depth of perception a deterioration. It was his family and heirs who gave it the present title, with the subtitle, *The Growth of a Poet's Mind*. Of the long poem originally planned, *The Recluse*, he wrote only two books of Part I, Part II (*The Excursion*), a sad falling off from *The Prelude*, and nothing of Part III. And *The Excursion* owes as much success as it has to the contrast between the recluse and the solitary who symbolizes an earlier state of the recluse, a state which the latter has passed through and outgrown. Even in a poem supposedly dedicated to a static vision, its only real source of vitality is in implied growth.

Now from his very principles one thing and one thing only can impair the imagination—"Positive Capability," to modify Keats' superb phrase, the arrestment of the mind at a single and exclusive orientation. Wordsworth grew up in the Lake District of northwest England, a place of rich valleys and almost Alpine scenery of awe-inspiring grandeur, a miniature Switzerland. It is astonishing that an area but twenty miles wide and thirty miles long can be so imposing. Culturally it was an area of a traditional and non-intellectual but ancient and reverent Protestantism, crossed with folkways more ancient still. It was a primitive and almost inaccessible world. Here, he later thought, he had been "fostered alike by beauty and by fear"; here he first encountered those contradictions in experience which came to play a part in his thinking like that of the antinomies in Kant's.

He grew up, then, in a pre-Enlightenment culture, nor did his stay at Cambridge, sunk like Oxford in a mindless somnolence, make much difference. When, on a walking trip through France, he encountered the French Revolution in its initial joyous urgency, he experienced for the first time the full force of the Enlightenment in its apparently irresistible sweep toward triumph and the establishment of heaven on earth. Under the pretense of studying French he returned to the country where everything suddenly made sense; and there he embraced revolutionary republicanism and sentimental "natural" love. Indeed, he became so solemn in his later years and his public image as laureate was so cleaned of his youthful radicalism by himself and his worshipers, that it came as a relief in 1916 to learn that he had had an illegitimate daughter.

In spite of his bliss, his uncles, who had charge of his patrimony, insisted that he return to England, and in 1793 he was horrified to learn that England and France were at war. All his new beliefs allied him with the French republican effort against his own country. But that emotional conflict was not to last long. The Revolution rapidly revealed its inescapable tendency toward terror and tyranny. Now the problems of the Enlightenment rose before him. Passionately he studied schemes of human regeneration, of social perfection—all the marvelous fantasies of the late Enlightenment. Inevitably he was led to logical contraries with which the reason could not deal. This shattered his faith that a solution to moral difficulties could be found in the study of the empirical world. The result was despair. He fled from London to a farm in southern England, where his sister joined him; and there he did a most interesting thing. For a year and a half he studied mathematics. Like Kant he found that only in mathematics could be found a perfect self-consistent order. That order was in the mind, not in reality. But whereas Kant, with his devotion to the technicalities of academic philosophy, buried deep and almost completely suppressed the emotional drives, in Wordsworth they were right at the surface.

Indeed, that was all he was really interested in. His devotion to mathematics can be seen as a turning away from reality and society in order to regain orientative equilibrium, in order again to release from the "under-consciousness" the orientative drive, the imaginative power. He had had a sense of emotional vitality; it had disappeared; how was it to be recovered? With the aid of the emotional ambience of his sister Dorothy and of his inspiring and philosophically learned new friend, Coleridge, it was recovered; and once he had found it again, he reinforced it by recalling in his new tranquillity those exaltations and agonies of his childhood and youth which originally brought his imagination to life. And he wrote *The Prelude*, his interpretation of his experiences.

"There are," he said, "in our existence spots of time,"

> passages of life in which
> We have had deepest feeling that the mind
> Is lord and master, and that outward sense
> Is but the obedient servant of her will.

Innumerable passages in this poem enable us to comprehend and experience the emotional vitality and force that must have lain behind the academic and abstract style of Kant. Yet because Wordsworth was an amateur philosopher and more interested in emotional vitality than correctness and impregnability of reasoning, Wordsworth said things that Kant would never have said. The mind, he was convinced, was exquisitely adapted to the outer world, and that world was equally adapted to the mind. Of the union of the two he speaks as of a wedding and a consummation, the offspring of which is creation. Yet in comparison to the mind, the world is passive, although a wise passiveness is necessary to prepare the mind for the consummation. That passiveness is necessary to free the mind from its superficial drives toward rational comprehension. Without that initial passiveness before nature, the mind does not wed; it seduces and rapes. Once the mind is released by contemplation and passiveness and tranquil restoration, the deeper forces begin to work and to appear in the guise of "love and holy passion." From the inviolate self issues forth the power to relate man to his world, and this act of relation is the act of the creation of value. We see intuitively, through unconscious powers, into the structure of order of which the visible universe is a symbol. Really it is not too distant a position from Kant's notion that the structural power of the mind is a guarantee that the world has structure, even though the mind cannot create a structure which corresponds to the structure of the world.

In the moments of revelation, then, the spots of time, the world is seen as a symbol of the self which underlies the conscious rational powers. But the world and the self have the same origin— the divine. The imagination closes the gap between man and the world, and the divine current, as it were, runs unhindered through the great triad of God, man, and nature. The results are exciting, or at least Wordsworth makes them so when we read him, for no author has succeeded so well in communicating the feeling of the aroused imagination "when it sees into the life of things." In such states the ordinary rational distinction between organic and inorganic life disappears. At that time there was no possible way to explain the origin of life, or at least the distinction between the organic and the inorganic; and the nature of life was a problem that Goethe and Coleridge, among others, wrestled with rather profitlessly. Wordsworth's simple assertion is more convincing, for he *feels* the life in rocks and stones, and he can make that feeling almost unbearably moving. We cannot believe it, yet it is irresistible. It is as if a poet of today could make us feel the life in atomic particles and the continuity of that life with our own, even though we know that we are not talking about levels of reality but levels of analysis, or different kinds of scientific constructs, made for different purposes. The hypothetical organicism of Kant has been metamorphosed into an experienced reality.

Not Chaos, not
The darkest pit of lowest Erebus,
Nor aught of blinder vacancy, scooped out
By help of dreams—can breed such fear and awe
As fall upon us often when we look
Into our Minds, into the Mind of man—
My haunt, and the main region of my song.

It is the imagination that redeems the world; in the deepest recesses of the self is the source of value. In opening ourselves to beauty and to terror we release its power.

Few understood Wordsworth. The high tide of his vision receded after 1805 and he regressed to embracing more commonplace orientative drives, became Christian and timid. Yet he had gone far; several profoundly important notions were implanted firmly in the minds of his readers: the sacredness of the poet, who through the exercise of his imagination releases value (or indefinable "truth") into the world and makes it available to the rest of us; and the necessity of engaging with this world, of finding our relation to this world, the world of the senses, of ordinary human experience, not of dreaming up fantasies of an unreal world to which we may escape, now in reality and in spirit after death. For though the world is a symbol, it is not only a symbol, not nothing but a symbol. There is no Platonizing reductivism in Wordsworth's vision. The imagination does not leap across to the divine beyond the world; it finds its path and its expression through the senses. The world does not vanish when we see a blinding radiance behind it. It becomes pellucidly beautiful as the divine glow shines through each particle of it. But Wordsworth was much misunderstood. His subjects, nature and simple and ordinary men, were confused with the imaginative power he used to look at them. His failure to publish *The Prelude* was, for English and American literature particularly, something of a disaster. The guidance—and the problem—which the next generation received came not from Wordsworth but from Goethe's *Faust*.

Much of *Faust* was written before Wordsworth began *The Prelude*; indeed, while Wordsworth was entering on his first abandon of enthusiasm for the French Revolution, Goethe published *Faust: A Fragment.* Yet he did not complete Part I and publish it until 1808, and he worked on Part II for the rest of his life, until his death in 1832, when it was published posthumously. But even that is not the whole story, for he first began to wrestle with the subject as early as 1770, even before he wrote *Werther*, and from the period 1770–75 there is preserved a fragment known as the *Urfaust*, not published until long after his death.

His first engagement with the Faust theme, then, overlaps the Werther period, and as one might expect the *Urfaust* shows the same negation as the novel. Nor is it difficult to see why he was pulled by this old story of the man who sold his soul to the devil for the sake of infinite knowledge, gratification, and riches. It symbolized precisely that negative defiance of the existence of divine value which poor Werther was driven to. But the completed *Faust*, the *Faust* of more than forty years of work, is entirely different; or rather, it is the solution of the problem of Werther, carried through the stages Byron, Stendhal, and Wordsworth worked out, and farther.

It is an almost incredibly complex work, and yet for every oddity there is a reason. It begins, for example, with a prologue to be spoken by the poet to the audience and then, on the stage's bare boards, comes a discussion between poet, actor, and director. (It must always be remembered that *Faust* was written for the stage, although it was not presented in both its parts until 1876.) Although these introductions say various things with which we need not be concerned, they do emphasize that the opening scene in heaven is part of a play, not a poetic description of an actually existent divine super-world, such as we get in Dante's *Divine Comedy* or Milton's *Paradise Lost*. As we come to understand, Mephistopheles is a symbolization of certain forces within the human spirit; and so is God. Neither is, in the theological sense, a person. Mephistopheles is the spirit of denial; he symbolizes the forces in man which are responsible for the negation of Werther, while God symbolizes the affirmative power. Faust's problem, it turns out, is not, as we might expect, either to succumb to the devil or to deny his existence; it is to learn to hold in a single vision the two forces symbolized by God and the devil. Like Coleridge, he needs to reconcile them without draining them of their contraries and oppositions.

In accord with his principle that poetry should not be didactic, should not have an easily extractable moral lesson as a sermon has, Goethe offers us in *Faust* not an explanation, rational, logical, philosophically consistent, of the reconciliation, but rather the opportunity to experience it. This is the high nineteenth-century notion of the work of art; like life itself, it should offer a rich complexity irreducible to simple statements; it should defy reductivist interpretations. Always, with *Faust*, we feel that the work presents an infinitude of possibilities; just as in interpreting life itself, we feel, or should feel, that we have done so only by an abstraction which leaves heaven only knows how much unaccounted for. So it is with the greatest works of that century. We feel that any interpretation leaves more to be said, that something capable of contradicting our interpretation is still lurking within the work, that there is always a disparity between the orientation we have derived from the work and the complex interactions of the artistic data itself.

About this opening scene there is a quality totally unexpected. A scene in heaven, with God speaking? Surely this is a scene of high solemnity; and in that tone most translators have operated. But Goethe surprises us; the scene is comic, although what God and Mephistopheles talk about is profoundly serious. For they are making a wager, and it is not for the soul of Faust. He is only the subject for the experiment. Mephistopheles insists that in creating the world, and especially in willing man into existence, God has made a horrible mistake in judgment; for the labyrinthine ways of God are so beyond the capacity of the human mind to comprehend that to man the world is a meaningless chaos. The little gleam of reason that God has given him he can use only to debase himself. Indeed, Mephistopheles is sorry that his own task is to torment the poor creature. But God wagers that even with an absolutely free hand, which he has anyway, Mephistopheles will not be able to tempt Faust to degrade himself utterly.

And by that Goethe means: to deny the value of human existence, and of Faust's own.

As the play proper opens, when we meet Faust alone in his study he has sunk almost to that point of despair. He is a Werther who has not quite given up, but in this very scene he is on the verge of poisoning himself. A subtler temptation, however, is reserved for him. He is a man who feels trapped and betrayed; betrayed by his success as a physician, which he feels he does not deserve; betrayed by his success as a professor, which forces him to teach students with an assurance he does not feel; betrayed by success itself, which confines him to academic life; but above all betrayed by organized knowledge, which he has exhausted. For he is driven by a demand for the absolute, for philosophical and scientific certainty, for one ultimate answer. He is totally isolated; violated by his role-playing and hopelessly frustrated in his desire to make sense out of the universe.

He is tempted, therefore, to achieve by magic both the understanding he cannot achieve by reason and the gratification his social condition denies him. And magic is precisely the temptation Mephistopheles is going to use; whenever the situation is too much for Faust, when he is impatient, weary, maddened, or proud, he lets Mephistopheles resolve the problem by magical means. And it always turns out, in the long run, not to have been resolved after all. In this opening scene the psychological roots of reliance on magic are revealed. Faust represents the human spirit at its best, not at its worst, as in the old Faust plays and stories; but even for the best of men, total frustration tempts one to rely on magic. Even the great Dr. Samuel Johnson, whose emotional life was a horror of frustration, had to touch fence palings as he went by them; the act was his magical way of grasping an emotional security that would compensate for the deep and terrible sadness and inexplicable grief that his inner life was steeped in. Magic, in the profoundest sense, is what man resorts to when any frustration is so bewildering that, for the time being, he can make no sense of reality at all. It is the charmed spear of the primitive and the great theological systems and the imposing constructions of Platonizing idealism. It is the imposition of the orientative drive upon all other human drives, especially the drives to art and beyond art to reality. To Goethe it was any illusion that there are superhuman forces, transcendental powers which man can call upon, whether demons or gods, or God. It is the self-indulgent righteousness of the Puritan, who can perform the most frightful acts without turning a hair. For evil always comes from turning one's back on art and reality. (Goethe was as profoundly opposed to escapist art as he was to didactic, and for much the same reason.) To surrender to any kind of magic is to cease to struggle.

But even before Mephistopheles appears, Faust has made the first movement out of his waste land. In translating *The Gospel According to St. John* he decides that the rendering "In the beginning was the *word*" must be wrong. Nor can he accept "thought" or "power." All of these are identifiable with magic, for none of them engages with reality. But now he has it. "In the beginning was the *act*," for only in the act does the self assert itself upon reality. His first positive position has been seized, and so it is clear to us that when Mephistopheles appears he comes as the symbolization of Faust's own powers of self-temptation. This marks Goethe's vision as an important step forward from Wordsworth's and explains, perhaps, Wordsworth's ultimate failure. For the Englishman felt that the soul having once been reborn, value having once again been achieved, the task is accomplished. But Goethe sees farther. It must be achieved over and over again; it is a daily job, and more than daily. But every time it is achieved, it takes the self a little farther, with a little more stability, toward its engagement with reality.

And so when Mephistopheles appears, Faust is not frightened at all. He already knows all about him. Yet the devil surprises him at a moment of utter despair and negation, of denying the value of all aspects of human life; and he offers him a life of total gratification. He will serve him in this life, if afterwards Faust will do his bidding. This is no wager for Faust, who is convinced that his identity is an inseparable part of earthly existence. He will, however, give up his existence, that is, his desire for a meaningful identity, if Mephistopheles once, just once, can tempt him to say to the moment, "*Verweile doch! du bist so schön!*" "Linger with me! you are truly beautiful," or perfect, or totally gratifying. Now this looks like just the reverse of Wordsworth's notion of the "spots of time," or moments of value. But in fact, it is the same idea. Wordsworth's moments take their value from the emotional reconciliation of opposites, but Faust here means moments from which opposites are excluded. If, he says, I ever accept a static, one-sided vision of experience, my identity will vanish; for selfhood is maintained only under tension. And indeed over and over again Goethe shows his agreement with Wordsworth that value is but momentary and depends upon an awareness of opposites. Hence Mephistopheles is at Faust's side until his death, for it is only by being aware, always, of one's capacity for denial that one can affirm; and whenever Faust forgets and surrenders to Mephistopheles' magic, evil results.

Faust's first temptation is sexual. His youth renewed, he falls in love with a charming young woman, Margarete, usually called Gretchen. He seduces her; her mother dies; she kills her child; she is condemned to death. Faust calls upon Mephistopheles to rescue her magically from prison, but she refuses to go. Part I ends here, and to most people, and all opera-goers, that is the story of Faust, the affair with Gretchen. It is only the beginning. It is only the first temptation, and from it Faust learns that good and evil are inseparable and that they cannot even be weighed one against another. Man's ways are truly labyrinthine. But he learns something even more important.

If value is to be derived from the self, how are we to know the difference between the vision of value and the illusions of transcendental magic? How is the assertion of identity to be distinguished from egocentricity? How are we to break through, from within, the limits of personality? After he has seduced Gretchen in a mood of sentimental eroticism, and abandoned her, Faust is heart-stricken when he learns she is to die. Her refusal to escape reveals her simple religion and her simple self-respect; her determination to accept responsibility for what she has done; her realization that her dream of eternal love and happiness with him was an illusion, and that, after what has happened, she could never be happy with him, or with anyone, ever again. Her sufferings have forced him to love her and, for the first time, through that love to recognize and affirm her identity. The barriers of egocentricity are burst, and Faust enters into a wider world. The process is precisely the reverse of the guilt of Manfred, who proved the reality of the chaos within him by violating another personality and infecting her with his own negation. But Faust discovers that only by affirming the identity of another can he confirm his own. Now he can enter the great world. Sure of his own selfhood he can seek for and choose a role to play. He can genuinely play a part in society, instead of being trapped and violated by a social role forced upon him. His powers begin to be released.

As Part II opens we see Faust do an extraordinary thing: he turns his back on the sun. This act marks what he has learned from the Gretchen episode: the difference between identity and egocentricity. For in earlier scenes he has perceived nature as a symbol either of his superficial and sentimental emotions or of his magical drive to achieve an orientative absolute. Not the sun, now, but the rainbow symbolizes his new interpretation of the phenomenal world: reality lies not beyond the appearances but in them. Value is to be derived not from the permanent but from the changing. This transition from the Gretchen story has been the source of the greatest difficulty for readers of *Faust;* it seems to justify those who maintain that the two parts are essentially unrelated, or connected only tenuously. Faust is in splendid spirits; but, so runs the argument, shouldn't he be overwhelmed with guilt for what he has done to Gretchen? Goethe thinks not, for guilt leads to despair, and despair to reliance upon transcendental and religious magic. Faust's task is to put his experience to use. Nor does this mean that his egocentric and sentimental cruelty is any way justified or to be condoned. It simply is, because he is human. Man's fundamental power, his "goodness," lies not in knowing the difference between good and evil, in acting with scientific certainty on the basis of known good, or if he is a wicked man, of known evil; rather it lies in knowing that there is a difference between good and evil, but in any given situation not knowing what that difference is. And man knows only given situations. Here Goethe marks as sharply as possible his departure from the Enlightenment, which believed that an examination of nature would lead to moral certainty. Morality, then, is the opposite of moral responsibility; morality's aim is to reduce the freedom of choice to the minimum, to non-existence, if it can; but the aim of moral responsibility is to increase the realm of moral choice. Here is the true moral opposition, the real ethical paradox: on the one hand the terrible drive toward the good act; on the other, the impossibility of ever knowing in advance what the good act is.

Consequently, in the traditional sense Faust is never redeemed, for a final position of moral "truth" is never achieved, any more than a final absolute value is ever achieved. The rest of this vast drama is concerned with exploring the implications. It proceeds on two levels, historical reality mingled with magic, and dreams, which comprise huge chunks of the work, so long that the reader is often in danger of forgetting that they are indeed dreams. In the world of reality and magic, the power of Mephistopheles to tempt Faust remains stable, but in the world of dreams it grows progressively weaker, less sinister, and at the end, when Faust is dying and experiences his final dreams, Mephistopheles is reduced to low and obscene comedy and disappears.

At the level of historical reality, Faust with Mephistopheles' magic saves the emperor's finances, then saves him from destruction by justified rebellion, and finally creates his own kingdom by rescuing a vast plain from its daily invasion by the ocean. As he is dying, he is busy building a canal to drain a marsh; that done, his kingdom will be perfect. But all this, because it is done with magic, results in error and evil, after temporary success. The empire is not saved from economic disintegration; the defeat of the rebellion serves only to preserve a decadent social structure which ought to be permitted to collapse; the land saved from the waves leads Faust to destroy an innocent old couple, and once again it will be conquered by the ocean; the canal is never finished. It looks like total pessimism, but it is not quite that.

During all this Faust has long dreams, particularly an immensely long vision of the classical world, which comes between the two emperor episodes. For the emperor's pleasure, and with the aid of magic, he has summoned up the spirit of Helen of Troy; but he is caught in his own device. He falls in love with her, whom he sees, ultimately, as a new embodiment of Gretchen. What he has fallen in love with is a sentimental and illusory vision of the past. One of the great achievements of the nineteenth century is its wholly new concept of how to deal with history. We shall return to this theme, but its essential significance is explored in the great Greek section, which takes up nearly a quarter of the whole drama. Throughout this marvelous phantasmagoria Faust is constantly tempted, by mythological beauty, by Helen, by historical glamor, by the Greek equivalent of the Jewish paradise, Arcadia, to assert the beauty of the moment. But it is art that saves him.

Here Goethe makes a wonderfully subtle distinction. The power of memory is a magical power; it brings the historical and mythological and personal past into such illusory reality that we cannot tell it from the present. But art gives the phenomena of memory the same reality as the phenomena of the immediate real present. Hence at first Faust wants to participate in the world of Helen, the symbol of the glamor of the past; but after investigating the past and seeing the ugliness as well as the beauty of the Greek imagination, the obscenity and absurdity—identical with the obscenity and absurdity of the present—he marries Helen, and their child is the Poet, who seeks to escape from the Arcadian world—and dies in his efforts. Instead of becoming by magic a part of the world of Helen, by the power of visionary dream Faust brings his own present, the late medieval and early Renaissance world, along with him. He embraces in a single vision those two contraries, past and present, and thus rescues and confirms his own identity. We rarely live in the present; and art rescues us from absorption in memory and time past.

Art, then, is different from transcendental-religious magic, for by embracing contraries it symbolizes the labyrinthine ways of God and the incomprehensibility of the order of nature. And thus when Faust emerges from the dream, he is not in a beautiful landscape, as at the beginning of Part II, but amid high, jagged, cloud-swept mountain peaks. Nor is this any Enlightenment notion of mountains as a sublime part of God's plan, nor a pre-Enlightenment notion of mountains as evidence of earth's fall from perfection and descent into old age. Rather, it is a recognition that nature is as inimical to man as it is friendly. We see that Goethe is telling us not that man is perfectly adapted to nature but that he is not, that man is a stranger in a world he did not make, that nature is indifferent to us, that there is no natural power which has but to be learned in order to make us perfectly happy. Wouldn't it be terrible, we cry today, if atomic warfare wiped out the human race? There is no reason, Faust would now tell us, to think so. If nature has purposes, we cannot know them; certainly there is no reason to think those purposes are directed to our benefit.

Faust's symbol of the natural world has shifted from the sun to the rainbow to the devouring ocean, from which he determines to wrest a living space for happy millions. But, as we have seen, his success, impatiently achieved by magic, is no success at all. In his last words he arrives at his highest wisdom. "Only he deserves freedom and life who conquers them every day. If I could see, in my newly claimed land, men living in these terms, then might I say to the moment: 'Linger with me! You are truly beautiful!'" But the whole play has told us that men cannot live like that; nor has Faust himself ever succeeded in thus living and acting. And so Mephistopheles loses, and in Faust's next to last dying dreaming vision, angels descend, defeat the demons Mephistopheles has summoned, burn him with their showers of rose petals, and while he is distracted by his lust for the angelic boys, bear off Faust's soul. Poor Mephistopheles is crowded out of the stage, into the proscenium toward the audience by the hosts of angels, and as they disappear, with obscene comedy he curses himself for being diverted from his task. The final failure of transcendental magic is that its charms can divert us from what is genuinely inimical. An egocentric sexual thrill interferes between Mephistopheles and the reality which is making him lose his wagers with God and with Faust.

The last scene is rich with the Catholic symbolism of his

early training to which in his dying moments Faust's dreaming visions return him. He sees his soul brought to the company of holy hermits in high mountain gorges; and the souls of sainted women, including the soul of Gretchen, sweep down from heaven to receive him and bear him aloft. From off-stage we hear a final mystic chorus. "All that is passing," the changing and impermanent phenomena which we encounter in life and in art, specifically, this work of art, *Faust*, "is only a symbol"—but of what we can scarcely know. "Experience is insufficient" to justify our existence; "yet here"—in life and on this stage—"it becomes sufficient"; life's process, not its achievement, is its justification. "The indescribable is here described"; the contraries of existence have been embraced in a single vision; we can live only in tension with the destructive forces within us and without us. "The eternal feminine draws us onward"; it teaches us, as Gretchen rescued Faust from egocentricity, and Helen rescued him from memory. For a woman, to a man (if he genuinely loves her, as Faust came genuinely to love Gretchen and her reincarnation, Helen of Troy), is the other, the not-self, without which the self cannot exist. Her very ambiguity as a mother, source of affirmation and negation, her insufficiency, her indescribability—make her the perfect symbol for the elusiveness and contrariness and ambiguity of experience. Value and identity lie neither in the goal nor the achievement but in the eternally frustrated act; they can never be certain and absolute.

Goethe called *Faust* a tragedy, for like the tragedies of the past it reveals man as inadequate for the demands which the conditions of experience make of him, and our satisfaction with traditional tragedies comes from the public statement that the best of men are in the same trap as we are. But *Faust* places tragedy in a new light: man's adequacy lies in his power to face his inadequacy; his tragedy lies in his inability to accept that adequacy. He cannot live without Mephistopheles. He can love, for a while, Gretchen and Helen—humanity and art—but he cannot exist without the devil of orientative illusion.

# CHAPTER VII

# *Explorers: 3*

Beginning in the 1790's, here and there throughout Europe, now in England, now in Denmark and Sweden, even, timidly, in France, but especially in Germany, at first individually, then later by twos and threes, frequently associated with the poets and thinkers, painters began to experiment with, to acquire, to express, a new vision of the world. Of these perhaps the greatest, certainly among the two or three greatest, was Caspar David Friedrich; little known in France or England or the United States, for some time he has been recognized in Germany as the most complete visual symbolizer of the new orientation. Although his landscapes are of the North Sea and of Rügen, a then Danish island on which he was born, of Dresden, where he lived after the turn of the century, and of the Riesengebirge, the mountains on the border of Silesia and Bohemia southeast of Dresden, the spirit, the vision of Wordsworth finds an almost perfect parallel in Friedrich's art.

If one has any sensitivity at all to the culture of this period the paintings of Friedrich are profoundly moving, and when one looks at them against the background of his immediate predecessors, almost inconceivably original. Sometimes when one walks in the woods after a rain, a wet leaf brushes the cheek. That indescribable quality of freshness, of new birth, of experiencing like Adam the world for the first time, is the feeling that Wordsworth and Friedrich alike convey.

Born in 1774, the year of *Werther*, four years after Words-worth, his first great picture was exhibited in 1808, the year Con-stable, as we shall see, made the leap to the new vision, the year Part I of *Faust* was published. It was a crucifixion, but such a cru-cifixion never was painted before. The title is "The Cross in the Mountains," and ostensibly it is a wayside cross. But that has only been the point of departure. We are shown a landscape, restricted to the very top of a mountain peak. It is rocky; but a little grass grows, and a few great evergreen trees have rooted themselves in rocky crevices and struggled into burgeoning life. It is sunset; the clouds are an exquisite shell pink, and three rays of the setting sun shine up from below. Silhouetted against them is an immensely tall, thin cross, on which is hung a tiny figure of Christ. But most ex-traordinarily, whatever material the figure may be carved in, it is utterly different from the wood on which it is hung, for lit by the pink glow of the setting sun, the Christ appears to be not a statue but a human body, not corpse-like in death but alive. It is impossi-ble not to think of this as a crucifixion. Unlike every picture of the cross I have ever seen, the figure is turned *away* from the specta-tor, looking down on the sun setting far beyond and beneath the mountain peak; and the figure is absolutely alone. There are no thieves, no human beings, none of the traditional drama and fellow-suffering of others. This is a totally isolated Jesus—but not isolated by his reabsorption into the Godhead. Friedrich explained what he meant by this baffling picture: the dying sun signifies the death of the old world which dies as Jesus' teaching dies. Nevertheless, the cross stands as unshakably as our faith, surrounded by evergreen trees, which flourish in all ages. An equivocal and paradoxical ex-planation, it can only mean that Christianity dies, but the truth which Christianity symbolized, the triumphant suffering of man, isolated in the gathering darkness, remains amid the emergence of life from the very stones of the earth itself. In a later, unfinished painting he presented the imagined ruins of a still unruined cathedral to symbolize "the destruction of the church and its master, out of the ruins of which a new quest for clarity and truth is arising."

It would be impossible to express more clearly the cultural crisis as Friedrich experienced it and understood it. He belonged to a group of young authors and thinkers, men who had rejected even the modified optimism of Goethe in the 1790's, which resembled, to their taste, too much the secularized optimism of the Enlightenment. For it they substituted a realistic pessimism. They were determined to see, if they possibly could, the conditions of life as they actually are. They refused even to be caught up in the forces of the German nationalistic effort which were gathering to oppose Napoleon's challenge and invasion. To the greatest author of the lot, Heinrich von Kleist, the vision was of the individual, absolutely alone, facing an indifferent and hostile society and universe. In his extraordinary story, *Michael Kohlhaus*, he presented an individual determined to force justice out of the world even if it cost him his life. But it is no sentimental humanitarian tale of a man dying to bring about justice for humanity. Michael goes to his death calm and even happy, because the absurdity of the price he pays for justice emphasizes the absurdity of a world which demands such an enormous price if we are to force any sense out of it all.

With one exception Friedrich painted no more crucifixes. Instead, almost his next work was that of a monk absolutely alone and infinitesimal on a vast stretch of empty and lifeless seashore; he faces away from us toward the immensity of sea and sky, which come together at the horizon in an equivocal blur. Now a monk is not a hermit. He has withdrawn from the company of man into a smaller company of like-minded men. But this monk is alone. His special cultural sub-group is not, for him, functioning. There follows a series of similar paintings, of which perhaps the most powerful is one of a pair of figures in a clearing near the edge of a forest. They are very small and beyond them, through the tree trunks at the forest edge, can be seen the glow, white, then orange, then at the horizon smoky gray, of the dying sun. In another, a woman stands absolutely alone, with her arms half raised and half welcoming, half despairing; she faces the rays of the sun rising from behind a mountain. In still another series human figures disappear entirely, but in the foreground is a dying tree, or even more suggestively, a pool which reflects the sky and a bit of the landscape. It is like an eye, disembodied; it is almost a Kantian symbol of vision, as if the figures and even the lonely tree, or the grave of a hero, were too human to express what he meant. From 1824 comes one of his extraordinary series of mountain landscapes, the high peaks, covered with snow and glaciers, like a setting from the last scene of *Faust*. But there are no people; only in the center foreground, in the place occupied in other paintings by human beings, stands a single dead tree trunk, stripped of branches and with its top shattered and swept away in some terrible winter storm—or so one feels.

When we read a scrap of a letter to a friend who wanted his company on a trip to Switzerland, which he never visited, we begin to understand. "You want to have me with you, but the I which pleases you does not wish to be with you. I must be alone and know that I am alone in order to see and feel Nature fully. I must perform an act of exchange with what surrounds me, unite myself with my clouds and mountains in order to be what I am."

From this we gain an insight into both the amazing technique and the extraordinary symbolic power of these landscapes. For their technique is one of a closely observed realism, of a photographic precision of observation, hitherto non-existent in European art. Indeed, a hasty glance at black and white reproductions of some of his mountain paintings in particular can delude one, for a moment or two, into judging that he is actually looking at a photograph. But the photograph was, when Friedrich established his style, still a quarter of a century in the future. That is, we of today have something to compare the paintings to, and we automatically make that comparison; but his contemporaries had nothing. They must have felt that they were looking at nature with their eyeballs skinned. The letter just quoted makes certain what one can guess. The landscape is simultaneously itself and a symbol of the self of the observer. The parallel to Wordsworth is astonishing, even to the notion of an exchange between the self and the world—"both what we half create and half perceive."

Yet one may well ask, "What is the evidence *in the picture* for that self-projection? Suppose one has not examined the documents, suppose one has not compared the pictures with an eye to discovering certain thematic symbols, such as resemblance of figure to tree to pond? Where is the source for a Wordsworth-like notion of the creative imagination? The individual symbols are, perhaps, 'literary'; certainly they are conceptual. That is, they may be presented in verbal signs, or language. What is the *pictorial* evidence?" Such questions are pertinent; and they can be answered. Although at first glance the paintings appear to be of a photographic realism, a second glance—yet one that does not recognize the symbolism—reveals something different. Indeed, what this second glance discovers, perhaps unconsciously, is the stimulus for the third, which begins to look for the "literary" symbols. Previous painters had obviously selected from the visual world. Their clouds, their trees, their flowers, their human figures, were of a "heightened" reality. The imagination was clearly at work in creating a "true" nature, one better than the world we see—paradisiacal or representative of the perfect structuring of nature which only the imagination of painter and scientist and poet can grasp. But Friedrich does something different. His details are as literal as he can make them. The way he paints his rocks and trees seems, by comparison with the great tradition of the fifteenth to eighteenth centuries, dry and hard, as if he refused to permit any imaginative or emotional coloring to distort his vision. The detail of nature is, as it were, freed from the controlling grasp of the imagination. And this in one way or another was to be the painterly ideal of the whole century.

Yet that does not mean that the imagination was not at work, that Friedrich was a literalistic imitator of natural phenomena. The imagination is in fact powerfully at work—in the overall structure of the painting. Just as *The Prelude* consists of innumerable exactly reported events and images, yet is given a grand and powerful coherence by the river which appears in childhood, plunges below the earth during the years of Enlightenment sentimentality and of negation, and then rises, as the imagination is restored, in a bursting torrent of life; so Friedrich's pictures are organized by powerful and often very simple shapes. A regressing series of acute triangular mountain shapes, thrusting upward, is seen from a gorge, the sides of which form a powerful triangle pointed downward, and the apices of the triangles are almost exactly in vertical line and in the dead center of the picture. The ruin of a monastery apse with three intact lancet windows is almost exactly in the middle of the picture; it is flanked in the foreground by two giant and dying trees, leaning away from it at almost the same angle; in the background a half circle of similar trees echoes the semicircle of the apse; directly below the center lancet of the apse is the central door of the façade, its sole survivor. In other paintings immense mountain landscapes seen from a mountain top are composed of ridges, irregularly placed but each a low triangle; and rows of these are set one behind the other as precisely as the rows of a theater audience seen from the stage. At times this principle of regression by rows is combined with the mountain triangle. The landscape flows, like waves, up to the base of a mountain, the low triangle of which dominates the landscape by its almost absolute centrality.

Here, then, is the contrast with previous painting and the source of Friedrich's peculiar power. In earlier paintings structure and detail are alike informed by the imagination; but in Friedrich, the perception of details is sundered from the structural vision of the whole. It would be almost impossible to conceive a more striking symbolization of the separation of the ordering imagination from the phenomena of nature. The world of nature is here unequivocally split from the human imagination, which is firmly located within the mind and vision of the artist, from whom order emanates. Order and therefore meaning, or the sense of meaning. We see the details, we feel, unconsciously, the order; unconsciously, because the clarity, the freshness of the observation of detail distracts us from perceiving the imposed order. But it is that sense of order which forces us to look more deeply, to compare the paintings, to look for their thematic continuity, to discover the artist's system of "literary" or conceptual symbolizations. Without that imposed order of which we are unconscious, it would not,

I think, occur to us to look for the symbols. For that unaware sense of order ascribes to the painting a value which persuades us to search for meaning.

The greatness of Friedrich, then, lies in his power to use the death of the old orientations—Christian and Enlightenment— to break through to an entirely new mode of the painter's vision. And like Wordsworth, like his friends, like Goethe whom they scarcely understood nor could without the complete *Faust,* he was determined to wrest value from reality itself. It is the unflinching directness of Friedrich that is most disturbing, for he unites, even better than Wordsworth, terror and beauty in a single image. For always in these august and withdrawn landscapes, whether of the uttermost peaks, or whether of a breath-taking vision of range upon range, waves of mountains and clouds, disappearing end- lessly toward an infinitely distant horizon, there is a touch of life. The central tree may be blasted, but at the side there is a tree still alive. The mountains may be rock and snow, but the eye of the pool and a little thin grass symbolize the presence of life-giving water, of life, of value. Further, in spite of his letter, sometimes there are two trees, or even two figures, as if he were saying that it is not enough that the beautiful and terrible world of nature be a symbol of the divided and all but unconscious soul; really to feel our own existence, we must be aware in friendship and love of at least one other human identity in order to feel sure of our own. "You call me an enemy of mankind," he wrote in a little poem, "because I avoid company. You are wrong. I love you. But in order not to hate men, I must abstain from their society."

A love that forbids companionship; here is the paradox of the isolated and alienated nineteenth-century artist. That Friedrich means it we know from the one group of works in which a figure faces us directly. These are his self-portraits, all drawings, as if to make the impression hard, sharp, sensuously unseductive. The face occupies most of the picture area in these pencil drawings. It is enclosed and almost framed by hair lower over the forehead and long, not curly but writhing, sideburns. The eyebrows are arched like a madman's. The preternaturally wide-open eyes look directly at us; they bore into us with a fixed and terrible gaze. It is as if only the most fearful self-restraint were holding him from flight or madness, so agonizing is it to look at us at all. But the lips are about to open, to speak, prophetically utter a message of burning significance. He cannot endure us; but he loves us. At once we know that the vision of not one of these men, not Wordsworth's, not Goethe's, was of classic calm, of an orientation which ensured equilibrium before reality; it was a perilous balance of perception and vision.

Yet not Friedrich but John Constable was to be the founder of modern painting. Part of Friedrich's magic arises from the absolute stillness of his landscapes. They seem frozen in a timeless vision. Even a rainbow, because of the perfect symmetry with which it is placed in the picture, gives us no sense of change, of evanescence. He parallels one aspect of the Wordsworthian vision, certainly, but the other aspect, the momentariness of the imaginative act, the sense that less exalted moments precede and follow it, the spottiness of the spots of time—all this is lacking. And thus the Englishman Constable, born in 1776, only two years after Friedrich, was able to go beyond the point Friedrich reached; for Constable for the first time successfully pictorialized the early nineteenth-century orientation in its fullness, expressing both the autonomy of the imagination and the evanescence of the autonomous moment. Nevertheless, he was like Friedrich in this: he too had had his literary sources, Coleridge and above all Wordsworth himself.

Like Wordsworth's, Constable's emotional life was deeply rooted in a circumscribed area of England. Only it was not the miniature but grandiose spectacle and melodrama of the "mountains" of the northwest corner of England. It was the gentle, quiet, unspectacular valley of the River Stour, on which his father had a mill, on which he was born, near which lived his patron, Sir George Beaumont, and which he painted over and over again, in a thousand aspects, as long as he lived—although to be sure he painted other places as well, particularly the area around Brighton on the south coast and Hampstead and its heath, a then still unspoiled suburb of London.

The river Stour runs between Suffolk and Essex, between Colchester and Ipswich. On it are towns still old and lovely, East Bergholt itself, Stratford St. Mary's, and above all the quiet dreaming town of Dedham, lost, one almost feels, in a timeless past. East Anglia, the bulge of England east and north of the Thames, northeast of London, composed of Norfolk, Suffolk, and Essex, was once, in the late Middle Ages and into the seventeenth and early eighteenth centuries, an active and wealthy country, the center of wool and silk weaving. Its churches are among the most splendid and luxurious in England. But today, and since long before Constable's time, it has become a backwater, preserving its earlier aspect, almost untouched by the industrial revolution and modern life. Unvisited by tourists, it is hardly known to the traveler and the vacationer, except for the Norfolk Broads, the labyrinth of natural and artificial waterways in the northeast corner. Once its ports were busy with trade with the Lowlands and Germany; now they are but dull seaside resorts. Only the numerous airfields of the Second World War have brought it into any real connection with the twentieth century. It is a countryside of unutterable sweetness; its only life is the quiet growing of trees, of flowers, of wheat, and the still, lazy flowing of the waters—and the skies, the ever-changing, the always dramatic skies of England. And here, where so little else obtrudes upon one's perceptions, the skies have a singular significance. That emotion-laden life of the skies became Constable's profoundest symbol, reflected with what frequency in the slow-moving waters.

With earlier painters and poets we feel that the aspects of nature they chose to paint were selected either because they were at hand, or because they were particularly expressive of natural laws, or because by chance they exhibited the compositional order of artistic tradition. They chose spots that looked like paintings—unlike Friedrich, who from his sketches in his studio made up paintings that looked like real "unpicturesque" places. Yet even his landscapes can be localized; we can go and see them. But the landscapes of Salvator Rosa, of Fragonard and Gainsborough, are anonymous, placeless. Like the parks of Watteau, we do not ask of them, "Whose park was it? Where was it?" They were abstractions from nature. With the nineteenth-century painters, however, we are convinced that the place the painter gives us, and even the spot where he stood, can be found; and we often long to go and find them. We feel that Monet's Lombardy poplars are still waiting for us at the very bend of the Seine where he found them. Further, with great frequency, especially in the early part of the century, it is true that the painter loved and returned again and again to the landscapes of his childhood. Even Friedrich kept returning to the shores and harbors of Rügen. Now from Wordsworth we know what this return meant. Thus the painter and the poet drank again from the deepest wells of emotional life. By returning to the landscape where his emotional life began, in which he first felt his identity and first experienced an oriented relation to the surrounding world, he renewed and revitalized the current of his truest feeling. It was in the very quietness and lack of drama of the Stour valley that Constable discovered one of the most important aspects of his art. It enabled him to go beyond Friedrich.

As we have seen, in Friedrich there is almost always some kind of "literary" or conceptual symbolism. To earlier painters the value of the painting lay at least in part in the subject chosen to be represented; and for this Friedrich substituted a subject that functioned as a conceptual symbol. But Constable fought passionately against the doctrine still official in the academic painting of his day, a degenerate form of rococo and Enlightenment neoclassicism, the notion that the subject had any importance in itself. Constable, with great effort, freed himself from the tyranny of the subject. The task of the painter, as he saw it, was not to paint something, but to make something out of nothing. Subjects, he insisted, could be found "under every hedge." The Stour country he chose because he knew it well and because to him it had a profound emotional value. But there is no attempt to dragoon the spectator into sharing that emotional value. To him it could be any place; and indeed to Constable it could have been any place. It was important only because it was his; just as, most of the time, for Wordsworth the Lake District was important solely because he grew up there and there first became aware of his identity. What the terror and the beauty of that country was to Wordsworth, so to Constable was the neutrality of the Stour valley. It could be anything to anybody, because it forced no one to identify a mountain as a symbol of divine grandeur, or a lovely valley, nestled among the mountains, as a symbol of paradise. It just was. It was himself. It was Constable's very knowledge, it would seem, that the emotional associations of his country were emotional and associational only to him, which released him to concentrate directly on rendering the phenomenal world itself; and that is where he began.

It is not where he ended, for to imagine that Constable, as Ruskin thought, saw nature with the direct and naked objectivity of an eagle or a sheep would be to make a profound mistake. Actually, in the beginning, and for over a decade, for his development was slow and painful, he attempted to do just that. He took seriously the attitudes of the late Enlightenment. For the significant subject he substituted significant nature, believing that he had only to record nature in its infinite aspects in order to create art. He was mistaken. His early sketches, up to 1808, and his first attempts at landscape show him simply floundering. There is no coherence in these works. They are as tedious as life itself. We can see his technique growing, to be sure; and we know that he studied the landscapes of his predecessors, especially Rubens and the seventeenth-century Dutch masters of landscape; he became an increasingly able craftsman, in the traditional sense; we also know that he talked to other artists, that he asked for their advice, that he was much concerned with theory, that he was trying to discover the secret of the "right" way to be a landscape painter. Suddenly in 1808 everything changed.

In his youth he had been a great reader of poetry, and apparently as a young man he still was. At any rate, his patron, Sir George Beaumont, was a kind of clearing house for most of the arts of the day. Sir George exhibits almost to perfection one of the prime functions of the cultivated amateur. He did enough painting himself to know what the problems of painting are; but above all he acted as a medium of communication between the painters and the poets with whom he surrounded himself, whom he patronized, whose works he bought, and whom he helped with money, encouragement, and influence. Among the artists in whom he was particularly interested, besides Constable, whose talent he recognized early and encouraged, were the two great literary figures of the day, Wordsworth and Coleridge.

Yet to refer to these two poets as great is to participate in an error. They may be great to us. They were not great to their contemporaries. To the fashionable aesthetes, critics, and connoisseurs of the first decade of the century they were absurd and, because of their one-time radicalism, perhaps dangerous. Who knew how radical they still were? A good many people thought them enemies of England in its great struggle with Napoleon. To recognize their genius, to encourage them, to praise them in public, to force upon reluctant friends the *Lyrical Ballads* of 1798, of 1800, 1802, and 1805, to insist that others share his own enthusiasm, mark Sir George and his wife as courageous, modern, and forward-looking readers, the kind that every poet is always longing for. That Wordsworth was grateful—almost, in his emotional austerity toward others, pathetically grateful—comes through strongly in his letters to Sir George. But most important is the fact that Beaumont, outside of Coleridge, was almost alone in knowing about *The Prelude*, that he and Lady Beaumont were perhaps the first people outside of Wordsworth's immediate family circle and the tiny group of his intimate friends, including Coleridge and Robert Southey, who even knew of its existence. Wordsworth certainly planned to read the whole thing to the Beaumonts, and when in 1806 the fair copy destined for Coleridge on his return to Malta had at last been finished, it was sent to Sir George to read and to have bound. Further, we know that Beaumont talked about it to other people, praising it with the highest and most extravagantly enthusiastic compliments, and retailing Wordsworth's ideas, which, it would seem, he loved to relate to the already famous "Tintern Abbey," a poem he had read "hundreds of times."

Now during precisely these years, 1805 to 1808, when he

was constantly in communication with Beaumont, Constable was at the height of his struggle against the intractability of nature, its refusal to become a picture just because it was carefully imitated. Then with dramatic suddenness, in the spring of 1808, the year of Friedrich's "Cross in the Mountains," Constable made an extraordinary leap into a new mode of seeing. He had left London and returned to the Stour valley; and there he painted, with astonishing rapidity, a series of oil sketches which sing of spring. One of them shows a farmer sowing his fields. He strides across the new-ploughed ground; birds whiz about him; clouds rush across a blue spring sky. It is drenched with wind and sun. Instead of the painstakingly, wearisomely detailed oil sketches he had been doing, Constable, in a single stride, paints a picture which seems to have been executed with a single brush stroke, as if all the brilliant and intense colors had been loaded on an eight-inch brush and rolled onto the canvas with one dash of the wrist. It is not so, of course. The effect is a consequence of an entirely new integration of manual dexterity and absolutely fresh vision. "There are in our existence spots of time," Wordsworth wrote, and this is one of them. This picture looks as if it might have been done today, as if one of our contemporary abstract expressionists should suddenly start painting landscapes; the effect would not be too different from these 1808 sketches of Constable's.

The affinity is instructive. As we shall see, our mid-twentieth-century painters are the product of nineteenth-century creativity, of the quest for the absolutely spontaneous. Nothing is more difficult to achieve. It requires not an automatic repetition of culturally transmitted Gestalten or forms of perception, with perhaps a slight shift, something a little new, but rather a new and complete integration of personality, perception, and manual dexterity of technique. Since it is so rare, it is probable that few paintings of our abstract expressionists will, in the future, be considered worth preserving, for these painters seek nothing else; but those few will be golden and treasures.

And that was Constable's problem. Although these oil sketches, which he continued to do the rest of his life, often with

marvelous, with breath-taking results, are entrancing, they are not
in the end satisfactory. So we feel, and so Constable felt. He knew
he had hit upon something genuinely new; and it is impossible for
me to be convinced that something as little as a brief conversation
with Beaumont about Wordsworth was not the trigger that released him. Certainly he no longer sought anyone's advice; he
even refused to discuss what he was doing with other artists, who
were quite useless to him, for they were still working mindlessly
in an exhausted tradition or were attempting to reconstitute it according to a no longer meaningful Platonizing idealism. By symbolizing the autonomy of the artist in his capture of the visionary
moment, Constable had moved into the nineteenth century. The
rest were still in the eighteenth, or earlier. But his problem was
how to use this vision in a completely satisfactory work of art.

For some years he struggled, producing, to be sure, a number of splendid pictures in the process; and in these years he developed three very important ideas from the great breakthrough
of 1808. One was freshness and vividness of color. Friedrich's
colors were often of a brightness startling for the time, but he still
worked with the older notion that colors should be harmonized by
a predominant tone. It was his detail that was so startling. What
Friedrich did with detail, Constable did with color. We are so used
to brilliance of pure color in modern art that now even Van Gogh
seems sometimes rather pale and washed out; but the colors of Constable's sketches and some, or some parts, of his worked-up paintings can still impress us, can still make us unaware of the passage
of a hundred and fifty years. Their color is still modern. To his
contemporaries, of course, Constable's colors seemed crude, un-
harmonized. He had to fight against not only the theory of color
harmonization but also against the accidents of age; for the con-
noisseur and collector desired above all what they called "gallery
tone," the rich yellowish brown with which they thought the old
masters had glazed their paintings. Unfortunately, they were mistaken. Gallery tone was simply a combination of yellow and yellow-
ing varnish and dirt. It is heartbreaking to see, as we often do in
our museums, Constables smeared with brown varnish before the

paint had cured to the point where the varnish would not make an insoluble chemical bond with it. Such paintings cannot be cleaned. To live, Constable had to sell, but to sell often meant to see his work destroyed.

His next idea was sparkle, the sparkle of sunlight on leaves, on grass, on water, on clouds. And this was an idea of the greatest importance, for to capture that sparkle, often with touches of white which his contemporaries called Constable's snow, was to capture light itself. If change is both the character of the world and the character of our autonomous vision of the world, the most intense mode of symbolizing that change is to paint the evanescence of change itself, light. Light governs what we see, governs our perception, and is inseparable from the emotional moods which at once control our sight and are symbolized by our vision. Light changes in itself, and changes as our feelings change. It is the quality which unifies the perceiving subject and the perceived object; value arises from that momentary synthesis. Light is the perfect symbol of the transitory and momentary orientative relation of the self to the world. The history of painting in the nineteenth century becomes the history of the capture of light.

The third innovation which he carried from sketch to finished painting was what his contemporaries thought to be "lack of finish." You were not supposed to be conscious of brush strokes, even to perceive them. To be sure, a few earlier painters, Hals and Rembrandt, for example, had experimented with the visible brush stroke which forced itself on the perceiver, and on close inspection Titians can dissolve into abstract color. But these are exceptions, and certainly in Constable's time the ideal was "finish," a workmanship which on the closest inspection continued to be recognizable as the representational image. Constable, however, used his sketching technique, restrainedly at first, with far less restraint as he grew older, in his finished paintings. Thus he was able both to preserve the spontaneity of creation and to symbolize that spontaneity; but above all it illustrated a new idea. Heretofore, the artist was considered the sole creator; the observer was the passive receiver of the artist's vision. Here again Constable went beyond Friedrich. In Constable's paintings the observer becomes himself a creator. The painter, as it were, presents us with the raw material from which we create our own painting. The autonomy of the imagination, here meaning almost literally the power to create an image, is seen at work in painter and observer alike. Wordsworth's line from "Tintern Abbey," "Both what we half create and half perceive," comes irresistibly to mind.

Yet Constable had not yet adequately solved his problem of symbolizing the moment in a finished painting, worthy to be preserved in the great collections, to hang beside the old masters. In 1819, therefore, in an attempt to find the answer, he set about a series of skyscapes. He had come to the conclusion that the light on the ground is determined by the kind of light from the sky. In this new series he set about to examine the skies, and in particular the clouds. Again, as in the sketches of eleven years before, we are aware of a step forward into a new vision; for in clouds he found a way of unifying the vision of light with the perception of objects. He felt that in his earlier paintings his skies were but theatrical backdrops. But now we find a subtle gradation in degrees of movement, from the permanence of buildings through the stillness of green meadow, the shifting but rooted shapes of trees, the sparkle of light on leaves, to the constant moving and unpredictably changing shapes of clouds. And beyond the clouds is the sky, now deeply blue, now half-concealed, now exquisitely tender, now half-veiled, or heavy with rain and storm and drama; but whatever it is, it determines the quality of light which governs and moves through the whole landscape. Light, the symbol of change, is itself in motion. The whole picture is now unified, not merely by the rough finish, the impasto, not merely by sparkle, not by traditionally harmonized color, not even by light, but by motion. The landscape is seen in the moment of illumination. Solid as it appears, we half expect it to float away and to be succeeded within its own frame by what is just outside.

As early as 1821 French connoisseurs began to buy Constable's, and in 1823 he began to exhibit at the Salon in Paris. His pictures were admired, above all by the painters, but the critics were dissatisfied. "Yet they want the objects more formed and defined—etc., etc.," he wrote a friend, "and say that they are like the rich preludes in musick, and the harmonies of the Eolian Lyre —which *mean* nothing and they call them orations, and harangues, and highflown conversations affecting a careless ease—etc., etc., etc., . . . . Is not some of this *blame* the highest *praise?* What is poetry? What is Coleridge's *Ancient Mariner*—(the best Modern poem) but something like this." Music and poetry which refused, so it then appeared, to be conceptually interpreted; the arts of time, the arts of flowing, the arts of the shifting changeableness of the world and of our perception of the world; music which has no subject in the real world; a poem which, whatever it may mean, is clearly and above all the exquisite and artistic shaping of the fantasy of the imagination—these are Constable's models and the analogues of what he was doing. The subject is of no importance; it serves only as a nothing upon which the artist can project his something, his vision, unique to himself and in its momentariness, unique for himself. The painting becomes not a means for symbolizing concepts, or sentimental feelings, or even the profounder emotions; but in the indifference and neutrality of the subject, it becomes the vehicle for embodying the artist's experience of relation, of orientation, of his profoundest self, of his sense of value.

# CHAPTER VIII

# *Explorers: 4*

IT IS SCARCELY without import that Constable should have compared his painting to music. One of the central statements of the latter part of the century is Walter Pater's, "All art approaches the condition of music"; and a thousand and one times it has been reiterated that the great art, the central art, of the nineteenth century was music. Even the men of the century seemed to have thought so, for as the century proceeded poetry began to lose its primal place in the hierarchy of the arts and to be displaced by music. We have encountered several times the notion that reality lies in the processes of the phenomenal world; if there is a permanent substratum behind the world our senses present to us, we cannot know it; and as we shall see, it is but a step from saying it cannot be known to saying that we cannot know whether it is there or not; and but another step to saying it is not there at all. But we have also seen that the notion that the structure of reality as process was derived by analogy from the necessity to restructure the world from inside the subject out. The character of the superficial part of the personality—emotions like rage and love, and the social roles we play—is process; while the deeper side, the self, comes into being, or at least comes into perception and awareness, by a mental process. That was a basic notion of Kant's.

The shoe was now on the other foot. Heretofore the task of the architect, the painter, and the sculptor had been easy; for them there was little problem in symbolizing on the one hand either a static world at the end of time or a static world outside of time, or on the other hand the fixed laws of nature. Nor was there a particularly dreadful difficulty in developing conventional sign systems for rage or love, or for the qualities necessary in particular social roles. For the poet and musician, however, who operated in time, only the fallen world could be the proper subject. Both arts, therefore, tended to be descriptive, and even in the Enlightenment with its regard for selecting details of experience which represented most perfectly the underlying and permanent character of nature, their primary task was descriptive and representational with particular regard to the subject.

Now, however, as the new orientation emerged, music and poetry, and the novel with its possibilities for immense length and the presentation of a whole life, became the arts which could achieve success with comparative ease. Painting renewed itself only slowly and with difficulty; architecture, perhaps, never succeeded until the twentieth century; and the solidity of bronze and marble was an embarassment to the sculptor, presenting a problem not solved until the last decades of this extraordinary period.

We see this in Arthur Schopenhauer's striking philosophical work, *The World as Will and Representation*. I shall have to say more about Schopenhauer later. Here I wish to say just enough to make, if I can, his notion of music comprehensible; for it is highly typical and was to have immense influence. He was perhaps the first to place music apart from the other arts and to insist that it is the greatest and the profoundest of them all. His notion is strikingly like Constable's; he denied utterly that the relation of music to any subject matter in the real world was of any importance or value, or even that it existed. He pointed out that the same music could be used with equal effect to accompany words and stage action that presented the struggle of heroes or that presented the household quarrels of a very ordinary family. Any association between a piece of music and an objective event, then, is purely arbitrary. He denied further that music does or can present concepts, abstract ideas, such as causality, or eternity, or immortality. He would only have been contemptuous of William Lyon Phelps' contention that a passage in Beethoven's "Appassionata Sonata" proves the immortality of the soul. But he went beyond the eighteenth-century theorists, for he denied that music presented even such passions as rage or love or religious yearning. The same music could equally well accompany a storm in the mountains or the anger of a god or of a contemptible criminal. What then does it do? Simple. It is *a copy of the will itself*. The italics are his.

To be fair to Schopenhauer, I must point out that this statement comes in the middle of a five-hundred-page book, most of which is devoted to explaining what he means by the will. Nevertheless, his concept is not really that difficult. Most philosophical ideas are simple enough once you grasp them. The difficulty of philosophy comes when the philosophers attempt to prove they are right, and Schopenhauer, like almost all other philosophers, shows how impossible that ambition is by continually writing in a tone of contempt and anger. After what the reader has gone through already, I do not think Schopenhauer will present any very difficult problem.

Schopenhauer took up where Kant's theory of knowledge left off, with the notion that the reason can create structure, and although no such structure will tell us what the world is, since both the mind and the world are natural products, we can assume by analogy, and act accordingly: structure is the ultimate character of the world. Not so, said Schopenhauer. The basic character of man is not reason but will, the will to live, the will, in spite of all obstacles, to continue to live. Its whole experience is one of a wearisome round of frustration and gratification, the only alternative to which is even more depressing, boredom; for the will's activity is pointless, purposeless. Deluded by the charms of reason, we ignore the fact that reason can give us no reason to live. Further, reason has no interest in individualities, which it cannot know, only generalities, what Plato called the ideas, the only thing it can know. But the will is unconscious; we are aware of its power but not of its character; nevertheless, because of the conditions under which it must operate, the will-to-live must take the form of the will-to-individuality, to identity, to selfhood. It forces us into a meaningless, purposeless, valueless drive to create and maintain our identities. One of the results of this drive is the mind's creation of the Platonic ideas, which the arts copy—all except music. Music is a copy of the will itself.

As with Constable, it is not the subject that is important but what the artist does with it. But there is even more. The true analogy by which we can grasp the world is not from the structure of the mind but from the drive of the will. The reason can only represent the world to the mind; it can only give an idea of a world, with no way of telling whether it is a true idea or not. But if we conceive the world as a pointless, purposeless, valueless drive toward existence and individuality, if we take our analogy from the will, then we have grasped the world's true nature. Music, then, is not merely a copy of the human will; it presents to us the real nature of the world, for the world is not representation but will. It is consequently the greatest, the profoundest, the truest of the arts.

The structure of music, the way it is put together with rhythm, harmony, and melody, gives us nothing but the pure activity of the will—tension and relaxation, frustration and gratification. Life is not one damned thing after another, for things we cannot know, only the ideas or representations of things. Rather, life is one damned impulse of the will after another, continually renewed after each frustration. Hence music can accompany with equal success any representation of human activity, whether a quarrel of heroes or the love of a pimp and a prostitute; for the will, which is indifferent to good and evil, makes no moral discriminations. A pimp is a hero if he wills to think of himself as a hero; and a prostitute is Helen of Troy if she so wills, as she necessarily must in her submission to the drive of the will toward individuality and identity.

But if this is what music does, how can we find it beautiful? For the same reason that causes all the arts to be beautiful. They look at experience as a significant spectacle. In art the will is short circuited. The arts do not require us to do anything except to contemplate them; and thus they offer us, though only temporarily, a release from the will's intolerable drive. But for this offering to humanity and to himself as part of humanity, the artist pays a fearful price. He can get to the artistic vision only by willing to; thus he suffers from the lash of the will like everybody else. Others, however, can act blindly; he must tear himself from willing, must isolate himself from mankind. His consolations are great, but his suffering and his desert loneliness are greater. Nevertheless, he can free himself and us from the lacerating will. Absorbed in the work of art, we can for a moment experience life as pure value, pure significance, free from the guilt of will and existence. Aesthetic contemplation is our only innocence.

Although Schopenhauer's words are different, we can recognize the pattern. Out of the unconscious emerges identity, which is given its fullest realization in the work of art. The isolated artist, though but for a moment, redeems the world. Through him, value enters the world. For a moment, for artist and observer alike, identity swims up to consciousness and is crowned with value. Self-generated order and meaning are experienced, not merely longed for in an agony of frustration. Consider the ideas of the inarticulate and verbally clumsy Beethoven, as translated and given form by Bettina Brentano. "When I open my eyes I must sigh, for what I see is contrary to my religion, and I must despise the world which does not know that music is a higher revelation than all wisdom and philosophy, the wine which inspires one to new generative processes, and I am the Bacchus who presses out this glorious wine for mankind and makes them spiritually drunken."

For a purpose which I shall make clear in a moment, I should like to translate Schopenhauer's terms into the vocabulary of this book. I have suggested that the orientative drive keeps us from seeing reality, locks us into the illusory embrace of given orientations. Art, on the other hand, by breaking up those orientations releases us to see aspects of reality which orientations conceal from us. And it can do this simply because it does not require us to act, action inevitably demanding that we use an orientation to select from and deal with the blizzard of sensation and phenomena. For the orientative drive we can, without confusing things too much, substitute Schopenhauer's will to existence and identity; and for his notion that art frees us from the will by engaging us in the act of contemplation, we can, I think, substitute the corresponding notion that by not requiring us to act art frees us to perceive more adequately. From the point of view of this book, then, we can say that music differs from other arts by reason of the fact that the others (except architecture, which Schopenhauer does not trouble with) present some aspect of reality in order to show the orientative-disorientative activity at work, while music presents that activity in itself.

The advantage of such rather dubious substitutions is this. In writing cultural history it is extraordinarily difficult to talk about music and to relate it to other cultural activities. Generally, as historians of music are wont to complain, it is ignored; we have the spectacle of a very great art, a human activity of the profoundest importance, omitted from such histories, not because the historian does not wish to talk about it, but because there is no language to talk about it with, which can be integrated into the conceptual language available for the other arts and the rest of human culture. The question as to whether or not music has meaning is absolutely unresolved. Yet even those who insist that music is a purely autonomous manipulation of forms quite untranslatable into other languages because it is not a language at all, or even a system of signs, tend to admit that somehow or other it is permeated with human values.

If, as I have suggested, the basic and most general human drive, a consequence of man's organism and his necessity to relate himself to his environment, is the orientative drive, we can, tentatively and vaguely, identify music as a symbolization of orientative activity itself, divorced from image, from concept, from objects, from the sensory world. But if we can do that, though with only a trace of legitimacy, we can go a step further and state that at the time of a profound cultural reorientation music should go through more violent changes than the other arts. I think it can be said that at the beginning of the nineteenth century it did.

The popular repertoire of serious music is today almost

entirely composed of nineteenth-century compositions, plus a few symphonies of Mozart and Haydn, both of whom are thought of, in comparison with the composers from Beethoven on, as light and a little frivolous. Until the 1920's that attitude was typical of all but a few of the most advanced connoisseurs, who mounted in that decade a great campaign, centered at Salzburg and its annual Mozart festival, to convince the music-loving public that Mozart was to be taken very seriously indeed. In other words, so profound was the revolution effected by Beethoven and his successors that for a long time earlier music was regarded as rather primitive. Only with the advent of the long-playing record did it become possible for most people even to hear music before Beethoven; even so the basic orchestral repertoire has been extended only a little in the direction of the pre-nineteenth century, and the same condition is true of basic piano, violin, and chamber music. A still surviving tradition, then, preserves the early nineteenth-century recognition of Beethoven's musical revolution.

Yet, paradoxically, it was more difficult for Beethoven and his first great successor, Schubert, to free themselves of eighteenth-century music orientations than it was for practitioners in the others arts. The second half of the eighteenth century was exceedingly barren of lasting artistic productions in poetry, the drama, painting, and though to a less striking degree, architecture; but in Haydn and Mozart it had two richly productive figures, who seemed to have carried music to its absolute heights. In the last decades of the century, when Bach was virtually forgotten and Handel comparatively neglected, as he still is, it seemed impossible to create better music than Haydn's and Mozart's. It probably is, but it is possible to create something different. Other artists had a relatively clear field; it was only too evident to them that the exhaustion of their arts indicated the failure of the orientation which they symbolized. But to Beethoven, and even to Schubert, who started composing after Beethoven had achieved his revolution and in the same city, that kind of evidence was missing.

Beethoven's struggle, then, to free himself was titanic, and not until 1808 was it obvious that he had effected something entirely new. Indeed, he is sometimes even bracketed with his two great predecessors and excluded from the nineteenth-century pantheon, which is stated to begin with the late Schubert, Chopin, Schumann, and Berlioz. But such a notion is an error. The passage I have already quoted is almost sufficient evidence by itself when we contrast it with the eighteenth-century conception of the role and the task of the musician.

Born in 1770, of the same generation as Wordsworth, Friedrich, and Constable, Beethoven grew up during the late Enlightenment and the period of the French Revolution. His political opera, *Fidelio,* and his original conception of Napoleon as liberator, show his conception of freedom as a free man in a free society; but what he said to Bettina Brentano arises from a profoundly different orientation. In that statement it is not a free society which frees man, but the artist who redeems humanity from the terrors of life. Religion can neither explain nor justify the human condition, nor can philosophy. A Catholic critic has seen in Beethoven's "Missa Solemnis" an anti-mass, a mass of the devil, a black mass. Absurd, of course; yet it is perhaps a kind of evidence that to Beethoven it is the artist who redeems religion, not religion that redeems the artist. Only the divine artist can liberate the human spirit into an ecstatic experience of absolute and pure joy.

There are then, two sources, or two stages of his self-conception, which was so often expressed as truculence, savage misanthropy, and even shady financial dealing with publishers and patrons. As a man of the people he welcomed the equalitarianism of the Revolutionary spirit, just as Wordsworth did. But as a nineteenth-century artist, his refusal to play the aristocratic conception of the musician's role had a different source and a different meaning. For his music and his personal life show a remarkable consistency and parallelism. The Enlightenment composer was essentially a servant of a nobleman; that is, he had a specific socially-structured role to play. In the same way the Revolutionary French painter, David, conceived of himself as the servant of the state, or, more largely, of mankind; for to David and his fellows, as with Beethoven until his disillusion with Napoleon, to serve the French state and its symbolic representatives was to serve mankind. The individual still found his identity and his value in a role. Just so Alcestis and Admetus, in Gluck's Enlightenment opera, *Alcestis* (1767), are saved from death and hell because they have shown themselves to be the model wife and the model husband.

*Fidelio,* written between 1803 and 1805 but based upon a French Revolutionary play of 1798, exhibits much the same conception of social redemption achieved by a perfect wife. The rescue of the heroine's husband is consummated by a political redemption, and the most moving scene in the opera, one of the most emotionally rending in all theater, presents political prisoners let briefly out of their dungeons to enjoy a little sun and air. They too, of course, are freed from tyrannical oppression at the end. However, there is a vast difference between conceiving oneself as the servant of mankind who writes an opera to further political freedom, and conceiving oneself as the spiritual liberator of mankind, who raises human beings to a Dionysian ecstasy. The remark to Bettina comes shortly after 1810; the Seventh Symphony (Wagner called it "The Apotheosis of the Dance"), which has always been recognized as Dionysian and ecstatic, was written in 1812. Isolated by his deafness, lacerated by physical suffering, Beethoven had by then determined, by fair means or foul, to achieve a financial independence which would free him from all social dependence. What the artist does for mankind, not as political and ideological servant but as spiritual liberator, deserves support.

Here we strike the apparent paradox of the nineteenth-century artist's notion of his economic place in society. Alienated from his culture, despairing of its adequacy for any human being, refusing to amuse it, or console it, or play its game, refusing to give it what it wants, let alone what it thinks it wants, arrogantly consenting only to give it an incomprehensible art which if understood would destroy its orientative foundations, the artist of this tradition nevertheless insists on his right to an income, to comfort, even luxury and splendor if he needs them. His justification? He brings to society not what it wants but what it desperately needs. Almost echoing the words of Friedrich, Beethoven asserted to his fellow man, "You think I hate you. I love you. Only I can't stand you."

This new conception of the artist's economic place in society, which perhaps Beethoven was the first to work out, parallels what he did to music. The Enlightenment composer had two tasks, to amuse and to be serious, but even when he was serious, he had to amuse. Mozart was never so serious as in his Enlightenment opera, *The Magic Flute*, but even he was rarely so amusing. Only in certain very late works does there seem to be an incipient rebellion, an echo or parallel to Wertherian negation. There should have been; he was seven years younger than Goethe. But Beethoven, after his youthful period, refused progressively to be amusing at all. Furthermore, his seriousness took an entirely different form, one that completely reorganized the forms he had inherited from Haydn and Mozart and the other eighteenth-century composers.

The sonata (called, according to the instruments used, also a symphony or quartet or trio, and so on) was a hundred years old when Beethoven started writing. It consisted by his time of either three or four movements, and a very limited set of possibilities for the musical structure of each; moreover each possibility had fairly binding rules. The sequence of movements was ordinarily fast, slow, fast, fast, though on occasion the slow movement came third. To listen to such a work was to go through a familiar structure with few surprises. The surprises were in the detail, not in the form. At the same time, each movement had a defined emotional character; if there was a contrast, it was a contrast of related moods. As much as music can be, it was a static structure, its various parts sharply delimited and marked off from one another, even within the movement, its primary interest the presentation of musical material, not its development. Music, it was felt, imitated specific emotions, nobility, anger, love gaiety, charm. In the art of making music express specific emotions Mozart reached an altitude of perfection, grace, and subtlety which had never been achieved, nor has been matched since. But there is no development of personality in his operas, only an endlessly fertile depiction of emotional states of individual personality, which is identified with a socially-structured role. Likewise in his instrumental music there is never the slightest ambiguity about which emotion he is imitating. Thus he has been called, in contrast to Beethoven and his successors, and sometimes to disparage them, "objective," and socially and emotionally objective he undoubtedly was. This whole system of structure and emotional depiction, Beethoven simply blew up.

For clarity he gives us ambiguity; for a clear and stable structure, he gives us the same structure pulled awry, immensely developed, utterly changed; for an unmistakable convention of emotional delineation he gives us the tidal flux and flow of psychic energy. Like Goethe and Byron and Stendhal and Friedrich and the rest of the writers and artists we have examined, he plunges below the social level of role and emotion. How to present the heroic in music was perfectly well known to Handel, Gluck, Haydn, and Mozart (though in opera, judging by his comparative failures, Mozart was not very much amused by the heroic). Who would guess that Beethoven's Third Symphony is about a hero, if the title page hadn't said so? Clearly, we have a new conception of the heroic. Instead of a firm, bold melodic outline, with the tread of heroes in the rhythm, presented unequivocally and at once, initially we do not even get the main theme in its complete form. And what a theme for a hero! Wavering, almost waltz-like, ambiguous in its shiftiness from major to minor, syncopated—even, when we think of Handelian heroics, indecisive—it does not at its first appearance have any heroic energy at all. But it gathers it. It develops into it.

At this point we arrive at another difference. In the traditional first movement of the sonata or symphony or quartet, the presentation of the melodic material is the important thing; between the two presentations occurs a development of those themes, rarely elaborate and usually fairly short. But even in the Third Symphony, the melodies are closer to themes; they are not presented so much for themselves as they are as possibilities for development. The development section becomes immensely long, and the second presentation of the themes is followed by a second long development. Nor is this development simple; everything Beethoven can think

of doing to a theme he does, so that at times between the theme
and its developed form, the connection, especially in later works,
can scarcely be grasped. Is it a development, or entirely new material? It is both; it is ambiguous, equivocal.

Yet even in the Third Symphony Beethoven had not fully
arrived at a new conception of music. The general eighteenth-century practice, in this form, whether for one instrument or many,
was to be serious and amusing in the first two movements but only
amusing in the last two. To be sure, it was often the amusement of
angels, amusement raised to the highest level of which human beings
are capable; nevertheless, it was amusement. After the terrors and
ardors of the first two movements of the Third, the last two are
infinitely less demanding. They have something of the eighteenth-
century sugar-coating on the pill, a reward for being good and
paying attention.

In the Fifth Symphony, however, the development of a
new conception is complete. It was written in the culturally crucial years of 1805-7, when Wordsworth was completing *The Prelude*, Goethe finishing Part I of *Faust*, and Constable and Friedrich
making their breakthrough into a new pictorial vision. The Fifth
gave Beethoven a very hard time indeed. If it is the greatest symphony ever written, it is so because it has within it the inexhaustible
freshness of an entirely new musical world. For the presentation
of emotional states Beethoven substitutes drama and conflict. For
the display of aspects of the self completed and stabilized by its
social role, Beethoven gives us the terrible struggle of the self to
come into existence. For a sequence of movements, two serious
and two amusing, Beethoven presents an integrated emotional
continuum. For melodic presentation he substitutes the germinal
theme, four notes, initially, from which almost everything in the
first movement develops. For two clearly defined movements, each
with its own melodic material, he employs that same theme, melod-
ically changed but rhythmically identical, or perhaps the rhythmic
energy itself; again in the third, and to carry us from the third
movement without a break into the fourth. In the fourth movement,
with extraordinary novelty, he uses the structure traditionally re-

served for the first, which in this symphony the first does not have. It is as if Beethoven were asking, "These structures, these formal organizations of the emotions, are all very well; but how do you get to them?" The Fifth Symphony ends where the traditional symphony began. If that is the case, under the cultural circumstances it would seem that this symphony must be about how psychic energy is marshalled, organized, and released so that it may arrive at an orientation which will enable the self to confront reality.

Everyone knows the da-da-da-DA with which the first movement opens. When he was asked what he meant, Beethoven is said to have replied, "Thus fate knocks at the door." The first thing to note about this famous story is the nature of the question. The questioner assumed that music has meaning, presumably the emotional imitation of the eighteenth century; but the meaning of this music he could not grasp. As for Beethoven's answer, one aesthetician, committed to the position that music is a manipulation of forms without any meaning at all in the ordinary sense, though it is permeated with "human values," maintains that Beethoven simply meant, "Don't ask silly questions." Aside from the fact that everything human beings do or come in contact with is permeated with "human values," aside from the fact that we cannot even imagine what "non-human values" could or would be, this interpretation ascribes to Beethoven a capacity for irony and intellectual sophistication which nothing whatever he ever said or wrote, judging by the records, would show him capable of or interested in. On the contrary his humor was gross, peasant-like, crude, and preferably scatological. He liked to shock refined people, presenting himself as a man of the soil. He was not, so far as we can tell, interested in intellectual teasing. Let us assume, rather, that he meant the explanation seriously.

"Fate" is a word variously used, but if any word has a root meaning, it refers to the conditions of human existence and experience as something no man can escape. Now when someone knocks at the door, he either wants to come in or wants you to come out. Specifically it is a request or a demand that a separation between the knocker and the knockee be removed. A door is a removable barrier between an enclosed area and an open area. Since fate is knocking, since one rarely knocks to get out, the person who hears the knock is within the door, inside the closed area. Now in nineteenth-century literature rooms, houses, caves, castles, courtyards are used over and over again to symbolize the idea that the self is an entity and that it is closed against or at least separable from social and empirical reality. This is the age of the discovery, or invention, of the self. Under the cultural circumstances, it seems more than likely that that is what Beethoven is concerning himself with. It is as if he said, "Thus the conditions of human existence force themselves upon the sensitive human organism and require that it come into existence as a spiritual entity."

But fate is always thought of as both uncontrollable and oppressive. Perhaps it would be better to interpret the remark a little differently. "Thus in its first encounter with reality, which summons it into the light, the self experiences frustration." Certainly the struggle and frustration and defeat of psychic energy of the will, to fall back on Schopenhauer, appears to be what the first movement dramatizes. The second, in contrast, is paradisiacal. An exquisitely beautiful melody, one which Beethoven worked years to perfect, is presented, and then transformed, metamorphosed, and restated in an astounding series of variations. It is astounding now. In 1808 it must have been a revelation. But this paradise is rejected, though innumerable facets of gratification, with just enough tension to be convincing, have been presented and enjoyed. Or rather, the actor in this drama is forced out of paradise; the triumphant assertion with which it ends is succeeded, in the third movement, by a return to the threatening and sinister encounter with frustration. (Compare the identical pattern of Byron's *Don Juan*.) And once again we hear the four notes of the opening theme, only instead of the downward minor plunge in the first movement, now, although still in the minor, the rhythm is repeated again and again on the same note. It can go either way, now, up or down, but the motion of the initial theme, though in the minor, and very soft, is upward.

If that downward minor plunge has been pushed back and held at one level, cannot it now be forced upward toward triumph? Consequently, the second part of the movement is a marvelous release, in the major, of pure energy, plunging up and down, like a dolphin, with superb effortlessness. The sinister opening returns; once again we hear the threatening four notes, only now instead of a conclusion there is a transformation. Suddenly the four notes are heard in the major; there is an immense jubilation; and there streams forth not, as in the eighteenth century, a stated, an asserted heroism, but an earned affirmation, the leap upward. And the succeeding notes of this theme echo the leap upward which we heard at the end of the second movement and the notes which followed it when the melody of the second movement had its complete form. The last movement is a tremendous drama of struggle with frustration, of encountering it directly, and of celebration, of joy, of pure affirmation.

If there is such a thing as cultural convergence, if among people of great intelligence and sensitivity there is at the same time but independently a reorientation in a new direction, and if orientations can be symbolized in a variety of ways, in philosophy, in fiction, in poetry, in painting, in music—and all of these possibilities seem to me usable in creating constructs of cultural history— then it seems to me I am justified (though not "right," since one can never be "right") in finding in the Fifth Symphony what we have seen elsewhere conceptually and pictorially symbolized: The self, stripped of its social roles and its traditional orientations toward reality, encounters the ambiguity and terror of a meaningless world; it turns aside into a paradise of value, of identity, and order, where a single structure underlies all variations of it; it re-encounters the frustrations and anxieties of existence; but with the pure value, underived from any traditional justification of man's existence, which it experienced in the withdrawn paradise of the self, it can encounter experience, and though it suffers, it has a self-derived orientation with which to face reality. Its sense of value can be damaged; it canot be destroyed. Before he died Beethoven was considering music for Goethe's *Faust*.

# Part Three

# The Heroic Redeemer

# CHAPTER IX

# The World without Value

WHAT BEETHOVEN DID to the eighteenth-century sonata forms in the Fifth Symphony seems almost trifling when we listen to his later works. From 1817 to 1823 he worked on two astonishing compositions. The Ninth Symphony was unprecedented in its length and its use of a great chorus and soloists in the last movement, a setting of Schiller's "Ode to Joy." The "Missa Solemnis" was simply a musical puzzle to his contemporaries, and remains today one of the most severe tasks a conductor can undertake. Successful performances are still rare. But these were easy, both to perform and to comprehend, compared to the astounding series of string quartets he worked on from 1824 to his death in March, 1827. In less than a year and half he created five works of such fullness, length, complexity, and difficulty of comprehension and execution that decades passed before they began to be performed with any regularity. Indeed, by the end of the century they were still comparatively neglected, and even today a good many performers insist that parts of them are unplayable.

The first of these works (String Quartet No. 12, Opus 127) is astonishing enough; it moves steadily, from movement to movement, from a quiet beginning through increasing tension, violence, and exaltation to a wild outburst at the end. In this psychological unity of plan, although the conventional four movements are still present, the old four-part structure is not merely subjected to extraordinary stresses and distortions, as in the previous works; it begins to dissolve. In the next quartet (No. 15, Opus 132) the dissolution of form and the emergence of psychological continuity is carried still further; while the third (No. 13, Opus 130) was so strange that his frightened publisher persuaded him to substitute a rondo for the original final fugue, which was published separately (No. 17, Opus 133).

For a long time the altered version of Quartet No. 13 was performed, and still is, but now the original version, though not yet standard, is presented with increasing frequency. In any case, today recordings make it possible for anyone to hear the original form; only then does the final Grand Fugue make musical sense, for when the quartet is heard in its original integrity, the fugue emerges, almost without a break, from the preceding movement. The first movement nearly destroys the first-movement form, for it consists of an extraordinarily abrupt and discontinuous alternation of fast and slow sections. The next three movements, together with the first, form something very much like the traditional four-movement plan, although the slow movement is third, in itself not too great a departure, one with eighteenth-century authority. But then Beethoven adds two movements: a slow movement and the Grand Fugue. If any music seems genuinely to deserve the epithet "divine," the final movement deserves it. Even Wagner, who learned how to write music from these works, and so was musically far in advance of his own contemporaries, did not achieve until *Parsifal*, fifty years later, such a fusion of unbearable tension with exalted ecstasy. When you can find players who can perform the fugue, a lucky and infrequent accident, it is possible to hear one of the most thrillingly raucous pieces of music ever imagined. It has everything, every imaginable shade of desire and satisfaction; but it is a brutal assault on the listener.

Nevertheless, in the fourth (String Quartet No. 14, Opus 131) Beethoven went even beyond this. The dissolution of the four-movement plan, threatened in the first of these works and almost achieved in the third, actually occurs. Beethoven states that it is in seven movements, but he could just as well have said five, for two are very short introductions to what follows. The preceding quartet ended with a fugue; this begins with one. The appearance of these fugues is doubly odd. By the end of the eighteenth century the fugue was almost an outmoded form, used for church music and musical pedagogy; its appearance in string quartets still seems to be very strange. In fact, the dissolution of the individual movement had, and has, the effect of powerful disorientation. Musical predictability virtually disappears; consequently, emotional tension rises. It is impossible to get accustomed to these works.

By contrast, the last (No. 16, Opus 135) is, instead of being tremendously long and discursive, terse; yet its structure is in some ways the oddest yet. The most peculiar thing of all is that the last movement is headed "The Difficult Resolve" and under the opening phrases is "Must it be? It must be! It must be!" All kinds of interpretations have been given to these mysterious statements. Most of them try to locate a referent for "It" but, at least from the point of view I am using in this book, it seems to me that to ask what Beethoven meant by "it" is indeed a silly question, silly because it cannot possibly be answered. Rather, the pattern exhibited appears to be the significant element: the facing of the unendurably conditional; the acceptance of the unacceptable. Artistic forms and patterns are invariably associated, perhaps quite arbitrarily, with specific orientations. To subject them to distortions and unprecedented strains, to dissolve them, certainly suggests that the corresponding orientations are themselves no longer emotionally functional. What was seen as necesary order is no longer perceived as inevitable but rather as arbitrary and meaningless. In these quartets in place of the dissolving forms emerges a new structure, but it is no longer a structure characterized by familiarity and predictability; its character is precisely that it presents us the unfamiliar and the unpredictable.

Beethoven said that the fourth of the series (No. 14, Opus 131) presents a day in the life of the composer. He has come to agree with Schopenhauer and Constable; the ostensible subject or referent of music does not have to be "fate" or "joy" or "a religious ritual"; it can be absolutely anything. Anything at all can be the "it" of "It must be!" Further, what the day exhibits is what every day for every human being exhibits: the failure of traditional ways of structuring experience, the randomness, meaninglessness, and pointlessness of events-in-themselves, and the continuous struggle, the asymmetric, non-rhythmic, irregular effort of the perceiving subject to shape order out of life's chaos. Beethoven's epigraph cannot be an echo of Part II of *Faust*, for it was not yet published, but it is remarkably like the words of Goethe's dying protagonist, "Only he deserves freedom and life who conquers them every day." Beethoven's day may end in joy and triumph, but it is only the triumph of a day; there is no final achievement at which the human spirit can rest. So it must be, whether we like it or not; certainly we cannot understand why it must be; we can only accept it, for a moment. And from that momentary acceptance, the most that any human being can achieve, emerges value.

Of all the artists and thinkers of the first stage of nineteenth-century culture, Beethoven in these last quartets was the most profoundly original, the most advanced, the one who by 1830 had departed most widely from the Renaissance and Enlightenment traditions. He is the first in whose work style catches up with orientation. In Wordsworth, in Goethe, in Friedrich and Constable, even in Byron, whose *Don Juan* stanza and style were imported into English from an Italian tradition going back to the fifteenth century, there is much that reminds one of the eighteenth-century Enlightenment. The dream phantasmagorias in *Faust* are derived from the seventeenth-century Spanish playwright, Calderon, and much of the stage spectacle comes directly from seventeenth- and eighteenth-century opera, pageant, and festival, superb displays of the most elaborate theatrical devices and stage effects imaginable. If it is true, as Schopenhauer and Beethoven felt, that music is profounder and truer than religion and philosophy, than all conceptual thinking—that it is a copy of the will, that it presents the real character of the world, or, as I would put it, of the orientative drive itself—it is only fitting, it is necessary, inevitable, that at this time music should have been ahead of the other arts. And in fact later musicians could draw on the late Beethoven as none of the subsequent artists and thinkers in other areas of culture could draw on the men we have examined or their contemporaries.

How far Beethoven went in his conceptual thinking, which explored oriental philosophy and religion, poetry of the present and the past, and the works of a number of the profoundest of his contemporaries, we do not know. Perhaps it went as far as his music; perhaps not. Certainly, no one else went as far as Beethoven did in his last quartets in structuring a new orientation. For what the men of this first stage had achieved, though extraordinary, was unstable. Perhaps, as we have seen, Wordsworth was the first to feel that instability; for he shrank from it and turned back, with a consequent drying up of his poetic powers. The great bulk of his poetry, and by far the best of it, was written by 1807. He could not face, or could not imagine, the continuous renewal which Goethe and, it would seem, Beethoven achieved. But he may have failed simply because he recognized sooner the nature of the problem.

Now the problem was this. Value had its source in the self; but it also could be symbolically perceived in nature. This appears to be the idea behind Beethoven's "Pastoral Symphony," his Sixth, written in 1807-8, directly after the Fifth and a kind of complement to it. After the struggle for self-realization in the latter he turned, one is perhaps justified in thinking, to the consolations of nature, in which he saw the divine as immanent; for he specifically noted that the Sixth was not to be conceived as descriptive music in the eighteenth-century manner, but rather as the feelings of the individual self before nature. Value, then, by a mode of intuitional perception, could be perceived as immanent in the natural world, in its ugliness and terror as well as in its beauty and grandeur. That perception was not a rational perception of structure; it was a way of seeing nature as a symbol of the divine reality that was immanent in it, but not rationally perceptible or comprehensible.

Value, then, had a dual authority. The self arose from the unconscious, but the unconscious was thought of not, as we think of it, as biologically earlier in origin than the conscious and therefore analogous to less developed forms of life; but rather as something outside of, something enveloping, something even, for some thinkers and artists, as above the conscious. It was, in short, divine. Value flowed from the divine, from God, in two currents, one into nature, including the physical part of man, and one into the human spirit. Man was lost, alone, isolated in a nature which he could not understand unless he joined the two currents by the spark of intuitive symbolic perception which leaped across the gap between soul and matter. When that was done, the whole world of matter and spirit came alive and was experienced as one living organism. Though the orientative drive cannot find final satisfaction there is always, built into the universe, a metaphysical satisfaction for it to find.

Such a notion is all very noble, and beautiful, and exalting, but in the long run it is terribly unsatisfactory. For one thing it is unstable. With tremendous effort the individual wrests value from the self, and then all of a sudden he discovers it was right in front of him. In all the figures who held this position, there is a confused flickering of thought and orientative behavior. In effect, value has two sources, the self, and the natural world; and that is one too many. The whole drive of the new orientation was to hold opposites in tension, not to submerge them into an imagined unity; it was to experience the conflicts, the contradictions of existence, not to think them away; it was toward reality, not toward a metaphysical escape from reality.

Yet these men, though they felt themselves isolated, were not, of course, living in cultural isolation. On the contrary, they were just like us; they lived in a cultural ambience which was wholly alien to them, but to which part of their personalities belonged. There is a limit to which one can, without total disorientation, symbolize in one's activity a disagreement with the illusory orientative satisfactions of the people around him. And the limit is soon reached. Just a little too much oriental religion, or sexual transgression, or addiction to drugs or alcohol, just a few too many violations of the cultural norms of one's society, and the fragile structure of the personality, or, as some of these men called it, the phenomenal self, collapses.

However, any metaphysical escape from reality looks very much like any other, and feels very much like any other. It is exceedingly difficult to maintain the distinction between perceiving nature as a divine symbol and perceiving it as divine because it was made by God. And that distinction smudged, it is even harder to maintain the distinction between perceiving the irreconcilable opposites of life, and thinking of them as representative of good and evil which God has put into the world both as our punishment and as our opportunity for salvation. These distinctions were difficult for nineteenth-century men because the whole pull of their culture, including all the great philosophy and literature and art inherited from the past, insistently offered a solution. Wordsworth, for one, could not maintain the distinctions; he lost his intellectual original-ity and his poetic power alike.

The difficulty became very obvious, indeed, when it was fully conceptualized, as with Kant. For what Kant took away in *The Critique of Pure Reason*, he restored in *The Critique of Practi-cal Reason*, by which he meant "the rational process of making moral judgments." The self? What is our decisive evidence for its existence? The fact that it can make moral choices. The self, then, is the conscience. Morality is characteristic only of man, not of nature. By analogy we may claim that nature has a structure which we cannot know; we may claim only that it has structure; yet no analogy will permit us to perceive that nature has a conscience. The real infinity and divine authority of man's spirit lies in his sense of duty. And at a stroke, Kant restores everything which *The Critique of Pure Reason* had done away with: God, immortality, moral abso-lutes, and all the rest of it. Nor is that all he was responsible for. His followers, of whom Hegel was the most conspicuous and influential, put these two ideas together—the mind is a structural analogue of nature; and man is above all a moral being—and rapidly arrived at a more complete and gratifying orientation than had existed for cen-turies, perhaps ever. It was also more terrible in its consequences.

Fearfully oversimplified, but not, I hope, with utter false-ness, Hegel's thinking went something like this. If the pure reason is an analogue of nature, there is no way of denying that the practi-cal (that is, moral) reason is also such an analogue. To be sure, we can no more say what the morality of nature is than we can say what its structure is. But that it has morality as well as structure we can be sure. Now the characteristics of our reason, whether pure or moral, is that it comes into existence by a process, the shape of which is given by the rhythmic systole and diastole—like the pumping of the heart—between seeing opposites, then reconciling them, then on the basis of that reconciliation seeing new opposites, and so on. The structures it creates, whether moral or metaphysical, are only temporarily true, but the temporary truth is always an organic part of the new stage of truth. Since nothing is ever lost, nothing is really untrue. This, then, must be the structural character of the phenomenal world, whether natural or social. Since the mind must work as it does, so, by analogy, nature and society must work as they do. The explanation is that this process, since it is progressively more complete and inclusive, must achieve perfection in infinity, both perfection and infinity being characteristics of the divine. Whatever is, inside or outside, must be from necessity, divine necessity; it must be as it ought to be; it must be as it is. Whatever is, is as it ought to be. Whatever is, is right.

The organic perfection of the absolute is not before us, to be sure. Neither the mind of any any man (except Hegel's!) nor the natural and social structure, which is now seen once again as natural, can be thought of as fully organized; nevertheless, the organic absolute is coming into existence by an organic process. After all, since it is organic, it *must* come into existence by an organic process. Further—and the reader, I hope, will give a start of fright and recognition here—whoever understands this process cannot make a moral error. If he is a Hegelian ruler of the Prussian kingdom, he will proceed to organize the German empire, which is sacred because it alone among social structures has taken the next step toward the political absolute of total organization. And if he is the inheritor of the German empire—if he is Hitler—he will proceed to the creation of a total European organization and beyond that to a total world organization, dominated by its "natural," "absolute," and "ideal" leader, Germany itself. But life, alas, even Hegelian life, is full of surprises; we cannot be sure we are doing the right thing until we have done it. For after all, there might be opposites not yet sufficiently integrated. Yet these lapses of the inevitable process toward total political organization, though inevitable, can only be temporary. Unless, of course, there happens to be another Hegelian state around, of the Marxist variety, which thinks that it and no other government understands the Hegelian "Science of History," and that its morality, being inevitable, justifies it in any act. After all, so runs the argument, Marx stood Hegel on his head and correctly located the absolute in "matter" not in "spirit."

As if it made any difference. How familiar all this is! By an extraordinarily complex and even perverse path, we are right back in the moral dead end of the Enlightenment revolution. Here is Robespierre all over again. It is only the last stage of the Enlightenment upside down. Moral problems can be solved by appealing to nature; or moral problems can be solved by appealing to the absolute. The terrible impudence of this kind of thinking, the unfortunately not incredible arrogance shows, better than almost anything else in cultural history, better even than Christianity, which is humble and tentative in comparison, the fierce resistance the orientative drive will oppose to any threat to its fancied divine right. The men we have examined are united by one impulse: the subjection of the orientative drive to the drive toward reality. But here, from these post-Kantians, we can understand why those who love the earlier poetry of Wordsworth, who are profoundly moved by the 1805 *Prelude*, are saddened and angered by his betrayal of himself and his great task after 1807. But Wordsworth's surrender was almost harmless, though he wrote sonnets in favor of capital punishment, compared to what Hegel was responsible for. Perhaps Hegel himself never went so far; perhaps he was was far more subtle than his followers, more complex, full of misgivings and tentativeness. Even so, the whole episode shows what happens when lesser men are given a chance to absorb an orientation which gives them the right to resolve moral questions by recourse to morally stainless and incorruptible power.

If we ask how this happened, it is instructive to remember that Hegel also, like Wordsworth and Beethoven, was born in 1770, that he too felt the fascination and promise of the French Revolution; but that his disorientation, compared with that of his greater coevals, was superficial. He was always, in spite of his superficial Kantian intellectual trappings, a man of the late and morally bankrupt Enlightenment who never saw its moral impasses. When we consider Wordsworth's lesser failure, perhaps lesser only because of political conditions, or Coleridge's, who also lusted after the absolute, as compared with Beethoven's success (if I am right in my suggestion of the significance of the late quartets), we can perhaps agree with Schopenhauer that music is a profounder and more important and truer symbolization of the will (or the orientative drive, I would say) than philosophy or any conceptual thinking. To accept bluntly the unacceptable without for a moment forgetting its unacceptability, is a far different thing from saying that the unacceptable is, after all, in the long run, really, if we only understand it rightly, acceptable.

It is no wonder that one man in Germany, a man neglected in his day and only rediscovered and properly assessed toward the end of his life, a man whose writings are still refreshing and bracing, hated Hegel with a deadly savagery, for he saw where Hegel was headed. That man was Arthur Schopenhauer. Born in 1788, exactly a month after Byron, he lived from 1814 to 1818 in Dresden, Friedrich's town, a center of realistic pessimism, and there he wrote *The World as Will and Representation*, published in 1819. As I have pointed out, he kept the notion of analogue between self and world; the characteristic of both is blind striving, aimless and purposeless. But he saw the dangers. If there are two sources of value, the self and the world, composed of nature and society, the drive to orientative satifaction irresistibly tends to merge them, and inevitably does so. A genuine metaphysical dualism in which there are two distinct, separate, and sharply and easily distinguished sources of good cannot be maintained. Even if, as sometimes does happen, one has a good mother and a good father, they merge into "parents" and melt into "parenthood."

Further, the Kantian-Hegelian and Wordsworthian lines of thinking inevitably led to a restoration of value to nature and society, as they exist. And that affirmation of an absolute morality stripped the individual of moral responsibility, leaving him only conformity to a morality maintained by power, as in the past. Though such thinking started by deriving value from the self, it ended by stripping value from the self. Clearly, the only way to prevent this sequence of steps was to begin by stripping value from the sensory world. And that is precisely what Schopenhauer did.

The will blindly strives, and so does the world. So far so good, but now the process tends to work the other way. If thus the world has no value, the same is true of the will. We are left with an oddity; the aimless striving of the will is a negation of order. But to say "The world is without order," is a very different thing from saying, "I don't know whether the world has order or not, nor do I know any way of finding out." Actually, then Schopenhauer is really saying that the world has order, but that that order is without value. Indeed, he describes the biological world in terms of a kind of primitive and metaphysical evolutionary theory. He has, then, separated order from value. Further, the ascription of purposelessness to the world implies that the world has meaning; for traditionally to state that the world has purpose was to find a reason for stating that it has a meaning. Schopenhauer, then, has sundered order and meaning from value. This achievement is an advance, for by reducing the possible gratifications for the orientative drive he has come closer to isolating its essential gratifications. He has now a very precise field in which to operate. He has only to discover a way in which value can be achieved without letting it spread into the pure non-value of the world.

Actually there is only one solution. If the will is the source of this ordered disorder, this meaningless significance, the way to stop the disgusting process is to negate the will. Here is the act of value; thus the world is redeemed. This act has two further advantages: first, it can be done only by the individual, alienated from his own will and equally alienated and isolated from nature and society. Thus alienation and isolation are made the only possible orientations from which to achieve value. This idea was to have immense force when Schopenhauer began to attract attention in the 1850's. We will see why in due course. Second, since the area of the phenomenal self, or the role, is the area where the personality participates in society, and since only such participation can make the self known at all—for the noumenal self can only be experienced and not known—the denial of the validity of the phenomenal self, which occurs when the will is denied, is the only way to bring actively into recognizable existence the buried noumenal self, the real self of the individual.

This is a very neat trick if one can manage it, and one can scarcely avoid, no matter how impolite it may appear, asking Schopenhauer how all this is to be done. *How* does one deny the will? But he is ready for us. He is ready for anything. First he points out that suicide is not the answer, for to commit suicide is merely to surrender to the frustrations of the will; it is not to deny it. Since the willing individual dies, he has not performed an act of value. That is possible only if he stays alive. In life there are three steps to denial of the will. As we saw in discussing his concept of music, the arts can only give us a brief vacation from the will; they do not genuinely quiet it. But at the same time we saw that the principle according to which the will operates is the principle of individualization, achieving its highest degree in man, in whom the will becomes, or can become, self-conscious.

The first step in achieving the self-consciousness of the will is to recognize that principle of individualization: all individuals are, from this point of view, precisely alike; all are equally subject to to the demanding and inexorable will. On this basis, and on this basis alone, a genuine justice is possible, because you see yourself precisely as you see others. The second step is affection, non-erotic love, or, as it is traditionally called, *agapé*. After justice comes morality, not the rational recognition of other individuals, but the "intuitive knowledge that recognizes in another individuality the same inner nature as in one's own." It is the love that penetrates behind the mask that the will places upon other selves in order to make them the object of its striving, to subject them to its own demands. It is empathy. We have seen it before, negatively in *Manfred*, positively in what Faust learned from the episode with Gretchen. The reason can only act from self-interest, that is, subject to the inexorable will. Only empathy can create morality. This is to become the leading moral idea of the nineteenth-century vision.

Finally comes the third step, the denial of the will, which is to be accomplished by asceticism, by frustrating the will, by demanding nothing of existence, by refusing to play any social role at all. Thus only can come any genuine value, any genuine happiness. To refuse to demand is to experience no frustrations. The individual must destroy his very will-to-live, must develop an indifference to all gratifications. Thus, and thus only, can he contemplate life and see it as it is, and in the face of what he sees experience a total gratification in having no desires to be gratified. He develops the holy indifference of the great saints of Eastern and Western religion, of St. Francis and the Buddha. But even this cannot be depended upon. And we receive the warning we heard from Goethe and from Beethoven. This denial, this indifference constantly wavers and falters. "It must always be achieved afresh by constant struggle," every day, every moment that we live, until we arrive at the ultimate beatitude of seeing the body and the world fade into nothingness, the only state that is to be truly desired, for it is the total negation of the will in all its forms.

When he was a little more than twenty years old, Schopenhauer said, "Life is a ticklish business; I have resolved to spend it in reflecting upon it." If we wish, we can regard his whole life of writing and publication as a paradoxical rationalization of his emotions, for after all to publish is to act, to engage in life; and the professional frustrations he suffered aroused in him the wildest anger of what we can only call a baffled will. But this is not to invalidate what he had said. It is proof that his knowledge of the difficulty with which the will is quieted came not from manipulating concepts in a comfortable academic niche but from the realities of his own experience. Schopenhauer, like all the men we have so far looked at, shows what terrible effort it takes to reach the truth of your own feelings, how hard it is to feel what you do indeed feel, not what you feel you ought to feel.

Once again we see from another point of view why the great men of this century insisted upon the importance of the life of the emotions, and how different their emotionalism is from the sentimentalism of the Enlightenment. His emotional response, if he can only discover what it is—and that alone is immensely difficult—is a man's only evidence as to the character of experience, which exists only because he responds to it. To dig out and control that response was the ambition of all of them. In that voyage of discovery Schopenhauer made the next step possible, for he stripped the phenomenal world of value. For the first time the self was truly adequate. Perhaps he hated Hegel so because he had but achieved a negative reversal of Hegel's system.

Marx may have stood Hegel on his head by converting spirit to matter (not much of a trick, really); but Schopenhauer was Hegel inside out. For Hegel's order and significance he substituted orderly and significant meaninglessness. Both men depended upon the analogy from self to world, from subject to object. Clearly, if the self was to be genuinely free, that analogy must be abandoned. By inversion Schopenhauer had shown the orientative regression which Hegel and Wordsworth, Friedrich and Constable, and even Goethe led to; and Byron and Stendhal could only offer an ultimately untenable self-in-hiding. What these men had learned had to be preserved, but Schopenhauer had to be surpassed. Somehow value had to be located within the self and stripped from the world. Schopenhauer's negative symmetry between self and object had gone beyond everyone else's positive symmetry. Now it was necessary to move into an asymmetrical orientation. No one did a better job of it, at least for a time, than Thomas Carlyle.

# CHAPTER X

## *Transcendental Authority*

IN STYLE AND THOUGHT *Sartor Resartus* is one of the most difficult books in English; it is also one of the most moving and beautiful, once you have mastered Carlyle's extraordinary way of writing, Carlylese. As we shall see in a few chapters, however, a fantastic style is the character of the art of the 1830's and 1840's, of the period in the development of the nineteenth-century vision called transcendentalism. Beethoven and a few other artists had already moved in this new direction, and the late works of Schubert baffled his contemporaries because of their extraordinarily free and anti-traditional modulation from one key to another. There was good reason for this stylistic fantasy, but before looking for that reason it is necessary to begin with transcendentalism itself.

One of the curious things about the nineteenth century is that by 1830 its heroic age of philosophy, particularly metaphysics, had ended. From now on philosophy becomes academic; philosophers are engaged not with constructing vast structures but with the analysis and testing of structures already created. Possibly the nineteenth century is not unique in showing this pattern. The Enlightenment began with a philosophical reconstitution, its rationalistic stage. It is one of the assumptions of this book that the orientative drive can be symbolized in a variety of ways, in philosophy and metaphysics, in the various arts, in science itself; for although science is the systematization and purification of the drive toward reality, it can only start from an orientation, and it can never leave it. In the nineteenth century, certainly after 1830, the main forward drive toward the development of novel orientations is found in the arts, though always the philosophers we have examined remain active in the culture and are returned to again and again to make a fresh start possible.

Thus *Sartor Resartus* is a philosophical work; but it is also a work of the imagination; it is a novel, such a novel as had never been written before even though Carlyle got some of his ideas from Goethe's *Wilhelm Meister*, which he had translated into English. Yet in spite of the fact that something also came from Jonathan Swift, who wrote early in the eighteenth century, and from Laurence Sterne's *Tristram Shandy*, written in the 1750's and 1760's, in the heart of the Enlightenment, these derived elements have been so thoroughly assimilated that *Sartor* is stylistically novel and entirely a work of Carlyle's own century. Except for the last quartets of Beethoven, it is the first such work we have yet encountered.

One reason is that Carlyle was born in 1795 and grew up in a cultural environment in which, for advanced people, a number of nineteenth-century works of the first importance were already accepted and firmly established as presenting at least the outlines of a new culture. As a young man Carlyle shows a pattern of development we have already encountered. Born in an out-of-the-way corner in southwest Scotland, less than thirty miles north of Wordsworth's birthplace, he started in an atmosphere of rigid and even rabid Presbyterianism, untouched by Enlightenment thinking, except for the dubious influence of Robert Burns, who lived, loved, drank, was ostracized for his revolutionary opinions, and died a few miles from the infant Carlyle. Sent at the age of fourteen to Edinburgh to be educated as a Presbyterian minister —such was the miserable destiny of bright Scottish boys—he read Gibbon's *Decline and Fall of the Roman Empire* and lost his faith, for Gibbon was in history what Hume was in philosophy, an expression of extreme late Enlightenment skepticism. A wave of Enlightenment thought swept over him, but it was too late for him to be drowned. He survived, a little damp, and incapable of accepting either his childhood religion or eighteenth-century attitudes.

The negation of Werther and the Harold-Manfred of Byron overtook him; the first gleam of a new way of ordering experience came to him from Madame de Staël's book on German culture, published in France in 1810 and in English in 1813. It opened up a new vision; the great creative power of the new Germany streamed in upon him. He corresponded for some years with Goethe; and he became a cultural focus of the highest importance to England; for England and Germany were the geographical areas in which the orientations of the nineteenth century first began to take shape. He spent the 1820's translating German works and writing essays about German literature for various magazines. The public was hostile, suspicious, and inclined to disbelieve that anything good could come from a country so recently but a minor and culturally derivative province of European culture; it was exceedingly indisposed—such was the power of the great English empirical tradition of the Enlightenment—to do anything with German metaphysics except make fun of it. Only a few Englishmen and some Americans, particularly Emerson in Boston, saw the importance of what Carlyle was doing.

Consequently, when he wrote *Sartor Resartus* during the first half of 1831, he had the devil's own time getting it published. At last *Fraser's Magazine*, the most daring and original of the day, ran it as a serial in 1833 and 1834. Few understood it; almost everyone was bewildered; most detested it. Emerson got it published in Boston, but not until 1836; and only after Carlyle had made a tremendous hit with his *History of the French Revolution* in 1837 could he get *Sartor* published in England. After that, nothing could stop it. It became the central work of nineteenth-century England. All the bright young men read it, generation after generation, and in England and the United States special annotated college editions continued to be published through the 1920's and are still in print—though now little used.

In the 1838 edition Carlyle included an appendix of selections from hostile reviews, inverting normal publishing practice. Thus he asserted that he too was among the alienated and the isolated, and that he accepted that condition gladly and without hesitation. Nevertheless, his was the typical problem of the transcendental period. After alienation had made it possible for the artist to mature and solidify his new vision, how was he to get back into society and put it to work without compromising it? At the profoundest level, that is both the subject and the problem of *Sartor Resartus*.

The first bit of mystification is the title itself. What can be the meaning of *The Tailor Retailored?* But the whole book is an elaborate mystification. Its literary form is that of the hoax. The narrator pretends to be a magazine reviewer who has received from Germany an extraordinary work. *"Die Kleider, ihr Werden und Wirken:* von Diog. Teufelsdröckh, J.U.D. etc. Stillschweigen, und Cognie. Weissnichtwo, 1831." *"Clothes, their Origin and Influence:* by Godborn Devilsdung, Doctor of Civil and of Canon Law, etc. Keepsilence and Co. I-know-not-Where, 1831." The book has been sent to him because he once lived and studied in Germany at Weissnichtwo, and knew Teufelsdröckh. Astonished and bewildered by the work, he writes to his correspondent, Herr Heuschrecke, for further information. Mr. Grasshopper sends him numerous paper bags, stuffed with Teufelsdröckh's papers, for the great philosopher has disappeared. From these the reviewer constructs an autobiography, or what appears to be an autobiography, for he has his doubts about the factual reliability of these documents. With their aid, he expounds Diogenes' book on clothes, at first commenting on the fantastic absurdity of the passages he translates, then gradually beginning to think there might be something to it after all, and finally having arrived at full understanding, asserting that a new gospel has been delivered.

Carlyle's predecessors had redeemed the world, for themselves; Carlyle sets out to redeem society. And we perceive both the hoax and the reason for it. The anonymous reviewer serves as a model for the reader—British, bristlingly empirical, antimetaphysical and almost anti-German. His original position only slightly in advance of that of the typical British reader—at least the reader who could be expected to try the work at all—he gradually leads him, with mad humor, dramatic suspicion, wild and savage outbursts of rhetoric, irony, exaggeration, sentiment, and profound emotion, to a comprehension of what he wants him to understand. The structure, like the so recently composed last quartets of Beethoven, is one of psychological continuity, from the confrontation of opposing orientations, through the breakdown of the old to the emergence of the new. It has been done often, but rarely with such imagination, fantasy, and coruscating brilliance.

For those in the know, it was obvious that Carlyle was taking off from Kant. To be sure, he did not have a technical and academic comprehension of either of Kant's *Critiques*. Most of Kant he got at second hand. But it makes no difference, for he grasped surely and firmly the heart of the matter, the Kantian revolution, the turning of the world inside out. He *felt* Kant, and for the artist—and for anybody—that is an infinitely more important thing to do with philosophy than to have the kind of understanding that can be tested in university examinations. But more; Carlyle communicates that feeling, including the initial dizziness of grasping Kant, to the reader; better, he stylistically and rhetorically symbolizes it. First, he presents his theory of symbols, somewhat cryptically; next in the pseudo-autobiography of Teufelsdröckh, which is an imaginative autobiography of Carlyle himself, he dramatizes the cultural battle which irresistibly, so we feel, forced him to that theory; finally he shows the application of that theory to the contemporary social, cultural, and political situation. At the end Teufelsdröckh, on the outbreak of the French Revolution of 1830, disappears, rumor says, toward France. The alienated visionary makes the symbolic re-entry into society.

Of the central section it is enough to say that it presents in the development of one person the whole orientative breakdown —negation, indifference, and rebirth—which we have seen at work, in its various stages, in various individuals. It is the best possible summary and model of the whole process—Wertherian sentimentality, orphan foundling, meaningless education, concentration upon one woman, failure of that symbol of value to respond, cosmically isolated wandering in the waste land, assertion of pure selfhood, socially alienated wandering with but the self restored, rebirth of world and social values from the wanderer's unconscious, escape from the limits of egocentricity by empathy, denial of the value of word and fact, assertion of the value of act, denial of the possibility of final gratification, acceptance of the necessity for creative frustration in the struggle with reality, and finally readiness to return to that struggle in the social arena. Precisely at this point, however, Carlyle returns to his theory of symbols, which enables him to escape from the trap of analogous symmetry between self and the empirical world.

The theory of clothes, their origin and influence, is a theory of symbols. Man is the clothes-making and clothes-wearing animal. When Adam put on the fig leaf he became man, for that act symbolized his shame when he emotionally confronted sexuality. Naked man is not man; the criminal goes mildly to his execution because judge and executioner wear clothes, symbols that he automatically submits to. Man is conditioned to respond to symbols of power, of social roles, of religion, of status, of everything that determines his behavior. Anthropologists have often praised Carlyle for defining man as the tool-making animal; but they rarely realize that Carlyle gives this definition only to show that man's most important tools are his symbols. The visible symbols, or clothes, are symbols of the phenomenal self, or social role, but the social role is but the symbol of the eternal infinite ego. To complete his scheme, the physical world is but the symbol of the divine.

In this scheme are several novel ideas of the first importance. Profoundly original is his conception of man as *homo symbolicus*. He has taken the first step toward a general theory of signs, a satisfactory semiotic, as the professionals call it. We tend to think today that the modern recognition of the importance of symbols is due to Freud, and perhaps that is true when we consider popular suburban culture. The fact is, however, that Freud's thinking arose in a cultural context in which *homo symbolicus* was a widely current notion. He simply took a literary tradition and translated it into psychological terminology. From the earlier notion that nature is a symbol of the divine that lies behind it Carlyle has proceeded to the idea that in the same category of human behavior are both the clothes that bookies and policemen wear to identify themselves to themselves and to others, and the ritual of the mass. According to the older notion this symbolic activity took place only in special circumstances and was a means of intuiting the divine value and reality that lies behind phenomena. But Carlyle showed not merely that it is a common everyday occurrence, but rather that it goes on continuously, that it is the identifying character of man. Indeed, it is not merely true that society exists by virtue of symbolic behavior; one can go further and identify the two. Society *is* symbolic behavior. The two words are interchangeable.

Carlyle's recognition that symbolic behavior is not a special but a universal form of mental activity, that all behavior, indeed, may be reduced to symbol-making, saved him from the dangerous tendency toward the old symmetrical scheme with its threat, and more than threat, to lead back to the Enlightenment impasse of "Whatever is, is right." The reason is that if to perceive nature symbolically is not a unique intuitive act, then such perception cannot give a special kind of knowledge. To comprehend the identifying marks of a bootblack is precisely the same activity as intuiting the divine in nature. The symbolic act makes everything sacred. But there is a big "if" here. *If* the symbolic act is not a ritualistic repetition but an instrumental dealing with reality.

As with all advanced men of the nineteenth century (we must always remember that there were very few of them), for Carlyle the sweetest bone to gnaw on was a fact. Here he is perhaps most original, for he sees the symbolic act not as an intuitive perception into what lies behind phenomena but as a tool with which to deal with the phenomenal world itself. Let me give a lurid example. Certain modern Freudians have said that Balzac's novels are so much concerned with money because their author was anally regressive. As everyone knows, for such a person money is a symbol of feces. The implication undoubtedly is that since Balzac's concern, being regressive, was neurotic, his preoccupation with money in his novels is an indication of his sick failure to grasp reality. But look at it from the point of view to Carlyle's theory of symbolic instrumentalism. The *fact* is that, according to *all* accounts, the nineteenth century created the modern money economy. If we take the Freudians seriously, not the easiest thing in the world to do, admittedly, we can say that Balzac's symbolic anal regressiveness enabled him to grasp a reality which only a few people were beginning to see at all. Balzac thought a money economy was a social deterioration. Perhaps it should properly be valued as a good thing. Possibly Balzac's ascription of negative value to the new money bond between men was his defense against a threatening neurotic regression. His evaluation might have been neurotic, but not his perception. The truth is, of course, that he objected to the fact that his contemporaries *thought* that money was the basic social bond and were wrong. In their anxiety to find unconscious symbols, Freudians rarely read very carefully.

In any case, Carlyle conceived of the mind as a tool, as an instrument. Pure reason is the mind's capacity not merely to structure data, as in the Kantian scheme, but to use that structure to look for new data. Such a notion was implicit in Kant, but Carlyle was the first to bring it out powerfully. He also saw the inherent tendency of the mind to be satisfied with its structure; instead of using its powers to engage with reality, it tends to sink back into a gratifying manipulation of the symbolic structure, or to think that its structure is final. For this reason, symbols can lose their power. Or rather, they maintain their power over men's minds without leading them to the instrumental symbolic act. Further, symbols, like any other tools, wear out; they lose their usefulness. They become both blunted and inapplicable, because the reality they were designed to deal with no longer exists. In the nineteenth century it was above all religious tools that had worn out, and the rationalist-empiricist tools of the Enlightenment. Now we can penetrate the mystery of the title. Man's clothes are symbols. In creating those clothes, he is a tailor. But his clothes wear out. He must, therefore, retailor himself, make himself new clothes. At certain periods in history his most important clothes, the ones he sews to symbolize the self, are in rags. Such a period was the nineteenth century.

Carlyle now takes another important step. His predecessors had thought of the artist as the primary symbol maker. Carlyle sees symbol-making as an activity common to all men. Everyone, from the lowliest ditch digger to Goethe is, in this sense, alike. Anyone who works uses symbols instrumentally. Salvation, redemption of the self and the world, are within anyone's power in the value-creating act, which reduces the chaos of experience to order. The only order we can know is the order we create by work. At a stroke the worker and the artist are put in the same category, for the symbolic imagination is no longer the prerogative of the artist. Nevertheless, there are degrees of adequacy. The great man is the one who, by experiencing within himself the failure of the old symbols, perceives that new symbols must be created. In that sense he is ahead of his society. Carlyle has here alit upon the idea that individuals vary in the degree of their modernity, according to their perception of the extent to which clothes have become rags, or symbols have worn out. So Teufelsdröckh had found himself in rags, had stripped himself naked, and had woven himself a new set of clothes. But if he had, then the rest of European men must. He waits in the little German town, where he is the Weissnichtwo University Professor-of-things-in-general, without salary, until the signs of the times should show him that enough other men had seen what he had seen—the rags of contemporary society. The French Revolution of 1830 breaks out. The time has come; and he rushes toward Paris.

Carlyle did something the German followers of Kant did not do. He readjusted the relation of moral to pure reason by showing their identity. Duty is infinite not because man has a conscience but because the mind must use its symbols and engage with reality in order to survive. Nevertheless, from his own remote Presbyterian background and from Kant himself he keeps the notion of the divine. In the symbolic act man repeats the symbolic act of God in creating the material universe. Man is, therefore, divine. Yet all men—and this is why he breaks with Christianity and cannot return to it—are sacred. The symbolic act of Christ is universal. In the act, all men sacrifice themselves to the divine self that is within them in order to realize it. All men, not just Christ, are incarnations of divinity. Ultimately, the self of each man is divine, and takes from the divine its authority for duty, for moral responsibility, for the symbolic act. The symbolic act is divine because it creates, like God, order out of chaos.

In what appears to be a remarkable similarity to the late Beethoven and certainly goes beyond Schopenhauer, the orientative drive is identified as the divine. The source of order, it creates meaning and value. This is what is meant by transcendentalism. It is not *what* the symbolic and imaginative power perceives—the noumenal behind the phenomenal, the divine behind the natural—that is the source of value and leads to the experience of divinity, to the moment of value; that was the old symmetrical thinking, dangerous and to Carlyle outmoded. Rather it was the act of symbolic-instrumental perception of the phenomenal that was in itself the noumenal. Order and meaning and value are solely in the power of the self which comes from God, which unconsciously is God. The world is valueless chaos.

Thus Carlyle created a genuinely asymmetrical thinking. The mind is divine, for the divine enters the world through the self and only through the self. The value of the mind, which is the instrument of the self, transcends absolutely the value and the reality of the empirical world, which is chaotic and worthless. Yet this is no escapist mysticism. All that we consciously experience is that world of empirical fact. Therefore the literature and the art of transcendentalism are realistic. The divine and transcendental self forces the mind upon reality; there is no escape. The fact, every fact, is miracle.

Once this pattern has been grasped, it is possible to comprehend the unity in Balzac's thinking. Mixing realism and the wildest transcendentalism, it has bewildered his critics, who are always trying to throw out either the one or the other. Yet the pattern of Balzac's thinking shows the most striking similarity to Carlyle's in spite of the fact that Balzac's mind was not so tough as that of his great contemporary. (Balzac was born in 1799, four years after Carlyle.) The Frenchman had a tendency, much mocked by his contemporaries and by subsequent critics, to exhibit the truth that man is an animal capable of believing anything, especially if it isn't true. He could absorb and apparently accept the most fantastic pseudo-sciences as well as illuminism, the occult, and wild new religious and metaphysical doctrines. In that respect, his mind resembled the popular and uneducated mind of his century. High-level culture, beginning with Bacon, had decreed that magic, witchcraft, demonology, and angels were insane delusions; an intellectually chastened Christianity agreed. But the popular and undisciplined middle-class orientation could scarcely get along without something of the sort. Mesmerism, phrenology, Rosicrucianism rushed into the vacuum. Today we are in no position to sneer. Astrology is one of the most popular and lucrative professions a twentieth-century American can take up, and fantastic religions flourish throughout the country, not just in southern California.

Yet in Balzac's thinking these things had a place. It is hard to say, but there is a possibility that he himself did not take them too seriously but regarded them as symptomatic distortions of the transcendental capacity. For one thing, like Carlyle, he probably began from Kant; for he had the greatest admiration for Madame de Staël, whose most important work was her book on Germany, which presented Kant to the West. To Balzac matter was a form of spirit. Weird as his thinking often seems, it must be remembered that much of science itself was still primitive, and that in particular the concept of energy had not yet been worked out. In one of his novels, *La Recherche de l'Absolu* (*The Quest for the Absolute*, also called *The Alkahest*), a monomaniacal Flemish scientist destroys his fortune and almost destroys his family in his determination to discover the unknown force which is the principle of electricity and which by encountering resistance brings about the myriad forms of the material world. Although Balzac has his hero achieve success, it was not in fact achieved until 1945, with rather disagreeable consequences.

Force, motion, energy—this is the fundamental character of the universe. In man it becomes self-conscious, or can become so in certain types of men; for man can be aware of the difference between spirit and matter. The "instinctive man" only acts, without thought; he is unconscious of the difference. The "abstractive man" lives in the realm of ideas; he is the man of genius, aware that the relations he perceives among objects are his own mental creations and that therefore his mind creates and through the will governs the world. The oddly named "specialist," who speculates, who sees everything, exists above the level of ideas; rapt in a state above consciousness, he experiences the force, the motion, the energy, the basic character of the universe, and he experiences it as divine. That ultimate ground of being, pure energy, is God, into which the self can enter, which transcends space and time, existent only at the level of abstractive man and his ideas—to experience that ground makes it possible for a living man to see the past and the future; the divine energy is eternal.

Things get a little wild at this point; nevertheless more sophisticated intellects, even of the twentieth century, have had similar notions. Physicists like Sir James Jeans—who had, shall I say, the orientative drive under insufficient control—have a very strong tendency to leap into the godhead when they reach what they fancy are the limits of science because these are the limits *they* have reached. Balzac's thinking is, to use Carlyle's expression, natural supernaturalism. Far more interested in science and pseudo-science than Carlyle, he had the same love for the fact but was considerably more interested in doing what has since been often the mark of transcendentalism, to establish metaphysical certainty by founding it on scientific and empirical knowledge, to prove the scientific truth of an orientation. Such affairs as Christian Science, the perennial philosophy, theosophy, anthroposophy, and the practice of yoga to earn admission to the movie palace of the spiritual absolute, show that a somewhat debased form of transcendentalism has become a popular and important pattern in the orientational repertoire of Europe and America. The human mind can go in two directions. By separating himself from instinct and abstractions, the level of ideas and self-conscious will, by entering into a state Balzac describes so accurately that it can be immediately recognized as schizophrenia, the individual can enter, while living, into the absolute. That path is the subject of *Louis Lambert*, the principal repository of Balzac's transcendentalism. But the sacrifices are appalling; to other men it is insanity. Only the most devoted care by a loving wife keeps Lambert alive for a few years. Then he dies from the unendurable strain he has put upon himself. Perhaps after death the self survives and lives an angelic existence which Swedenborg, the eighteenth-century Swedish mystagogue, claimed to have seen. That possibility Balzac explores in *Seraphita*, which contains an exposition of the doctrines of Swedenborg and other mystics. Obviously, absorption into the divine absolute is not possible, at least for long; man must take the alternative path, he must go not against the current of energy as it encounters resistance, but with it; man must confront reality.

In talking about three types of man, Balzac does not use "type" in the modern weakened sense of "kinds" or "categories" into which actual living human beings may be sorted. "Type" is used, rather, to mean "character," "mark," "distinguishing feature." Each individual man is to a greater or lesser degree specialist, abstractive, and instinctive. The possible combinations of infinitely varying proportions of each type make up the myriad kinds of human individuality we find in the world, no two men being similar, just as no two stones are similar. Similarity is order, but the character of the empirical world is infinite non-similarity, or disorder. For order is a creation of the mind.

In the same way there are three types of human behavior: *savoir, vouloir, pouvoir*. Knowing, that is, generating ideas; willing, that is, converting the ideas into a desire or will-for-gratification; being able to act, that is, to impose the will upon reality. (The resemblance to Carlyle's transcendental instrumentalism is sharply obvious.) Thus in the behavior of human beings is evinced the encounter between energy and resistance, the result of which is life. These types of behavior are also infinite in their patterned and variously proportioned combinations in existing human beings.

When the two systems are put together—personality and behavior—by an astoundingly inventive mind, as Balzac's was, the possibilities for imagining an incredible range of human personalities are obvious. Balzac's psychological system certainly seems to account for the almost unbelievable number of unique individual characters which appear in his thousands of pages of fiction; no two are alike, yet the configuration of each is sharply and unmistakably clear. Whatever else may be said of his system, it worked.

This mode of thinking did even more for Balzac. It explained himself to himself. And that, perhaps, as in the case of Schopenhauer's system, was its real purpose. One of the most commonly encountered personalities in Balzac's work is the monomaniac, the man who has generated one idea so powerfully that it dominates him and eventually destroys him while frequently laying waste everything around him, family, fortune, health, sanity. Such was the hero of *The Alkahest;* such was Louis Lambert; such was the grotesque and utterly convincing miser, old Goriot. Such was Balzac. His monomania was not to write novels, or to write at all. His monomania was the word, the form the idea takes when the force of energy brings it into the world of life: the word is the incarnation of the idea; and incarnation is the correct term, for in the word the divine energy takes the purest form man can know, its instrumental form. Here we meet an old friend, the redeeming artist who introduces order and value into the world. Such an artist, as Balzac was—the type was by now culturally fixed—is the alienated artist, to whom society no longer makes any sense. Balzac's monomania of the word took the specific form of using the word, and the capacity for creating order incarnate in the word, to comprehend society, specifically society as it existed and functioned in France in the first half of the nineteenth century.

Nor was *pouvoir* neglected. His ultimate gratification would be to explain that society to itself, to raise it to self-consciousness, to self-control, and so to social reform and regeneration. Posterity may think of Balzac as a novelist, but Balzac thought of his task and destiny as infinitely nobler and more meaningful. Like

Carlyle's hero, his task was to show society where it had failed, where its strength lay, and the direction it must take. Only such a self-conception could have sustained him through twenty years of creative and economic struggle, could have brought him so near to completing the vast structure of *The Human Comedy*, which was to consist of one hundred and twenty separate works, from short stories to novels constructed on an epic scale. He completed, or nearly completed, ninety-nine; several were finished by other hands after his death, for his monomania, as all monomanias must, destroyed him.

Neglecting and ignoring the transcendental thinking that shaped his imaginative production and gave the force to continue his colossal task in the face of difficulties that would have destroyed far sooner a lesser man, readers and critics have simply classified Balzac as a realistic novelist, one who merely observed and wrote. The famous, and apocryphal, story that he had himself run over by a cab so that he might describe the experience of one of his characters is symptomatic of this essentially naïve thinking about Balzac. Technically, he began as an historical novelist; as a novelist, though he was a transcendentalist, he took off from Sir Walter Scott and the American James Fenimore Cooper. How he moved from historical to realistic fiction throws into the sharpest profile one of the central modes of nineteenth-century culture.

More than any other writer Scott was responsible for the historicization of the nineteenth-century mind. From 1814 to 1832 he published a series of historical novels which fascinated all Europe and America. In almost every way a conservative, he reacted against the French Revolution. Its failure was what he expected and hoped for, yet it made him realize that eighteenth-century conceptions of society were inadequate. He wanted a fresh vision into human nature and social interrelationships, but to achieve that new insight detachment from the present was necessary; for the present was confusing; there was too much of it, too much detail; too many forces were at work. He too experienced the negative isolation and alienation of Werther and Harold, and thus he, too, lost control of the present. The past was simpler, if only because limited quantities of documents and artifacts had survived. The present was infinite, but not the past. The past, he saw, could be used to create an analogy to the present, for the limits of information about the past could impose limits upon the present. The past would make it possible to handle the present without getting lost in a maze of incomprehensible detail. But that analogy, of course, could not be random. It had to have structure. Where was that structure to come from?

Others had used the past at random without structure, to create a fantastic background against which to isolate that area of their personalities which was alienated from society and its orientations. Such "historical" isolation served to dramatize the self and to protect it from the criticism and irony which would inevitably have functioned if the self had been projected against a contemporary setting. Werther had revealed precisely that difficulty, and Goethe had placed Faust in fantastic medieval and classical environments. Wordsworth and Coleridge and a multitude of others had done the same thing, and so had Byron. *Childe Harold* also showed the difficulties of the contemporaneous setting, and in *Manfred* Byron turned to medieval fantasy. Even *Don Juan*, though it is easy to forget, is an historical poem, as are all of Byron's plays. Scott himself had done the same thing in his early long poems, the heroes of which were the models for Harold and Lara and Manfred and the rest of Byron's stable of alienated figures.

In these works the protagonist is, of course, all important, for he symbolizes the poet's orientation. He alone has structure, while the background is random, accidental, decorative, unrealistic, at best emotionally symbolic. Nevertheless, the basic principle had been discovered. Scott took the next step, applying that principle to the historical novel. The structure of the analogy between finite past and infinite present is to be derived from the artist himself. Thus the past becomes a symbolization of the novelist's orientation. Not his self-conception but the order he imposes upon society becomes his subject. Consequently, in Scott's novels the main characters are stereotypes from the theater and from earlier fiction; they simply serve the conventions of the novel. What

Scott is really interested in is his conception of the web, the warp and woof, of society. He created the novel as social history which made sense out of the present. Finally, to give the whole structure depth and convincingness, he set that imagined society against a landscape and in a geography which had remained unchanged from the historical period he was using. You could, and still can, go and see where favorite Scott characters lived and fought, loved and wandered. Untold thousands of tourists have subsequently done precisely that, and the whole fake system of the Scottish clan plaid was invented by Scottish tailors to please them. Scott was responsible for the first of the literary tours.

Even while Scott was still alive and writing, though no longer very well, Balzac had carried over the technique of the great wizard of the north into his own mode of transcendental realism. What Scott's readers thought of as a summoning forth of the past from its black nothingness, Balzac could see as a summoning forth of the structure of the past from Scott himself. The way to deal with the present was not, as the eighteenth-century realists had done, merely to observe and include enough detail to create the illusion of reality. Like the medieval decor of the Scott of the poems, of Goethe and the rest, all that was merely stage setting. No; it was to select so that every detail, every piece of furniture, every stain on a slum wall, every little French town, every item of landscape and geography, every line on a face, every expression, every garment, illustrated and symbolized the idea which was the theme. Thus truly the word was incarnate in empirical reality, and mastered it. From Scott's poems and their equivalents in other writers, the stage of historical decor, came the technique of structuring the personality on the pattern of an orientation, of the idea. From Scott's novels came the technique of controlling and structuring the personality's environment, including other people, in the same way.

Everything in a Balzac novel serves a symbolic and intellectual purpose. Everything is related to the idea. Now Balzac was well aware—it was a cardinal idea with him—that relationships are the creations of the mind. As he wrote he began to see new possibilities of relationships, not merely within each novel but between novels. By 1830 he had written a number of stories and short novels; from these he selected six and republished them under the title, *Scenes of Private Life*, and he projected a *Scenes of Political Life* and *Scenes of Military Life*. Already his vast idea was beginning to germinate. By 1834 he had conceived of organizing these groups into a single gigantic structure, its general title, *Social Studies*, the subdivisions, "Studies of Customs," "Philosophical Studies," "Analytical Studies"; how people behave, the immediate causes for their actions, and the ultimate, fundamental causes. Thus he works back from action through the will to the generation of ideas in the pure self. This grandiose scheme was not actually executed, but it led to the next important development. Now he began to rewrite to bring his characters in line, to change names so that the same character appears in several novels, to rationalize and relate the chronological scheme. And in his new work he picks up minor characters from old stories and develops them; he writes new stages in the life of old major characters. He sets out to bring into his scheme each major province of France, each level of society, every significant gradation of personality and behavior. All of French society in the nineteenth century is to be embraced, from top to bottom, and from one side of France to the other.

All this indicates that by now he has fully developed his system of transcendentalist realism. He has his mind firmly in control. His grand monomaniacal idea can manage anything it is faced with. Consequently he explores science and pseudo-science, the evolutionary thinking of Geoffroy Saint-Hilaire, the extremely popular phrenology of Gall and Lavater, every system of establishing relations that he can seize with his voracious mind and put to use. He can use them because each is but an instrument of the will informed by the idea. What he is doing seems almost impossible. For years he has been turning out immense quantities of fiction, much of it good, all of it getting better. The occasional masterpiece begins to become the norm of creative activity. And at the same time he is absorbing from every possible source floods of information, of data, of facts, and endless patterns of organizing ideas. He is now ready, and in 1841 he announces that he now knows what he is doing; he is creating a colossal organization of philosophy, psychology, and sociology which shall be at once an immense imaginative structure and a scientifically reliable social history of France in the first half of the nineteenth century. With what he would have called sublime audacity he adapts the title from Dante. It will not be *The Divine Comedy* but *The Human Comedy*.

Such a fully structured imaginative creation, unequalled in size and in scope, had never been projected before. No one has ever dared to rival it. Had he not died of exhaustion, of his own monomania, which he understood as no man has, of his rage for order, had he lived but five or six more years instead of dying in 1850, he would have completed it. From the chaos of experience his magical imagination summoned forth a world. He gave it order; he gave it meaning; in spite of its brutalities and horrors, which are utterly irreconcilable with its nobility, its passion, and its beauty, he gave it value. There are, to our modern taste, absurdities in it; but these are trifling. *The Human Comedy* is absolutely convincing. No man, at least not yet, can understand and comprehend a society. But only Balzac can make one feel the experience of luminous social comprehension.

# CHAPTER XI

# *The Transcendental Ear*

ONE OF THE BEST CLUES to how Balzac thought of himself and how he placed himself in his society is to examine his dedications. His problem was that of all the transcendentalists: How is he to re-enter society without compromising his vision? How is he to make the notion of the alienated artist into a socially integrated role? It was the problem of re-entry, and one of the best analyses is the English Alfred Tennyson's "Lady of Shalott," an excellent example of turning a medieval legend into a modern myth, of using a fantastic historical setting to isolate and dramatize a modern problem. Tennyson's lady lives alone in a castle on a river island. Far down the river is the city of Arthur, Camelot. Here are two of the most important symbols of nineteenth-century art: the isolated tower ("isolate" is derived from the Latin *insula*, an island), and the city—the artist and society. The tower we have seen before; it is an assertive equivalent of the cave, the house, the enclosed room, the courtyard. It is not the self-in-hiding but the self affirmed. What is new is its juxtaposition with the city. Who the Lady is and what she does is a mystery to the world around her, which only hears her song. Within the tower, however, she weaves an endless tapestry, depicting the world in the work of art. But she does not see the world directly. Her knowledge comes from watching a magical mirror, and she knows that if she turns from the mirror and looks out of the window, if she abandons the artistic imagination which isolates and protects her, a terrible fate will

196

destroy her. Yet she is tempted; in the mirror she sees human life, peasant and burgher; she sees Lancelot in all the splendor and beauty of his strength, his youth, and his human pride and self-sufficiency.

> She left the web, she left the loom,
> She made three paces thro' the room,
> She saw the water-lily bloom,
> She saw the helmet and the plume,
> > She look'd down to Camelot.
> Out flew the web and floated wide;
> The mirror crack'd from side to side;
> "The curse is come upon me," cried
> > The Lady of Shalott.

Perhaps because he was ten years younger, perhaps because the nineteenth-century orientation was older and better established in England than in France, Tennyson saw the danger more sharply than Balzac; for the Lady leaves her castle, lays herself down in a boat, and drifts down the river to Camelot, singing as she dies. When the boat with its dead body reaches Camelot, Lancelot says merely, "She's lovely; I hope she goes to Heaven." He is totally uncomprehending.

Balzac had other hopes for relating tower to city. His dedications are not only clues to his attitudes; they are an integral part of *The Human Comedy*, for by bringing his friends and the men he admired into its structure, he identifies himself with them, thus attempting to establish a group of individuals large enough and important enough to fix a pattern of personality which might function socially without damage. Alienation is difficult, dangerous, and exhausting; most of the advanced artists and writers of the nineteenth century attempted to solve it by forming around themselves a little group, or creating with other artists a miniature social world, often with its own economy, its own home, and its own medium of publication. The pattern appeared early, when Wordsworth and Coleridge together with Dorothy Wordsworth formed a little *avant-garde* group, lived near one another, and found a sympathetic follower, a publisher who would get them into print, not in London, but—and this is often a significant part of the pattern—in provincial Bristol.

The people in Balzac's dedications were a similar group, friends who understood him and artists whose work paralleled his own. Victor Hugo, George Sand, Franz Liszt, Heinrich Heine, Théophile Gautier—to know their work is to understand the cultural ambience of *The Human Comedy*. But greater than any of these, more profound and more original in their grasp of the artistic and orientative necessities of the time were the painter Eugène Delacroix and the composer Hector Berlioz.

*The Human Comedy* is a vast work of imaginative historical and realistic sociology; but it would be a mistake to imagine that Balzac was concerned alone with ordinary sensual man—and woman: *l'homme moyen sensuel*. If he was to create a true picture of his society, at least as his imagination conceived it, it must include himself. It must present the thinker and artist alienated and detached from his society but struggling to find a means of livelihood, an audience, a recognition of his self-conscious transcendental and redemptive genius. The great cultural model for the artist and his group of followers and worshippers was Christ and the apostles, and the dominating theme of Balzac's portraits of artists was the search for an understanding group and the genius' self-sacrifice to the divine energy of idea, will, and power, for the good of mankind. The biographies of the artists in his dedications paralleled with the utmost precision the appalling lives of his Christ-like geniuses of art and thought. If anything in *The Human Comedy* has absolute authenticity it is these figures. The terrible lives of Delacroix and Berlioz might have been written by Balzac. Both left memoirs and journals, documents which could be made a part of the *Comedy* and published in it, with the same format and Balzac's name on the title page, without changing a word.

Delacroix was born in 1798, a year before Balzac; Berlioz in 1803, four years after. All three were in Paris in the 1820's, young men savagely struggling to get started in a complacent, orthodox, and reactionary social situation. It was the time of the

Bourbon restoration, and the comparatively mild regime of Louis XVIII was succeeded in 1824 by the brutal political and religious repression of Charles X. It is no wonder that the Revolution of 1830, which flung Teufelsdröckh out of Weissnichtwo and overthrew the moribund monarchy and an aristocracy which had lost its power of political and cultural leadership, appeared to be the beginning of a new era; for the Bourbons had done everything they could to contain and destroy the new cultural forces fighting for survival in France, although they were already firmly established in England and Germany. What followed the glorious days of 1830, however, was almost as bad, perhaps even worse. The middle classes, which had been released by the Revolution of the 1790's and only barely restrained by Napoleon and the restored Bourbons, now took power. They were interested in one thing, money, the control and exploitation of the new industrial giant that was extending his strength from England into Europe. It was the era that shaped Karl Marx, the same kind of personality as Delacroix and Berlioz. Thinking of himself as a Christlike genius and alienated redeemer, as much a materialistic transcendentalist as a materialistic Hegelian, he belongs in *The Human Comedy*. His life should be printed under Balzac's name.

Critical as was the problem of Delacroix, that of Berlioz was worse. The painter had a language still partly comprehensible to the general public; but the composer had none. How was he to make the transcendental harmonies audible to the physical ear? How was he to translate into music the divinely justified and authorized imposition of the will upon the realities of life, that imposition which would redeem the world and permit the artist to take his rightful place in it, as hero and Christ of the new gospel? Only Beethoven could be his model. But who in France understood Beethoven? One thing was clear to the young Berlioz—he must create that language himself and it must be unique, immediately and absolutely identifiable as his and no one else's. It was a decision that immediately exposed him to the rancors of musical pedagogues, such a man as Lesueur who, having at last permitted himself to take the risk of listening to Beethoven's symphonies, was utterly overcome but could insist to Berlioz that such music ought not to have been written. "Music that ought not be written," that was the kind of music Berlioz wanted to write.

In 1828, when the Lesueur incident took place, he himself heard the Beethoven symphonies for the first time; and he discovered the only possible point of departure for his unique style. Stylistically the solution to his problem began to assume some clarity of outline. Beethoven had freed music from the demands society made upon it; it would be Berlioz' sublime task to carry even further what Beethoven had done. But if the stylistic direction was clear—to follow the direction Beethoven had pointed to without imitating him—the problem of musical language was not, for in creating a new style Beethoven had destroyed the old musical language of emotional symbolism, of which Mozart had been the master and which Rossini and Cherubini could still use. It was still, consequently, the official doctrine that instrumental music was inferior to operatic and religious music, in which the musical language was unmistakable; but it was apparent to Berlioz that Beethoven had established instrumental music, particularly orchestral music, as superior to all other kinds. That it was some kind of emotional language Berlioz could feel in the vibrations of his nerves, in the beating of his heart. But in his youth, his ignorance, and his almost insane daring and ambition, and in his determination to create a unique style, it was apparent that some way must be found to control that language as he made it his own. The old system had been expressive through well established conventions, but if he wished to say something new and say it in a new style, he had to discover not only something to say but also some means that would perform the function of the dead conventions. Paradoxically, he had to create conventions that would be operative only in his unique works.

If we look at it this way, we will not be surprised at the fact that the dominating mode of transcendental music is apparently inspired by literature. It is quite a different matter from the program music of the eighteenth century, which Beethoven, for a sum, did not hesitate to turn to when he composed that horror,

"Wellington's Victory." Such music is imitative; it copies, sometimes with grotesque results, sometimes charmingly and movingly,
the sounds of the natural world, or it imitates them: the barking of
dogs, the songs of birds, the facile gliding of a skater. It must not
be confused with the "literary" music of Berlioz, though he, on
occasion, would employ imitative devices—with a difference. To
understand what he did it is necessary to look at his cultural situation, which was precisely the same as Balzac's and Carlyle's. Beethoven's music may have profoundly excited him, but it did not give
him the conceptual, or verbal, comprehension of what he was.
That came, and for a non-philosophical temperament like Berlioz',
could only come, from literature.

In the same years that he was experiencing the revelation
of Beethoven, he was swept off his feet by Shakespeare, whom he
saw acted in Paris in 1827, and by Goethe, whose *Faust*, Part I, in
the translation of Gérard de Nerval, appeared in the same year.
Byron and Scott also became his gods. The freedom of Shakespeare, the flow of his emotion, his language, and his action, his utter
transcendence of what to a young Frenchman were the formal
limits of the theater, gave him a pattern and a justification for his
own transcendence of traditional forms. And the nineteenth-
century authors made him understand himself, his cultural position,
his task—to realize the uniqueness of the self in the uniqueness of a
style. He also saw how to do it.

If we look at his early works we find titles like "Waverly"
and "Rob Roy" (Scott); "Eight Scenes from Faust"; "King Lear,"
"The Tempest" (Shakespeare). And later were to appear "Harold
in Italy" (Byron), "Romeo and Juliet," "The Damnation of
Faust," "Two scenes from Hamlet." Further, his two first great
successes, the "Symphonie Fantastique" and the strange "Lélio,"
were works for which he himself created the plot, deriving his
ideas from Byron, Scott, Shakespeare, Goethe, and DeQuincey's
*Confessions of an English Opium Eater*, the predominating idea
being alienation.

One of the curious things about Berlioz is that while he
reviled anyone who violated the artistic integrity of a work, who

changed Beethoven's scoring or notes, who cut and rearranged Shakespeare, who freely moved arias and scenes from one of Mozart's operas to another, he himself behaved with utter freedom when he used literary sources. Those who look for a setting of Shakespeare's play in "Romeo and Juliet" will be disappointed and puzzled, or who look for a musical imitation of Part IV of *Childe Harold* in "Harold in Italy," or for the equivalent of Goethe's play in "The Damnation of Faust." That is not what Berlioz was doing. On the contrary, with astonishing originality and genius he seized upon the chance to do for music what Scott had done with history. He used literary works as analogues. "Harold in Italy" is not "about" Byron's work nor even about his hero. Just as Scott's "history" was an analogue for his conception of his own society, so the orientation of Byron's hero is an analogue to the orientation Berlioz presents in the music. Like Beethoven, he wished to symbolize the orientations and disorientations of the self; like Balzac and Schopenhauer he was concerned with the will. From Beethoven he learned to write music in which no element is present merely to fill the requirements of a form. From Shakespeare he learned to be absolutely free in his form. From both he learned what Balzac was learning at the same time, how to make every detail fulfill an expressive function. And from the great literature in his cultural ambience he learned to understand what he was saying.

To be sure, he wanted fame and fortune; he had the transcendentalists' urgency to find a heroic place in society; he wanted, undoubtedly, to be understood, so much so that in "Lélio" he mingled spoken monologues with songs, choruses, and orchestral passages; but his essential reason for drawing upon literature was to create a kind of double or parallel symbolism, the musical and the verbal. In this way he solved what seemed to be an almost insuperable problem, the creation of a way of establishing conventions that would function only in unique situations. A convention that exists only once is scarcely a convention; but the device of literary analogy succeeded in creating such conventions. Nothing is more of a mistake than to think of Berlioz as a writer of "program music"; he was nothing of the sort. Like Beethoven's his subject was the unique self; his music is a dramatization, a symbolization of its activities. Even the "program" for the "Symphonie Fantastique" is not, in the ordinary sense, a "program" but rather an independent prose poem, the psychic movements of which parallel those of the music.

This is the reason for the peculiar symphonic form he developed, first adumbrated in the "Eight Scenes from Faust," but established in the "Symphonie Fantastique" and "Harold in Italy," a kind of viola concerto originally written for Paganini, and fulfilled in "Romeo and Juliet," "The Damnation of Faust," and "The Infant Christ." It permitted, in Shakespearean and Goethean fashion, a variety of movements or "scenes," but it was unified in two ways. First was an idea he probably picked up from Beethoven, the repetition of a theme from movement to movement. Each movement had its own set of themes, but in addition at dramatically appropriate points the *idée fixe*, as he called it, would reappear. This repeated theme invariably recalled the basic attitude with which the work was concerned, love in the "Symphonie Fantastique," isolation in "Harold in Italy," while the variations and the differing musical and psychological environments of the theme indicated the transformations that basic attitude was going through. Love could become hate. Isolation could be absorbed in joy before nature or lost in the bacchanalian orgy of brigands. Further, the reappearance of the theme made it unmistakable that behind each "scene" or movement was an individual who was organizing the material in order to symbolize his attitudes. It was not, like eighteenth-century music, saying: "This is love, this is nobility." Rather, it said, "This is the joy, this is the sorrow, this is the ecstasy of the same person." The artist is present in his own work. To make the presence of the artist felt, to make it unmistakable that the work exists in order to realize the existence of the artist, his will, his organizing powers, and his grasp of experience—this was the drive that unified into a single cultural convergence, in the same stage of the development of the nineteenth-century vision, all of the artists of the time. Each of Berlioz' major works is the equivalent of a Balzacian portrait of a monomaniac.

Berlioz triumphantly carried this drive forward and broke through the barriers of an extraordinary new musical technique. It is a peculiarity of his music that the piano arrangements of his orchestral scores sound uninteresting, platitudinous, cliché-ridden, and dull. Yet when you hear the same music played by an orchestra it strikes the ear as profoundly original, fascinating, ravishingly beautiful, unlike anything else ever written. If there was one area of music still unexploited in Berlioz' time it was the area of orchestration. It was not that the earlier composers had no sensitivity to orchestral sound, and Beethoven had made important developments. Rather, their music was not primarily conceived in terms of orchestral sounds. It sounds just as well, and not very different, in piano arrangements, and in the eighteenth century the composers themselves were constantly presenting the same music in different orchestral dress. Berlioz, however, seems to have *thought* orchestrally, as if the sound of the work came to him before the melodies, or the harmonies, or the structure. He listened to the orchestra as Friedrich and Constable looked at nature, with the naked ear. It was as if no one had ever really heard the orchestra before. His orchestration is his most perfect success in symbolizing his transcendental orientation, his asymmetrical vision of reality.

For it was reality he was attempting to seize, the only reality music can seize, psychological reality. He was successful because to the nineteenth-century mind that was the most important reality, for it is the reality which orders experience and makes it valuable; and because to the transcendentalist of Berlioz' generation, psychological reality was the only reality, or at least the only reality that counted. The function of the objective world, whether the Alps amid which the viola wanders in the opening of "Harold in Italy" or literary masterpieces, was not to "inspire" the composer to try to represent them in music. Rather, they served as symbols which triggered and released attitudes which the composer already had and had experienced but could not understand or grasp conceptually without some kind of verbal control. Images from nature and symbols and dramatic situations from literature became analogous parallelisms which served composer and audience alike in guiding their understanding during the artist's voyage of discovery into the divinely ordering self.

At the same time Berlioz was finding out how to create a new convention for musical meaning by turning to literature for an analogue, Robert Schumann, the German composer, born in 1810, seven years after Berlioz, quite independently was doing the same thing. His familiarity with literature was even greater than Berlioz', for it was not merely reactive; he was a writer himself. Indeed, throughout his adolescence he spent as much time writing as composing, and in the 1830's, when he had matured as a composer, he continued to write, not imaginative literature but musical criticism, among the best ever done. In this also he resembled Berlioz, who often virtually supported himself with musical journalism, brilliant and wickedly clever, but not so penetrating as Schumann's. For this there was a very good reason. The French with a few exceptions—Chateaubriand, de Sénancour, Madame de Staël, Constant, the painter Géricault—were at least a generation later than the English and the Germans in grasping the new conception of the world, the world turned inside out. French culture, from this point of view, had been distorted by the Revolution, by the Napoleonic empire, and by restored Bourbonism. The whole society was involved in a series of fearful crises, and artists were required by the state to create symbols of the national effort. Themselves caught up in the cyclonic politics of the time and the hurricane of social revolution and reformation, like everyone else they participated with all their emotional force in the activities the state exacted.

At a time when European culture demanded that the artist —with painful effort—wring his new vision and the symbols for that vision out of himself, that the artist make the journey into the innermost depths of the personality, the French artist was caught in a situation which forced upon him a structure for experience, the state, and dictated its symbols. The result was rhetoric, superb and even convincing rhetoric, to be sure, but nevertheless rhetoric, the aim of which is always not to illuminate but to persuade to a specific action. When the advancing European mind was struggling to distinguish between social morality and individual moral responsibility, the French artist was deprived of his opportunity to participate in this aspect of the development of the nineteenth-century vision. The self could not be separated from the social role. The very success of each of the metamorphoses of the state—Revolutionary, Napoleonic, and Restoration—though each was temporary, made this culturally false position all the more seductive.

The French yearned for *la gloire*—a peculiarly French concept, synthesizing individual achievement with the state's grandeur and power—for the sublime, for the publicly exalted. They developed a taste for rhetoric, a taste which they have not lost, which survives today in the speeches of De Gaulle. His utterances may be as necessarily meaningless as those of American politicians, but he always has what the Americans invariably lack: grandeur, nobility, aesthetic form, emotional force—*la gloire*. Consequently even the greatest of the French transcendentalists—Balzac, Hugo, Berlioz, Delacroix—created an art often subtly corrupted by rhetoric. This temptation was reinforced by the necessity to make up for lost time; they were seduced into trying to achieve by sheer force of personality and style what the Germans and the English had achieved by psychological and philosophical depth. Consequently the transcendentalists' effort to find a social function became in France an almost uncontrollable passion. The result was a frustration of corresponding violence. It took the generation of Flaubert and Baudelaire, both born in 1821, to discover and rebel against the taint of rhetoric in the French art of the 1830's.

From all that, Schumann, of course, was spared. There was for a time, especially in Prussia, a national effort against Napoleon, with its rhetorically distorting effect; but it did not last long, it affected only a part of Germany, and it could not seriously damage an orientation already firmly established and kept in line by the grand power of Goethe to maintain a perilous balance. Further, where Berlioz and Balzac had to get the new German and English culture at second hand, by report and in generally inadequate translations, the language of the German form of the nineteenth-century vision was his own, while English, being closer to German, can be translated more powerfully into that tongue than into French. Nor did the translations of the time suffer either from French literary regressiveness or from French rhetoric. Schumann could experience the literary achievements with a subtlety, a quietness, an interiorness which was difficult, almost impossible, for Berlioz. Berlioz' instrument was the orchestra, sometimes of mammoth size and supported by great choruses, though not in his finest works; Schumann's instrument was the piano. Berlioz could be heard only in concert halls, opera houses, public buildings, by masses of people. The only intimate musical experience available to Paris was through Chopin, an immigrant Pole. But Schumann's work of the 1830's could be played by the talented amateur; it could be heard alone or in small and intimate groups of likeminded people. The very circumstances of performance made it personal, like reading poetry or fiction or philosophy. And this was true of Schumann's great contemporary, Chopin, who was also born in 1810. Never before had the piano been the vehicle of such important music, with one exception.

So true was this that the piano is often thought of as a nineteenth-century instrument, while in the popular mind the harpsichord is identified with the eighteenth century. But in fact the piano was invented, simultaneously in Germany and Italy, in the second decade of the eighteenth century, and by the 1750's was well established and beginning to make the harpsichord appear oldfashioned. The harpsichord is abrupt and limited to dynamic levels; the pianoforte, to give it its full name, means "the soft-loud" instrument. The harpsichord jumps abruptly from soft to loud; the piano is capable of infinite dynamic shadings. The harpsichord player must sustain a note by holding a key down with a finger; the sustaining pedal makes it possible for the pianist to sustain a note in the bass while both hands are busy in the treble. This is the technical reason for the eventual extension of the range of the piano some octaves beyond what was customary with the harpsichord. The piano is thus capable of an infinite variation of harmonic modulations and suspensions which the harpsichord cannot achieve. To increase emotional intensity and to sustain sounds the harpsichord-ist must trill on two notes; the pianist can create emotional inten-sity by harmonic suspension and enrichment and by sudden or gradual changes in loudness and softness. It is not surprising that the piano became the favorite instrument of Enlightenment senti-mentalism.

Nevertheless the full possibilities of the piano were not begun to be explored until larger, more powerful instruments were developed, with a range extended upward until it matched and sur-passed the range of the orchestra. Now it could be a rival to the orchestra, and from 1816 to 1822, almost precisely the period he was working on the Ninth Symphony and the "Missa Solemnis," Beethoven created a series of five piano sonatas which almost match the last quartets in their beauty, their psychological depth, their extension and violation of traditional form patterns, and their profound originality. The piano was revealed as the one instrument of musical communication over which a great artist-performer could have entire control, the one instrument which was capable of almost anything and which one individual could completely dominate. Beethoven revealed the piano as the perfect instrument for the objectification of the socially alienated self and will. The transcendental piano virtuoso became the dominating figure in the nineteenth-century musical world, and insofar as nineteenth-cen-tury culture has survived either at the middle cultural level in western Europe and America or in Russia, which has been cultur-ally sealed off from the twentieth century, he remains so. From these last piano sonatas of Beethoven Schumann began.

His problem was consequently the same as Berlioz', who started from Beethoven's orchestral works: how to comprehend and control the new musical language Beethoven had created, to find verbal and conceptual equivalents so that he himself and his auditors could understand what it was saying. Like Berlioz he rev-eled in the worlds of Byron and Goethe, Shakespeare and Scott, as well as the lyric poets of early nineteenth-century Germany, especially Heine, from whose *Intermezzo* he selected in Berlioz fashion the lyrics for his miraculous song cycle "Dichterliebe" ("A

Poet's Love") with its exploration of erotic bondage, terror, and freedom. From Jean Paul Friedrich Richter he learned how late Enlightenment sentimentalism could be transformed into nineteenth-century imaginative fantasy by using it to symbolize the symmetrical idealism of the century's first decades. But the profoundest revelation came from the stories of E.T.A. Hoffmann (1776–1822), composer and short story writer. From him Schumann probably got his adolescent desire for a dual career as musician and writer, but Hoffmann's genius lay in writing, and Schumann, whose real talents were musical, achieved in that art what Hoffmann accomplished in fiction.

Born in the same decade as Scott, only five years younger, Hoffmann did precisely the same thing as the wizard of the north, in precisely the opposite direction. Scott gave Europe its historical imagination; Hoffmann gave Europe a symbolic path to the unconscious mind. Scott turned historical decor into orientative analogy; Hoffmann used history, myth, fable, and ghost stories as an analogy, a means of selecting and controlling those psychic forces of which Wordsworth was aware but could only symbolize in nature. In "The Ancient Mariner" Coleridge had hit upon what Hoffmann did, but Coleridge used the technique only twice again, in "Kubla Khan" and in "Christabel." Hoffmann created a mass of fiction which was imitated, pillaged, drawn upon, and developed for the rest of the century throughout Europe and America; for prose can be translated as poetry cannot. The stylistic and formal symbolization of poetry cannot get from one language to another; but symbols of prose fiction can move across linguistic boundaries almost without loss, at least when they are novel and not bound up with the traditions of national culture. If influence alone were to be the test, Hoffmann would be ranked among the greatest artist-visionaries of the nineteenth century.

Hoffmann achieves his effects and transmits his sense of deeper psychic levels, which had perhaps been made accessible by his addiction to alcohol, by a sharp juxtaposition of realism and fantasy. The two worlds exist side by side. The world of conscious experience is symbolized by daylight and ordinary life; the world of the unconscious by darkness, night, and history, myth, fantasy, insanity, and ghosts. One of his titles is "Nachtstück," a nocturne; and this word Schumann used for an extraordinary series of piano pieces (Opus 23, 1839). One of Hoffmann's figures was a mad musician, Kreisler, modeled on himself and his own disorientations and probings into the interior life; and this figure Schumann used for another series of piano pieces, "Kreisleriana" (Opus 16, 1838). Among Hoffmann's finest stories is "The Golden Pot," which was to become a favorite of Wagner's and one of the central literary documents of nineteenth-century Germany. Here the world of myth and primeval history is made simultaneously existent with the ordinary world of the 1800's. The student Anselmus, through his love for a girl who appears sometimes as a human being and sometimes as a magical green snake, leaves the "commonplace" and enters the world of pure spirit. Thus he enters into "possession of his inner self," sharply differentiating that self from his social role.

Indeed, there are few other nineteenth-century works in which are so explicit the psychic process of bringing the self into existence by separating it from the role, and by distinguishing between the consciousness of reason and the unconsciousness of spirit. Although Hoffmann himself held, like Jean Paul, the symmetrical vision of nature and self unified in the divine, his technique of symbolizing the dichotomy between self and nature not by transforming the world of nature through visionary intuition, in the manner of Wordsworth, Friedrich, and Beethoven's Sixth Symphony, but by creating an independent world of history, myth, and fantasy, made it possible for his symbolizations to be used by the transcendentalists as they could not use those of his contemporaries.

It is impossible for me not to believe that his experience with music, that most sensitive indicator of disorientation and reorientation, was the determining factor in releasing his literary power. Just as Constable saw that "The Ancient Mariner" was like music, so Hoffmann could create in literary fantasy the verbal parallel to music. So Schumann wrote in 1837 a piano cycle called originally "Phantasien," and later "Fantasiestücke" (Opus 12), and the "Intermezzi" of 1832 (Opus 4) were originally called "Fantasy Pieces." This form of the word has quite a different meaning from the musical term "Fantasy," a work in free form, which Bach had employed early in the eighteenth century and which Schumann used for his great C Major Fantasy (Opus 17), which is a Beethovenesque development of the sonata form and which was conceived as a musical memorial to Beethoven.

The Hoffmannesque sense of fantasy Schumann used again in "Faschingsschwank aus Wien: Fantasiebilder," "A Carnival Prank from Vienna: Fantasy Images" (Opus 26, 1839), and in this title he united literary analogies from Hoffmann and Jean Paul. Schumann was particularly entranced with Jean Paul's masquerade scenes, and three of the piano cycles of the 1830's use the masquerade as their controlling literary analogy, "Papillons" (Opus 2, 1832), "Carnaval" (Opus 9, 1834-35), and the "Faschingsschwank." The original title of the first was "Larventanz," "Dance of the Masks," but later it was changed to "Papillons," "Butterflies." Now the butterfly is an ancient symbol of the soul or psyche, and a proper title for this work would be "Masks of the Psyche," "Disguises of the Self."

If this seems far-fetched, there is other evidence. In 1831 he started to work on a novel to be called "Davidsbündler," "The Companions of David." David destroyed the Philistines, and by this time Heine had already established "Philistine" in the metaphorical sense it still has, the commonplace, unimaginative middle classes, inimical to the divinely chosen artist. The enmity of society and artist is the theme, and the notion of "companions" indicates the presence of the group of allied and like-minded fighters against society. The companions of David are the equivalents of the artist who received Balzac's dedications and of Berlioz' public bid for a following in the production of the "Symphonie Fantastique" and "Lélio." When he established a musical journal in 1833, Schumann brought into reality the ideal of an *avant-garde* group. The "Carnaval" ends with a "March of the Company of David against the Philistines," and in 1837 he wrote "Davidsbündlertänze," "The Dances of the Company of David." In the original edition of that work, the various pieces were signed either "E" or "F," "Eusebius" or "Florestan." The names, which also appear in "Carnaval," come from his novel and are again used with similar names to identify the points of view from which his musical critiques were written. "Florestan" is passionate, assertive, aggressive; "Eusebius" withdrawn, contemplative, gazing into the interior world. "Florestan" is the tower opposed to the city, the self in its assertive and antisocial aspect. Eusebius is the cave, the self-in-hiding.

The piano cycles of the 1830's, then, are cycles of dramatizations of various aspects of the self. Like Berlioz Schumann uses the sequence controlled and made specific by literary analogy in order to symbolize to himself and to his auditors that the new musical language finds its proper function in symbolizing the orientative-disorientative activity of the self. Within the cycles or sequences of both men, each unit or movement is a mask. It was a brilliant conception, for it made accessible to composer and to auditors a verbal instrument which could open up the interior meaning of the work. Again, as with Berlioz, the device left him free to develop the formal structure.

Some of these cycles of the 1830's are in the form of theme and variations: "Variations on the Name Abegg" (Opus 1, 1830), "Impromptu on a Theme by Clara Wieck" (Opus 5, 1832), the great pianist, whom he later married after great difficulties, and "Symphonic Études" (Opus 13, 1834), one of his most irresistible marvels. These, of course, are modeled on the variation sets of the later Beethoven. They are not eighteenth-century formal transformations of a theme with a specific emotional significance; rather, they are metamorphoses of an orientation. The device is similar to Berlioz's *idée fixe*, and Schumann also uses that technique of repeating a theme in different parts of each work and from work to work, though not so systematically as the Frenchman.

It is but a step from formal metamorphoses to the cycle or sequence of emotional masks, for each has the same kind of unity, while the sequence is also held together by a style which, developed out of Beethoven and Schubert, is as unmistakably and uniquely Schumann's as Berlioz' is his. Although it is true that the individual members of each sequence are simple in structure, being basically a dance or a song, the sequence itself gave him opportunities for a musical organization without precedent. Each cycle becomes a drama in many scenes; again he resembles Berlioz, whose "Romeo and Juliet" and "Damnation of Faust" are similarly put together. Berlioz, however, in his orchestral works tended to stick with the traditional four-or five-part pattern, as Schumann did in his sonatas. In the piano sequences, however, there was no limit to the number of parts, just as there had never been a limit to the number of variations. Undoubtedly, this undefined number of sections came from the variation tradition, but as important a source, considering his literary interest and knowledge, was the free stringing together of scenes by Shakespeare and Goethe, for Schumann too wrote a set of scenes from *Faust*.

For the first time music had the formal freedom of poetry; nor is this comparison without significance. On the contrary, Schumann thought of himself as a poet whose medium was music, not words, or with some assistance from words. The nineteenth-century identification of poet with imagination, of the poet with seer and the redeeming priest, made the term "poet" the primary term for any artist. Instead of providing amusement, no matter how refined or noble, instead of representing the real world for our delight, the musician and the painter identified themselves with the poet, the divine illuminator. It is fascinating to see how Schumann gradually grasped and extended his conception of the poetic sequence in music. At the beginning each part was independent, and each was about the same length, and each had the same musical character, that of the dance, for one of his few precedents was the dance suite. Gradually other forms are mingled; the length freely varies; tempos change within each section; in the "Symphonic Etudes" variations are mingled with sections having no relation to theme, that is, sequence sections; gradually, though with caution, unresolved harmonies turn up at the end of sections, so that one flows uninterruptedly into the other; themes and motives recur; and the whole sequence becomes longer, fuller, richer, infinitely varied. In the last works of the 1830's one feels that a whole life has been dramatized and heard; the listener has something of the satisfaction which only the greatest music can give, the sense of having encountered the full range of human experience. Schumann achieved a freedom even Beethoven had only tasted. Even more than Berlioz, he transformed the forms of the past, a task which takes greater genius and greater care than to invent new ones. Without a trace of rhetoric or stylistic violence, he had subjected a living tradition to his will, and left it living. Berlioz' successors could use his orchestral discoveries; that was all. But the later Schumann—for he was his own successor—and those who followed him, particularly Brahms, could use his stylistic inventions and his freedom of form. His formal revolution in the piano sequences of the 1830's was to lead to the free accomplishments of the late nineteenth century and of the twentieth.

# CHAPTER XII

# *The Transcendental Eye*

WHEN DELACROIX DIED IN 1863, Charles Baudelaire, the poet, wrote a long letter to the editor of the *Opinion Nationale* on the great painter's achievements. A couple of extracts can catch the tone of the essay:

> The important thing . . . is to show, as far as the written word is capable of showing, the magical art with whose help he has been able to translate the *word* by means of plastic images more vivid and more appropriate than those of any other creative artist of the same profession—to discover, in short, what was the *specialty* with which Providence had charged Eugène Delacroix. . . . This strange, mysterious quality . . . is the invisible, the impalpable, the dream, the nerves, the *soul;* and this he has done . . . with no other means but colour and contour; he has done it . . . with the perfection of a consummate painter, with the exactitude of a subtle writer, with the eloquence of an impassioned musician. It is, moreover, one of the characteristic symptoms of the spiritual condition of our age that the arts aspire if not to take one another's place, at least reciprocally to lend one another new powers.

Although Baudelaire himself had gone beyond, as we shall see, and rejected much of transcendentalism, here he catches the character of Delacroix in the language of the painter's own time. In the first sentence, for instance, the contrast between "written word" and "the *word*" suggests that he is using Balzac's meaning in the second instance; while the italicization also of *specialist* confirms that interpretation. Baudelaire had known Delacroix; he understood his paintings and his cast of mind, his attitude toward his art, how his personality functioned in mind and art alike.

Baudelaire, born in 1821, grew up in the high times of transcendental realism; in the essay on Delacroix, for example, he quotes from Emerson, the American counterpart of Carlyle and Balzac, Berlioz and Schumann, in order to establish his comprehension of Delacroix as the transcendental hero. But above all, he points unerringly to the unique quality in Delacroix that symbolizes the domination of the subject by the heroic will, which is the realization of the "soul," to use Baudelaire's word for the noumenal self. The invisible made visible—the ambition of the nineteenth-century artist, and above all of the asymmetrical transcendental realist. Finally, the classification of Delacroix with writer and musician and the emphasis upon the unity of the arts as different modes of symbolizing the same invisible reality, the only reality that counts, indicates Baudelaire's insight into the spirit of the 1830's.

And indeed, in his journals Delacroix writes almost as much about music as about painting, although, as is so often true of painters, he did not grasp the similarity of the music of his own time to what he was doing. To him Mozart was the man of divine perfection, yet, in spite of his uneasy feeling about Beethoven and his conviction that much of the great German was commonplace, he realized that Beethoven had disclosed a "horizon" which Mozart had never seen, that among himself and Beethoven and Byron's *Don Juan* there was somehow an affinity. No, it was not the music of the nineteenth century which he grasped, but its literature. Like all the men we have examined, he discovered an unsurpassable revelation in Scott, in Byron, in Goethe, and in Shakespeare, whom the early nineteenth century remade into a nineteenth-century poet. Like all the advanced young men growing up in the 1820's, he found in these men of letters a bomb that blew up the old orientations. In 1827 he made a tremendous sensation with his lithographs for *Faust*, Part I. These nineteen sheets, like Berlioz' "Eight

Scenes," were inspired by Gérard de Nerval's translation. Later series of lithographs were based on Goethe's *Götz von Berlichingen,* an early play of his negative Wertherian period, and on *Hamlet.* As for his large oil paintings, again and again Delacroix drew upon these same writers for subjects.

That his illustrations for *Faust* were lithographs is significant. In making a lithograph the artist draws directly on a piece of limestone with a greasy crayon. The technique permits the taking off on paper of a reversed copy of what the artist has drawn. It is, above all, direct and rapid; unlike etching or engraving, processes which force the artist into a certain rigidity and objectivity of line, lithography is as personal as handwriting, while the use of the broad-lined crayon and its possibilities for shading, for smearing, for indefiniteness, make it infinitely more flexible than other techniques of the graphic arts. It combines the personality and individuality of water color, of sketches, of brush drawing in ink, with reproduction for the purposes of publication. Those techniques permit the existence of but one specimen; lithography, which made possible reproduction in hundreds of copies, permits the effect of uniqueness to be combined with graphic reproduction for comparatively wide distribution. When Delacroix made the *Faust* lithographs, the technique was only a couple of decades old. For the nineteenth-century artist, and particularly for Delacroix' generation, it had unique advantages.

To the transcendentalists the value of the moment lay in the encounter of the mind with reality, not in what the mind discovered. From the beginning the nineteenth-century artist, poet, musician, and painter had the problem of symbolizing that moment; he had to dramatize spontaneity. Nineteenth-century art often looks spontaneous; it often seems to be the record of the moment. But it never is. The nineteenth-century artist, on the contrary, had to exploit every technical means, to work long and laboriously, in order to give the observer the impression that the work had been spontaneously and immediately brought into existence. However, what in the period of symmetrical intuitive perception into the noumenal behind the phenomenal was a desirable quality—dramatizing and symbolizing that perception as the experience of a moment—became for the transcendental artist a necessity. For him, as we saw in discussing Balzac and the instrumentalism of Carlyle, the moment of encounter, the flash of reorientation, of experiencing a wholly fresh, unique, and unprecedented encounter of the will with the world, of force with resistance—this experience was in itself the experience of the noumenal, the rising to the surface of the unconscious, the realization, as Baudelaire put it, of "the invisible, the impalpable, the dream, the nerves, the soul."

Clearly, a publicly available technique for such symbolization was immensely important; for the sketch and the drawing were considered private, preparatory, preliminary work not for the public eye. It was, in fact, only as a result of nineteenth-century art that drawings began to be collected not as indications of an artist's technique or as sentimental memorabilia but as works of art in themselves. The lithograph could be at once public yet as personal, as intimate, as spontaneous as handwriting. Like calligraphy, moreover, but unlike sketches, the lithograph was not a note made for one's own subsequent exploitation but a letter, a message, addressed to another, to the public. Paintings, even after public exhibition, ended up, if they didn't return to the artist's own studio, in private collections. When bought by the state they were in museums; but the lithograph, like Schumann's piano cycles, could be studied in intimacy. And there is another similarity between these two forms, for one organizing drive behind Schumann's work was the urge to create a highly wrought work of art that sounded like an improvisation.

A kind of calligraphy, then, the lithograph technique permitted an extraordinary development of the expressive power of the line. When we consider that a psychiatrist has been able to predict an attempt at suicide by examining the handwriting of a patient about whom he had no other information; when we look at our own handwriting and see how its changes, its pressures, its variations in the inscribing of particular shapes, shift with our moods, with our attitudes toward the person to whom we are writing, it is obvious how important it was for Delacroix to capture in a public, finished medium a quality always present in drawings but eliminated in finished paintings. If we contrast an early painting like "Scenes from the Massacre at Chios" (1821-24) with the famous "Liberty Leading the People" (1830) (his memorial to Teufelsdröckh's revolution), a striking contrast is obvious. Baudelaire expressed it perfectly. From the calligraphic experiments of 1827 Delacroix has learned to retain in the finished paintings a freedom of contour with a consequent capture of movement which makes the earlier painting, splendid though it is, seem posed, static, rhetorical, a studio production.

The *Faust* lithographs set free Delacroix' line to become the source for a personal contour. It is not merely that the figures in the painting seem to be in motion. The whole painting, as a two-dimensional surface, seems to be alive. The sinuosities, the writhings, the violently abrupt shifts in the twistings and turnings of the contours, their absolute freedom no longer contained within an implied triangle, as they are even in the "Liberty" of 1830—these characteristics in his later paintings express a vitality not derived from or justified by the subject but emerging from the artist himself and justified by the implied uniqueness of the moment of vision. Friedrich gets his personality into the painting by relying upon an unnatural symmetry or an equally unnatural regression of planes, thus symbolizing the noumenal order behind the phenomena he paints. Delacroix organizes the whole painting in terms of an apparently wilful system of writhing contours. As with Balzac, though the mind is engaged with reality, the relations set upon between unique objects are derived entirely from the mind of the artist.

What Delacroix did with contour he also did with color. He set it free to live its own life, independent of line and almost independent of subject. In this development the sight of the Constables exhibited in Paris in 1823 had a revolutionary effect, and his visit to London in 1824 confirmed and enforced his new realization of how color could be used. Throughout the history of European painting there has always been a struggle between line and color.

When you look at a square green sofa-cushion, what do you see? A patch of green color or a shape that happens to be green? Which should you do, if you are a painter, relate the shape to adjacent shapes or relate the color to adjacent colors? If you think that the shape of an object can be defined by line and shading, then the shape is identifiable with the three-dimensional reality. And from the point of view of the color, which changes as the light changes, your task is to catch the "real" color of the object. Again, since the shape is fixed, real, definable by line, the color, being less definable, should be subordinate to the shape.

As a result, European paintings, from the Middle Ages to Constable and Delacroix, were colored drawings. Color was imitative, or symbolic (the Virgin is always in blue), or during the Enlightenment harmonized to reveal the underlying unity and rationality in nature. Not even Friedrich, nor even Blake, whose color was regressively symbolic, had set color free. Constable made the first step when he painted in terms of light. Light, however, controls color. Color is still subordinate to a higher "reality." Delacroix, his eyes cleaned by Constable, was able to go even farther than the Englishman. He made color emotional, personal, subjective, irrational, determined neither by verbal concepts nor by moral symbolisms. Nor is it a color language in which a specific color can be equated with a specific emotion, or even serves to reinforce that emotion. Titian, Veronese, Rubens, and Watteau—all the painters in the Venetian tradition—used color that way, a device analogous to the "affects" of Enlightenment music. Their color was rationalized by association with emotions, appropriate to the roles of the figures in the painting and to the moral and social judgment made upon the events by the artist, who was a public servant of the social morality. Crucifixions are dark; royal triumphs are brilliant.

But consider "The Abduction of Rebecca" (1846; the subject is from Scott's *Ivanhoe;* the painting is in the Metropolitan Museum of Art in New York). Baudelaire tells us that Delacroix kept an extraordinary clean palette; the colors were so arranged that it looked like a bouquet of flowers. When we examine this

painting, we have no doubt of the accuracy of Baudelaire's reporting. The scene is of terror, abduction, warfare, physical suffering,
violence, the burning of a great castle; but the colors are as
splendid, as rich, as superbly sumptuous as if Veronese were painting the "Triumph of Venice." The blue of the sky is as limpid, as
pure, as "joyous" as a Poussin painting of Apollo driving his sun
chariot through the heavens. The artist is indifferent to what he
sees; or rather he is so armed by his free contour and free color that
he can gaze on anything. Like Carlyle's, like Balzac's, his gaze is
heroic; passionate, yes, but the passion does not arise from his emotional reaction to the subject. He serves as no indignant public conscience; he does not serve at all. The passion is the result of the
encounter between his will and the reality; it is the consequence
of the self realized in imposing transcendent order upon a reality
which has significance only because it is the occasion of the self-realization.

His subjects are massacres, revolutions, horses fighting,
abductions, imperial suicides, Don Juan and his companions drawing lots, imperial conquests, Medea killing her children, or they are
Bacchus and Ariadne, the Good Samaritan, Christ on the Cross,
Virgil presenting Dante to Homer, or Apollo victorious over the
serpent python. Whatever he paints, he confronts it with the same
unshakable emotional detachment. "The hero is he who is immov-
ably centered," said Emerson, and Baudelaire quoted him to focus
upon the heroic quality of Delacroix. This is what makes Delacroix
the greatest painter of his generation; an artist's style, his unique,
inimitable formal power, is his heroism. Here is the beating heart,
the quivering nervous system, of the transcendental vision.

Great as Delacroix was, important for the future as were
his achievements, although he was undoubtedly the greatest artist
of his generation, there was a greater artist of transcendentalism.
Delacroix had lost one thing that Constable had won, freedom
from the subject. In that area he was regressive, limited by the
strained and forced version of the nineteenth-century vision which
was almost all the French had so far achieved. In the freedom from
subject and the freedom of color he was surpassed by a man older

than himself, whose accomplishment is all the more impressive in that he belonged to an older generation. Joseph Mallord William Turner was born in 1775, the decade of Friedrich and Constable. The first part of his career was spent in doing what they were doing, but less adequately, more regressively bound to earlier centuries, particularly to Claude Lorrain, the French artist of the mid-seventeenth century. But when he was past fifty he suddenly, with a surprising forward leap, revolutionized his style and emerged as the greatest transcendental artist.

So long as Turner was understood merely as a forerunner of the triumphant impressionists of the late nineteenth century, he was misunderstood. Light is less his concern than color. To think of him as an early impressionist is to make as bad an error as to think, with Ruskin, that his chief merit lies in the accuracy of his observation and his power to record that accuracy in paint and pencil and water color. The truth, as we are beginning to see, is that he was not a few decades ahead of his time, but a full century. Only with the development of abstract expressionism in the 1940's and 1950's has it become possible to realize what his real concern was, although it should have been possible when Van Gogh emerged in the last decades of the nineteenth century. But then Turner was in eclipse, and the acceptance of Van Gogh was very slow. Turner's first reappearance occurred when impressionism had finally been accepted by museum directors and the general public, at least in England, in the first decade of this century. His second is occurring now, in the early 1960's, with the public acceptance of abstract expressionism. Today it is possible to see that the real "subject" of Turner's late period is the encounter of the loaded brush with the canvas.

We have few clues to Turner's interior life, but one is of paramount meaning. For years he labored on a long poem, written in a turgid debasement of Milton's style; sections of it occasionally appeared as epigraphs for his pictures. It was called *The Fallacies of Hope.* Does the title imply the negation of Werther, or the pessimism of Friedrich and Kleist, or the perilous balance of Goethe? It is impossible to tell, for the full manuscript, which is almost undecipherable, has never been published. In any case it appears thoroughly consistent with the intense conviction we have met so often that to hope for any final orientative gratification in human existence or after it is a mistake. Certainly the title and the epigraphs express the drive toward reality as it is, not as we would like it to be; and his paintings up to 1828 are characterized by an almost inconceivable fullness of detail, closely observed and exquisitely presented. This is what Ruskin admired him for.

Suddenly, in 1828, in a small painting never exhibited at the annual shows of the Royal Academy, for which he almost invariably painted enormous and brilliantly-colored show pieces— he was always cynical about the public—a wholly new style appears. The canvas is swept clean of the detail which had overloaded his previous work and made them almost oppressive. We see nothing but a strip of beach, a child, the sea, the sky, a single star reflected on barely breaking wavelets. Only Richard Parkes Bonington (1802-28) had achieved anything approaching such simplification, and Friedrich in the "Monk on the Seashore." Although in previous pictures the subject had always been subordinated to the landscape, now it virtually disappears or is reduced to tiny figures whose activities would be incomprehensible where it not for the title. Color becomes increasingly free, not as in Delacroix, in a continuous shifting and change of small areas of color across the surface of the canvas, but in great patches. In 1834 the burning of the Houses of Parliament in London gave him an incomparable opportunity; in an extraordinary series of oils and watercolors he used the conflagration as an excuse to drown the canvas in light and color, and the glare made it possible to suppress detail into blobs, patches, and streaks. It is impossible to see the significance of what was happening in these pictures if one examines reproductions. Only the originals can show how the laying on of the pigment, the wild sweep of the brush, can give the observer the sensation that he is repeating Turner's tactile excitement. Subsequent works, the famous "Rain, Steam, and Speed," and the "Steamer in a Snowstorm" of 1842, carry the process still further.

It is true that at the time he was experimenting with Goethe's theory of color, which involved the coordination of color and emotion, but even where he appears to use this theory, as in "Steamer in a Snowstorm," the supposedly gloomy effects of blue, dirty greens, gray, and black are utterly dominated by the wild swirling of the paint itself. Perhaps the most extraordinary are among his very last paintings, done shortly before he gave up working in 1847. These have the same subject, a ship at sea in a snowstorm. One is in the Metropolitan in New York; the later one, perhaps his last work, is in the Tate Gallery in London. In the second the development begun in the first, really begun in 1828, is completed. Ship, sea, and snow have virtually disappeared in a passion of pigment. The storm is not at sea, nor in the unbelievably imaginative handling of infinite shades of white; it is in Turner's wielding of the brush. The expressive symbol is neither in subject nor in color; it is in the brush stroke itself. He has arrived at a line of development which was not continued until almost a hundred years later, in contemporary abstract expressionism. The encounter between the creative and ordering imagination and reality has achieved a symbolization in the encounter of loaded brush and canvas beyond which, even now, it is scarcely possible to see. Far more than Constable he forces the observer to become a creative eye.

Yet when we compare Turner with Delacroix, we can observe remarkable resemblances; the drive of both artists was the same. Delacroix also, in his later works, uses a very loose technique which suppresses detail for contour and color. But where Delacroix' contours are justified by the outline of the object depicted, though not derived from it, Turner's whirling brush strokes are justified only by fire, by steam, by whirling snow, by wind, and ultimately are quite independent even of these. As for subject, even though Turner goes far beyond the Frenchman in breaking with it, there remains a residual justification for passion in the fact that he paints fire, storms, and wind-torn sunsets, as well as translucent misty dawns. In one strange painting of his later years, however, he goes as far in denial of the subject as anyone went until the twentieth century. It is an interior at Petworth, the castle of Lord Egremont, who, in spite of Turner's plebeian origin, was his close and dear friend. There are no people, only walls, windows, draperies, and furniture. And even these disappear in the color that floods the room and drowns its objective phenomena. But it is more than color; it is pigment, which appears to have floated onto the canvas from some unknown and unimaginable world, some universe different from ours and more intensely vital. For a moment, Delacroix, in the *Faust* lithographs, which catch and preserve the nervous movement of the crayon over the stone, moved in the direction Turner was to take; but he turned aside and anchored his contours to the object. Not so with Turner. He carried almost to its final point the freeing of the movement of paint-loaded brush across canvas. Through the incomparably exquisite control of the impassioned nerves, the brush engages the artist with reality; but his imagination is almost utterly free. With the utmost effort and a just not completely uninhibited severity of the will, the artistic, redemptive imagination all but transcends reality. It is the farthest point of transcendental heroism.

# Part Four

# Illusion and Reality

# CHAPTER XIII

# Transcendentalism
# in Difficulty

Ιτ is no accident of meaningless randomness that the
farthest or highest point of heroic transcendentalism should be
as remote from ordinary human affairs as the delicate movement
of an artist's brush from palette to canvas. At least, the randomness can be eliminated when we examine Turner's final paintings
with the instrumental construct I am using. As it turned out, the
heroic redeemer could be successful only in the realm of art. The
transcendental redemption of society could be symbolized, but
only symbolized; it could not be accomplished. The opposition
between tower and city, as Tennyson saw early in the 1830's, was
too profound for the artist successfully to re-enter society. There
were several reasons; some of them were inherent in the character
of the city, of society itself; some were immanent in the transcendental version of the tower. For there were difficulties, not
immediately apparent, in the transcendental stage of the nineteenth-century vision which forced the next generation to abandon it and go farther than the transcendental heroes had thought
necessary or possible.

The reasons for the resistance of society to the transcendental vision I have already touched on, particularly in the
Introduction and again in Chapter XI. The 1830's saw the ac-
cession to political power of the middle classes, which had already

seized economic power, throughout western Europe and in the United States. The rise of the middle classes—when were they not rising? They always seem to be rising through the whole course of European history, but the industrial revolution of the eighteenth and nineteenth centuries finally gave them freedom from any control by the landed aristocracy, whom they gobbled up by all kinds of devices, including marriage. The absorption of hereditary privilege by economic privilege through marriage is one of the great themes of Balzac. Yet at the same time, and almost in spite of themselves, both Balzac and Carlyle had a great admiration for the captains of industry, and a profound hope that they would be true social leaders. For a time both men hoped through their writings to seize imaginative control of the minds of the leaders of business and industrial enterprise—of the entrepreneurs—and turn them into transcendental heroes. So, in America, did Emerson. The reasons for this mad optimism are not difficult to find. It was apparent to everyone that industrialism was creating a new kind of society, new forms of social interaction, new bonds for social cohesion, new economic relations among men. It was not quite so apparent, though many were aware of it—Thomas Babington Macaulay, the English historian, for instance—that only the middle classes had a living cultural tradition in the kind of social organization necessary to control and exploit industrialism.

For centuries the European nobility had thought in terms of campaigns and seasons. Their orientation was simultaneously military and agricultural; the rhythm of their wars was determined by weather which makes army movement possible; the rhythm of their farming was equally determined by the seasons. In the second the aim was to ensure enough food to last to the next harvest and enough seed to plant it. In the first, it was to win a particular year's campaign; wars went on until one side or the other was exhausted or bored. Wars, consequently, were long, lasting years, even decades. Indeed, periods of peace were statistically abnormal. Even to think of alternate periods of peace and of war, in the modern fashion, would be a mistake; war, with small armies, was like agriculture, simply a normal cultural mode for the aristocracy.

The aristocracy thought a year ahead; their expectations were set for immediate gratification. Their vocations were farming and fighting; their avocations were love and gambling. An action was a good action if it produced immediate or short-term results, whether those results were favorable or unfavorable. The imagery of the seventeenth-century aristocratic poets of England is based upon an interchangeability of the military campaign, the seduction, the throw of the dice and the turn of the card, the plunge of the plow into the earth. They too, however, accomplished a revolution in the eighteenth century, the agricultural revolution, achieved mainly by the agricultural sword, the moldboard plow. And they had one great merit: *noblesse oblige*, moral responsibility for the economic and social welfare of their subordinates. A nobleman was morally judged by the degree to which he accepted and carried out the responsibility conferred upon him by the privilege of controlling the wielding of sword and plow by the lower social orders.

The middle classes, however, thought in different terms with different sets of expectations. The successful businessman, investor, and entrepreneur has to think in long terms. He has to be able to postpone gratifications. In the very earliest days of European business enterprise, when European civilization was still very young, the merchant trader had to be able to endure a suspense about the success of his pack train or ship which might last for years. Therefore he had to have the imagination to manipulate a variety of enterprises simultaneously, to control and marshal unseen resources. Daniel Defoe's making an inventory of the natural and industrial resources of England and reporting to his fellow middle class projectors and entrepreneurs what could be developed and exploited was a typical acting out of middle-class morality. The discipline of postponed gratification is the basis for middle-class morality. Psychologically, the aristocrat could afford failure; he did not have to endure the emotional ravages of suspense. But the business failure for the bourgeois is tragic, shameful, and terrible; if gratification is postponed, its failure is extremely hard to take. In the middle-class twentieth-century morality of the United

States the goal of psychotherapy is to train the social deviant to postpone gratification and to endure the frustration of that gratification when it is not forthcoming. It is the middle-class conception of mature behavior. It identifies Russian Communism as a belated middle-class morality, with the usual conflict between long-term industry and short-term agriculture.

The American Civil War was the first modern war because it was the first middle-class war, the first war that was a war and not a campaign or a succession of campaigns. "Campaign" came to mean not a seasonal but a geographical military effort. The North won not merely because it opposed industrial strength to agricultural strength, but because Northern government leaders began to think about war in terms of business and industrial enterprise, in terms of marshaling resources and postponing meaningless small victories for one overwhelming defeat of the enemy. War became a middle-class enterprise when Lincoln stopped thinking in terms of capturing Richmond—that was an aristocratic conception—and got Grant to forget about symbolic victories and to postpone triumph until he had totally defeated Lee's army, a victory made possible by Sherman's business enterprise in slashing through the South and eliminating the essential agriculture and transportational margin that enabled Lee to sustain his military power.

The vocation of the middle classes is long-term investment and exploitation of natural resources; its avocations are religion and scientific technology. Like the aristocracy, it betrayed its moral weakness in its avocations. Aristocratic religion is a mere ritual of immediate gratification, emotional conversion, and relief from anxiety. Undisciplined in postponed gratification, the nobility requires the drama of mass and confession and prayer to a patron saint and in a splendid church, to tolerate postponed gratification. The people, for similar reasons and because they have been trained by the aristocracy, follow suit. Methodism was a popular movement. Middle-class religion thinks more in terms of salvation after death, postponed gratification, of long sermons, of prayer to God in an environment of domestic simplicity. To the middle-class businessman, religion is a training in postponed gratification; one endures the suspense by surrendering to the will of God. The Enlightenment notion, therefore, that order and value are structured in nature by the will of God, and that gratification necessarily results from a patient overcoming of ignorance of natural law, was perfectly tailored for the middle classes. It was no trouble at all for them to think that the "invisible hand," in the long run, served both entrepreneurship and the people the enterpreneur had to exploit in order to carry it out.

From the religious and technological avocations of the middle classes, reinforced by the Enlightenment conception of perfect adaptation to nature and the necessarily man-directed purposiveness of nature, of the wisdom and benevolence of God as manifested in natural law, rose the failure of middle-class morality, its social irresponsibility. The beauty of European and American cities was the creation of the aristocratic morality; that so little of that beauty remains, and that almost all of the nineteenth- and twentieth-century urbanism is hideously ugly, is the consequence of middle-class morality. Enlightenment ideas could be used either way, with or without social responsibility. But only the middle classes had the emotional and social discipline to create and exploit the industrial revolution. Only the middle classes had the gall to use every propaganda instrument in their power to persuade the miserable working classes that their standard of living would automatically rise, and to attempt to train them to postpone that gratification to the lives of their great-grandchildren, long after their own lives had ended. Russian Communism, of course, is doing the same thing today.

Obviously the orientative drive toward moral irresponsibility which operates by draining away the opportunities for moral choice was profoundly reinforced by the middle-class morality of social irresponsibility. This is that Philistinism—that moral, religious, and aesthetic complacency and self-satisfaction, that brutal middle-class self-indulgence—which Heine and Schumann raged against in literature and in music. When the redeeming transcendental hero, armored in his new vision and the acceptance of his alienation, issued from the tower and descended upon the city, he encountered impregnable walls, walls of mockery, walls that simply ignored him, walls that admitted him only in the role of social pet. His devaluation of society was countered by a social devaluation that turned him into a bohemian. Society was convinced it had no need of him; its redemption was assured by the will of God, the orderliness of nature, and the laws of economics. It was redeemed in every way except economically, and economic redemption was surely on the way. Further, it had economic control of the publishing business, and the socio-economic forces of the time, as I pointed out in the Introduction, worked only in the direction of increasing that control. Philistinism could only be continuously reinforced.

The result was peculiar. During the nineteenth and twentieth centuries, when a new vision of man was being forged in the desolated hearts of a few geniuses, quantitatively the most important cultural circumstance was the spreading of medieval and Enlightenment orientations, as well as peculiar middle-class hybrids of the two. Outworn orientations were being reinforced with infinitely greater rapidity and power than the various stages of the nineteenth-century vision could be developed and uttered. The transcendental hero found that the very attitudes he had rejected were by the 1830's far more powerful and widely diffused and socially rooted than when the rejection first began in the 1770's. Innumerable people were discovering the Enlightenment, were just beginning on its first stages, when the transcendental hero was attempting to bring to their attention the second stage of what had superseded the Enlightenment. If nineteenth-century minds multiplied arithmetically, Enlightenment minds were multiplying geometrically. Nor was that all. The half-unconscious pre-Enlightenment orientations were being made conscious for millions of the newly literate. In the nineteenth century the Enlightenment was constantly fighting against what it had superseded, the dissemination of which had the same ratio to the dissemination of the Enlightenment as the latter had to the dissemination of nineteenth-century orientations.

The cultural situation was further complicated by the fact that while some minds were leaving transcendentalism, others were just entering on the first, symmetrical stage of the nineteenth-century vision, and still others were just leaving the Enlightenment and entering into the negation of Werther and Byron. And it was still further complicated by the fact that any individual mind was very likely to exhibit attitudes derived from all three dominant orientations and the transitional stages between them.

The cultural situation, then, was bad enough; but transcendentalism itself suffered from certain shortcomings and inconsistencies. A glance at the career of Benjamin Disraeli, one of the few transcendental politicians, will bring them out. In the 1830's he attempted to create a new political party, a kind of third force, which would combine the social responsibility of the old nobility's *noblesse oblige*, the moral responsibility of the nineteenth-century orientation, and the social aims of the late Enlightenment. The subtitle of *Sybil*, his social novel of 1845, reveals one of his most important influences; it was *The Two Nations*, and it came from *Sartor Resartus*. Disraeli's political style, as well as his personal style, particularly his clothes, had the fantastic quality of transcendentalism. It was the equivalent of Berlioz' music; like Marx, he was a Balzacian hero and monomaniac. The climax of his career was the creation of universal manhood suffrage and of the British Empire, the attempt to extend social responsibility to all classes, and the effort to create an imperial supernational transcendental authority.

Carlyle and Balzac also showed, in the long run, the same desire to impose heroic authority. In Balzac it took the form of the imposition of moral authority by the Catholic church and of political-economic authority and responsibility by a revitalized monarchy. One of the more peculiar results was the revaluation of Catherine de' Medici into a great heroine. Carlyle became more and more enamored of the dictator who ruthlessly imposed his will on society for its own good. The results were remarkably like those of Hegelian thinking and are often confused with it. Where Hegel ended up with "Whatever is, is right," Balzac, Carlyle, and

Disraeli ended up with "Whatever the transcendental hero wills is right." Emerson, a milder type, created a doctrine of "self-reliance" which could be and was absorbed by the anarchic individualism of the socially irresponsible middle-class Philistine.

It became apparent that it was impossible for the nineteenth-century artist to re-enter society, not merely because society was becoming progressively more inimical, but because the imposition of the will upon reality, when given political and social instrumentality, meant the denial to others of their own moral responsibility. To redeem society could only mean to do for others what the nineteenth-century vision had made possible for the alienated individual to do for himself: the creation of a genuine moral responsibility in everyone. The difficulty of this aim was not only that these "others" did not want it; it was also that to create the social conditions necessary for the assumption by all men of moral responsibility meant a temporary and perhaps permanent—who knew?—denial of the very responsibility the imposition of the will was designed to create. Further, any exercise of power over another denies the basic principle of nineteenth-century morality: the empathy which Byron negatively discovered in *Manfred* and which Goethe and Schopenhauer and Carlyle had already seen as the only adequate basis of morality since it was the only way to break through the ring of egocentricity consequent upon deriving value from the self. When the transcendental hero set out to translate what he believed into a political program, his actions, through the exercise of power, reinforced the egocentricity which his beliefs were designed to break down.

Paradox upon paradox! Nor were these the only difficulties with transcendentalism. There were also the problems of authority and of style. The authority of the transcendental hero derived from the unconscious noumenal self, not from the role he played in a social structure; and that noumenal self was conceived either as divine in itself or the incarnation of the divine. Since it lay below the level of rational and empirical inquiry, the self could only be symbolized and its divinity only asserted. Traditional theology, because of its paralogisms, its unconsciously bad logic, could go through the motions of rational and objective inquiry and examination; furthermore it had a sacred text to comment on, or, in its Enlightenment mode of natural theology, it had a sacred world to discuss. It could imagine it was talking about realities, but that illusion was forbidden the transcendentalist by his own principles. Authority, and acceptance of authority, are social acts; authority does not exist unless it is recognized by others. Transcendental authority, authority derived from the self, turns out to be a paradox, an impossibility for the socially alienated. To the person who refuses to accept it and challenges the transcendentalist's right to assume authority, no answer is possible. The acceptance of an authority is a socially transmitted orientative pattern. Acquiescence can be forced by power, but only psychological violation can induce consent when hostility or lack of sympathy is present in the challenger.

Indeed, many have felt psychologically violated by Carlyle, by Balzac, by Berlioz, and also by Wagner, whose roots are deep in the transcendentalist tradition, though he went beyond it. To accept transcendentalist authority one must first be sympathetic, but to be sympathetic one must first have already gone through at least some of the transcendentalist's experiences. Then, and then only, can one accept what the transcendentalist says, for only then can one perceive it as what the transcendentalist says it is, a symbolization of a basic reorientative experience and the discovery of a new, asymmetrical source of value. The initiate knows that the adept's symbolization is valid and authoritative because he has experienced what is being symbolized. The only way to that vision is forever and inevitably the path of alienation and isolation, of extreme psychological suffering, which no one will follow unless he has no other recourse.

Thus what was intended to be a vision available to all men turned out to be an exceedingly closed vision, available only to a very few; what was supposed to come to man in an aura of divine authority turned out to have no social authority whatever. Even today it takes the utmost sympathy to penetrate Balzac's vision, to see its unity, and to accept its validity—to comprehend his whole vast fictional structure as a symbolization of a profound insight.

This very sympathy, however, created another difficulty. It first appeared, or perhaps most glaringly appeared, in the application of the transcendental scheme to Christianity. In 1841 Feuerbach stated that God is but the projection of man's inward nature, of the self. Here was not only an attack on Christianity itself; it was more uncompromisingly anti-Christian than Carlyle or Balzac. It brought to the fore another transcendentalist difficulty. If Christianity is but a symbolization, it is no different from other symbolizations. All symbolizations, then, are of equal validity; for they all symbolize the same thing.

Feuerbach, born in 1804, was younger than Carlyle and Balzac. They had depended, though unconsciously at least in part, for the divinity and authority of their symbolizations upon Christianity. It was an inconsistent position, and Feuerbach revealed its inconsistency. Feuerbach makes every individual into Christ; every individual is a hero; thus, in effect, no individual is any more heroic than any other individual, and no symbolization has any more validity than any other symbolization. Symbolizations have only functional and instrumental validity. And suddenly the self is divested of divinity; there is no divinity. Feuerbach himself shuddered away from this conclusion and developed an elaborate and complex metaphysic to keep man, somehow or other, rooted in the divine. But he revealed an internal weakness of the transcendental position and adumbrated an essential characteristic of the next stage.

Truly, Balzac was right; he and his contemporaries were all monomaniacs. In the 1830's and 1840's the Philistine mind called them crazy, and in the 1960's it still does, not least because of the transcendentalist style. The style of the first, symmetrical stage was sufficiently like traditional styles not to cause too much alarm, but the asymmetrical style—because it had to symbolize a unique vision of value—was the truly fantastic style. It set people's teeth on edge; it caused riots; it aroused the most passionate detestation. But its greatest difficulty was that it could not be used, or developed; it was a dead end.

Such a style created a problem unique in European cultural history. Style had heretofore been continuous. The sharpest stylistic break had been the shift from Gothic architecture to Renaissance architecture. Even that was not only sharper than the corresponding stylistic shifts in the other arts; it was more a matter of a change in ornament than a change in structure, and it was, in comparison with the sudden and dramatic appearance of the transcendentalist style, extremely slow. The transcendentalist, on the other hand, plunged the observer, the listener, and the reader into a wholly new stylistic environment. The notion of a style that could not be transferred to followers and disciples, the notion that every artist had to create his own unique style, was so profound a break with the stylistic experiences of man that both observer and practitioner were quite at a loss. Even if you recognized this art as new, original, authentic, and great, what did you do with it, if you were an artist yourself?

These, then, were the problems that transcendentalism created: society was increasingly hostile; heroic redemption began to appear an impossibility; transcendentalism contained a moral paradox; its authority was convincing only to the already sympathetic; its divinity was threatened; social power and aesthetic style became novel cultural problems. The dual career of Richard Wagner, dramatist and composer, gives historical reality to these abstractions.

# CHAPTER XIV

# *The Hero Frustrated*

THE HYSTERICAL ADULATION and the furious hatred which have always been the norm of judgments of Richard Wagner's music dramas are alone almost enough to mark him as a transcendental artist. The world is still divided into Wagnerians and anti-Wagnerians, though it is the latter who are now beginning to appear old-fashioned. However, a third party is currently developing whose attitude is simply that he is one of the great classics of European culture and should be treated accordingly. The violence is subsiding, and it is becoming possible to examine him as a human genius, and not as God nor yet the devil.

But there are more marks of his transcendental origins, his unique, novel, and extravagant style, his youthful conception of himself as a world-redeemer, his control of musical meaning by literary analogues, and especially his idea of the *Gesamtkunstwerk*, a fairly common idea of German transcendentalism. The notion of a work of art that would synthesize all the arts is a logical consequence of the transcendental notion that each of the arts says the same thing in a different way, but that each of those ways is necessary because each corresponds to a different facet of human behavior. If the work of art is to be fully functional, it must appeal to and make use of the whole range of human personality and behavior.

As we have seen, Baudelaire also noticed the same tendency in the arts of the 1830's and the 1840's, and he was, naturally enough, particularly engaged in the phenomena of synesthesia, of hearing paintings, seeing music, and experiencing the vowels by means of color sensations. To the transcendentalist determined to play the heroic redeemer of society, the *Gesamtkunstwerk* was precisely the aesthetic form to be used, for it could appeal simultaneously not only to all facets of the personality but to all types of human beings, no matter which aesthetic and sensory sensitivity was dominant. Furthermore, if the task was to create a functional substitute for religion, there was already in existence ample proof of the social and individual efficacy of the *Gesamtkunstwerk*—the Catholic Mass, which even appealed to the sense of smell, a device that Wagner never cared to try.

Yet Wagner, born in 1813, and therefore younger than the generation of Carlyle and Delacroix, was not one of the creators of transcendentalism, as the slightly older and more rapidly maturing Schumann was, but rather, by growing up in the transcendental ambience, was highly sensitive to the problem of how the heroic redeemer could fulfill his destiny without exerting morally irresponsible power. Even before he had fully realized the question and worked out the implications he was somehow aware that the transcendental attempt to redeem society was not going to work.

Here, perhaps, a word of explanation is necessary. Wagner has been so identified in the popular mind and among high-level anti-Wagnerians with Hitler and Nazism that he has become almost a kind of symbol of the brutal and irresponsible wielding of social power. Actually, a graver mistake, a more erroneous misreading of Wagner's libretti would be impossible to imagine. If the Nazis had understood Wagner they would have banned him; if they had been capable of believing him, they would never have been Nazis. Unfortunately, this misunderstood power complex of Wagner's—for, as we shall see, he was profoundly concerned with the nature of social power—has been extended to a judgment of his music, which many experience as a violation. When a great genius, like all of the transcendentalists I have touched on, as well as a good many others I have not, creates a profoundly original and new style to convey an equally original and novel orientation, the shock of disorientation is almost unbearable.

The effect of Wagner is constantly compared, by the unsympathetic, to emotional rape, to being violated by an irresistible emotional power. To the sympathetic, however, the effect is precisely opposite. It is intensely emotional, to be sure, but it is an illumination, not a rape or a violation. Further, the full response to Wagner is as intellectual as it is emotional. This is related to another commonly encountered misjudgment of his work, in this case one simply based on inadequate evidence. The most familiar parts of Wagner, especially in the United States, are certain excerpts, "The Entrance of the Gods into Valhalla," "The Ride of the Valkyries," the overtures and preludes to *The Flying Dutchman, Tannhäuser,* and *Lohengrin,* and so on. From these the naïve concert goer judges what he has not heard, the total work, thinking that such concert excerpts are typical. The contrary is true. When a Wagnerian opera is properly produced, it is given in a fairly small theater; it is intimate, it is highly intellectual, and much of it, most of it, even, is closer to chamber music than to grand opera. Further, the excerpts when given a concert presentation, are in themselves often misunderstood. A couple of examples will suffice. "The Entrance of the Gods" is often sneered at as musical pomposity. Such a judgment does credit to the sneerers. It *is* pompous; it is supposed to be; it is an ironic comment on the hollowness of Wotan's victory. Likewise the "Love Death" from *Tristan and Isolde* is thought of as a marvelous apotheosis of erotic love; actually it is ironic. As we shall see, the whole point of *Tristan* is that erotic love is an illusion.

In truth, few nineteenth-century artists have been so grossly misunderstood, as much by his adorers as by his haters. Actually, he was concerned with only one problem, though with endless ramifications of it: Art, through the artist, is the source of human value. The artist cannot re-enter society. How is the value of which he is the bearer to be made socially valid? The gap between artist and society cannot be closed; neither can it be permanently bridged. How can it be crossed? Is it the artist's responsibility to cross over to the public? Is it the public's responsibility to cross over to the artist? Must the lightning the artist wields be tamed, channeled, masked, perhaps, to make it available to others? And if it should be, how can that ultimate responsibility of the artist be discharged?

All of Wagner's creative career and of his practical career, as a man of the theater, as a public figure, was devoted to this one problem. Nor is he in this sense atypical. From the beginning, as we have seen, the nineteenth-century thinker, in making the distinction between self and role, makes the distinction between moral responsibility and morality. Should Wagner, like Balzac and Carlyle and Berlioz, tell people directly what they should do? Impossible; he was young enough to see that that tactic would not work.

From this standpoint it can be said that his ten major works from *The Flying Dutchman* to *Parsifal* in reality compose one gigantic work in ten acts. It is useful, at this point, to have a list of them with the dates of composition.

| | |
|---|---|
| The Flying Dutchman | 1841 |
| Tannhäuser | 1843-44 |
| Lohengrin | 1846-48 |
| The Ring of the Nibelung | 1853-74 |
|     The Rhinegold | 1853-54 |
|     The Valkyrie | 1854-56 |
|     Siegfried | 1856-71 |
|     The Twilight of the Gods | 1869-74 |
| Tristan and Isolde | 1857-59 |
| The Meistersinger of Nürnberg | 1862-67 * |
| Parsifal | 1877-82 |

(* These two works were composed between Acts II and III of *Siegfried*.)

But this list gives a somewhat distorted picture. Actually even before each work was finished, the new one was germinating in his mind, and the libretti were, of course, written before the actual musical composition was begun. Wagner's creative life, then, was virtually continuous for more than forty years; and it was devoted to an exhaustive exploration of a single intellectual problem and of a single musical problem. Since the musical problem was the one we have already explored in Berlioz and Schumann, how to control musical significance through literary analogy, it is possible, though somewhat unrealistic, to take up the two problems separately. But if we do so, at least it will make a fearfully complicated matter somewhat easier to handle and to grasp.

## 1. WAGNER'S DRAMAS

*The Flying Dutchman* (the story came from Heine) revives an older symbol and gives it a new significance. The Dutchman is an outcast and a wanderer, modeled on the Ancient Mariner-Harold-Manfred tradition. He is cursed to sail forever, with no hope of death. But there is a difference from the older figure. His crime is known and he has hope of redemption. He refused to submit to the arbitrary and cruel jokes of nature and of God; he will be saved if he can find a woman who will be true to him even to death. Every seven years he is permitted to come to land and seek such a woman, but he has never found her. He is, then, alienated from society and isolated in a universe which derives no meaning from either nature or nature's God. The ocean, in a fairly well-established tradition, is a symbol of the valueless self; the land, of the valueless society, in which the bad are strong and the good are powerless.

Senta, however, whose father is willing to sell her to the Dutchman, has long loved his portrait and his story. When her father brings the Dutchman to her, she swears undying love; but the suspicious Dutchman, overhearing a conversation between Senta and Erik, her now rejected suitor, misunderstands the distinction between Senta's love for Erik, which is of the land, of society, only a social role, and her love for him, which is of the ocean, of the self. He rushes back to the sea; Senta leaps after him into the waves. The ship sinks, and he and Senta soar upward over the wreck, in each other's arms. The wreck of the accursed ship and their salvation above the sea indicates that the ocean is itself cleansed and redeemed. That is, the self is redeemed and made radiant with value, while the land remains valueless. What appears to be death to the onlooking landsmen is in actuality life, the life of the self, redeemed by love.

Nor is it by any means an accident that the staging requires the audience to be of the party of the landsmen, of social death. They think of the Dutchman as a terrible and cursed ghost, something supernatural. Only Senta is capable of escaping that orientation and recognizing the Dutchman's human identity, a spiritual redirection which she is able to achieve only because she is familiar with the song of the Dutchman (known as Senta's ballad) and with his portrait. That is, her redemption from society, which accomplishes the Dutchman's redemption from the valueless self, is brought about by her contemplation of works of art.

Redemption through woman and woman's love is one of the great themes of transcendentalism. Goethe was by no means alone in his use of *"das Ewigweibliche"*—"the eternal feminine" —as the intrument of redemption. At the end of *Faust*, he was extremely close to asymmetrical transcendentalism; and woman occupies the place in that stage of the nineteenth-century vision which nature occupies in the symmetrical stage. The men of the first stage could break the bonds of egocentricity by the intuitive, analogous, vision into nature as a symbol of value; but that way was closed to the asymmetrists. Only another human being could make that break possible by accepting the love or empathy of the alienated outcast and by returning it. In either case the process was a recognition of the self beneath the role. Woman was selected as the proper symbol because of her power to love in spite of society, of her biologic and economic necessity to think more in terms of individuality than of collectivity. That it was not a matter of erotic love is apparent from the frequency with which a friend of the same sex performs the necessary act of recognizing the self beneath the role, a symbolization which found its most important literary embodiment in Tennyson's *In Memoriam*.

In spite of the fact that art releases Senta, and Senta redeems the Dutchman's selfhood and sense of value, the outcast is still dependent upon a force within society for his redemption. Although Wagner has gone beyond the point where social re-entry is seen as the consummation of redemption, he is not free of social dependence. How was redemption to be achieved independently of social recognition? He returned to the problem in *Tannhäuser*. Here the protagonist is an artist, specifically a musician and poet, like Wagner himself. It is Wagner's most intensely personal work. At the same time it marks another step out of the transcendental position; the symbolism is almost entirely Christian and it is extremely easy to give it a traditional Christian interpretation as a conflict between profane and sacred love, between *eros* and *agapé*. Wagner here begins to use a solution to the problem of the gap between artist and society which others of his contemporaries, Tennyson, for example, also adopted. It is an exoteric-esoteric device; that is, it presents to society a perfectly consistent structure of meanings which conforms with its dominating orientative symbolism; but on the other hand, it holds an interior meaning which is quite different, indeed, quite opposed.

*Tannhäuser* replaces the ocean with the cave, and Senta with Venus-Elisabeth. As the work opens, Tannhäuser is in the cave of Venus; he is the self-in-hiding in the paradise of total gratification—but he can't stand it. Urged by the drive toward reality, he rejects paradise and returns to the world. There at the contest of song he mocks the sentimental eroticism of the Minnesingers (the knightly love singers) and praises the erotic realities of Venus. Horrified and shocked, the knights would destroy him, but he is saved by Elisabeth, who insists that he have the chance to redeem himself by going to Rome. The pope, equally horrified at his worship of a pagan goddess, condemns him to hell. Bitterly, Tannhäuser sets out to return to Venus, but the utterance of the name of Elisabeth stops him, and her death permits him to die, while the chorus sings of her entry to heaven and her pleading before God for Tannhäuser's soul. He is saved. He is saved not because of institutionalized Christianity but in spite of it. Elisabeth, it turns out, not only loves Tannhäuser; she em-

pathizes with him. In her prayer to the Virgin she admits to precisely those same erotic desires which the sentimental knights
refuse to accept, and it is the stifling of those desires, their denial,
which kills her. To clinch this, the dead staff of the pope, which
he said could no more put forth leaves than Tannhäuser could be
saved, is brought in at the end by the young pilgrims; it is in
full leaf.

Tannhäuser, then, dies because there is no one left in the
real world who can accept him with his erotic desires, in the
totality of his personal identity. From Tannhäuser's point of view,
the Venusberg, the paradise of erotic fulfillment, is a bore, but at
least it is better than the sentimentalities and falsehoods of society.
Nevertheless, Elisabeth's position is equivocal. On the one hand
she wishes to return Tannhäuser to society; on the other, her
identification with Tannhäuser kills her. Further, Wagner still
has not resolved the problem of making the hero independent of
someone within society who will confirm his sense of identity and
release him from egocentricity. He has to re-examine the problem
in *Lohengrin*.

This work is a political drama. The transcendental hero
descends into the world at a time of political-social crisis, when
the heathen hordes are attacking the old Holy Roman Empire
from the east, and the concealed heathens within Brabant have
spirited away the heir to the throne. Only when the crisis within
Brabant has been solved can its resources be added to the empire's
and the threat to European civilization be met. Emerging from the
realm of pure value, Lohengrin at first appears to solve the crisis
by saving Elsa from the false accusation that she murdered her
brother, and by his marriage to Elsa becoming himself the ruler of
Brabant and the ally of the emperor. Nevertheless he fails. Elsa
insists on knowing his name and his origin; that is, she demands
his authority as a representative of society and the heir of its
leadership.

At this point Wagner perceives the limitations of the
transcendental effort to redeem the world. Elsa the Christian has
been seduced into doing what she promised not to by Ortrud, the

secret pagan. They are, in short, sisters under the skin. Between paganism and Christianity there is no difference. Both are merely instruments by which society exerts its control over mankind. Both are implements of social power. The failure in *Lohengrin* is dual. When the hero at last achieves complete independence from society, his redemptive power is compromised by his lack of authority. At the same time the orientations of society are seen as invalid. Wagner attempts to resolve the problem by having Lohengrin restore the Prince, whom he had saved from Ortrud by turning him into a swan, and give him his own sword, horn, and ring, standing for a prince's power and duty to defend his people, to summon them to cooperation, and to pledge his life to the values of Lohengrin.

The transcendental hero, then, cannot himself redeem society, but he can make the natural leader—as Balzac and Carlyle hoped—into a redemptive instrument. Yet this solution also leaves unsolved difficulties. If society stubbornly resists redemption by the hero, why cannot it just as well resist the hero's representative and surrogate? And further, is not Lohengrin's preservation of the Prince in the shape of a swan somewhat equivocal? If Ortrud had not uttered her triumph, would not the Prince have remained a swan? Is not Lohengrin, then, exerting arbitrary power? Is he not violating another identity in order to wield social power? And does not this compromise his whole position?

To answer these questions Wagner set out to write another work, which developed into a tetralogy and took him nearly thirty years to complete and bring to the stage. To do so he had to create a new kind of singer, a new kind of orchestra and orchestral conducting, a new kind of theater—the best theater for opera ever built—and a new kind of financing, the festival. It also took a king and the cooperation, not always willing, of a small bourgeois German city. But he did it.

There are two ways to discuss the *Ring*. One way takes hundreds of pages, even if one neglects the music; the only other way is to be exceedingly brief. I shall, perforce, take the latter. Like *Faust*, the *Ring* seems inexhaustible—certainly no one has yet exhausted it—and as rich and complex in meaning as life itself. Like *Faust* it is in the high nineteenth-century style; it defies final interpretation; for it evolves from an irreducible paradox. Yet the delights of returning to it are endless, for one always finds another bit to be fitted in, or something ignored that puts much of the action in a new light. I can only hope to say enough to induce the reader to continue his own investigations with the interpretative instrument I offer.

The first thing to be noted is the mythology. To root out the cancer of humanity's social life, Wagner uses ancient German and Scandinavian mythology and legend, just as in *Tannhäuser* and *Lohengrin* he had used Christian mythology. In the manner of Feuerbach, whom he had just read, he sees all mythologies as equivalent. Before he finishes the *Ring*, he will see none as valid. For the moment, in the tradition of Herder, he sees German mythology as particularly appropriate for a German artist and a German public. The second point is to note the order in which the *Ring* was written. It is not enough to say, as is often said, that he wrote it backward. Actually he wrote backward, forward, and sideways. After he had worked from *Siegfried's Death* back to *The Rhinegold*, he reworked the tetralogy, changing *Siegfried's Death* to *The Twilight of the Gods* and to it adding a prologue which explains events before *The Rhinegold* begins. The work would be more immediately comprehensible had he preceded *The Rhinegold* with another short work called *The World Ash Tree*. For the events of the *Ring* really begin when Wotan breaks off a branch from the tree that supports the world, shapes it into a spear, and carves on it his runes of world governance.

The meaning of the *Ring* emerged slowly, over many years, and the history of its composition is the history of how Wagner, who thought symbolically before he conceptualized his insights, worked out the problem he had set himself. The original ending was to have Siegfried reconciled with Wotan, in Valhalla, and this reconciliation was to symbolize the solution of society's ills, the successful excision of its cancer, the patient restored to health. The Wotan-Siegfried relationship is a repetition of the Lohengrin-

Prince of Brabant dualism, the self-conscious transcendental hero and his unself-conscious instrument. It is precisely the same relationship as was to exist between Carlyle-Balzac and their captains of industry.

Wagner begins, then, at exactly the point *Lohengrin* leaves off, with the morally equivocal problem which was left hanging in the air as Lohengrin returned to Monsalvat, the realm of pure value. It is no surprise to discover that the sword, the horn, and the ring, are carried over from *Lohengrin* into the next work. To them is added the spear. But after Wagner's encounter with Schopenhauer's philosophy, which crystallized conceptually what he had already begun to see symbolically—indeed had felt even in *The Flying Dutchman*—the whole character and point of the work changed. In the new ending there is no redemption of society, no reconciliation between Wotan and Siegfried, no after-life for Siegfried and Brünnhilde in Valhalla; Valhalla is itself destroyed, and the ring goes back to the Rhine, from which it had been torn. The writing of the *Ring* is the history of Wagner's solution of the problems posed by *Lohengrin:* that solution is the failure of the transcendental hero, the impossibility of an adequate society.

The *Ring* is usually discussed as if Siegfried were the transcendental hero. But Siegfried is unself-conscious, unable to use the sudden insights he occasionally has, fearless only because he is ignorant and stupid. No, Wotan is the transcendental hero who attempts to introduce pure value into society by his control over the ultimate source of human and social energy, unconscious psychic life, the ash tree that supports the world. By identifying the transcendental artist-hero we can understand that this shaping of the spear broken from the ash tree symbolizes how the transcendental poet-hero controls the world by controlling the human imagination. In the terms of this book, whoever controls the shaping power of men's orientations controls society. Yet Wotan desires to use this power responsibly; he carves upon the spear the laws that bind him to man's service, laws which sustain his power. If he transgresses those laws, his power is lost. Wotan symbolizes, then, one kind of social power, from which he successively creates social order, freedom, and love.

But there is another kind of power in the world also, economic power, the treasure of gold guarded by the daughters of the river Rhine. It is natural power. The ash tree supports the world, true. The world is, in Schopenhauer's form of Kantianism, representation (or idea). But this is no Platonic idealism. The world is there, it exists. Man cannot know it, but he experiences it through the will, and above all through the frustration of the will. Alberich, the gnome, baffled, mocked, and humiliated by the Rhine daughters, whom he attempts to love, seizes upon the gold as compensation for his frustrated eroticism. (The significance of the erotic problem in *Tannhäuser* is thus clarified and made certain: sexuality is a reality which cannot be idealized away.) The desire for economic power over society takes its origin from the frustration of the human will as it expresses itself in erotic love. Freud himself could say no more on the subject.

Wotan is now faced with an appalling paradox. There are two kinds of power in the world, imaginative and economic (or natural). Economic power cannot of itself become morally responsible; it is compensation for frustration, and no compensation can ever make up for what frustration loses. Imaginative power, Wotan thinks, can be made morally responsible by self-limitation. But because it is limited, such power cannot endure the existence of any other kind or source of power. *All* power must be under control. Wotan, too, has been motivated by love for man and by his desire to create for man a satisfactory world. His love is now frustrated; to overcome that frustration he must break his own laws; he must win the gold from Alberich by thievery and trickery. His moral position is now fatally compromised. His paradox is this: to be morally responsible, power must be self-limiting; but limited power is a contradiction, a paradox. Power, therefore, cannot be made morally responsible. Erda, the earth goddess, the goddess of things as they are, the goddess of the impregnable resistance of reality to human desire and will, warns Wotan that he must give up the ring or lose his power; and that even if he does, he will lose his power anyway. *"Ein düst'rer Tag dämmert den Göttern."*

Erda's sentence is almost untranslatable, for *"dämmern"* means both to dawn and to become dark or dusky: *Götterdämmerung* should really be translated "The Dusk-Dawn of the Gods." The pun symbolizes the whole paradox of Wotan and the *Ring*. Wagner here exhibits the kind of thinking we have seen before, and seen as one of the central ideas of the nineteenth-century vision; not the reconciliation of opposites and antinomies but the full exposure to them and acceptance of them in all their irreducible polarity—this is the task of the thinker-artist.

Once the paradox of Erda's warning is grasped, the rest of the *Ring* is comprehensible. Wotan himself, however, does not, cannot, understand her. He will refuse to accept the unacceptable. He is determined to find a solution to the unsolvable. He gives the ring to the giants—he turns over the economic nexus of society to the workers, who have so little idea of what to do with it that one giant kills the other and makes off with it, to become a dragon and sleep on it forever, if possible. But Wotan enters the newly built Valhalla from which he hopes his power will emanate to establish order and value in the world. And as he and the gods march over the rainbow bridge the Rhine daughters sing from below that only in their world is the true, that the world of the gods is false and cowardly.

With this much understood, the rest of the story, the working out of the consequences, can be examined rapidly. Wotan first establishes social order among men and then attempts to create a hero (Siegmund) who will be the instrument of his will and capture for him the ring. But as Fricka, the goddess of social morality, points out, in doing so he has violated his own laws. Wotan realizes that he has deceived himself. He has destroyed the very social order he has created. (The Lohengrin-Prince of Brabant equivocation is here finally admitted.) He cannot create a free man. His will simultaneously desires social freedom and social slavery. The paradox of reality has invaded the personality of the transcendental hero. He thinks now of only waiting for the end, and he sets out to destroy his will, Brünnhilde, his daughter by Erda, the offspring of the union of idea and reality. But once again he deceives himself, for he thinks that by releasing his will into society, by freeing it of its responsibility to him, he can enable it to control the free hero, the child of Siegmund, who is an accidental result of Wotan's attempt to create a redeemer. (The Siegmund-Siegfried pair correspond to the Prince of Brabant as a swan and as restored to his human form, with sword, ring, and horn. Mime, Siegfried's foster parent, makes him a horn; he himself forges a sword; and from the slain dragon's hoard he takes the ring.)

As I suggested above, the shift from Siegmund to Siegfried corresponds to the cultural shift by which the transcendental hero stepped back from attempting to control society directly to attempting to control it indirectly. His power over the imagination conceals itself behind freedom—Siegfried—and love—Brünnhilde—the two forms of the hidden will. Yet love in its boundless desire to have complete control over its object, destroys freedom; woman, in her determination to make man submit to biological necessity, destroys his autonomy. And freedom, in its fearless and blind and stupid conviction that it is adequate to the conditions which reality imposes upon man, destroys love; man destroys woman in the effort to maintain his autonomy. To gratify man's free exercise of his power over reality, one woman is as good as another; Gutrune can serve Siegfried's purposes as well as Brünnhilde; to gratify woman's biological drives, only one man will do. (Thus the sentimentality of *"das Ewigweibliche"* is exposed.) Siegfried consequently underestimates the capacity of reality to frustrate his will; he is destroyed through the machinations of Hagen, the son of Alberich. In fact, Hagen, whom in his fearless illusion of adequacy Siegfried has failed to understand, kills him; the uncontrollable and frustrated desire for economic power destroys the instrument of the transcendental hero, Wotan. Wotan can no longer avoid recognizing his self-deceptions and the unresolvable paradox of reality. Love achieves its only gratification possible, death. The ring returns to the Rhine daughters, who drown Alberich in the flooding waters of their river. Valhalla burns; the gods are destroyed. In the orchestra the theme of the will-to-live finally reaches a resolution on a major chord, which dies away into silence. The will can be gratified only when the world of man ceases to exist; that is, it can never be gratified.

In a word, or a few, Wagner's point is this: the transcendental hero cannot redeem society. Not because he does not have access to value; he does. But that value cannot be realized in a world impregnable to morality. The attempt to make social power morally responsible only reveals the morally irresponsible power of nature. From the power of the imagination imposed upon reality flow social order, love, and freedom, but the imaginative and value-laden will, when it encounters the unshakable amorality of nature, can only destroy the very values of order, love, and freedom which it has created. The transcendental hero cannot solve the problems of society because the problems of society, since it is a natural product, are unsolvable.

To clarify what has happened to the nineteenth-century vision, let me summarize the developing issues as sharply as I can. After the negative phase, value was found immanent in the self, and symbolically in nature. It was then drained from nature and found only in the self, but capable of being embodied in society. At the end of the *Ring* society and nature are placed in the same category, valueless, unredeemably resistant to being impregnated with value. Nor is this all. The gods die. Wotan, unlike Lohengrin, does not leave the world; he is destroyed with it. The transcendental vision of value is shorn of its transcendental authority, of its divinity, of its godhead. The question now remaining is this: Does value exist at all? Or are we back to the total negation of Werther and Manfred? Does the world offer no gratification for the orientative drive?

Before Wagner finished the *Ring*—before he could finish the *Ring*, or better still, before he could bear to finish the *Ring*—he wrote *Tristan and Isolde* and *The Meistersinger*. Wagner did not commit suicide, even symbolically. He not only finished the *Ring*; he carried through the almost inconceivable financial and theatrical labors required to stage it in Bayreuth in 1876, the year, it is worth remembering, all of *Faust* was first staged. Either he did not take the *Ring* seriously, did not believe what it said, or he had found an answer to it. After all, although Schopenhauer had clarified his deepest convictions, he had gone far beyond Schopenhauer in the depths of his pessimism. It is much more difficult, because more convincing, more real, more irresistible for creator and receiver, to symbolize a vision than it is to conceptualize it. Schopenhauer is bracing, even amusing, clever and witty; but the *Ring*, when it is intellectually, symbolically, and musically experienced, is chilling, terrifying—or would be, were it not for one thing. The *Ring* is, ultimately, not tragic but triumphant.

Man's tragedy, Goethe had said in *Faust*, comes from his inability to accept his inadequacy before the demands which the conditions of experience make of him. Hence he must always have a Mephistopheles at his side. Before the nineteenth century, tragedy reconciled man to life by persuading him to submit to the orientations of his society. It continued to be what it was in its origins, a religious ritual. Wagner, however, by destroying society *and* the hero, not just the hero, achieves his triumph by enduring and making it possible for us to endure the vision that man's problem cannot be solved, that man is inadequate. He goes beyond the negative symmetry of Schopenhauer and also beyond Goethe, who said that man cannot live without Mephistopheles, without a magical or transcendental or religious or divine prop for his orientations. Wagner disagrees; man, he says, *can* live without Mephistopheles. Hence Wotan dies. The completion of the *Ring* was preceded by the creation of a realistic comedy; but that in turn was preceded by an exploration of the illusions of transcendentalism.

*Tristan and Isolde* was written after Wagner had composed the *Ring* through the second act of Siegfried. Immediately before him lay Siegfried's awakening of Brünnhilde and their love. Since this love was to lead to disaster, and love was to be revealed as destructive, Wagner had to run counter to the whole transcendental tradition of erotic love, which was, as one might expect, one of the few transcendental notions which had penetrated deeply into the public mind. In a society which was becoming steadily more puritanical, any thing that sanctified sexuality by coloring it with a quasi-religious light was bound to be popular. That the public still does not comprehend the real meaning of transcendental love is plain when one examines middle-class fiction today, particularly as it appears in magazines and moving pictures. *Tristan*, as a result, has always been the most completely misunderstood of all of Wagner's works. One of Freud's least popular remarks is his statement that he regarded love as the model psychosis; Wagner would have agreed with him, and he said as much in *Tristan*.

Yet when he came to the third act of *Siegfried*, he himself still accepted the tradition. *Tristan* is an exploration of its significance. Once and once only, in a passage usually cut in performance, partly because most tenors are afraid to sing it, does Wagner's real meaning come through explicitly. In the third act, Tristan curses the drink, the love potion, which ostensibly was the cause of his and Isolde's fatal passion. But then he penetrates to the perception that he himself brewed the drink, that the poison of love in it came from his father's need and his mother's sorrow. And he curses the drink, and he who brewed it—himself. The sorrowing Kurvenal bends over his master's prostrate body and cries out against love, "the world's fairest illusion." Erotic love, then, is a projection, a self-created mask which the lover places over the face and the form of the beloved. Lovers do not see each other at all. They see only themselves. Thus Tristan reaches an emotional consummation of his love when Isolde is not with him, and he is dying; and Isolde reaches her ecstasy when Tristan is dead, though she is firmly convinced, to the moment of her own death, that he still lives. Further, the climax of her emotion is identical with her total loss of identity and her merging with nothingness.

Thus, the love scene in the garden is entirely an analysis of how two lovers exploit each other's emotions. Their whole effort is to merge their two identities and together vanish away into night and nothingness, to become one with the universe. Unfortunately reality intrudes, as it always does. Death is the only gateway that leads to this goal, but when you are dead you can scarcely enjoy the loss of identity. Transcendental erotic love, then, is an unrealizable ideal, because it pursues a symbol and not a reality. It is an insanity. Far from being an apotheosis of love, *Tristan* strips the mask from one of mankind's most cherished orientative gratifications and reveals it as an illusion. But even more is involved.

The weakness of transcendental love, even when, as it often was, it was recognized as a symbol, was that it was a resolution to the problem of transcendental authority. As we have seen, if the beloved confirmed the identity of the transcendentalist by loving him in return, thus confirming him as a bearer of divine value, the lover then became dependent upon the beloved. The situation exhibits the same pattern as the transcendental heroic redeemer whose unself-conscious representative and instrument is within society. The lover is therefore exploiting the beloved; at the same time his dependency upon her denies the very thing his love is designed to achieve, a confirmation of his independent identity and selfhood. The pattern has the weakness of all forms of transcendentalism; it imagines that the not-self can in fact be redeemed into value by the activities of the self at the level of the social role. A dual violation takes place. The lover violates the beloved by exploiting her as a symbol; and he violates himself by making his identity depend upon a symbol. If identity can be affirmed only by affirming another's identity, transcendental love is unable to turn the trick.

Attention, therefore, shifts to the reason for this inconsistency; and it is what we have already seen: the need for authority, the need for the confirmation of the divinity of the self. Wagner has taken the whole problem of the *Ring* and narrowed it down to the relation between two people. This pinpointing enables him to see that the illusion of love is caused by the illusion of divinity. Consequently, the divine world of value which Tristan and Isolde strive to reach cannot be reached, because it doesn't exist. The divine, unconscious ground of the universe is mere night and nothingness. The problem he had to solve in the *Ring* is now clear, but to finish it he had first to write *The Meistersinger*.

Even anti-Wagnerians like *The Meistersinger*, but they understand it no better than their enemies do. The symbolic structure is extraordinarily complex. Hans Sachs, for instance, is also God, John the Baptist, the self-conscious nineteenth-century artist free from transcendental illusions, and the mature Wagner. Walther is Adam, Christ, the unself-conscious nineteenth-century artist still caught in the illusions of religion and love, and the young Wagner. This is just a bit of it, and to work it all out is a delightful—and instructive—exercise in literary interpretation. But the whole thing is masked in an adept historical realism. To distinguish it from transcendental realism I shall call it objectist realism, for reasons to be discussed later. Here it is enough to say that this kind of realism is the artistic expression of seeing transcendental divinity as pretension and illusion. For this orientation there is no divine ground to the universe, no opening out of the unconscious self into the Godhead. Since the artist cannot claim a transcendental authority for his style, he must turn elsewhere, outside of art, or to earlier art, for a model; he derives his controlling structure from science, from history, from pre-nineteenth-century or "classic" models, from folk art, from medieval and Greek and Roman art. Thus *The Meistersinger of Nürnberg* is not only, literarily, a "classic" and highly traditional comedy, modeled on eighteenth-century intrigue-comedies; it also is more traditionally operatic than anything since *Lohengrin*, with choruses, duets, concerted pieces, and even something like the old-fashioned aria. Its musical texture is very close to that of Bach; and the general atmosphere, flow, and easy continuity are closely related to the great Mozart operas, particularly *The Marriage of Figaro*. But it is no mere revivalism. It is vitalized by Wagner's controlling vision, which is wholly of the nineteenth century.

The theme is *Wahn*, illusion. The question of the opera is how a new art is to supersede an old art, when the old art has the political and social power and the new art has none. Clearly, put in this form, the problem is one that Wagner struggled with all his life. But it is also to be noted that this, the problem of social power, is precisely the problem of the *Ring*. Hans Sachs is the transcendental hero shorn not only of any hope of redeeming society but also stripped of transcendental illusions. Not only does society refuse to recognize his authority; he himself refuses. Consequently it is only with the utmost hesitation, doubts, self-questionings, and modesty that Sachs interferes with the situation at all, to unite the young lovers, Eva and Walther, and to have Walther's genius recognized. But he has one powerful weapon. Stripped of illusions he can recognize and identify the illusions of others, particularly those illusions which persuade people who have social power that they ought to have social power because they deserve it. In his great monologue he says, "Illusion, illusion, everywhere illusion." But his analysis leads him to his solution. "If you would do a great thing, you must manipulate people's illusions." To free mankind of its illusions is impossible. Illusion is the mode in which man exists.

Only one thing in the world is free of the curse of illusion: art, because it does not pretend to anything else. Consequently Walther is no transcendental artist-hero. He is simply a nice young man who can write beautiful poetry and set it to beautiful music, once he has learned how to integrate his own natural genius into the great stream of aesthetic culture and tradition. (It is worth remembering here that even as early as 1838 Wagner was already immensely learned in the whole history of European music; and The Meistersinger shows greater contrapuntal mastery than any European composer had demonstrated since Bach.) Walther introduces value into the world solely because he creates a beautiful work of art. Man lives in a world of illusions which he hangs onto by deceiving himself that they have either natural or divine authority and right. He can do no other. He is dependent on illusion because illusion sustains him. Only art can give him freedom from illusion ; for art now claims no illusory authority.

In precisely those years when Wagner was working on The Meistersinger, Robert Browning, the English poet, was saying the same thing in The Ring and the Book. Art is "true" because it is a lie and doesn't pretend to be anything else. Art cannot redeem the world, but it can give the man who looks at the world the experience of value. By manipulating illusions and releasing the power of art, Hans Sachs establishes a relation among the artist, the people, and the holders of social power. The power of art is now clear. It introduces value into the world by creating in the hearts of men the experience of order and meaning. To assert the existence of order, meaning, and value, whether natural, divine, or transcendent, is an illusion; to experience them is essential to maintaining life. Art is the source of that experience.

Nevertheless, a moral problem remained unresolved. The Sachs-Walther relationship retains traces of the Lohengrin-Prince of Brabant equivocation, and the Wotan-Siegfried-Siegmund situation. Sachs manipulates people; he plays God; it cannot be said that he violates them, except indirectly. Yet the moral task of the nineteenth-century man is not fulfilled if he simply helps people to release their natural talents. This is not to confirm their identity but only to involve them in a social role. From this point of view, the task is to free people from their illusions. *Tristan* and *The Meistersinger* gave Wagner the insight to complete the *Ring* and the moral courage to carry through the gigantic task of staging it. Yet his original question, "How is the ultimate responsibility of the artist to be discharged?" had not yet received an adequate answer. After the *Ring* had been triumphantly produced, he turned almost at once to *Parsifal.*

As we have seen, Wagner had long since carried Feuerbach's ideas to their logical conclusions. In conceptualizing orientations man only talks about himself. Religions, constitutive metaphysical systems, and similar symbolizations are useful only when their symbolic nature is realized. Asserted to be true, they are all illusions. In writing *Parsifal*, Wagner, with joking irony, employed the dominating illusion of Europe, Christianity. It was a joke Nietzsche never caught on to, unfortunately. For Wagner presented the work with all the panoply and seriousness of a religious festival. It is absurd that it should always be given at Easter; it is absurd that applause should be forbidden; intellectually serious Catholics—of whom there are a few—are quite right in their suspicions of it. Wagner turned Bayreuth into a religious temple not because he took Christianity seriously but because he took the theater—art—seriously. As Francis Bacon might have put it, the proper place for the idols of the theater, those religious and philosophical fancies men entertain each other with, is the theater.

Religion does not redeem art when *Parsifal* is produced; art redeems religion by exposing it as a symbol and thus releasing the individual to see what is really going on in the work. It is hardly necessary to say that almost no one ever takes the opportunity Wagner offers him. *Parsifal* is like the Bible; people are so overcome by the religious aura that they fail to understand what it says. If they understood the Bible, they would certainly keep it from their children, nor would they read it themselves except behind closed doors. Today, in Germany, Catholic clergymen are beginning to urge their flocks not to attend *Parsifal*. It must be admitted that Wagner is beginning to be understood.

In actual fact, *Parsifal* is far easier to understand than anything else Wagner ever wrote. It is perfectly plain that the Christian brotherhood of the grail and their leaders have failed, that they do not save Parsifal. On the contrary it is Parsifal who saves them. It is equally clear that Parsifal earns his own redemption not through religion but through psychological insight and empathy. Parsifal is a pure fool, free from social and religious illusions. Thus when Kundry attempts to seduce him, by empathy he feels the wound of Amfortas, whom Kundry has seduced and violated, and he realizes that it is not Kundry who tempts him but the mask of Herzeleide, his mother, which she is wearing. Here, then, is the root of the madness of erotic passion. Freud was to say no more.

Klingsor, the magician who has attempted to control eroticism by self-castration, hurls the sacred spear. Amfortas, the King of the Grail Knights, had lost the spear when he succumbed to Kundry. The attempt to control illusory eroticism by Christian repression is futile; hence his own spear, wielded by Klingsor, has given him his wound, which will not heal. But Parsifal, who has seen through eroticism, cannot be harmed; he grasps the spear. This spear is Wotan's spear, with a difference. It symbolizes power, to be sure, but not power over others; rather, power over the self, control of identity through insight, an insight, it must be remembered, made possible by means of the power of empathy. As we have seen, deriving value from the self leads to egocentricity unless that egocentricity is overcome. Wagner reverses this scheme. Identity and value are achieved at the moment of empathy and insight. The two psychic acts are simultaneous. The problem of egocentricity does not arise, for egocentricity is the consequence of believing illusions. Egocentricity is the character of the Christian Amfortas, wounded by his surrender of identity to the illusions of religion and love.

After years of wandering, fighting, and suffering, during which he confirms his insight by sharing the suffering of humanity, Parsifal returns to the temple of the grail. There once more the spear and the grail are united. The grail is the vessel of nurturance, of love, of true femininity, just as the spear is the symbol of true masculinity. Both of them are independent of biological sexuality. Men and women alike must be capable of both identity and love, with neither submissive to the other, nor dependent, nor exploiting, nor violating. This point is underlined by the death of Kundry, who appears in two forms, the household slave and the great whore, the eternal erotic enchantress—but in both against her will, violated. Women, Wagner is saying, have been denied their identity and their true power of nurturing others by being condemned by men to role-playing. It is curious that Leopold von Sacher-Masoch had made precisely the same point in the famous—or infamous—*Venus in Furs*, published in 1870. Masochism, he says, or submissiveness in men, and sadism, or psychic domination in women, will exist as long as women are condemned to these two roles and not permitted to be human beings.

In reuniting grail and spear Parsifal rescues the Christian grail knights from extinction. He does nothing, it is to be noticed; he simply displays the spear. Amfortas yields his kingship to Parsifal and in the dome mysterious voices are heard singing, "The highest wonder of salvation! Redemption to the redeemer!" Only the self-redeemed is truly redeemed. It is impossible even for the artist, even for Hans Sachs, to redeem someone else. Only he who has freed himself from the illusions of man and at the same time has seen them as necessary to man, is genuinely redeemed. Thus the equivocal Lohengrin-Prince and Sachs-Walter relationships are at last terminated. Gurnemanz attempts to instruct Parsifal but fails. Parsifal must instruct himself. The moral responsibility of the re-deeming artist, therefore, cannot be discharged by giving freedom, identity, and love to another, for the gift cannot be made. He can only construct a work of art which shall reveal, at least to those who take the trouble to look, beliefs for what they are, illusions. Like Parsifal, he can only display what he knows. Wagner, like Parsifal, became a Christian only in the sense that out of pity for men he pretended to share their illusions so that he might free them.

Wagner had now concluded his vast ten-act drama. He had solved his problem of how the artist discharges his moral responsi-bility to introduce value into the world: the artist offers the oppor-tunity for self-redemption. Whether anyone took that opportunity or not was beyond his control; the attempt to achieve that kind of power he had long since abandoned. It is doubtful that he thought very many people would or could use what he offered them. He, at any rate, could from now on devote himself to writing non-dra-matic music, to copying the will directly, without relying upon visual and verbal symbolization. But he never did. Within six months after the first cycle of Bayreuth *Parsifal* performances in 1882, he was dead.


## 2. WAGNER'S MUSIC

If Wagner's dramas have rarely been understood, his music has always been met with an intense reaction, whether of passion-ate adoration or equally passionate detestation. It is hard to say which is the greater tribute to its power. I have called the transcen-dental style "extravagant," wishing less to imply any judgment of excellence or failure than to emphasize its power of going "beyond reasonable limits," as the dictionary puts it. For transcendentalism brings out with extreme violence the question inherent in the whole nineteenth-century vision. What is a "reasonable" limit?

Who determines that "reasonableness"? To the nineteenth-century artist "reasonable" means only "common sense," society's "consensus." It is a culturally transmitted orientation that seeks to establish, to fix, to standardize aesthetic qualities. It shoves aesthetic possibility under the iron paw of the orientative drive. But above all, since it is culturally transmitted, it is not earned by the individual self; "reasonable" aesthetic styles are but the clothes of the social role, the rags of the past which keep the Philistine snug and warm, though dirty. The transcendental artist wishes to be cleanly exposed to aesthetic possibilities; he wants to be naked and cold to the hurricanes of stylistic creativity.

This ambition explains what has sometimes been disparagingly called the "eclecticism" of nineteenth-century art. Just as all religions and mythologies symbolized the self, so did all aesthetic styles. Syncretism was, for example, one of the marks of transcendental theological writing: the effort to relate all religions by aligning doctrines that functioned in the same way in each system —the equivalence of Christ and Buddha, for example. (A late descendant of this sort of thinking is to be found in the efforts of Jung and his followers to discover the universal language of symbolic archetypes.) The greatness of an artist, consequently, lay in his power to combine styles of the past into an entirely new style, an absolutely and unmistakably individual style that would serve his purpose, to symbolize the uniqueness of his own transcendentally justified self.

Like Delacroix, who integrated the baroque style into his own art without for a moment compromising its originality and its nineteenth-century character, the artist had to be both original and learned. This was the weakness of Berlioz. This is why so much of his music has the character of a period-piece, why his works are uneven, for all their beauty and brilliance and imaginative originality. From this point of view, Schumann was a far stronger composer; and so was Chopin. One is always surprised to learn—and to remember—that the latter's style is firmly grounded on Bach's *Das Wohltemperierte Clavier*, properly translated as "Compositions for any equally-tempered keyboard instrument." (That is, the pitch has been adjusted so that the same piece can be played in any key.) But Wagner was the strongest of them all: his musical knowledge was the profoundest; and he continued learning and studying as long as he lived. He constantly fed into his style ever-new knowledge of other styles, including, at times, those of his contemporaries, Berlioz and Liszt and Mendelssohn. Thus his style is ever-growing, constantly increasing its formal and expressive power. Again, although it is always his style, unmistakably his, yet it is impossible to say that there is a Wagnerian style. There are, rather, Wagnerian styles. And so true is this that as one becomes thoroughly familiar with his music, each work seems to be in a different style, and even each act.

One of the best examples is the difference between the music of Act II of *Siegfried* and that of Act III. Between the two acts he wrote *Tristan* and *The Meistersinger*. When the curtain goes up on the third act, one is in a new musical world, yet it un-mistakably belongs to the same musical universe as Act II. This is not a matter of dramatic contrast; it is a matter of steadily growing musical development for fifty years, from his student attempts in the early 1830's to the last touches put upon the *Parsifal* score when it was in production in 1882. He is the strongest of the transcen-dental composers because he was the most learned—the most eclectic and the least eclectic.

Initially his problem was the same as that of Berlioz and Schumann. How was the new language of Beethoven, which some-how or other found its vital current below the level of the emotions of situations and roles, to be understood and controlled? As soon as his musical apprenticeship was finished, he became an opera com-poser. Three operas, *The Fairies*, *The Love Ban*, based on Shake-speare's *Measure for Measure*, and *Rienzi*, which was highly suc-cessful for many years, preceded *The Flying Dutchman*. More than Berlioz and far more than Schumann, he was subjected to the influences and requirements of the operatic world. Opera, it must be remembered, was then a very popular form. As normal to the theatrical life of the time as the musical comedy is to our Broad-way, it was more an entertainment than high art. Thus Wagner was torn between a musical language he had learned from the highly rarified and non-popular late Beethoven quartets, which he was among the very first to study, to comprehend, and to assimilate, and the demands of a musical tradition which required that music be illustrative according to a well-established system of conventions which associated certain musical devices and forms with particular situations and emotions.

Schumann and Berlioz could select from already existent and publicly familiar literary works analogues that symbolized the streaming life of the self, of the will, of orientative-disorientative behavior; while Wagner, from the nature of the form and from the nature of the public conventions, had to work at the level of the role, of the social side of the personality. To integrate the musical and the dramatic demands, he had to do what all transcendental artists had to do, subject everything to his own will. Like Balzac, he had to make everything into a symbol of the activity of the self. At the literary level he turned from adapting plays, then the standard source for operatic libretti, to writing his own libretti by re-handling for symbolic purposes, as we have seen, old legends and mythologies. For this reason, his true career begins with the *Dutchman*. But how could he introduce the self into the music as well?

In Beethoven's last quartets he found the first clue. The four-part sonata form was analogous to the traditional operatic form of "numbers": recitative, arias, duets, choruses, and so on. Just as Beethoven dissolved the sonata form and gave it a psychological continuity in order to symbolize the self structuring the objective world, so Wagner could break down the numbers system of the opera for the same end. His first step, already timidly appearing in the *Dutchman*, was to link the numbers as Beethoven had sometimes linked movements, by not employing a cadence at the end of a number. At the same time he began to repeat melodies and themes where they were dramatically appropriate. And there is reason to believe that at one time he intended that each act flow without a musical break into the next, that the work be presented without intermissions. Thus we see him using two devices Berlioz and Schumann had been working on for a decade, the *idée fixe* and the psychological flow.

Neither of these men, however, quite got beyond the movement-number tradition. Both, when they turned to traditional forms in the 1840's, began to regress to the formal and non-symbolic system of movements and numbers with final cadences at the end of each. Not Wagner. With him the difficult problem of opera was the cause of an aesthetic tension sufficient to keep his direction steady. In *Tannhäuser* the unbroken flow was further developed, and in Act II of *Lohengrin*, the last act composed, it reached its highest form. Here, although numbers are still identifiable, they are joined by long passages which are neither recitative nor melody. That is, the singer—and Wagner had a lot of trouble with his singers over this—had to sing the notes as written, whereas the recitative tradition permitted the singer almost improvisatory freedom of rhythm and pitch. On the other hand, this new kind of melody did not conform to the tradition of set length for the melody and of specified repetitions. The numbers were now embedded in an unbroken stream of melody. Obviously, the next thing to get rid of was the numbers. His struggles to solve this problem account for the five-year delay before he could start composing the *Ring*.

During this period he conceptualized what he had been half-consciously doing for nearly a decade. He integrated his experiments into the ideas of endless melody and of dramatically significant motifs. These two were themselves aspects of one conception. For endless melody he had two traditions, the fugue, and the development section of the sonata first-movement form. Repetition and variation is what makes a succession of notes into a melody. Embedded in fugue and development sections are melodies, parts of melodies, and variations of melodies which are first presented when the fugue or movement begins. What Wagner did was to introduce new melodies *after* the fugue-development flow had already begun. Thus at any time he could introduce new melodic material, musical phrases to be repeated and varied. Nor was even this device without precedent; double and triple fugues introduce new melodies in the course of the musical process, and Beethoven and a few others had tried such introductions during the development of the first-movement form. What was new was the introduction of new melodies at dramatically appropriate points. This made the repeated musical "motto" of the *Dutchman* and the *idée fixe* technique into the "leitmotif" system.

When most people become enthusiastic about Wagner, they begin to learn the names of the leitmotifs, the "leading motifs," a singularly inexpressive term. They are all carefully extracted and named in special sections of piano scores and often in performance programs, and modern recording companies reprint them and conscientiously indicate in the margins of the libretti where they appear. One envies the early Wagnerians to whom this information was not available. For "leitmotif" is not Wagner's term, nor did he name his themes. To think of them in terms of their names is to turn them into conventional signs. The word and the motif become interchangeable. As Debussy said, each character when he appears presents his calling card. To identify them verbally as one listens to the music is to miss their whole significance. The endless melody, including the motifs, exists, according to Wagner's own statement, below the conceptual level. It cannot be conceptualized, only experienced. It is the psychic flow of the self, of the will.

When Wagner read Schopenhauer's theory of music, he felt that what he had been trying to grasp was there successfully explained. The stage presents the fusion of self and objective world, symbolized verbally and visually; the music, the flow of the self's orientation toward that fusion. The leitmotif, then, is not a melodic conventionalization for some fragment of that objective world, nor the equivalent of a verbal or visual symbol. It is a symbolization of the psychic orientation of the self toward the self's dealings with the objective world. Thus "sword motif," for example, should be interpreted as "the musical symbol of the orientation of the self toward what the sword symbolizes." The most important thing about any appearance of a motif is not the fact that it appears but rather the musical environment from which it emerges and the form it takes, whether major or minor, for example, or more or less rapidly than its original appearance, or with its melodic curve and range distorted or extended or compressed.

The success of the system is indicated by how easily long sections of the *Ring* and of later works can be detached and performed in the concert hall with instruments substituting for voices. Then one perceives how fully even the vocal line is an integral part of the melodic flow. For this there are two very good reasons. One is purely musical. Wagner never discussed it and it was not even worked out until the 1920's. The fact is that the melodic flow is not merely a flow; it is an ordered flow. Although on a vast scale, as musical forms go, there is an internal order of a purely musical nature. Thus segments can be lifted out which are musically and formally coherent. The types of musical form Wagner uses are endless, but they are there.

The other reason is more subtle. The music has a life of its own because it symbolizes the activity of the self. The stage is the self engaged with reality; the music is the self detached, isolated, alienated, regarding and responding to that engagement from a distance. This is why the stage action of the *Ring* can be thoroughly pessimistic, yet value remains in the world of human experience. It is the self, embodied in the music, that endures even though society and the hero have both been destroyed, even though the divine world has been eliminated, even though the problem of society is seen as absolutely unsolvable. We have seen the engaged self symbolized as the tower, the withdrawn self symbolized as the cave. The power of the *Ring* rises, at least in part, from this simultaneous parallelism of tower and cave. Nor is it accidental that the completion of Wagner's musical system coincided with the composition of the *Ring*. In the transcendental era the self depended for its value upon divine authority, on the one hand, and on the other, its heroic effort to manipulate society for society's own good. The *Ring* strips the self of that divine authority and asserts that the heroic effort is futile and must necessarily be frustrated. The self is now absolutely—and terribly—free, neither supported nor justified. For the first time it is really stripped bare, its value entirely self-generated. Was it for more than acoustical and dramatic reasons that when he built Bayreuth Wagner literally hid the orchestra in a cave?

The final solution in *Parsifal* of the question Wagner had

started out with—the discharge of the moral responsibility of the artist—brought about a final stylistic evolution. From *The Rhinegold* through *The Twilight of the Gods* the system he evolved in the early 1850's was developed and refined, continuously becoming more supple and expressive. In *The Rhinegold* it is almost naïve, at times it seems externally applied rather than felt from within, although that very naïveté gives the music a classic simplicity wonderfully appropriate to the freshness of a primeval world. At the end of *The Twilight of the Gods*, however, it is under perfect control. Throughout this period the predominating function of the music is expressiveness. *Parsifal* is first of all sensuously beautiful. And this corresponds with the moral orientation of the work, with the judgment that the only valid redemption is self-redemption. No longer is the music primarily devoted to urging a particular succession of orientations upon the listener. Like Parsifal displaying the spear, it is simply there; it offers the opportunity for self-redemption. Whether we take that opportunity or not is our business. The music of *Parsifal* is first of all a work of art, and secondarily a structure of meanings. The art justifies the meanings; the meanings do not justify the art; just as on the stage art justifies religion, the religious illusions do not justify the art. The primary source of the redemption is the music itself, and the singers who chant the final words—"Highest wonder of salvation! Redemption to the redeemer!"—are invisible.

Wagner looms colossally in nineteenth-century cultural history for a dozen reasons, but most of all because he responded so deeply to its cultural forces that he alone moved through all of its last three stages, transcendentalism, objectism, and stylism. To a group of objectists I shall now turn, and then to their stylistic problem.

# CHAPTER XV

# *Self and Object*

ALTHOUGH WAGNER'S DEVELOPMENT shows what are at once the profoundest and the most subtle reasons for the failure of transcendentalism, it is worth examining how and why other individuals central to nineteenth-century culture went through that reorientation. Generally speaking, the 1850's was the decade in which appeared the major cultural monuments marking the break, monuments which established the new orientation and also established the style or, more precisely, variety of styles, which symbolized the objectist orientation.

I use this term because the standard terms—"realism" and "naturalism" and "objectivism"—have too many meanings and not enough. Besides, transcendentalism, as we have seen, also had its own mode of realism. Indeed, in the broadest sense realism, naturalism and objectivism are characteristic of the whole nineteenth-century vision, with its drive toward reality, away from constitutive orientations and toward instrumental orientations. This third stage, which perceives both transcendental authority and social redemption as illusions, leaves the self in direct confrontation with the object in the empirical world, with no recourse but to look at it as best it can.

However, it is impossible to look at an object without a Gestalt, without some orientation that will structure it. The weakness of objectism was precisely that; during this period John Ruskin (English, born in 1819) insisted that the task of the artist was to look at the world with the naked eye. To him Constable saw nature with the eye of a sheep. However, to be a human artist one must have some other reason for looking than for food. Or rather, some other reason as well. Ruskin's thinking about art and architecture, therefore, was forced to go outside of art to find some way of controlling the artistic vision, and justifying it. One way was functionalism, which established itself at this point. Using an Enlightenment notion of adaptation, Ruskin demanded that architecture be fully functional, in every structural detail, and that the structure express the function. Likewise painting must be psychologically functional, by making us aware of and adapted to the beauty of the natural world.

But this functional notion was insufficiently humanized. Architecture and painting, therefore, must be moral; they must recommend particular moral attitudes toward experience, not necessarily those which society approves of. Quite the contrary. Very much in the manner of the *Ring*, the artist and the architect were to make perfectly clear, directly and indirectly, what a shambles middle-class business and industry were making of the world and what a horrifying and non-functional, non-adaptive society they were creating. Art and architectural decoration, therefore, were to be exquisitely transcriptive of the appearance of the world, but controlled by biological function and a human morality, derived from biological and social adaptation.

It is apparent how easily this aesthetic ideal could align itself with the rapidly spreading Enlightenment ideas of social reform. Today, when middle-class society, so far as it is modern at all, proceeds on Enlightenment assumptions, the objectism of morality and natural transcription is its predominating aesthetic mode. The popular middle-class novel presents an Enlightenment version, or perversion, of moralized Freudianism in an objectist style and technique. Thus when a young man of the mid-twentieth century grows out of Enlightenment attitudes, he usually begins with the works of this period as the most accessible—Melville, Baudelaire, Turgenev, Tolstoy, Dostoyevsky, the early impressionist painters, Brahms, Dvořák, and so on. Stylistically, they are closest to what he is already familiar with, and the transition is easier than it would be with the first stage, which usually takes him some time to comprehend, or transcendentalism, which takes a long time to comprehend because the naïve mind easily confuses it with eighteenth-century deism or even pre-Enlightenment Christianity, that is, with one of the religions in which he has been brought up and against which very often he is rebelling.

Yet even though objectism became established in the 1850's, a few individuals had experienced the failure of transcendentalism even before. One, Robert Browning, anticipated Wagner's rejection by nearly fifteen years. Born in 1812, he wrote *Paracelsus*, his first important work, before he was twenty-three and published it in 1835. It is strangely mature in style and thought for so young a man, but as one might expect, it exhibits a confusion of the first stage in the developing nineteenth-century orientation with the second. Paracelsus is determined to wrest the truth from the world by scientific investigation, and to comprehend and to reveal to mankind God's plan and purpose. Yet he is aware that no raw, naïve empiricism will serve his purpose. The truth is not a light that comes into the mind from without, but rather it is a light within the mind which goes forth and illuminates reality. The problem is to let it out, for its emanation from the mind is hindered by our culturally inherited and socially reinforced ideas, particularly Platonism.

In only two states can the mind let the ray of truth issue forth: one when the mind is like a gnat half-suspended in air on a perfect autumn day, when it has no purpose, no aim, no ambition; when, to use Schopenhauer's term, the will is quiescent. The other state is when the mind is profoundly disturbed, either emotionally or physically. But Paracelsus cannot use his own insights. He can neither achieve a will-less state nor make use of his disturbances to break through to a new vision. Only at the point of death, when he no longer wills and when his whole body is breaking up, can he finally transcend his mental sets and see into the life of the world. What he sees, of course, is the world as process. Like Schopenhauer and Balzac he arrives at a kind of primitive and metaphysical evolutionism. It is impossible not to think that when he went to press Browning was perfectly satisfied with what he had said; yet *Paracelsus* contains a profound inconsistency. If truth is the light of the mind issuing forth, it is non-constitutive, it cannot tell us what the world is really like. Yet the hero's final vision *is* constitutive; by intuition he sees how the world is really structured. In the first act Paracelsus is a transcendentalist; in the last he is a kind of Wordsworthian-Hegelian intuitionist. To get out of this difficulty Browning embarked on another long poem.

*Sordello* was five years in the making and was completely rewritten twice, finally being published in 1840. It is almost precisely analogous to the *Ring*. Its theme is the frustrated transcendental hero. The narrator's tone is ironically sympathetic throughout. Sordello attempts to embody the transcendental vision in poetry, but the public cannot understand him. He then attempts to redeem society; but his father, a typical early medieval fighting politician, laughs at him. He then realizes that neither of his failures makes any difference. As a transcendentalist, with an insight into the divine process of the world, he sees the whole world, as it is, to be radiant with value and order and meaning. Since there is no reason to write or to act, to be moral or to be morally responsible, since the world is perfect when seen from the transcendentalist point of view, there is no reason even to live. And so he dies. The narrator washes his hands of him, but does admit that after all his life was not entirely wasted: he did write one poem a few lines of which are still remembered—by a child.

In a most unusual, perhaps unique, way Browning here reveals the moral weakness of the transcendental position, its dangerous temptation to impose moral authority by force. In *Sordello* Browning shows up the egocentricity which Carlyle and Balzac could not quite overcome, and which makes the Lohengrin-Prince of Brabant relationship so morally equivocal. At the same time he pinpoints the other danger of transcendentalism, its tendency not to act at all, to subject, in spite of itself, the drive toward reality to the orientative drive.

For the next twenty-five years, in a series of poems with

historical and contemporary settings, Browning concerned himself with the illusions of the mind and of society. *In a Balcony*, a one-act poetic play published in *Men and Women* in 1855, is a work of central importance. Here two human beings finally break through the web of illusions their wills have spun about them and achieve pure value by recognizing each other's identities and making their love for each other meaningful. But whether they are to be punished or rewarded or simply let go for the brutal way they have exploited the emotions of their queen we never know. The curtain falls as the tread of the guard is heard approaching.

Thus Browning indicates that the experience of value is but momentary; that the conviction that the world has order and meaning comes as a consequence of breaking through illusions. But, and here is the important point, no propositions, no conceptions, no metaphysical truths, no moral verities—nothing can be derived from that experience. It happens, and we must struggle in frustration until it happens again. Even if it never happens again, to have experienced it once is enough. We cannot *know* that redemption is truly redeeming; but we can support ourselves with the knowledge that the experience of redemption is both possible and, when it happens, convincing. The very fact that we can take nothing away from it protects it from skeptical analysis. Value, then, lies not in intuitively perceiving a truth or in embodying and incarnating transcendental truth in reality, but in breaking through an illusion.

In both *In a Balcony* and *Tristan and Isolde* transcendental love appears as justifying absolute non-morality, that is, as merely the reverse of social morality. Both works imply that to choose is the only way to come in direct contact with reality, and Browning makes it clear that choice can exist only when illusions are shattered, when all orientations are broken up. Thus he successfully establishes the insight of the first act of *Paracelsus*. The light from within the mind is not truth and certainly not constitutive truth, but value, and it can only be let out, be experienced, when at a time of either will-lessness or profound disturbance existing orientations are shattered. Therefore, in the 1860's in *The Ring and the Book* he concludes, as I have already suggested, that truth, historical, scientific, or moral, or metaphysical, cannot be known; but that the function of art, which makes no claims to truth, which is quite frankly a lie, is to so affect the mind of the observer that his orientations are shaken up and restructured, thus releasing him to do a significant act. The rest of Browning's career, therefore, was spent in developing a theory of moral instrumentalism, and of art as releasing the moral responsibility of the individual. His later thinking thus parallels the late Wagner's in *Parsifal*.

Gustave Flaubert worked out his break with transcendentalism differently. In *Madame Bovary* he directly attacked the one transcendental ideal that had penetrated deeply into middle-class society, transcendental love. It was only fitting, then, that when it was published in 1856, an effort was made to suppress it as obscene, and that when Charles Baudelaire's *Flowers of Evil* was published in 1857 it was successfully prosecuted on the same grounds. Both men, who were contemporaries, born in 1821, attempted to deal with erotic realities, particularly with the contrast between love as an illusion and love as it actually is, a madness. Flaubert, in order to get objectivity and to strip from love all of its transcendental trappings, turned himself, the artist, into a middle-class provincial doctor's wife; but he kept himself in the book by using something like Browning's device in *Sordello*, the ironic and detached narrator, telling the story of Dr. Bovary and his wife.

Baudelaire, on the other hand, remains in his book as both narrator and protagonist, turning his irony against himself and against the loathesome urban environment of Paris under the Third Empire; his only sympathetic figures are those outcasts, the artist, the poor, and the prostitute. Flaubert's device, which he uses again in *A Sentimental Education*, begun before *Madame Bovary* but published long after in 1869, is to make the self into an object. "Madame Bovary," as he said in his famous remark, "*c'est moi*"; she is a symbol of the transcendental area of his personality. Baudelaire also symbolized the self by taking transcendental symbolism, which suffused everything with value, stripping it of the divine, and using the world of objects to symbolize the states of his soul. "What do I care," he once said, "what the reality outside of me is made of, provided that it helps me to feel that I am and what I am."

"To feel that I am." As with Browning, the sense of selfhood and of its value is unstable. The first two stages of the nineteenth-century vision attempted strenuously to stabilize the self. It is the great merit of these men that they unflinchingly accepted as an unsolvable problem of subjective reality that the sense of selfhood and value flickers, comes and goes. With Baudelaire as with Browning, value appears only in the moment. It is the task of the artist to engage in a continuous disturbance, to open himself to a stream of disorienting experiences, so that that sense of value might appear, for himself and for his audience. In a way they had no choice. Once the self had lost its transcendental dimensions and had to assert its existence in the face of and in connection with real objects impenetrable to value, it had to submit to all the distortions, shames, and evils of the personality.

That the title of Flaubert's novel is *Madame Bovary* and not *Emma* shows that she struggles to escape from her role into a world of pure self, but that when she does she only plunges into a hell of undisciplinable emotions. The paradise of the self has disappeared. Its place of abode is the horrible inferno of the personality, filled with the shouts and screams of pointless desires, of shame, of guilt, of self-recrimination, and of a terrible boredom. Browning too, in the 1850's began to devote himself to villains, aware of their villainy, struggling to redeem it by some casuistry, some elaborate self-deception. The problem was, then, not to redeem the personality; it cannot be redeemed. The problem was to accept it, to pluck from that hell of evil a flower of selfhood and value. "To know what I am." Baudelaire plunged himself into hell, and Flaubert plunged Madame Bovary into hell.

But bad, stupid, immoral, self-deceiving, foolish, and eventually suicidal as Emma Bovary is, she is better than her environment. She is the victim of sentimental religion and transcendental love. She is an historical product, a necessary consequence of the process of a human culture. Her corrupted spirit is nobler, more beautiful than the man she seduces or the man who seduces her. Her suicide is an expression of her final refusal to be invaded and violated further by the world around her. Though she fails, her constant effort is to make her life into a work of art. At the end of the book, her decent, stupid husband, who has come to know all about her, her lovers, her debts, her neglect of her child, still cannot live without her; broken, prematurely aged, self-neglected, he dies. Whatever she was, she symbolized a human potentiality infinitely more significant than the stupidly vicious bourgeois around him. By objectifying in Emma his own personality, the ironic and detached Flaubert redeems himself. As with Wagner, value lies in the tough-minded power to look at things as they are, and at oneself as one really is. The task of the artist is too objectify and make inescapable the social world and the interior world so that the observer may see in himself and his world what his orientative drive normally persuades him to conceal and to ignore.

Thus Baudelaire, at the end of the opening poem of his book, writes his dedication "To the Reader": "His eyes filled with unconscious tears, he dreams of scaffolds, smoking his hookah. You know him, reader, you know this sensitive monster—hypocritical reader, my twin, my brother. He is myself. He is you." Like Emma, Baudelaire's journey into the personality leads to a desire for death. Yet again it is no mere Wertherian despair. Death will lead, he hopes, to something new. Nor is he talking about Christian immortality. Rather, it would seem that the conclusion of *The Flowers of Evil* is analogous to the end of Melville's *Moby Dick* (1851). There Ishmael, the outcast wanderer, who has been seduced by Captain Ahab's transcendental madness, his determination to impose meaning on a meaningless world, alone survives of the crew that had failed to capture the indifferent white whale. And he survives because he can seize upon a coffin, the only thing that is left of the sunken *Pequod*. The ultimate unfaceable fact of the hell of the personality is death and the knowledge of death.

Baudelaire, who after all did not commit suicide and had no wish to die, who had plans for further work, in this last poem symbolizes his acceptance of death, without any consolation of a paradise hereafter. When a man accepts his own death, which he bears with him in blood and flesh and in his desires, then he can truly begin to live, then he can truly hope for something new, for some relief from boredom. Thus Baudelaire, like Wagner in the *Ring*, converts his tragic pessimism into triumph, by looking at it, by enduring it. The self confronts the object, and uses the object to realize what it is. Baudelaire hails the death of the personality, not the death of the self. Thus Wotan dies, but he is reborn—his identity, not his deluded personality—as Hans Sachs. With these men, the nineteenth-century orientation went through a new and powerful transformation; they emerged with an iron power to confront the reality of the personality and the reality of society.

Indeed, they were iron years. The central theme was frustration, the frustration of the self's desire to find value anywhere but in itself. The fullest, most exhaustive exploration of that frustration, in itself, without reference to objects—at least to objects in the empirical world—is to be found in the symphonies of Anton Bruckner. It is a pity that the famous—and infamous—critic Eduard Hanslick never could abide the symphonies of Bruckner, though he was less harsh about Bruckner's religious music. For it would be difficult to find a composer whose music more perfectly conforms to Hanslick's notion of what music is and ought to be.

Both were Austrians and of the same generation; Bruckner was born in 1824 and Hanslick in 1825. In 1856 Hanslick published his famous *The Beautiful in Music*. His position was virtually the same as Schopenhauer's, divested of its metaphysical dimensions, and Wagner's, as it was conceptualized in the 1850's. Like the other men of this crucial decade, he stripped art of its transcendental dimensions and authority. He also denied to music any reference to situational emotions, such as love, or grief, or courage, thus divesting it of any social reference, leaving only the composer and the music. That there is a tradition of musical conventions tied to situations he resolutely refused to admit; in fact he never came adequately to terms with the problem at all. Yet, as we have seen, Wagner had to struggle fearfully against it and Berlioz and Schumann had to make up for Beethoven's departure from it by using literary analogues. Further, according to Hanslick, the feelings that music does express are below the conceptual level; they are from the unconscious. Music, consequently, is not translatable into words. Nevertheless, the process of musical structure is the embodiment of those inaccessible feelings. It has no reference to the world of objects. The object of the composer's individuality is the material of music itself. Thus Hanslick is typical of his period in placing self against object and seeing that from that struggle emerges pure individuality or selfhood.

It is apparent that his conception is almost precisely the same as Wagner's. Who would imagine, if he had not heard it before, and if he had no notion of the title, that the Prelude to Wagner's *Tristan* was the introduction to a music drama about love? No one, I venture to think. But I think anyone would say, just as Hanslick from his principles would have to say, that it is the embodiment of tension, a tension which arises solely from the manipulation of the musical material. As a work symbolizing tension, it could just as well be the introduction to an opera about a doctoral candidate about to take his oral examination, or about making business decisions at a high corporate level. Tension is tension; it can and does occur in any situation, depending upon the personality in it. Tension is a non-situational feeling, part of the psychic process and flow of orientation and disorientation. Why, then, did Hanslick so detest Wagner, in particular the Wagner from *The Ring* on, and Bruckner? The usual accounts tracing the enmity to gossip and the politics of the Viennese musical world are unsatisfactory. The venom and hatred with which Hanslick wrote about these two composers came from the heart.

The answer, I think, lies in the title to his book, *The "Beautiful" in Music*. In a note he agrees with Franz Grillparzer, a Viennese dramatist too little known outside of German-speaking countries, that Shakespeare could use the ugly but that the composer is confined to the beautiful. Ugliness, however, is a quality ascribed to objects in the empirical world, and so is beauty. Neither has anything whatever to do with the psychic process. They are judgments, not, to use one of Hanslick's favorite—and wrongly used—words, "scientific" statements about something's character.

Nevertheless, with his acceptance of Grillparzer's notion it becomes clear that to Hanslick music should not be disturbing. The weakness of his book lies in his failure to distinguish between what music is and what he thinks music ought to be like, what it ought to offer, pure contemplation of the composer's manipulation of musical material. The reason for his failure is that though part of him had broken with the transcendental tradition, part of him had not, the part that in the last paragraph of his book talks about music's having "the vital spark of the divine fire." There was in Hanslick an afterglow of earlier stages of nineteenth-century development, of Stendhal, for instance, whose image of the self was a closed paradise. Wagner and Bruckner he could not endure, therefore, because their music is profoundly disturbing.

It has been objected that there are sudden halts in Bruckner's symphonies, sudden stops in the flow of the music, that his music does not have the easy and beautiful flow of the great masters, Brahms, for example, whom Hanslick and his followers opposed to Wagner and Bruckner. (Brahms himself regarded both Wagner and Bruckner as great geniuses.) This sudden stopping and starting again in Bruckner as well as the great length of his works, two or three times as long as Brahms' symphonies, has indeed proved a barrier to many a listener. These unexpected interruptions or blocks in the musical current have often been explained as the consequence of Bruckner's musical ineptitude. Yet he was a famous and highly successful teacher of composition and of harmony. Harmony is above all a means of maintaining continuity of form, and of harmony Bruckner was a prodigious master. Ever since the early eighteenth century any conservatory student of most modest talent has been able to write music with a lovely flow; there is no problem to it at all, after a little instruction. But with the clues we already have to the character of this period, an iron time, a time of the frustration of the self before the object, the problem of Bruckner becomes immediately answerable.

If music is the embodiment of psychic process, surely one of the most striking characteristics of psychic process, or of any process—a river running through rapids or winds beating against a mountain range—is frustration. There is always some frustration in music; a variation is a frustration of our expectations for hearing a melody in its original form. From the great repertoire of kinds of musical process, Bruckner selected and enormously magnified and dramatized the frustrating elements. This also explains the length; to make us experience fully that frustration Bruckner has to use great length, first because we expect something much shorter, second because only continuously reiterated frustrations can break through our orientations, which demand immediate and continuous gratification from music with just enough frustration to put an edge on the pleasure. Wagner had done the same thing, although his operas are no longer than the typical opera of his time. Rather, there are only three acts with one stage scene for each act, as against four of five acts with numerous scene shifts, each involving a pause.

The length, then, is necessary to what Bruckner is doing. And he has a number of other devices. One is repetition. Listeners complain that the music is getting nowhere; they are quite right; that is the point. Another is immensely long cadences, four or five times the length of those other composers employ. Still another is exact repetition of a motif one half note above where it has been. A particularly powerful one is to conclude a movement by leaping up from the keynote to the fifth, and remaining there, instead of proceeding, as one would expect, to the eighth, the keynote, again. Nor is that enough; the brasses hammer on the fifth while the internal parts make tremendous efforts to push the main melodic line from the fifth up to the eighth. But of course the most powerful is the interruption itself. A favorite device is to build up a climax in the middle of a movement, the kind of climax normally found only at the end. Thus, instead of a harmonic resolution, he gives you perhaps a minor seventh, which he will hammer at with the entire orchestra, as loudly as possible. Suddenly everything stops. From the double basses there is a mutter, an harmonically undefined rumble, and the clarinet slowly, in the minor, picks up the theme which had so recently been unresolved, and starts, softly and feebly, all over again. Bruckner's invention—I have mentioned but a few of the more obvious devices—in symbolizing the frustrations of the psychic process is endless. And of course, when gratification is at length achieved, as it usually is, at least partially, the release of feeling is exalting to the highest degree. For this reason many commentators have insisted that the subject of the symphonies is religious experience.

I think this is an error; his religious works, his masses, his psalms, his "Te Deum," minimize the frustration. They have the same extreme beauty and nobility, to speak very vaguely, of thematic material, but they are beautiful in quite a traditional sense. Of these works Hanslick spoke favorably. They interested him; the symphonies he could not abide. Indeed, what is often called the Bruckner problem—the contrast between his peasant-like simplicity of personality and religious faith and the grandeur of his symphonies—is again no real problem. To him, the symphonies may have been his struggle toward God. To us they are the incarnation of psychic frustration in the self's effort to reach value. From this point of view, between his life and his symphonies there is no dividing line at all.

Few great artists have led such discouraging lives or made great achievements in the face of such difficulties. Without the brazen self-assurance of Wagner which carried him triumphantly over the heads of beleaguering creditors to the protection of King Ludwig of Bavaria, poor Bruckner had no self-confidence at all. He was a music student until he was forty, and the first symphony he dared give a number to—actually it was his third—was not begun until 1865, in his forty-first year. Neglected, humiliated, suffering a terrible nervous breakdown after his first symphony was completed, never well-off enough to marry, never even having the courage to find a wife, innocent, socially naïve to an almost unbelievable degree, he did not achieve any kind of financial security until he was fifty-six, and then he had a fearful teaching load, by modern standards, constantly occupying himself with other men's music when he should have been free to create his own. Even more than Wagner, at least as much as Baudelaire, his music, his one gigantic symphony in nine parts, written from 1865–96, with the fourth movement of the last left unfinished, symbolizes the frustration of the self engaged with the impenetrable object, in an iron time. Yet the heroic codas are heroic because they have wrested order from the frustration, from that engagement; they have brought forth from the deepest recesses of the personality an affirmation of value. In facing its terrors the self earns its victory.

# CHAPTER XVI

# *The Crisis of Style*

Ⅰ F BRUCKNER HAD NOT EXPERIENCED the stylistic problem of his generation, his music would probably have been recognized much sooner for what it is and his achievement in symbolizing psychic frustration much more readily honored. The roots of Wagner's stylistic evolution were in transcendentalism, and the initial impetus of the *Dutchman, Tannhäuser,* and *Lohengrin,* together with the tension between the operatic tradition and Beethoven's, could carry him through the stylistic crisis of objectism. Even so, as we have seen, *The Meistersinger* is full of stylistic revivals. Even in the *Ring* and *Tristan,* moreover, the vast formal structures that held the music together were, after all, external and arbitrary; they had nothing to do with the actual psychic flow of the music.

This arbitrary and external imposition and control over the work of art is the particular character of the period. Bruckner, who started to study only after transcendentalism had begun to break up, was exposed to the problem to a degree which Wagner never experienced in the same force. Actually, as early as 1840 Schumann had abandoned his free development of the suite-variation form and had begun to return to the "classic" forms of the eighteenth century. Technically, those forms had been developed to keep the music going, and emotional disturbances and frustrations of the flow were kept at a minimum, for the Enlightenment aesthetic ideal had been to create an equivalent to the order and structure of nature. The symphony, then, was traditionally associated with unimpeded movement, occasionally given tension by formal disturbance and by emotional symbolization. Beethoven had increased the tension very considerably, but he had not interrupted the flow, except in the introduction to the last movement of the Ninth Symphony. To interrupt the flow, to use the symphony to symbolize frustration meant, in the light of the tradition, to deny what was assumed to be its very character. Wagner could evolve his externally imposed form out of himself, but Bruckner could only arbitrarily impose an existing form upon what he wished to say. To use the symphony as he did meant that he involved his listeners in a frustration he had not counted on. Hence his bewilderment and deep hurt at his rejection.

Thus the disappearance of the transcendental authority left the objectist artist with no divine justification for an extravagant style; at the same time, the departure of transcendentalism left embedded in the cultural situation all those stylistic revivals which the transcendental artist had brought back to dominate, absorb, and synthesize into his extravagance. As Schumann's transcendental convictions paled, his style became more traditional and his extravagance faded under the power of pre-transcendental and eighteenth-century pedagogy. In his later works we recognize Schumann, but we are puzzled and dissatisfied by the steadily decreasing Schumannesque character. Indeed, Schumann himself, in his later years, suffered a steady deterioration of his own sense of identity. Since the artist was no longer in a position to impose a unique style on his material, to evolve his style from himself and his divine idea, and since it is impossible for the mind to encounter the objective world without a pre-existent Gestalt or orientation, the post-transcendental artist had no choice but to find outside of himself and his work of art a controlling orientation for his vision. That is what Bruckner did, and this imposition of an external control is the character of objectist culture.

The most famous documents which reveal the crisis of style are Flaubert's letters. *Madame Bovary* is not a long novel, yet it caused Flaubert the most acute agony. Every sentence was rewritten and rewritten; always there was the problem of what words, what phrases, what attitudes, what details, he should employ. Attempting a novel in the Balzacian tradition, Flaubert wholly lacked Balzac's power to convert everything into a symbol, a realization of the incarnate word. He could not be a monomaniac. In short, his agony over *le mot juste*, his famous phrase meaning "the exact, the perfect word for the purpose in hand," was a consequence of the fact that he had no basis for choice, no reason to choose one word rather than another.

In every segment of behavior, every human being exhibits style, a unique pattern or configuration which is different from everyone else's pattern. Each member of the English speaking world, for example, speaks a language which is uniquely his; he colors his vowels a little differently; he slurs certain sounds in a special way; he has a rhythm all his own; his intonations and his pitch variations are unlike anyone else's. Indeed, in this sense there is no such thing as a language. A language is an abstraction; there is only speech, and in each human being's mouth it is a little different. How this should happen is obvious; in the pronounciation of "i" in "milk," for instance, I have heard not only "milk" but "melk," "malk," "mulk," and even "molk." (These spellings, of course, are only very rough approximations of the actual sounds.) There is a range of sounds which can be used for the vowel position in "milk" without irredeemably hindering communication. The total of an individual's pronunciations is his pronunciational style.

But there is another level of style. Within certain geographical areas there is a selection of possibilities; no individual in that area will go beyond those limits. We can tell the Bostonian from the Charlestonian, but highly trained linguists can tell within fifty miles where an individual was born and brought up. The individual is trained unconsciously in a phonetic orientation which establishes a range of sound variation; within that range he creates his own style. Further, a geographical style of a couple of hundred square miles is part of a larger stylistic area with its own set of variations. For each stylistic level, then, there is an orientational level which sets limits. Thus the style of eating in Seattle, say, is limited by the Northwestern orientation, and the Northwestern style is limited by the Western orientation, and so on. When an individual creates a unique style, then, he has a certain range of possibilities within which to operate. That orientation may be conscious, or it may be unconscious. In the latter case, it is arrived at by consciously deduced principles, derived from another orientation farther in the mental background.

It is, of course, the assumption of this book that these principles may be traced back to basic psychic levels. In Balzac's case, his orientation was such that he had only to select from the stylistic possibilities in a given situation that particular one which he felt most successfully symbolized the uniqueness of the self and its divine authority. Decisions being relatively easy, he worked by drafting rapidly, not worrying about stylistic consistency, and revising proofs, sometimes two or three times, concurrently with creating new material. His whole career was organized around a continuous revision of his works, before and after original publication, so that the total body of his work evolved steadily in the direction of bringing every detail under the control of a highly conscious orientation.

Before the nineteenth century and to a lesser degree through its first stage, that of the discovery of the self, artistic styles developed, it would appear, more or less unconsciously, and for the most part without any awareness of the relation of the style to the dominating orientation. Only in the Enlightenment, as with Herder, did advanced minds begin to relate an aesthetic style to fundamental orientations about the character of experience. Certain Enlightenment artists self-consciously sought for a natural basis for style. When, however, the world was turned inside out and order was derived from the self, stylistic order began to be consciously derived from metaphysical principles. Flaubert, therefore, with no metaphysical principles, in a situation in which the self nakedly confronted the object, had no way to create an orientation which would limit the possibilities and, at its highest efficiency, select the most suitable. With such an orientation, Balzac was immensely prolific. Flaubert, who had at least as much genius, produced only a fraction of what Balzac did, and that with immense labor. But that continuous and almost overwhelming frustration was solely a continuous agony of indecision, for he had no orientation on the basis of which he could decide. The result, in *Madame Bovary,* was a verbal style so pellucid that it was virtually invisible. And that, of course, is why it is the most successful novel he wrote, or anybody else wrote, or ever has written, from the objectist orientation.

The invisibility of the style meant the elimination of personality; only the self confronting the object was left. That was the one way to solve the stylistic problem; not to have a style. To be sure, to say that *Madame Bovary* has no style is not true; rather, it does not share the stylistic selectivity and exaggeration which is the mark of artistic behavior as opposed to normal behavior. Artistic style exists only because it is perceived against a background of non-artistic style. The language of *Madame Bovary*—since it is a written language—melts almost imperceptibly into that abstract language which everyone is aware of but no one uses. Of all books it is the most difficult to translate. To create an English style as aesthetically neutral as Flaubert's would take his genius, his patience, his culturally determined ability to be endlessly indecisive. The effort almost drove him insane. What translator would want to take the same risk?

Flaubert's struggles bring out the crisis of style with unmistakable sharpness and explain why others turned to some external authority. To be indecisive one needs a monumental self-confidence; even Flaubert's was barely enough to sustain him. Others turned elsewhere to solve the problem. Ruskin's architectural solution is highly instructive. He found that an exquisite transcription of the natural world and a moral purpose derived from biological adaptation were not enough. The problems of how to put these two together, the problem of form, of style, of aesthetic organization, of how to create something moving and beautiful—these remained unsolved.

In the ordinary affairs of life, we determine our style by imitating a model, whether we are bankers, or teachers, or housewives. And art is no exception. As I suggested before, the disappearance of transcendentalism left the artists without a model. As

Baudelaire put it, there was no tradition. Transcendentalism in its syncretic eclecticism had used up and exhausted stylistic tradition. Ruskin solved his problem by selecting the military and domestic forms of Gothic architecture and by insisting that here was to be found the model for a re-created architectural tradition. It was his belief that in the course of time architecture would develop a new style from the functional and decorative principles of the Gothic.

This solution may be called the "classic" solution. "Classic" has two major meanings: the best of its type or class, and the Greco-Roman style, which got "classic" applied to it because the men of the Renaissance felt that anything Greek or Roman was the best of its class. Ruskin's solution was "classic" because he was convinced that of all attempts to solve the architectural problem, military and domestic Gothic architecture was the best. It was functional, its form had the vital springiness of the botanical world, and its transcriptions from nature were exquisitely observed. Architecture, then, must begin again on this model; as society became integrated and functional once more, as he thought medieval society had been, it would develop an appropriate architectural style. His solution demanded that architects study and practice the principles of Gothic architecture. The Houses of Parliament, however, is not objectist Gothic but transcendental Gothic. Its ground plan and the major organization of its form are based upon the Greco-Roman tradition, but its ornament is Gothic. It is, then, an example of the syncretic eclecticism of its period. Ruskinian theory demanded something utterly different, something Gothic all the way through. Its tendency was necessarily archaeological. Ruskin's tradition is responsible for the innumerable historically correct Gothic churches built in the past century.

At the same time Ruskin was creating his theory, architects and other theorists were making equally strong statements in favor of Renaissance architecture, Roman, Greek, Baroque, Rococo, different varieties of the Gothic from those Ruskin approved of, such as the ecclesiastical Gothic. As I have already suggested, objectism is the basis of middle-class culture today, and in architecture is the most visible evidence of that statement. Again it is the union of objectism with Enlightenment orientations that is responsible. These historically correct styles were familiar when they were revived, for almost all of the major buildings of Europe had been built in them. To the middle-class mind the styles were hallowed by familiarity and by association. The middle classes, particularly in the United States, still build in these styles when they can afford to, and split-level development architecture today is littered with pitiful and nostalgic fragments of the objectist styles.

However, it would be an error to dismiss the achievements of the objectist architects as not "modern." Here again the self is nakedly set against the object, the object being, in this case, the style. This is what accounts for the increasing archaeological and historical correctness of the buildings in this tradition. The architects developed a stylistic mastery which rivaled that of the original creators of the styles they were using. Furthermore, their buildings are unmistakably of the times in which they were designed. It seems to me that there is no denying the beauty of hundreds, thousands, of buildings created in this tradition. They are in the same spirit as *The Meistersinger* and as the symphonies of Bruckner.

A different attempt to find a stylistic authority led to an exploration of the possibilities of a natural language. In *Paracelsus* Browning used a high transcendental style, based upon Wordsworth and Shelley, but extravagant and grandiose. In *Sordello*, rejecting transcendentalism, he also rejected the transcendental style. His new style was extraordinary, and though it went through many modifications, he never abandoned it. On the one hand it is syntactically of extreme complexity, presenting such fearful barriers to the reader that *Sordello* is the most neglected poem of any importance in English literature. It makes the reader feel as if a gigantic hand were squeezing his brain. Yet it is by no means in a transcendental style. Rather, its stylistic models are on the one hand the poetry of John Donne, of the early seventeenth century, and with Donne's authority, the spoken language. Formal syntax, in which most poetry and literature was written until the twentieth century, is, of course, a convention, necessary because written language is stripped of those innumerable other devices which in the spoken language support, qualify, and determine the meaning. In reality verbal behavior takes place in an incredibly rich context of total linguistic behavior, and that in turn is inseparable from a virtually infinite number of other sign systems. Anyone who has studied only the literary form of a foreign language finds the actual spoken language practically incomprehensible. Browning created his style by violating the conventions of written prose and the more elaborate conventions of traditional poetry and by founding his style on the rhythms, the phrasing, the stresses, and the grammatical involutions of the spoken tongue.

Baudelaire's style shows the same forces and a somewhat similar solution. The structure of *The Flowers of Evil* is, by his own admission, entirely arbitrary and externally imposed. Originally divided into five "chapters," after its suppression and revision it was reissued in six; and had he lived to prepare his planned third edition, further structural manipulations would have appeared. It is possible to argue forever as to which edition, the first or second, is better organized; but the question is unresolvable, simply because the structure in both is arbitrary. The style equally depends upon an external authority. On the one hand the forms—the stanza structure, the line, and much of the language—were derived from the grand baroque and even from witty Enlightenment forms and manners of seventeenth- and eighteenth-century French poetry. But against this are placed the natural rhythms of the spoken language and a vocabulary drawn from the vernacular, even from the gutter. Such words had never before been used in French poetry, and the literary scandal was almost as great as the moral.

The English poet, Tennyson, used, though with less intensity, a somewhat similar contrast. Employing verse forms revived from early periods and hallowed by associations, he employed, after 1840, a diction drawn from the middle-class vernacular and refined, by the same laborious choice, to an almost Flaubertian neutrality. In the 1850's, the iron time, his major work was *Maud*, a study of a sensitive social and economic middle-class outcast, whose erotic frustrations, caused specifically by Philistine values, drive him into insanity and a total loss of identity. At the end he finds salvation by going off to war.

What the hero of *Maud* symbolized, Arthur Rimbaud, born in 1854, the inheritor of Baudelaire, acted out. By the time he was twenty he had plunged, in poetry and poetic prose, into the hell of personality, and the hell of middle-class society. Rejecting both these barbarisms, rejecting art itself, he went to Africa and became a slave trader. Cutting himself off from the European world entirely, he preferred to encounter a true barbarism, justified by its integration with an infinitely cruel natural world. His purpose is apparent, to seek a real identity by exposing himself as violently as possible to a world impenetrable to value. Whether he succeeded no one knows; but what little evidence we have suggests that he did.

Similarly, in the late 1850's Tennyson began working on *The Idylls of the King*, the publication of which stretched from 1859 to 1889. Tennyson never entirely lost his transcendentalism, but it became extremely attenuated. On the surface the *Idylls* entirely conforms with middle-class morality; that is its exoteric face. But beneath, esoterically, it is an utterly disillusioned demonstration, like the *Ring*, that society cannot be redeemed, that its ills cannot be healed, that the transcendental hero violates those he presses into his service, and that the artist-hero must forever remain alienated.

Shortly after completing *Sordello*, Browning embarked on a series of dramatic monologues, in which the speaker is neither the poet nor some aspect of the poet, but an individual drawn from the contemporary world or from the historical past. The device is not dissimilar to Flaubert's turning himself into Emma Bovary, and thus getting a stylistic control from the manners and behavior of the provincial middle class, from which, of course, he himself had come. Browning, just as he turns for his verbal authority to the vernacular, imposes upon the self a stylistic control taken from the non-artistic personalities, from, as it were, the vernacular of personality structure. It is by manipulating these personalities antithetical to himself that he finds a cultural style and an immense variety of orientations which he can use for his purpose, the encounter with reality. In this stylistic device his most astounding achievement is *The Ring and the Book*, in which the same story is told eleven different times by ten different people, one of them most subtly masked as himself.

But it is not a story. It is a matter of history, a long-forgotten seventeenth-century murder trial and what led up to it. The source for his material was a collection of documents made for one of the lawyers involved; Browning found it in a flea market in Florence. Here we find another kind of external authority, that of history, or rather, historical documents. This control is not to be confused with the classic control, which we saw in Bruckner and Ruskin and in *The Meistersinger*, though Wagner used sixteenth-century documents in preparing his libretto. Rather, it is the employment of recently developed techniques of historical research. It is not the use of history as an analogue, in which the artist selects from history in order to symbolize his orientation. For the objectist there is no orientation to symbolize. It is not "history" but the materials of history, the documents and the artifacts, which create for him an orientation which he can use to examine the objects of personality and behavior. In *Salammbô*, published in 1862, Flaubert imposed upon himself the same external control, dependent upon archaeological study of ancient Carthage.

This kind of historicism is the same thing as the artist's employment of recently developed tools of the social sciences. Instead of depending upon his intuitive knowledge of his own social environment, or using his insights to create a symbolic analogue, in the manner of Balzac, the novelist began to use governmental reports, newspaper accounts, the techniques of reportage and social research, the writings of sociologists and economists, and the theories of physiologists, of biologists, of geneticists. Of the novelists who employed this kind of control, Émile Zola, born in 1840, is undoubtedly the greatest, at least in the sense that his works penetrated into every part of Europe and America and created an immense following of novelists and readers. He established the technique of the researched novel. After several preliminary trials, he published in 1871 the first in his series of more than twenty novels devoted to the study of one family, in its various legitimate and illegitimate branches, under the Second Empire, the Rougon-Macquarts. Like Balzac, he attempted a Human Comedy, but where Balzac used scientific ideas as an analogue for his vision, and where Balzac hoped to redeem society, Zola used science, particularly the then rather primitive science of heredity, to control his investigation into the realities of French social structure.

Zola was especially inspired by the rapidly growing science of ecology—a word invented in 1873. Ecology is the study of the mutual and complex relationships between an organism and its environment. It was made possible by Darwin's *Origin of Species*, first published in 1859 and rewritten five times, the last edition appearing in 1872. The objectists were among the few who understood Darwin, whose scientific construct of evolution arrived at precisely the results they had arrived at. The idea of evolution had appeared recognizably in the eighteenth century, and we have seen how Schopenhauer and Browning employed early evolutionary concepts, which could easily be absorbed by the symmetrical stage of the nineteenth-century vision. Evolution was perfectly adaptive or teleological, in the Hegelian manner, its ultimate purpose and aim —*telos* means both—being perfect adaptation of organism to environment.

Darwin, born in 1809, was highly sensitive to the cultural forces of his time. He comprehended that if the organism were perfectly adapted to the environment there would be no reason for new species to appear, since the system of nature would already be perfect. And yet geology showed that new species do come into existence, and his study of domesticated animals proved it. On the other hand, if evolution were purposive, there should be a steady closing of the adaptational gap between organisms and environment, and man, being recent in origin, must be the best adapted of all organisms. When he considered Malthus' demonstration that human population growth outruns growth of human food supply (that nightmare which in the twentieth century has become a daymare), and when he had meditated about his voyage around the world from 1831 to 1836, he was forced to the conclusion that no organism is perfectly adapted to its environment, that species come into existence and disappear according to an immensely complex system of organism-environment relationships—ecology—and that that system was characterized by accident and randomness. Consequently species originated neither by the direct will of God nor by a metaphysical and divine principle of teleology which God had structured into the universe, but simply by chance. When the objectists read Darwin, they found the confirmation of their own naked experience with reality. Society cannot be saved, for it is a consequence of the random interaction of organism and environment.

When Zola looked at society with these controlling orientations, what he saw was, simply, hell. In his famous expression of 1867, conceived to justify and explain the art of Edouard Manet, he said, "Art is a corner of nature illuminated by a temperament," but as he discovered, and as Manet himself had shown, that artistic temperament needs an external controlling orientation if the self is unable to evolve one which is justified by transcendental authority. The transcendental hero is armored; the objectist hero is naked. He must seize a shield, almost at random, from the world around him. Zola's shield was science; his sword was a moral objectivity, an indifference to social morality, which revealed with an unexampled and brutal illumination—Rimbaud's word—the social irresponsibility of the middle class in all its orientative and moral complacency. That same apparent amorality is to be found in the extraordinary casualness of Manet's picture of the execution of the Emperor Maximilian, in one version shot by Mexican, in another by French soldiers. Over the wall of the court in which the shooting is so casually carried out gazes a bevy of pretty Mexican girls, mildly entertained by what is going on, but really rather bored, much more concerned with their own charm than with the death of three men in the courtyard below.

Manet was born in 1832. His youth, therefore, was dominated by the objectist revolution of Courbet, born in 1819, the same year as Ruskin. Like the little group of English pre-Raphaelite painters, whom Ruskin sponsored and defended, he attempted a direct transcription of nature by throwing over the whole academic tradition as it had developed since Raphael. I suggested earlier that Delacroix had failed to get rid of the notion that somehow the value of a painting depended upon the inherent

dignity of the subject; that even Turner could in only a few paintings rid himself of the notion that in the subject of the grandeur,
beauty, and violence of nature there was an intrinsic value. For
both, therefore, the choice of subject was a symbolization of the
transcendental self, of the power of the self to impregnate the object with value.

To Courbet such a hierarchy of subject was absurd; to him
there was only reality itself, or, as one twentieth-century critic
puts it, matter, so that human beings, often shown asleep, are revealed as neither more nor less than the nature of which they are a
part. Human beings are not presented against a background of
nature. Nature is presented—reality, matter—and human beings
may or may not accidentally, randomly, be there too. The external
control of the Pre-Raphaelites was moral, as well as transcriptive;
not so with Courbet. His choice of subject was determined by only
one thing, that it moved him. Courbet was anti-idealistic, anti-
intellectual. Basically, he had no interest in social judgments. He
put his friends and his relations in his pictures for exactly the same
reason that he painted the landscape around Ornans, where he was
born and brought up: he was moved. Like Wordsworth and
Constable, he continually returned to the environment and people
of his childhood and youth simply because they were his. Thus he
constantly renewed his identity and was able to face over and over
again the natural and human world with a directness of regard
which was uncompromising and, in French painting, absolutely
novel. His control was his personal emotion.

Manet's method was different. For his external stylistic
control, he used the recently invented style of the photograph. The
impact of photography upon the painter's vision was twofold. On
the one hand, it freed him from the traditional task of recording
appearances. As I suggested earlier, black-and-white reproductions
of Friedrich have a photographic look, although all his work was
done before photography was perfected in the 1830's. The reason
lies partly in his power to make minutely observed transcriptions
of natural appearances, and partly in the fact that reproductions
are themselves, of course, photographs. Eventually the camera

was to free the artist from the task of transcription; its immediate effect was to give him a new technique of transcription. To the ordinary, untrained eye, the photograph looks like a reproduction of reality. It is odd, however, that a very old saying asserts that the camera cannot lie; originally and for nearly a hundred years it omitted color. In fact a photograph is a surface made up of patches of different intensities of gray, with shading within the areas of the patch.

What this meant to the painterly eye comes out when we examine Ruskin's drawings and water colors. He used the line to establish the form, and the shading or chiaroscuro went across the forms. After he became acquainted with photographs of buildings, which he first saw in Venice in 1847, his architectural drawings and water colors adapted the photographic technique of shading within the forms, which were patches of tonal gradation. The line thus disappeared. It had neither a life of its own nor did it function as a boundary to forms or patches. Only in the twentieth century, in the work of Edward Weston, for example, was the line made significant and aesthetically meaningful in the photograph; but within the last fifty years the photograph has become an artistic medium in its own right, and modern photography should not be used as a basis for understanding the significance of the photograph to the painter's vision in the middle of the nineteenth century. Manet, adapting the photographic surface, painted in colored grays, in patches; indeed many of his paintings have almost no color at all. In the 1870's, however, impressionism took a new direction. With the generation of Renoir, born in 1841, nine years after Manet, colors were no longer mixed on the palette. Flecks of pure color were applied from the rainbow palette directly to the surface of the painting. The painter did not mix the paints. The eye did the mixing. The control was scientific, derived from recent developments in the study of color perception.

The vision of photography gave Manet another control as well. Heretofore a painting had been composed. The forms had been related by a subtle violation of symmetry known as balance. Further, the forms generally were complete, uninterrupted by the edge of the canvas or the frame. The photograph, however, revealed the possibilities of transcriptive composition. Forms were cut off by the edge of the photograph; a continuity of the scene with the rest of the world was insisted upon. The peculiar advantage of this spontaneous and random vision was stridently urged when photographers, seeking to make their technique into an art, employed traditional painterly composition in the studio. Nothing is less convincing or more absurd than the photograph of a still life or of a nude carefully arranged according to the compositional tradition of paintings. But the open-air, unposed photograph was seized upon by Manet as a way to solve the problem which had long haunted nineteenth-century painting, how to get the spontaneity of the momentary vision of value into the painting. Only Turner had solved it, and he of course was virtually unknown in Paris in the 1850's and his later work misunderstood and neglected in London. In fact, in the 1850's Ruskin was busy cataloguing the Turner bequest, and Turner's most important paintings and drawings were inaccessible.

The randomness of the camera eye, the utter arbitrariness of where the edge or frame of the photograph cuts off the scene from the rest of the world, showed Manet how to symbolize spontaneity. This, combined with painting in patches of colored grays, made it possible for him to complete a painting within a couple of hours, or at most a single day. Subtly sensitive to the objectist perception of the instability of the self and the impossibility of imposing order upon the undisciplined personality, he insisted that a painting must be finished in a single span, for the next day it is no longer the same person who returns to it. The photograph freed the artist from the draftsman's line, from detailed finish, and from the compositional tradition. It is no wonder that the public and official critics detested his work, while Zola could understand what he was doing and insisted in his brilliant articles and essays of 1866 and 1867 that a new painterly vision had come into existence. Cézanne celebrated these articles by painting his father reading the paper in which they appeared; and Renoir by painting Alfred Sisley, himself an impressionist painter, reading the articles in a café frequented by the followers and admirers of Manet.

Manet used also one other control for his vision, a device

which reveals in its full significance the continuity of objectism with the origins of the nineteenth-century vision, its realization of unresolvable antinomies, of irreconcilable opposites. During the 1860's he painted a series of pictures in which the composition and the subject were derived from the old masters but the material was taken from the contemporary world. The two most famous are "Le déjeuner sur l'herbe" ("Lunch on the grass," or "The Picnic") of 1862 and "Olympia" of 1863, exhibited in 1865. The first is derived from the "Concert Champêtre" in the Louvre, sometimes assigned to Giorgione, sometimes to Titian, and from a sixteenth-century engraving after Raphael. It shows two fully clothed men in the woods; with them are two women, both nude, one sitting next to the men and looking directly but indifferently at the spectator, the other paddling in a stream in the background. What are they doing there? For what purposes have the women undressed? The men are engaged in a conversation; they quite ignore the two women. The scene is as equivocal and shocking as the indifferent girls in the "Execution of Maximilian."

That is, it was shocking to the public, precisely because no explanation was offered, either of justification or condemnation. The figures are merely there. It was this indifference that infuriated the middle-class public. The picture is not erotic; it was its very lack of eroticism that maddened the Philistines. They were entirely accustomed to the all but pornographic eroticism of the official painters of the annual Salon. These painters used all kinds of historical and Biblical settings as an opportunity to display nakedness, male and female, as erotically as they could. They used the photograph, not to release their vision, but to give their nudes the vulgar reality of the indecent photograph. As Gauguin said a couple of decades later, "The Salon is an enormous brothel." The nude in Manet's painting neither invites violation nor suggests that you submit to her in a masochistic frenzy. Her admirable self-possession and unashamed failure to be coy locates pornography right where it belongs, in the spectator's mind. A controlling structure derived from the classic tradition enables Manet to look at a woman's naked body as an object, and to see her personality as a self-determined entity. Unlike Kundry, she is neither drudge nor great whore.

The "Olympia" is even more powerful, for this woman is quite clearly a prostitute. She is carefully posed in a picture arranged with all the balance of traditional composition. Indeed, "Olympia" is taken directly from the recumbent nudes of Giorgione, Titian, and Velasquez. But those nudes are goddesses; they are evocations of Venus, idealized out of the human sphere, symbols of a paradisiacal world of perfect gratification. Olympia says no such thing. Cool, untroubled, self-possessed, she looks directly at the spectator; like her earlier sister she is neither coy nor dominating; she is neither sacrificial victim of lust nor *femme fatale*. She pretends to nothing. She waits, ready to give value for payment received, her subtly braced and tense right arm revealing the presence of a genuine and human identity. In herself she is anything but pornographic, but Manet could not have said to the public more clearly, "This is really what you come to the Salon for. You want a whore? I give you a whore. But you will not be able to pretend that she is anything else." Is was no accident that so many of the academic Salon pictures, such as those of Bouguereau, ended up hanging above the bars in the saloons of Western gold towns, barrooms of hotels which were in fact brothels; or in the collections that wealthy Philistines made of pornographic and semi-pornographic art.

In precisely the same spirit Manet exhibited in 1864 a dead Christ, supported by angels. But Christ's eyes are open; his resurrection, if that is what it is, is painful. He is equivocal. Is he dead or alive? He exhibits his wounds, which are not prettied up. He looks directly at the spectator, but with an ambiguous withdrawn glance. But there is nothing ambiguous about his body. It is the body of a man, a masculine man, with hair on his chest. Fully to understand this picture, one must be familiar with the Christ of the Salons, that androgynous, eroticized being, blatantly appealing to the eroticism of women and the repressed homo-eroticism of men. Instead of that creature, Manet offers a real man, violated in body and soul, not sacrificed, his death thus justified.

For the theme is violation. This Christ does not say, "Come, violate me," or "Come to me and in your emotional surrender be violated." It says, "You have violated me." One is again reminded of *Parsifal*, in which religion does not sanction a false and pornographic eroticism, as it did in the religious art of the time and most Catholic religious art today, which turns churches into the reception rooms of whore houses; rather, Wagner's revelation of false eroticism in Parsifal's rejection of Kundry releases a profound and true sexuality to justify and sanctify religion.

These ironic controls of Manet's reveal the real function of the externally imposed controls of objectist art. The aim of these artists was to reveal the hell of personality and the hell of middle-class society, to force the self to encounter that hell with no illusions that it could redeem it, with no transcendental authority to penetrate it with value, with no illusion that behind the self lay an unconscious but divine support for identity. Therefore, the order arbitrarily and even randomly drawn from outside the self and outside the artistic tradition was in violent contrast with the disorder, the frustration, the suffering, the horror, the unredeemable randomness of subjective and objective existence. Thus order and disorder, value and failure of value, meaning and meaninglessness, identity and the instability of identity, are symbolized and suspended without reconciliation in a single vision. The dual vision of Coleridge's "Kubla Khan" is here renewed and given new power and authority. Hell and heaven, the sunny pleasure dome and the caves of ice, order and disorder, are contained in a single all-inclusive ironic orientation.

The strength of middle-class society today comes from its incorporation of the objectist tradition; its weakness arises from its subjection of that tradition to the non-ironic Enlightenment orientation which drains the opposites of their opposition and reconciles the irreconcilable, which has sentimentalized the great achievements of that iron time, which has converted moral responsibility masking itself as moral indifference into a traditional and socially acceptable morality. However, partly because the Philistines were beginning to capture the objectist tradition, as with the late Courbet, who became academic, pretty, and pornographic, but mostly because of the tension in objectist culture and its unresolved problems, the artist and the thinker went on to a new stage, in which the various styles of objectism were drawn together into a single powerful conception of style. Style itself was seen as the source of value.

# Part Five

# Style and Value

# CHAPTER XVII

# *Identity and Personality*

I<small>N SOME WAYS</small> the objectist artists were in the position of Stendhal and Byron and other men of their stage in the development of the nineteenth-century vision. Both groups were reduced to the naked confrontation of self and world. It is, for example, probably one of the consequences of the objectist orientation that Byron's *Don Juan* began, at last, to receive the admiration it deserved, and that this later Byron was seen as far greater than the Byron of *Harold* and *Manfred*. The morale of both groups, likewise, depended upon the capacity of the self to endure the vision of what it saw.

But there was also a profound difference, and the later group was in a more perilous and disturbing situation. Both Byron and Stendhal retained enough of the ancient way of thinking to be able to support that endurance with a vision of the self as paradise. Indeed, to individuals who had with great difficulty escaped from valueless negation, it is not surprising, indeed, it is inevitable, that the recovery of selfhood should be felt as an entry into paradise. But the successive attempts to find a metaphysical or divine ground for that paradise—the symmetrical stage and the asymmetrical or transcendental stage—had both failed. When the world was turned inside out, and when value, meaning, and order were derived from the self, a metaphysical ground for that self had to be created; that was the activity of the imagination, whether artistic, metaphysical, or moral. But with the failure of transcendentalism, there was no ground for the self. Consequently, the function of the imagination had to be carried on from without, by imposing upon the self an order not derived from the self. Thus the self could create value by gazing fixedly upon the hell, or meaninglessness, of society and personality. I have compared this imposed order to armor; it would be—or it came to be—better to compare it to stocks, in which the self was rigidly fixed.

In that very act, however, of imposing an external order lay the solution; for if the order was imposed from without, it was the artist who went out and looked for it. If he was in stocks, he was there by his own choice, decision, and moral responsibility. If the imagination chose, from without, a structure to sustain its fixed vision, the decision to choose and the choice itself were acts of the imagination. This realization united all of the formal activities of the objectist imagination; and it was perceived that each of the external controls was a symbolization of the self's orientation, of its creation of value by opposing self to object. It followed, therefore, that all of the various styles used by the objectist were united by the fact that each was an aspect of style.

In the terms of this book, the function of the orientative drive was seen in a new way. If it was no longer possible to validate the orientative drive and hence the sense of identity or selfhood by appealing to a transcendental source, it first appeared, in the objectist stage, that the orientative drive could be justified only by deriving an orientation from the empirical world. Now it could be seen that the act of derivation was itself the justification for the orientative drive; and that the validity of the orientative drive lay in its very power to seek an orientation for the purpose of engaging with reality. The artistic task, therefore, was no longer to find an external controlling form but to symbolize the orientative drive itself, the power of the individual to maintain his identity by creating an order which would maintain his gaze at the world as it is, at things as they are. In short, the orientative drive became an instrument.

But this was a far different instrumentalism from that evolved by Carlyle and Balzac. With them the instrumental symbol worked to embody, to incarnate the divine, to make the Word into flesh. This new instrumentalism was not a transcendental tool but an orientative tool. The order which style could create was not, then, a divine order which justified man in creating order out of the chaos of a world without value, but a purely human instrumental order which would symbolize man's power to create a subjective order which could fix his gaze upon that valueless world. Further, it was an impersonal order, and for this reason. In distinguishing between self and role, the first two major stages, through transcendentalism, had marked off a preserve within the personality from which redemption could flow. The task was to redeem the rest of the personality (the task of transcendental love) and from that redemption to move on to the redemption of the world. But the objectists had shown that personality is but an aspect of nature and society, and that therefore the personality was also hell. It followed that no area of the personality could be fenced off and designated as paradisiacal, as inherently structured, ordered, valuable, and meaningful.

Therefore, for the old distinction between self and role a new distinction was made, between self and personality. Style, consequently, could not be derived from an internal, accidental randomness which was no different from, which was indeed identical and continuous with, the accidental randomness of society and nature. Hence the new style, which symbolized the distinction between self and personality, could not be extravagant in the transcendental fashion. It could not symbolize the individual's power to maintain orientation in the face of that experienced world of personality, society, and nature. It was, then, the artist's task not to create and symbolize an orientation but to symbolize the orientative power itself. An orientation must necessarily be derived from the personality or, in the objectist mode, from outside the personality, from science, or history, or natural language, and so on. The capacity to find an orientation was, consequently, an impersonal potential. Stylism is marked by a peculiar impersonality.

But it is not marked by non-individuality. The self, even though it was now distinguished from the personality, could be experienced only by the orienting individual. Selfhood, though it was impersonal, was not objective; it remained and necessarily had to remain subjective. As Parsifal revealed, the hell of personality cannot be redeemed by concealing dependence upon the mother under the mask of transcendental eroticism. Personality, as he discovered in his wanderings between Act II and Act III, cannot be redeemed; only selfhood can be redeemed. The individual, therefore, cannot redeem others, for that would be to attempt to redeem their personalities; he can only demonstrate that he has redeemed his selfhood. He can only be a model to others, by exhibiting the power of self-redemption. Parsifal does not return from his wandering a conquering hero; that would mean a redemption of his personality. He returns exhausted, his personality reduced to valuelessness. Nevertheless, he remains Parsifal. He does not become "man" or "Christ" or anything of the sort. Nor, when he has touched Amfortas' wound and thus healed with the spear of selfhood the bleeding and torturing horror of personality, does he vanish from the earth or ascend into heaven. Quite the contrary, he becomes king of the Grail knights. The achievement of selfhood makes it possible for him to use personality as an instrument to empathize with other men's experience of the hell of personality, and his own sufferings enable them to empathize with his. He does not become Christ or a symbol of Christ. He uses Christ's suffering in the hell of personality and world as a model which gives him the power to perceive that world and personality are hell, are valueless. Thus he remains Parsifal, a unique individual; only the self-redeemed is truly redeemed. His individuality has value, though his personality does not.

For this reason, the new style was at once impersonal and individual, and the art of the past was neither a tradition to be triumphantly exploited by the personality nor the source of styles and forms to be arbitrarily imposed from without. Rather, it became a model; and the artist's task was not to imitate it but to grasp its essence. A tradition gave the artist impersonality; to make a unique use of the tradition gave him individuality or selfhood. Thus Wagner used, in *Parsifal*, the Christian tradition; but he used it in a unique way, in a manner that was uniquely his own, with style. Further, the essence of any orientative tradition is, of course, not what it says, not the orientation its presents, but its power to order and thus to symbolize value. This was what distinguished art from all other orientative activities; its power to symbolize individuality and selfhood as opposed to personality and lack of identity meant that it was the opposite of hell—personality and the objective world. Art, therefore, was not symbolic of paradise; it was paradise. In itself it was order, meaning, and value.

The men who came after the objectists, therefore, applied to the essence of art the word which had been traditionally applied to paradise: beauty. The religion of beauty, "aestheticism," was thus born; for the word "aesthetic" was traditionally applied both to "that which is characteristic of works of art" and "that which is beautiful." The relation between religion and art was conceived as symbolic; but the symbolism went in the opposite direction. Art was not symbolic of the divine; rather, the fiction or illusion of the divine was man's way of symbolizing the essence of art. As in *Parsifal*, religion did not redeem art; art redeemed religion. Indeed, it also redeemed science; and the vitality of this tradition appears today when the scientist attempts to demonstrate that his also is an aesthetic activity and worthy to rank beside the artist's. Beauty, then, is the union of the impersonal and of the individual's experience of selfhood; and beauty is immanent in the work of art. The task of the artist is to create that beauty.

Nevertheless, the position was not arrived at in one leap; two stages may be discerned. In the first there is a continuity of the objectist confrontation of self with the valuelessness of the world; but the function of the external and arbitrary control is assumed by the impersonal and individual style derived from artistic tradition. To the ugliness of personality and reality is opposed the beauty of selfhood. We have already seen that shift in *Parsifal*, in which expressiveness is subordinated to a stylistic continuity of aesthetic surface, to beauty. In the work of the English poet, Algernon Charles Swinburne, born in 1837, we see the poetic analogy to *Parsifal*, but the subordination of expression to beauty is even more striking than in Wagner's last work, even though Swinburne formed his style in the 1860's, when Wagner, still an objectist, was composing *The Meistersinger* and had still to complete *The Ring of the Nibelungs.* Swinburne's achievement may be brought out by contrasting *Atalanta in Calydon,* published in 1865, with Wagner's *Tristan and Isolde,* completed in 1859, when Swinburne, like Siegfried, was just beginning to forge his style out of the shattered fragments of the tradition.

That Swinburne belonged to a new generation, with an orientation profoundly different from that of his objectist predecessors, comes out in the way he trained himself to be a poet. No English poet before him had so thoroughly mastered the styles which tradition had already created. The traditional ballad style of the Scotch border (he grew up in Northumbria, the northernmost shire of England), the Chaucerian style, the various Elizabethan and seventeenth-century baroque styles, the styles of Dryden and Pope, and of the nineteenth-century poets, particularly those of friends and immediate predecessors, Rossetti and William Morris—he not only experimented with all of them, he mastered them so completely that he could write in each with the ease of the original poets who created and used them. He became a poetic chameleon, able to use any of the major styles of the tradition with stylistic mastery and expressiveness. From these he forged his own style, which began to emerge in the early 1860's.

The peculiar character of Swinburne's poetry, which is in general the character of the first stage of the stylistic era, is the contrast between the beauty of the aesthetic surface and the material from the world of experience which is the subject matter. In this he goes, as already suggested, beyond Wagner, for the aesthetic surface is far more non-expressive than it is even in *Parsifal.* In the ordinary, non-metaphysical and non-evaluative use of the word "beauty" it is a quality most commonly ascribed to sets of sensory data to which we can relate ourselves with the least loss of energy. It offers the maximum opportunities for orientation. Each discriminable element or entity within the situation offers of itself a minimum of emotional disturbance, to the point of being emotionally negative, and at the same time permits the observer to perceive readily a large number of relationships between it and the other elements or entities present. In short, it presents the maximum degree of structure which the artist can manage to create. Or the mathematician. The claim, constantly encountered in both the Platonic tradition and any form of the aesthetic or stylistic tradition, that there is an affinity between art and mathematics, and the continuous, though mistaken, efforts to solve the problem of artistic judgment by asserting that a work of art is beautiful to the degree its formal relationships may be mathematically described, are both instances of identifying art with structure. The offer by the work of art of a rich opportunity to experience a high degree of structure is precisely the character of Swinburne's style. In the ordinary sense, non-metaphysical and non-evaluative, it is as "beautiful" as Swinburne could make it. His study of traditional styles and the innumerable poetic exercises he wrote in them had but one aim: to discover the essence of their art, that is, by stylistic standards, the peculiar structural devices to be found in each. By abstracting these structural devices and coordinating them in his own poetry—poems, that is, which were not exercises—he created his own style. It was, then, at once traditional and individual, highly disciplined and unmistakably Swinburne's.

There is no device of poetic form which he does not master and incorporate: sound relations, that is, rhyme, alliteration (consonantal repetition), assonance (vowel repetition and similarity); stress relations, that is, rhythmical patterns and an extraordinary rapidity of rhythmical movement which makes the patterns of rhythm leap out at the reader so that he grasps them immediately; and syntax relations, long sentences of great syntactical complexity which are, however, given continuity and repetition of pattern by exploiting the possibilities of parallel syntactical structures.

This beauty of surface is responsible for very positive reactions from the reader. One reader finds it ravishing and enchanting, utterly irresistible; another, perceiving only the continuity of the aesthetic surface but incapable of responding to the variety within the patterning, to the subtle and constant play of discontinuity, finds it monotonous and excessively lengthy; a third, more perceptive, objects violently to the disparity between the extreme beauty of the surface and the highly disturbing content of the poems. It is notable that each of these objections has been made to *Parsifal*, and in general is constantly made to all of the work of this first stage in the development of stylism. Both of the first two responses are equally imperceptive; the one, carried away by the beauty, and the other, bored by it, experience the surface so powerfully that they are unable to get beyond it into what the poem is saying. To the one the poem is meaningless but beautiful; to the other the poem is merely beautiful but makes no sense. The third, however, sees what is there, but objects to Swinburne's work on the ground that the aesthetic surface is nonfunctional, that is, it is inexpressive of the emotions presented by the structure of the poem's meanings. Such critics are, of course, perfectly correct; but they miss the point.

To Swinburne, as a stylist, the emotion of situations is inseparable both from society and personality, while the self is not part of the personality but antithetical to it. The capacity of the self to create a world of order, meaning, and value, that is, beauty, is symbolized by the style, the consistency of aesthetic surface. Everything that the self experiences, however, is meaningless, chaotic, and without value. What the poem refers to outside of itself, therefore, is highly disturbing and intensely emotional. In the stylistic stage of nineteenth-century culture, the self functions both as gratifying cave and as observatory tower. The highly structured style, with its maximum opportunities for ready orientation and formal and sensuous gratification, offers a position or a stance from which one may safely observe and experience the chaos and ugliness of reality, whether that reality is within the personality or outside of it or lies in the relation between the personal and the non-personal. Thus the drive toward orientation is satisfied and simultaneously the drive toward reality is released. The chaos of reality can be permitted to invade the utmost recesses of the personality. Consequently Swinburne and his fellows and their successors have an extraordinary psychological penetration and a power to admit the existence within the personality, in society, and in the natural world, of horrors which even Baudelaire and the objectists had not quite been able to encounter. The first stage of stylism, therefore, involves the reconsideration of everything the objectists had looked at, but with a structured self, symbolized in aesthetic surface or style, rather than with an enduring self, the presence of which is only implicit.

The subject matter of Swinburne's poetry moves outward in steadily expanding circles; he begins with the horrors of personality, proceeds to the horrors of the family, goes on to the horrors of society, and ends with the horrors of nature, its indifference, its amused and equivocal juggling of creation and destruction. His early poetry, most of which was written before *Atalanta in Calydon*, though it was published in 1866, in *Poems and Ballads*, a year after *Atalanta*, is mostly concerned with one theme, the eroticism of submission and domination, with sadism and masochism, in this resembling *Parsifal* and *Venus in Furs*, published, it will be remembered, in 1870. Swinburne himself was a masochist; he knew what he was talking about, whereas Baudelaire, who inspired Swinburne to these themes, probably was less familiar than he with the actual practices, such as achieving erotic gratification by being whipped. It is an instance of how the stylists can go farther even than the objectists and can admit in themselves horrors which one is supposed to conceal, even from oneself, if possible.

It is not surprising, therefore, that Swinburne should also, in several poems, have written about Lesbianism, homo-eroticism among women. It is interesting, though anything that can be called evidence is wholly lacking, that a persistent rumor in the English literary world affirms that Swinburne himself was homosexual or at least, like Byron, bisexual. Were the poems about Sappho and her maidens a Proustian reversal of the actual state of affairs within Swinburne's own personality? Certainly, in his letters he vehemently denies such imputations and excoriates contemporaries, such as John Addington Symonds, who were homoerotic. Perhaps the tendencies were there, but repressed, Swinburne permitting them to reveal themselves only in reversal, in the Lesbos poems.

Whatever the biographical facts, it is not difficult to see the place of the Sappho poems in the psychological structure of *Poems and Ballads;* for both homo-eroticism and hetero-eroticism are seen as equally characterized by sadism and masochism, by violation of others and by submitting to others so that one may suffer violation. Further, this exposure of the true nature of eroticism as an excuse for violation and self-violation is no mere expression of tendencies in Swinburne's own personality. If they were that, the poems would be a defense or rationalization of sadism and masochism. On the contrary, they are an exposure of the failure of eroticism, which from its very nature produces a frustration which can be gratified only with destruction or self-destruction, torture and murder, or self-laceration and suicide. Eroticism is revealed as something inseparable from emotional and physical suffering and torture.

Swinburne's experience in publishing these poems was much like Baudelaire's with *The Flowers of Evil.* The outcry against them was so great that though no legal steps were taken, Swinburne's publisher refused to continue and the poet had to find another publisher, one with a rather unsavory reputation for publishing and dealing in pornography and semi-pornography. His fury against the Philistines is quite understandable. He was condemned for attempting a serious and poetic treatment of themes the existence of which the critics, those Cerberus guardians of the public morality, would scarcely even admit, ascribing everything in Swinburne's book to his own diseased imagination; yet while Swinburne was being attacked and an attempt was being made to drive his book out of the literary market, two streets in London were entirely devoted to selling pornographic literature, art, and objects which were not always *objets d'art.*

A similar attempt was made for the rest of the century to discredit the followers of Swinburne in this stage of his development, the decadents, who likewise created works of art characterized by great beauty or surface and style with an exploration of the most profoundly concealed and erotically sinister aspects of the personality. Their style was exquisite; their subject was sexual transgression and what the Philistine called perversion. The strategy of the attacks on the decadents was, of course, always to ascribe the creation of such works to the depravity of their personalities. The truth of the matter is that sometimes the transgressions of the decadents were imaginative and sometimes they themselves were transgressors. In either case their explorations into the horrors of personality were sustained by style. In art they were aesthetes or, to use the term of this book, stylists; in life they were dandies.

In considering this matter it is wise to remember that the market for true pornography, the purveying of pornography unredeemed by style, of pornography for its own sake, is primarily the well-to-do middle class. The respectable citizen buys the vast majority of pornographic publications. The high prices for such books are and always have been the proof; only the economically self-disciplined can afford them. As Wagner said in the opening of *The Rhinegold,* the lust for economic power is the consequence of frustrated eroticism. There is even some reason to believe that economic lust can be more easily controlled in a country in which little or no legal control is extended over pornography. There is certainly every reason to believe that pornography serves an important social function of some kind or other, and that it best serves that function when enough legal barriers are put up to make procuring it not really dangerous but truly venturesome, at least when, as in middle-class society, it functions in part as a reward for economic self-discipline.

The difference between pornography and the literature and art of the decadents lies precisely here. In pornography eroticism is not presented as a horror, as an illusion, as necessarily frustrating all true gratification. In the part of the Swinburnian decadents it is. The Philistine hates the decadents because they spoil his favorite reading matter, whether found forthrightly in pornography or concealed in sentimental novels, plays, magazine stories, movies, and television. The Philistine lives and loves under the illusion that eroticism is gratifying; that it is an illusion the active practice of psychiatrists—not to speak of those cassocked men in confession booths who serve the same function—demonstrates only too amply. The literature of the decadents reveals that illusion for what it is, something that invariably leads to domination or submission, or both, and thus invariably to violation of another human being. Pornography, however, not only does not reveal violation as violation; it positively approves it. It is a morality of immediate and total gratification consequent upon the erotic invasion of another personality. Pornography, then, finds its great market among the Philistine middle classes not because it is immoral but precisely because it thoroughly embodies the Philistine morality. The literature of the decadents is morally responsible; it reveals the horror of eroticism.

The interpretation of Oscar Wilde's *The Picture of Dorian Gray* (1891) is a case in point. Dorian remains forever young and beautiful, but his picture reflects the progressive effects upon his personality of his exploration of vice, which seems all the more vicious because it is so inadequately specified. But it was not Wilde's purpose to write a pornographic novel, nor yet a cautionary tale. Dorian is the dandy, the man of style. The point of the story is that such a man can maintain his identity while he investigates the most terrible pits of London's erotic and economic sub-world. The elegance of London civilization and the horror of the world on which it is built and on the existence of which its own economic and emotional existence depends are sharply juxtaposed. Dorian is the artist, the dandy, the stylist whose identity is presented as antithetical to his personality. True, he is destroyed by what he experiences, but not until he is an old man. And after all, who is not destroyed by the hell of the personality and the society which his identity exists in? If the novel were a mere middle-class morality tale, when he dies the beautiful Dorian should become as ugly, as depraved, as misshapen as his picture. But actually, as he becomes what his picture is, his picture regains all the beauty of Dorian as a young man, a beauty which he had kept throughout his long life. The end products of his life are a ruined body which is continuous with his personality and his society, and a work of art which will symbolize forever his power to explore the hell of reality.

Wilde's mistake was to attempt to live his novel, to use, as he said, his genius in his life and his mere talent in his art. He was condemned to prison and driven into exile and poverty because he had sexually cohabited with a few of the large class of London homosexual prostitutes. These male prostitutes would not have existed—and would not exist today, and not just in London—had there not been an economic demand for them. Like pornography, and for the same reason and in the same way, they were supported —in modest splendor—by the economic discipline of the middle classes, and had been for decades; and before them, so far as we can tell, by the aristocracy. Perhaps, after all, Wilde was not condemned for immorality but for poaching.

The contrast between Swinburne's presentation of eroticism as a destructive illusion and Wagner's in Act III of *Tristan* is the contrast between an aesthetic surface which is emotionally non-functional and one which supports, reinforces, and brings out as intensely as possible the emotional agony of slashing into scraps the veil which eroticism casts over the realities of the personality. This contrast is even more striking when *Tristan* is compared with *Atalanta in Calydon*. That this work made Swinburne a great reputation, which in the following year *Poems and Ballads* half ruined, can only be a consequence of the fact that his readers responded so powerfully to the extraordinary attraction of his now fully mastered style, the sensuously seductive aesthetic surface, that they scarcely understood what he was really saying. For *Atalanta* is an attack upon the family, which the nineteenth-century version of the Enlightenment asserted to be at once the natural basis of society and divinely instituted; in the Protestant middle-class culture of the time the focus of religious sentiment was a version of the Holy Family in which the equivocality of Joseph's role was minimized and usually entirely suppressed.

*Atalanta* is modeled on Greek tragedy, but only modeled. It is therefore quite different from, for example, *Merope* (1858) by Matthew Arnold, an objectist who used ancient tragedy as an imposed external control. Swinburne's theme may be variously stated. Perhaps the heart of the matter appears when the chorus, alone on the stage, chants, "Who hath given man speech? or who hath set therein A thorn for peril and a snare for sin?" and answers, "The supreme evil, God," the creator of the unresolvable antinomies which tear men apart, who makes language the instrument by which men establish relationships among themselves and the instrument which smashes those relationships, sets men in strife. Through language God is the source of order and disorder, of social creativity and social destruction, just as Aphrodite—goddess of erotic love, who "against all men from of old . . . hast set thine hand as a curse," who seems to offer men delight—is in fact "an evil blossom . . . born Of sea-foam and the frothing of blood," who destroys not only lovers but brothers, friends, armies, and cities.

The unresolvable antitheses of human experience, then, are the subject of the poem. On the one hand is Althea, convinced that man cannot trust the world, that the gods are jealous and destructive, and that only in the family and in sacrificing everything to the family is safety to be found. Meleager, her son, on the contrary is sure that man should trust the world, that the gods wish him well, and that social order is the necessary result of going out of the family to find one's love. Meleager, however, loves Atalanta, who, dedicated to the virgin goddess, Artemis, is unattainable, for she has stripped herself of her social femininity. To protect her, he kills his uncles, his mother's brothers. In fury at this double betrayal of the family, Althea plunges into the fire a log which, as it is consumed, destroys her son. Meleager dies, and Althea never speaks again. Swinburne has set in the most violent contrast two irreconcilable opposites; no solution is possible. Man, as the chorus chants in its final utterance, is helpless before his gods, the powers that determine the character of his experience; he can neither placate them nor destroy them.

As we have seen, *Tristan and Isolde* presents exactly the same pattern. On the one hand, the lovers insist that society is a world of illusion and that meaning and value reside only in the personality; on the other, Mark, Brangwaine, Kurwenal, and Melot are sure that the personality is a world of illusion and that meaning and value are to be found in the social order. Neither set can understand the other; poor Mark is so foolish as to imagine that he can give up Isolde, unite the lovers, incorporate them into the social order, and fix things up so that everybody lives happily ever after. In Wagner's work the self is implicit in the power of the music to endure and respond to what is happening in the drama. The music is emotionally functional. In Swinburne's poem, on the contrary, identity is maintained by the unbroken and consistently structured beauty of an aesthetic surface which is indifferent to the searing emotions unleashed by the struggle between Meleager and his mother, between erotic love and family love.

From the family Swinburne turned to society, and in a series of poems about Napoleon the Third's imperial dictatorship over France and the pope's emotional dictatorship over Italy revealed that the two forces, government and religion, which pretend to give society order, in reality lacerate the bodies and hearts of mankind. In place of these horrors, he offers society a vision of "love, the beloved republic," a society in which each human being maintains his own identity and confirms the identity of others, in which man will have gone beyond the eroticism and role-playing of masculinity and femininity. But like Wagner at the end of *Parsifal* he offers no recipe for how humanity can attain such a state nor what it would be like if man could, by some miracle, achieve it. One suspects that it is a negative ideal, one not to be hoped for but presented merely to reveal what the human state in actuality is.

The same equivocality is to be found in Swinburne's treatment of nature. Man is the product of nature, but the consequence of his appearance at the end of the evolutionary process is that to give himself importance, to find value in the world, he must project upon the universe the illusions of his religious insanity. Nature is herself equivocal, ambiguous, full of antinomies; she is the womb and the tomb, destructive and creative, equally indifferent to the joys and the sufferings of men, which are but by-products of her endless and pointless creative activity. In nature Swinburne finds but one positive symbol, the sea, "the great sweet mother." The best of Swinburne's poetry is not merely about the sea; it is about swimming. He was profoundly interested in the psychological gratification to be found in that sport, and there are astonishing stories about his own prowess and the extraordinary risks he ran to indulge it.

With him the sea changes its traditional nineteenth-century symbolic significance. Heretofore, it had symbolized an area of the personality in which the self might be found. The alienated man had gone to sea with other men, or at least in a boat. But in Swinburne there is only the naked body far out from shore. The land is both society and personality, for to the stylist there is no difference; society and personality form a single continuum. The sea, then, makes possible a separation from society and personality; it destroys both when men venture out upon it. In the sea the swimmer is aware only of his identity, which is confirmed by the even contact between the water and the surface of the naked body. Swimming brings to the surface of the consciousness the body-image, which is, to Swinburne, the profoundest symbolization of the sense of identity. From the sea, the swimmer can look back at the land and know what society and personality really are, and can gaze down into the depths of the sea, where wrecks and skeletons image their proper fate. In Swinburne's imagery, the sea performs, then, precisely the function that in his poetry is fulfilled by his style; it opposes antithetically the self and the personality, and beyond personality society and that world of nature, womb and tomb, where man finds his uneasy and bitter home.

The poetry of Swinburne has long been all but excluded from the canon of English poetry. Only since about 1950 has it been possible, so powerful was the influence of the critics and poets of the 1920's, to read him again with sympathy and to begin to comprehend what he was doing. A similar fate has been that of a French painter, Gustave Moreau. For half a century he was a joke in the art world. The Moreau Museum in Paris, willed, like Turner's collection of his own works, to the nation, was unvisited, or visited only by seekers of nineteenth-century curiosities; yet, suddenly, in the early 1960's, critics and the knowing public have begun to look at him seriously, or, more precisely, have become able to see his work. Every new stage in the development of art blinds us to what has gone immediately before, yet so cleanses our vision that we suddenly see what, before the coming of the new vision, we could not see at all. Thus the recovery of Moreau follows the recovery in the mid-1950's of the late Turner and the late Monet.

Moreau, born in 1826, eleven years before Swinburne, was slower in arriving at stylism. He began as an academic and salon painter, though under the influence of Delacroix; but his long stay in Italy from 1856 to 1860 completely transformed his art, and by 1865 his mature style had formed itself. His Italian sojourn nearly coincided with Swinburne's preparatory period; his aims were similar and the results were alike. Most nineteenth-century art students in Italy went to Rome and stayed there; a few might have wandered to the major galleries in Florence and Naples. But Moreau seems to have gone everywhere. Far from being solely interested in the "antique" as it was understood in the exhausted academic tradition descended from Raphael, he turned to archaic vases, Pompeian frescoes, Byzantine enamels and mosaics, and all the painters, it would almost seem, of the fourteenth and fifteenth centuries, the early Sienese and the fifteenth-century Florentines. Even more interestingly, he leaped across the later Leonardo, Raphael, and Michelangelo, to the mannerist painters of the sixteenth century who followed the High Renaissance artists. At that time the mannerists were pretty thoroughly ignored. Like Swinburne he renewed his art by a fresh examination of the tradition, and from that tradition he forged a style at once traditional and individual.

As with Swinburne's style, one is tempted to say that Moreau was intoxicated with the manipulation of the aesthetic surface. But it is no aesthetic drunkenness. Every traditional resource of the painter is studied, analyzed, mastered, and brought under control, especially the equivalent of Swinburne's rhythm, a color which rushes out of the canvas to embrace the observer in an immediate sensuous shock; yet it is a shock which is as gratifying as it is impossible to ignore. In his later years Moreau sketched in floods of pure color, with no line, no definition, no suggestion, or almost none, of any natural or human object. As his style matured, his control of line, derived mainly, it would seem, from the mannerists and certain fifteenth-century painters such as Mantegna and the fourteenth-century Sienese, became increasingly adept, so that the surface of the painting began to have the character of a two-dimensional arabesque, an almost calligraphic independence from the subject matter. Again, in his later years, other sketches show him substituting for the line long, unbroken, and sweeping brush strokes which of themselves form an over-all arabesque-like pattern. An even more individual feature of his style, however, was his exceeding complexity of minute patterning within relatively small areas. Leonardo, the late Michelangelo, and the mannerists had been particularly fond of creating elaborate and ingenious designs for jewels, headdresses, armor, and fabrics. No painter has ever gone so far as Moreau in creating fantastic adornments for his figures, for furniture, for architecture. Finally, color, line, and pattern are synthesized in "Jupiter and Semele," on which he worked from 1864 to 1895, a picture which seems all one gigantic and fantastic jewel, a style which, like Swinburne's, seems to offer nothing but sensuous gratifications, bizarre, utterly unrelated to anything in the world.

And of course it was thus unrelated, and for precisely the same reasons as the emotionally non-functional character of Swinburne's style. For Moreau's subjects are the nightmare, the dream, mythological terrors, and above all, in his two famous paintings of Salome (1876), an oil and a water color called "The Apparition," in which John's severed head hangs in the air before the half-naked and terrified princess and dancer, the destructive woman. These two pictures are magically evoked in Joris Karl Huysmans' *A Rebours* (*Against the Grain*), published in 1884, when Huysmans was thirty-six. This novel is so decadent that some critics, probably in error, think it a parody of decadence. Parody or not, the hero of *A Rebours*, which has been thought to be the evil French book which corrupted—or released—Dorian Gray, is typical of his time in possessing Moreau's two Salome paintings, for they haunted a generation and inspired Wilde's own *Salome* of 1893, originally written in French. Like Swinburne, Moreau symbolizes in Salome the horror of the eroticized personality, and in many of his paintings, though not these, he takes the androgynous figure of the salons and gives it a new significance. His style redeems it from the vulgar semi-pornography of its origins, and he uses it to indicate that masculinity and feminity belong to the world of personality, which is unredeemable, which can be endured only if seen through the sensuous jewel of his style.

Perhaps the reason that his "Jupiter and Semele" took him so long to complete was not merely its size—it is six feet high and every inch is incredibly rich with color, arabesque, and pattern —but its subject, its attempt to deal with the divine. It is, he tells us, a picture of regeneration, a hymn to divinity; but that divinity is entirely mysterious. Semele is bleeding and dying from the thunderbolt which the monstrous, jeweled, and terrifying Jupiter has hurled at her, yet she is lying across his knee; unsupported, she is half raised, her face turned toward the god in terror and adoration. Her death is a sacrifice; at the foot of the divine throne sit Death and Pain, and a sorrowful Pan, the god of nature, and below him are the forces of Erebus, strange gods and nightmares, symbols of the darkest forces of the personality. To these lower figures, the sacrifice of Semele offers hope of regeneration, fainter as one's eye moves down from the base of the throne. But the nature of that regeneration is as mysterious as the nature of the divine. One is convinced that no transcendental divine is here symbolized. It is a divinity like that of the only goddess Swinburne recognized, the sea. It is nothing in itself; it serves only to rescue the identity from the hell of personality, society, and nature. The real embodiment of the divine in Moreau's art is the style itself. The divine becomes, as in Swinburne's "Hertha," a mere psychological projection, an attempt to symbolize man's sense of identity and value, an illusion which only those released by art and style can penetrate. For the men of this first stage of stylism, the greatest work of art in existence, the greatest imaginable, was *Parsifal*.

# CHAPTER XVIII

# *Identity and Style*

I N THE YEARS WHEN SWINBURNE was creating his individual and impersonal style, Johannes Brahms, born in 1833, was doing much the same thing. In the early 1850's his compositions were of the objectist stage, with remarkable similarities to Wagner's work of that decade; about 1856, however, he began to move in a new direction, mastering certain forms, particularly the variation structure. He was especially interested in thematic transformation, but the themes for which he wrote variations tended to be taken from other composers. In this imposition of external control he was still objectist; nevertheless, his exploration of the aesthetic possibilities latent in the work of others was a means to discovering his own individual uniqueness and to creating his own unique aesthetic surface. For at the same time he renewed his musical studies, particularly concentrating on counterpoint and on the choral and instrumental contrapuntal music of the sixteenth, seventeenth, and early eighteenth centuries. The work which finally emerged from this, the work in which his style appears triumphantly established, was "A German Requiem," on which he labored from 1857 to 1868, just the years in which Wagner was working on *The Meistersinger* and Swinburne on *Poems and Ballads* and *Atalanta in Calydon*. Brahms' "Requiem" is much closer to Swinburne than it is to Wagner. Wagner used Bachian counterpoint as an externally imposed control; one is constantly aware of the continuous reference to Bach. But Brahms integrates baroque counterpoint into his own style. Like Swinburne, he derives musical and aesthetic essence from an older, pre-nineteenth-century tradition and synthesizes it in a novel way and an individual manner.

This presentation of a consistent aesthetic surface which must always be, in the most ordinary sense, beautiful, in which the emotional expressiveness is subordinate, has led to curious judgments on Brahms. He has been called cold, academic, forbidding, withdrawn, and emotionally superficial and timid. For those whose musical apprehension has been overwhelmingly dominated by earlier nineteenth-century music, particularly by the Wagner of the *Ring* through *The Meistersinger*, or by the violent and dramatic splendors of Bach's earlier organ compositions, the sustained tensions of his "Brandenburg Concerti," or the grandiose and dramatic power of his "Mass in B Minor" and "The Passion According to St. John," all this is undoubtedly true and is probably responsible for the senseless and rather disgraceful Brahms-Wagner controversy, in which Brahms, with his withdrawn and disengaged personal attitude toward experience, was certainly by far the lesser offender. Actually, in making such judgments his critics are pointing to precisely that withdrawn, disengaged, apparently timid personal and musical orientation which took the risks of neither matrimony nor opera.

As we have seen in the judgments made on Swinburne, not to speak of Wagner and Bruckner, it is always wise to pay the closest attention to a critic, such as Hanslick, for instance, who passionately and sincerely loathes what he is attacking. Even if such men are really talking about their responses and not about the work of art—and that is usually the case—they provide a clue to what is genuinely interesting in the work. For the same reason, in developing one's own taste, in freeing oneself of the aesthetic orientations imposed by the cultural milieu, the art to pay attention to is precisely the art which appears to be cold or frustrating or disturbing, not the art which is immediately gratifying, for there probably is little that the latter can teach us. At the present time, when Wagner is beginning once again to receive his proper due, a campaign of denigration has been launched against Brahms. As with Swinburne, the aesthetic surface is so seductive that there is a tendency to ignore the intensity of the psychic flow which the music presents.

It is by no means an accident that Brahms' mature style should have made its first extended appearance with a requiem, a lament for the dead, which he wrote with the recent death of his mother, whom he loved dearly, in mind. Of the emotional experiences that lay behind subsequent works we know little; but what little we do know suggests that the emotional material he was dealing with and which his style was making it possible for him to come to terms with, was invariably emotional suffering. Typical is his remark about a chamber work, that it was the music of a man ready to blow his brains out. If we think of his exquisitely beautiful and highly wrought and exceedingly learned style, such a remark is a mystery; but if we forget about the style, if we deliberately repress our stylistic awareness, it is clear that the emotional content is a psychic flow in which even moments of gratification are ultimately frustrating and the source of suffering. Thus even the triumphant finales—only Tchaikovsky had the courage to write a symphony which ends in pain and frustration—have a different character than the more equivocal triumphs of Bruckner. They are, one feels, dictated by the tradition of form and by the style. They are part of that aesthetic surface which from time to time opens up, as it were, to reveal the terrors that lie beneath it. In Bruckner the finales are earned by the struggle with frustration. In Brahms they are the reward for maintaining the style in spite of the human suffering of which the composer is only too well aware. In Bruckner, an objectist, the subject is the personality and its hell of frustration, and the style is determined by the necessity to present the subject. In Brahms, the stylist, the self is separated from the hell of the personality; the style has a life of its own.

In 1890, with the Second String Quintet, Opus III, Brahms formally and officially ceased composing. He had said, he thought, what he had to say, and he had created and fully mastered his style. He was probably afraid of the aesthetic composition undertaken just to keep busy, which was the case with Swinburne, for example. That tendency of stylism to become mannered indicated a weakness in this stage of nineteenth-century cultural development, an unresolved problem, or rather a problem which it created, which I shall turn to later. Brahms, with his extraordinary aesthetic subtlety, seems to have felt it as a threat. Certainly he rose to no bait which various conductors and admirers offered in order to get him to write another symphony after his Fourth, completed in 1885. Nevertheless, another wonderfully productive period lay before him. It lasted six years, from 1891 to 1896, and it produced works which are not only among his finest but are also at once his most Brahmsian and of an entirely different character from anything he had produced before.

Apparently he was stimulated by the playing of the fine clarinetist Richard Mühlfeld, for whom he first composed a trio (Opus 114), then a quintet (Opus 115), and two sonatas (Opus 120). The clarinet is an aesthetically penetrating instrument; its sound is unmistakable and it stands out in the sharpest contrast against any background. When it is not used merely for orchestral color, it is even more distinctly a solo instrument than the piano, which is easier to blend with the orchestra. In these works the contours of the clarinet's melodic line are so distinct that the color of the other instruments appears neutral. It is like a human voice, and we are astonished that it does not articulate itself into words. Brahms himself indicated that in the trio and the two sonatas the clarinet part could be played by a viola, but such a performance changes the whole character of the music, for the viola blends with the strings and even with the piano, as the almost human clarinet does not. In addition to the clarinet works, these six years of Brahms' life also produced twenty short piano works (Opus 116 to Opus 119), the "Four Serious Songs" (the texts are from the Bible), and a set of eleven chorale preludes for the organ. Almost all of these works are at once exercises in style and something far different. In a curious way the subject is the style itself. Particularly in the piano and clarinet works, the austerity of the earlier Brahms, or at least the withdrawn quality, has vanished; and in its place there appears a sensuous appeal as irresistible as the music of the Flower Maidens in *Parsifal*. These works have been called "autumnal," but that, I fear, is a mere sentimentality derived from the fact that he was near death. Actually, of course, he was not yet fifty-eight when he decided that his life as a composer was finished, and it was not until after the composition of the "Four Serious Songs," which were inspired by Clara Schumann's death, that his own health began to fail, in his sixty-fourth year. Indeed, the songs are a return to his earlier manner, even to the integration into his own style of the baroque church cantata. They are an interruption of the music written from the clarinet trio to the clarinet sonatas.

The character of this last style is more than sensuous; it is, as the parallel with the Flower Maiden music suggests, seductive. It entices the listener into a world of intricate and, especially in the clarinet works, arabesque pleasure. These works are not mere exercises in style; they are revels in an identity detached from the world. From the mid-1860's to 1890 Brahms' orientation was one of identity, symbolized by style and sustained by style, opposed to the horror of experience. In these works, on the contrary, the orientation is gratification in identity itself, symbolized and sustained by style but opposed to nothing. His very refusal to hear a concert performance of the "Four Serious Songs," which he composed by returning to an earlier attitude and only because of the death of a dear friend, once greatly loved, suggests that these works were done out of a sense of moral and aesthetic duty, that what he was truly interested in were the clarinet and piano works on which he had been working. In thus moving into an orientation in which style serves to symbolize and sustain identity without reference either to the horror of reality or the mystery of transcendence, Brahms entered the second stage of stylism.

This is the explanation of why he wrote for the clarinet and the piano. The first, as we have seen, stands out against a background which it turns into neutrality. Its voice is almost human, almost verbally articulate, and Brahms wrote these works for a particular human being, a virtuoso, a dandy, as it were, of the clarinet, a man who had realized his musical identity in a single and striking manner. Mühlfeld, born in 1856, had grown up in a culture in which stylism was thoroughly established. But Brahms too had been a virtuoso, a dandy of the piano, and the works not written for the clarinet were written for the piano, for himself. Nevertheless, the terms "virtuoso" and "dandy" are too harsh, too strident. The dandy and the virtuoso exist in terms of their opposition to the Philistine world. From this opposition, as we have seen, these last works are free. Here Brahms is resting upon himself, rejoicing in his own identity. The great traditional symbols of cave and tower are no longer apt and to the point. Perhaps a proper symbol would be the star, or a softly radiant constellation. So, at any rate, thought the French poet, Stéphane Mallarmé, who saw more profoundly than anyone else into the nature of the shift from the first to the second stage of stylism, from identity in opposition to personality and world to identity in itself, self-sustained by its own self-generated style.

Brahms reveals the problems of the first stage of stylism and the tendencies of the second, but it cannot be said that he fully enters the second; to do that he would have had to create an entirely new style. Mallarmé, on the other hand, born in 1842, younger than both Brahms and Swinburne, was able to do so. He was perhaps the first artist to experience leaving one and entering the other. Like Swinburne, he began by taking his subjects and his general attitude from the Baudelairean tradition, even to regarding it as his duty to translate into French what of Poe's work Baudelaire had left untranslated. Nevertheless there is a difference. To be sure, there is the same loathing for the Philistine world, for Paris, for French culture under Napoleon III, for the body, for the personality; but he does not wish to explore these things; he wishes to escape them. To have established his own style on the model of previous styles was not enough; the authority of a non-functional style was only its opposition to the horrors it confronts. It was all very well that style should symbolize identity; but this strategy meant that value appeared only as a result of that opposition, that confrontation of horror, that chimera, as Mallarmé called it, that impossible and absurd fusion of utter disparities. Further, that chimera was not the world itself; it was a creation of the mind. When the mind created a vision of horror, it was its own hell it symbolized, not the world's, for the world it cannot know. And the same relation existed when the mind created a vision of beauty. Both the horror and the beauty, then, were illusions; for both were but what the mind inherited from its predecessors. Thus a style derived from tradition, in the manner of Swinburne, Moreau, and Brahms, was of precisely the same character as the horror which that style made it possible to confront. To put it in the terms of this book, so long as style was derived from tradition, the drive toward reality was subject to the orientative drive. If the self, the *moi*, to use Mallarmé's French word, were to be genuinely free, it must be free from traditional orientations as well as free from reality. It could neither be sustained by tradition nor thought of as called into existence by its confrontation with the horror, the chimera. A way must be found to assert its existence and to symbolize that existence, yet to do so without depending upon the engagement with reality.

Mallarmé's cultural predecessors, as we have seen, used the orientative drive as an instrument to engage with reality, thus finding its justification; and they symbolized that drive in the order or structure of style. Mallarmé's task was to free the orientative drive, to assert its independent existence. Style, then, was not to be an instrument with which to engage with reality; rather it was to be an instrument to symbolize the orientative activity in itself. It must be pure structure, unrelated either to orientative constructs or to predictive constructs. It must be independent of traditional art, religion, metaphysics, or science; yet it must function emotionally as each of these functions. The identity, the *moi*, must be asserted to exist, and its existence must be symbolized in an individual, non-personal, and also non-traditional style.

Furthermore, style was not merely a handy or convenient way to symbolize the self; it was the only way. There are two reasons, or two ways of putting the same reason. First is the fact that all existent ways of symbolizing the *moi* were bound up with and had been achieved by art, religion, metaphysics, and science. Second, only aesthetic style, as it had been freed by Mallarmé's immediate predecessors and had been discriminated as something in and of itself, exhibited pure structure. Up to the first stage of stylism, style had always been the servant—the slave, Mallarmé would put it—of expression; it served either to bring out an orientation or to discriminate some aspect of reality; in everything but art that is all it can do. By making style non-functional the first stylists had discovered pure structure, which symbolized the orientative drive, that is, in Mallarmé's terms, the *moi*, the self, the identity.

And there are further reasons why aesthetic style was the only possibility for symbolizing the self. Only aesthetic style can exhibit individuality. Mathematics, at least as it was then conceived, is universal, as non-individual as it is impersonal. Moreover, only aesthetic style is sensuous, and if the self is to be given existence, and at the same time revealed as independent of the world of empirical reality, it must be symbolized sensuously. Thus it can be experienced sensuously, exactly as the empirical world is experienced. Only thus can we be sure of its difference from that world. Only thus can we discriminate it. The entire world, ideally, must be organized by aesthetic structure into a single book—which no one can possibly write, although all artists, according to Mallarmé, have done nothing but try to write it—so that the full independence of the *moi* can be achieved and realized, by artist and by reader. This book would exhibit pure uncompromised value.

However, since the poet must use language, he cannot be entirely free from traditional structure, and since poetry exists by conventions he cannot be entirely free from poetic tradition. The creation of pure style, therefore, completely free from tradition, completely individual, as individual as it is impersonal, is equally impossible. Thus what the poet must do he cannot do. This was to bring out the opposites, the antinomies, the irreconcilable opposites, the chimera of the nineteenth-century vision, with an almost unendurable sharpness. But if what he must do, he cannot do, the sensuous symbolization of the self in an aesthetic style cannot be achieved; the poem can only be a gesture toward its achievement. In that case the poet must have some non-poetic control by which to measure how far his gesture has moved toward this new concept of the absolute, and to comprehend the point from which he started. He must, then, have some non-poetic notion of what the *moi* is; he must have an anti-metaphysical metaphysics. In the late 1860's Mallarmé undertook this problem; it almost killed him.

Mallarmé set out to follow farther into the depths the riddle with which the nineteenth century had begun, which Goethe even in his Werther period had stumbled over, momentarily. If the world is to be derived from the self, if the self generates meaning, order, and value, what is the self? Above all, what is its authority? It is always necessary to remember that these were not abstract questions, and that the attempts to answer them were not academic toyings. They were questions asked by real human beings in a real social situation, and the nature of their relation to that situation, alienated from that society and isolated within it, meant that the pressures of the society upon the self were enormous. Further, as I suggested earlier, since there is no such thing as society but only human beings behaving, those pressures were felt as existing within the personality. It was the great achievement of the objectist stage to have discovered precisely that fact, that no one can separate his personality from society and the historical process; for one human being's personality is neither more nor less than continuous with society and historical process, which consists only of personalities. Indeed, from the objectist point of view, "personality," "society," and "history" all refer to the same thing; they are but three different words for the same entity. One uses one or the other, depending on how one wants to talk about it.

The alienated individual was driven back, therefore, to making a distinction between personality and identity, locating value in identity. But if style was based on tradition and if identity existed only because personality-society exists, then the alienation—and of course the moral responsibility that is the product of alienation— was compromised, and value was not truly located in the self or derived from it. Mallarmé's suffering was not only a consequence of the difficulty of his undertaking but also a result of his social position; it was, at the profoundest level, an emotional problem, inseparable from a real situation. It was to validate the alienation of the nineteenth-century man from the Enlightenment and pre-Enlightenment orientations of the culture that surrounded him. It was to justify the artist, to prove the correctness and moral responsibility of his judgment that the society-personality process was what Baudelaire and Wagner had said it was, a horror.

Following the line of thought Wagner had sketched, Mallarmé, apparently quite independently, began by thinking of the world as illusion, as a chimera. What exists, exists; yes, of course. But our knowledge of what exists consists only of relationships which the mind creates. Where Balzac had found transcendental justification for those relationships, Mallarmé, of course, could not. For he looked the other way, toward the transcendental, and saw the chimera there too, understood that whether or not there is a transcendental realm, what we know of it is again nothing but mind-created relationships. Meditating on these matters, his mind thought through itself. It saw itself only as the product of matter, and the self as a mere fiction. He experienced such a loss of identity that a mirror became pure horror. Yet as we have seen before, a total loss of identity is an unbearable experience. As he protested to a friend, he knew there was nothing novel about materialism, but the ordinary materialist does not experience the emotional consequences of his ideas. "His" identity is not threatened, because "he" knows the truth about life and matter. But Mallarmé experienced emotionally the consequences of materialism, for to him the self knows itself only as the mind is active. When the mind disappears the self disappears. He encountered, therefore, nothingness. He became nothingness. By the power of thought he had felt his way out of existence.

So long as we remember that his was an emotional problem arising out of a cultural situation, rather than a mere metaphysical problem, that his aim was an anti-metaphysical metaphysics, it is possible to grasp how he recreated himself. He struggled, he tells us, with God and overthrew him, the creature of ancient and evil plumage. But then in a burst of agony, God bore him "off again among the Shadows; then victoriously, ecstatically, infinitely, I floated downward until finally one day I looked again in my Venetian mirror and saw the person I had been several months before—the person I had forgotten." Mysterious as these words are, obviously there is an inversion, a redirection, and a rebirth. God is overthrown and cast to the earth; the world is nothing but matter. To overthrow God, then, is to think yourself out of existence, for the transcendentalists less than forty years before had stripped the world of value and made it impossible to look to matter for confirmation of identity, even by symbol and analogy. When God reconquers, when value re-emerges, two "I's" appear, as with Carlyle. One is borne off into the shadows, into darkness, into nothingness; the other descends victoriously. But he goes on to say, a few sentences later, that he is "not the Stéphane you once knew": he is "impersonal." It would appear, then, that it was the personality that God bore into the shadows, and this interpretation makes it possible to understand what has happened.

The pattern was: "self" equals "nothingness"; "matter" equals "being." The pattern now is: "self" equals "being"; "matter" equals "nothingness." If the self is nothingness and the world (empirical existence) is being, there is no place for value to reside, for the world is valueless. One must reverse the scheme. The world is nothingness; it is properly valueless. Empirical existence, too, is nothingness and valueless; the self, therefore, is being and value. If there were no nothing, there would be no self. "After I found Nothingness, I found Beauty," by which he means selfhood, meaning, value, and order. That is, the self emerges by contemplating that nothingness. As on a coin, the reverse is nothingness; the obverse is existence, which is the horror. The obverse face of the coin is what we know, existence; the reverse face, or back, tells us what power issued it, whence it comes, from nothingness. But the self does not depend upon that horror for its validity, but upon nothingness. Since the self can know itself only in terms of existence, it is therefore its task to redeem existence by turning it in poetry into a symbol of nothingness.

That this aim cannot be fully achieved necessarily follows, for words refer to existence and are governed by tradition. However, in the poem there are pauses between words, between sentences; there are blank spaces between stanzas; in music there are silences. By subjecting the sensuous world as it is grasped in words and sounds to order and to style, its disorder can be controlled. The blank spaces, the silences, thus can emerge as part of the structure, as part of order, not chance and disorder. And in contemplating those blanks, those silences, those symbols of nothingness which come into existence only when the chance and disorder of existence are structured by style, the self feels its own existence. Thus in "The Afternoon of a Faun" the faun feels his own selfhood only when the nymphs are absent. Only in absence, then, is there beauty. To create something which will make possible the experience of nothing, and thus of selfhood, was, as Mallarmé conceived it, the task of the poet. Thus life is redeemed and value may be experienced.

Drowned as we ordinarily are in the permanent cloudburst of phenomena, of chance and disorder, we could experience only our personality, were it not for the poet, whose style creates a structure in which absence is present, in which the contemplation of the *vanished* sail, of its no longer being before us, enables identity to be felt. Thus Mallarmé opened up in the Philistine world a hole in which the alienated artist could be free. Style, by its proud refusal to serve the horror, even to the degree of telling it what it is, and by its proud independence of tradition, which the horror steadily incorporates and absorbs, redeems the nineteenth-century man. Thus self-redemption is not dependent upon existence, as Parsifal was dependent, but is a genuinely free act. For the first time the self is truly free, transcendentally groundless, independent of empirical reality; it is a star; it is virginity; it is Hamlet, silent, reading in the book of himself; the swan in frozen water; the mirror.

With this non-poetic version of the *moi* we can now return to Mallarmé's stylistic problem, which was to create a nontraditional and impersonal style. Since he was a poet, the material for stylistic creativity had to be found in language, though as an observer he was equally interested in style in all of the arts, from music and ballet to women's fashions, to the analysis of which he once devoted a short-lived magazine. As a poet, furthermore, he had to wrestle with two forms of language, the natural language, the day-to-day speaking and linguistic drift of speaking of all men, and the conventions of poetic language. His struggles with natural language led him to what is at least one of its essential characters, syntactical patternings. Poets have always gained some of their effects by violating the syntactic norms of language, but in the past they had done so for expressive purposes. Mallarmé, of course, was interested in stylistic aims. Consequently, his dealings with syntax were not designed to reinforce the emotions in his poems, which by ordinary standards are quite emotionless, but rather to restructure ordinary language into syntactical arabesques, to raise the unconscious patternings of language into a conscious and free syntactical lace. And "lace," which is both highly patterned and transparent, is one of his metaphors for what he was doing. The *moi*, as we have seen, works through the mind; if the mind, instead of unconsciously accepting syntactical patterns, builds them anew, using existing structures for its materials, the self is realized in at least one area of existence.

Of the various conventions of poetry—and Mallarmé attempted to isolate and deal with as many of them as he could—he particularly selected metaphor as material for stylistic creativity. To be sure, metaphor is a normal carrier of linguistic innovation; in using metaphor everyone is a creator of new meanings. Metaphor is the most creative aspect of language; at least until modern scientific linguistics developed, it was so discriminated from other aspects of linguistic behavior. Thus, when the early nineteenth-century vision singled out the poet as the source of value, as the man whose imagination was radically creative, what was thought to be the most creative aspect of language was identified with poetic behavior. Metaphor was identified as the essence of poetry. Mallarmé continued this tradition and virtually identified the power of the poet to create new meanings with his power to create new metaphors. The normal function of metaphor, indeed, is to say something for which no word or expression exists. Mallarmé, who not only had something new to say but even had something to say which was not sayable, consequently made the structure of his meanings as dependent on metaphorical innovation as he possibly could. These two devices alone—not to speak of others—make his poetry enormously difficult. He once said, in mock modesty, that at least his poetry, if it did nothing else, would develop good readers.

His prophecy was perfectly correct. It is no exaggeration to say that because of the innovations of Mallarmé—which were developed not only by French poets, but also in Germany, England, and North and South America—anyone who can read twentieth-century poetry at all can read all poetry with a precision and a freedom unknown before the end of the nineteenth century. But the reader of Mallarmé must do what Mallarmé did; he must break through his orientations; he must raise to consciousness his sensitivity to syntax and he must restructure it. Likewise, he must raise to consciousness his sensitivity to meaning and he must learn to perceive and to respond to new meanings, meanings which put the whole world in a new light, which enable him to see it from an entirely fresh orientation. Syntactic and semantic self-consciousness and novelty are among the most difficult tasks the mind can undertake. But if the mind can manage to undertake them, the rewards are enormous. For these linguistic structures are the principal carriers of traditional orientations. When we raise these structures to consciousness, we raise orientations to consciousness. We see orientations for what they are, structures which the mind has made. But to see that is to be able to see their inadequacies, and thus the individual's mind is freed to attempt to create structures of greater adequacy, for in raising these structures to consciousness it gains an insight, ever increasing, never ending, into the nature of mental constructs, and thus it learns to be free and creative. Consequently Mallarmé's efforts to realize the self through style are anything but remote, anything but irrelevant to the individual's engagement with reality.

This is the great merit of the second stage of stylism, that instead of attempting, as its predecessors had done, to lead the mind to reality, which it could only do, as Swinburne, Moreau, and Brahms show, by developing and integrating existing orientations, it turned its attention to the creative destructuring and restructuring of the mind itself. It freed the mind to create the world, out of the materials of the world and the constructive power of the mind. "Faithful to some special vision deep within," Mallarmé said in 1894 to an English audience at Cambridge, "we may extend or simplify the world at will." Ultimately, Mallarmé does not lead us from existence to nothingness; he makes us free to find our own way from nothingness to existence. The problem of how the self-redeemer is to redeem himself is solved; for Mallarmé sees clearly what Wagner had but symbolically fumbled at: the profoundest satisfaction of the human identity is to create the world, for in creating the world, the identity itself is self-created.

There is another aspect to Mallarmé's thought which I have only touched on. Even before his plunge into himself, his discovery of nothingness and in nothingness, of beauty, he had formulated it. "Describe not the object itself, but the effect it produces." This, he said in 1864, is the task of the poet. It was, of course, nothing new. As we have seen, it had been the self-conscious task of the nineteenth-century artist ever since it had first appeared, seventy-odd years before. But after objectism and the first stage of stylism, with its non-functional aesthetic surface and its "realistic" and "naturalistic" technique, it appeared to be new. When he uttered this formula, Mallarmé himself scarcely understood what it meant; only after his great and terrible adventure in the ensuing years did he understand what he was really after, and was able to put the two aspects of his thought together.

The materials of poetic style, syntax and metaphor, not to mention other aspects which I have not touched on, are themselves part of existence, that existence which is to be redeemed by restructuring the ways we see it. They belong, further, to that area of existence which we categorize under the term "human behavior." Insofar as they are part of the cultural process, they are part of the personality. Feelings, i.e., "the effect that the object produces," are also part of the personality. If the mind is the source of structure, the feelings compose the medium through which we experience existence. By describing not the object but the effect it produces on our feelings, we bring the object within the control of the structuring mind. We extend or simplify the world at will by restructuring our feelings about the world. Therefore the identity has two ways to symbolize its coming into existence: first, by the novel structural arabesque which the mind creates; second, by restructuring the images which the personality has traditionally used to symbolize its feelings. This it can do in two ways, by distorting the image and by juxtaposing images which traditionally have been kept separate. From this point of view syntax—as in the structure of a question, an exclamation, a statement—is a symbol of a feeling state. A new feeling state may be summoned into existence by distorting the syntax. As for juxtaposition, consider the opening line of T. S. Eliot's *The Waste Land*, "April is the cruelest month." "April" is traditionally a symbol of affirmation, "cruel" of negation. To juxtapose them is to bring into existence a new feeling state for "April" to symbolize; it is to assert that to affirm the value of human existence in its natural aspect is the result of a fearful misapprehension of what human existence truly is. To juxtapose traditionally separate images, then, is to distort the valuation of traditionally approved or disapproved feeling states. Juxtaposition and distortion are indirect and direct ways of distortion.

Now distortion, in one way or the other, is the only way the identity can achieve realization, can come into existence, can be subjectively experienced when it deals with feelings. To create wholly new images for feeling states would be like creating wholly new structures with no relation to preceding structures. They would be absolutely arbitrary, totally random, completely accidental and uncontrollable. Such activity would surrender the self wholly to the world of disorder. It would make choice impossible, for there would be no reason to choose one thing rather than another. Structural arabesque and distortion of imagery, therefore, cannot be completely arbitrary; it is their difference from what tradition vainly imagines to be the only possible structure and the only possible imagery, which releases the freedom of the self and proves to itself and to others that it is independent of a transcendental ground and also of deceiving and illusory traditional orientations.

A painter and a musician, directly and indirectly under the influence of Mallarmé, did for their arts what Mallarmé did for poetry. He gave mankind a new experience of language. By the magical power of stylistic creativity, they gave freedom to painting and to music; they gave mankind new eyes and new ears.

# CHAPTER XIX

# Style and Freedom

$\mathbf{A}$s early as 1870 a subtle change began to come over impressionism. The appearance of Renoir on the impressionist scene, with his rainbow palette, meant a break from the photographic control established by Manet. Color began to have a life of its own, and the emphasis began to shift from the object represented to the aesthetic surface. It was not until the mid-1880's, however, that a real redirection became visible, and a younger generation of artists began simultaneously to subject the impressionist technique of painting in flecks of color to a more scientific control and at the same time to reintroduce a formal and spatial organization. Renoir, for a time, abandoned the impressionist style and returned to constructing solid figures in a Renaissance manner; even Pissaro made similar experiments. Georges Seurat (born in 1859) in particular set about creating paintings which established spaces and in those spaces, solid, static, and simplified forms. In the famous "A Summer Sunday on the Grande Jatte," painted in 1885 and 1886, now in the Chicago Art Institute, he made the first steps toward distortion, for the figures and the trees seem almost to be illustrations for a book on solid geometry.

Today it is hard to judge what the painting meant to his contemporaries. How did they see it? For that matter, how did Seurat himself see it? Did he see cones, cylinders, segments of spheres, masked as people and trees? Or did he see people and trees simplified to the point where the observer is reminded of the forms of solid geometry? What was he trying to paint? Figures or forms? Was he painting forms in order to realize people, or was he painting people in order to realize forms? Was he summoning an intellectual, abstract world of geometry from outside of the painting in order to control the images? Or was he painting figures in order to introduce into the world an individual and impersonal sense of form? Is he interested in externally imposed control or in style?

A few years later, after an interim in which he regressed from the questions he had posed in the "Grande Jatte," he moved in a different direction. In "Chahut," a picture of musicians and a chorus line of dancing men and women in a cabaret, he is unmistakably concerned with creating an arabesque, an aesthetic surface for which the scene is not much more than an excuse; yet even here, the elements of caricature indicate a lingering trace of social commentary, of objectism. The style does not quite live for itself. "Chahut" was painted in 1889 and 1890, but by then far greater men had solved the problem Seurat was struggling with. He died in 1891, only thirty-two years old, without, apparently, fully comprehending the revolution in European vision which was taking place.

That revolution was the achievement, above all others, of two men, Paul Cézanne, born in 1839, and Eugène Henri Paul Gauguin, born in 1848. Gauguin was particularly influenced by Japanese prints, which first began to circulate in Paris in the 1850's and were a very chic thing to collect by the 1870's. Perhaps the first artist to be influenced by them was James McNeill Whistler, the American, born in 1834, who lived and worked in Paris and London. But even he did not absorb in any profound sense the lesson they had to teach. Indeed, it is extraordinary how long it was before the influence of these works began really to be felt, hardly before 1888—at least in painting, for they did have some effect on typographical design and a little on book illustration. But their long-delayed effect indicates better than anything else the difficulty for even highly talented artists of breaking through the traditional forms and modes of perception.

Today it is no trouble at all to see the lesson that the Japanese prints were capable of teaching: the images which we use to imitate reality are conventions. But that is a paradoxical way of putting it. If they are conventions, the images can scarcely be said to imitate. I suggested earlier that the ultimate effect of the photograph was to release the artist from the necessity of copying appearances, but that its immediate effect was to give him, Manet in particular, a new way of copying, by patches of shades of gray. Simultaneously, the salon artists used photographs to make their images more "exactly" imitative. The notion of imitation, of "mimesis," had dominated not merely the painter but European art, in nearly all its forms, literature and theater, for example, for centuries. Even Schopenhauer could do no better than to say that "music is a copy of the will."

What actually happens, however, is something quite different. Any visual image of a discriminated area in the natural world, a human figure, for instance, presents multitudinous, even infinite aspects. The artist can only select. Even Ruskin had seen that no artist, not even Turner, can paint a sunset; he can only put down on canvas a narrower range of color and light which is the equivalent of the range the sunset exhibits, but not the same. He cannot reproduce the reflection of the sun on water; he can only put down the brightest color he has and adjust his other colors to it. What Ruskin had not seen, however, is that the aspects the artist selects to put down are determined by his cultural traditions. He does not imitate reality, because he cannot; but the images which he uses as signs of that reality are so controlled by cultural tradition that they are seen by himself and by his audience as copies of reality.

Even the impressionists, then, merely developed what they thought was a refinement of the tradition of imitation, of copying, of reproducing the visible aspect of the world. Nevertheless, as we have seen, from the time of Friedrich on, through Constable, Delacroix, and Turner, the artists, seeking constantly to symbolize the self, were experimenting with the conventions; but always their justification, since their aim was to come closer to reality, to engage with it, was to improve the conventions of imitation, which they did not yet perceive as conventions. They thought of themselves as improving the tradition of copying.

Now Japanese prints should, one would think, have made

the artist aware that ways of rendering distance, for example, are conventions, and that perspective as developed in Europe was but one of the perhaps infinitely possible conventions. Nor was it only these prints that made such a new perception possible. Gustave Moreau probably examined with care more that did not belong to the tradition of European painting than any artist in Europe; yet there is in his painting no indication whatever that he thought of doing anything but integrating Byzantine and early Sienese art into the European tradition. Likewise, in the Louvre, in the British Museum, from the 1850's on, there were placed on exhibition superb examples of Assyrian and Egyptian art. Always, however, there was a profound conviction that any way of rendering reality other than the European tradition was primitive, undisciplined, uncivilized. Byzantine art, so far as it was known at all, was simply thought of as degenerate Roman art; and when in the 1860's and 1870's William Morris revived the art of medieval tapestry, he did not develop medieval conventions in his images but nineteenth-century conventions. Apparently he thought he was making an improvement; he seems to have been quite puzzled that somehow or other the medieval tapestries were more impressive than his.

The other thing to be learned from Japanese prints, as well as Byzantine enamels and ancient art, was that a painting is a two-dimensional surface. The task of European "imitative" art, it was thought, was to create the illusion of three dimensions. The notion that a picture can be thought of as a two-dimensional pattern of line, color, and shapes was simply, at that time, impossible. For the vast majority of men in Western culture it still is, and in Russia to think that a picture is anything other than a means of creating a three-dimensional illusion is a political crime. In the United States only since the war have more than a few thousand people arrived at the point of judging a picture by any other criterion. When, in the 1890's, Oscar Wilde said, "Nature imitates art," what is now a commonplace was then almost incomprehensible. What he meant, of course, was that we see nature in terms of the conventions we have learned from our culture, and that art is the primary bearer of that visual orientation, or Gestalt. There is no such thing as the innocent eye, which Ruskin thought was the primary equipment of a painter. To break through that visual orientation and that tradition of imagery which it governs is an extraordinarily difficult thing to do. Tens of thousands of people even today wander through galleries and exhibitions of modern art in simple bewilderment. The question is, then, not, "Why were the painters not influenced by Japanese prints and other art in non-European traditions?" Rather, it is, "What made it possible for them to be influenced?" That is the mystery.

The answer, of course, is already before us. Those cultural forces that led from the first stage of stylism to the second were responsible. It was the necessity to symbolize the self in a way that would establish it as self-created, and order, meaning, and value as self-generated, that was responsible. We can see this in the work of Cézanne, who is justly called the father of modern painting. Apparently early in the 1880's he came to realize that although as an impressionist, indeed, as a European artist, he had set out to copy nature, he could not in fact do so. He carried to the next step Manet's effort to catch in a brief lapse of time what he was painting, on the grounds that if one returned to it the next day it was neither the same man who returned nor the same scene he returned to. Pursuing this idea to its necessary conclusion, one becomes aware that from minute to minute neither the same man nor the same scene continues. But this is to conceive the man as merely a machine for transcription. As soon as one realizes, as Cézanne realized, that continuity of thought lasts while the discontinuity of nature is ever-vanishing, then the task of the painter appears in quite a new light.

We cannot know nature; we can but make a mental construct of nature and transcribe that mental construct onto the canvas. But when we do that our unique individuality takes over, and the painting becomes not an image of nature but an image of the self that regards nature. The painter must study nature, then, to discriminate his feelings. He cannot know nature; he can only know his response to nature. A painting has its sources in nature and in the mind—nature only provides the sensory data; the mind furnishes the control. Order and structure come from the mind, and the establishment in the painting of order and structure symbolizes the continuity of the observing mind.

The task, then, as Cézanne put it, was to make pictures as solidly constructed as those in the museums—but not constructed in the same way. Objectism, as Baudelaire had seen, had destroyed tradition for the nineteenth-century man. Cézanne had to create, as it were, a new tradition, one that would have the solidity of the great masterpieces, but would also have the uniqueness of the structuring self. But that self must be an impersonal self; the personality is merely a matter of emotions, and his objectist tradition—his friendship with Zola, for instance—meant that Cézanne had no interest in expressing his emotions. The picture must, then, be at once impersonal, individual, and non-traditional.

Thus Cézanne passed directly from objectism to the second stage of stylism; or rather, like Mallarmé, who was but three years older than he, he passed through the first stage lightly, superficially, in Cézanne's case because of the subtle transformation of impressionism in the 1870's, which permitted the aesthetic surface, the style, to live something of its own life. And it was also apparent that he worked through in visual terms, as a painter's problem, precisely the same pattern of development which Mallarmé had to tear himself apart to achieve. Though Cézanne was reticent, there is evidence that underneath his almost peasant-like solidity a powerful struggle was taking place. Certainly powerful forces were released; for he broke through the whole European tradition of structuring a painting, and the whole European tradition of seeing. What he achieved can be expressed in a sentence: the task of the painter is not to imitate reality but to create a visual structure, self-generated, self-ordered, which symbolizes the self and is the incarnation of value. Thus the subject of one of his landscapes of Mont-Sainte-Victoire, for example, is not the landscape, the mountain, the village, the road, the trees, the viaduct. The subject is the style. The painting is not about a landscape; it is about structure.

Our knowledge of how he worked reveals a curious parallel to Mallarmé, a demonstration that in his talk about silence and absence Mallarmé was not discussing a metaphysical abstraction but an emotional experience. There are far more unfinished Cézannes than finished, and the unfinished ones are unfinished in a very curious way. In the midst of finished passages, entirely surrounded by such passages, there are blanks, irregular white spaces which have not been touched with the brush, nor with a pencil. It is apparent that he worked by adding touch after touch, gradually building up a structure of such extreme complexity—critics are still busy analyzing that structure as if they were exploring an unknown world —that every new brush stroke had to fit in perfectly, had to establish innumerable relations to every other brush stroke, and at the same time had to contribute in manifold ways to the color structure, the spatial structure, the structure of the forms, the relationships among the objects, to every possible kind of structured visual relationship which, it would seem, the human mind can conceive.

As the painting progressed each still unpainted area became more crucial. In the traditional manner of painting, so long as the forms emerged powerfully and the space was unmistakably illusionistic, a painter could be careless or trite in lesser passages without doing too much harm. And since he was painting in terms of conventionalized images, if these lesser passages served to bring the images out and to support the observer's recognition of them, all was well. Hence traditional painting was constantly threatening to dissolve into passages of varying significance and merit. The nearer the painter approached completion, the easier it was to finish it. Not so with Cézanne. The fewer and the smaller the unfinished areas, the more difficult it was to fill them. In some of his paintings, therefore, there are little white unfinished spots all over the painting. But the astonishing thing is that though the painting does suffer, it is only the suffering of absence. It is not an unfinished painting; it is a finished painting with unfinished areas. So long as it is carried to the point where the structure begins to emerge, it is complete.

The intellectual power exhibited in such a way of painting is worth meditating on, but the important thing here is the resemblance in his method of working to Mallarmé's analysis of the nature of silence, of absence, of what is not there. As we have seen, silence, absence, white pages, the spaces between stanzas, present opportunities for the self to achieve realization. This is exactly what Cézanne does with his white spaces. And there is a further parallel. In a letter Cézanne said that the method to be pursued "consists of looking for the proper expression of what one feels, and in organizing sensation in terms of one's personal aesthetic." To achieve the first of these, Cézanne introduced distortion; it is most obvious in his paintings of human figures. Here the traditional images are distorted; they break away from the conventions of imaging the human figure which still dominated impressionism and Cézanne when he was an impressionist. What we feel in the face of these icons is weight, solidity, imperviousness. They are, in any traditional sense, expressionless; but, untouched by human emotions, grief or love or anger, they are moving. What we feel symbolized by the distortion of tradition is the identity of the human being. Stripped of emotion, of anything that we might call personality, the image becomes the human being in his pure individuality. The structure has at once distorted the image and related it to a world of impenetrable solidity.

As for the second part of the remark, "organizing sensations in terms of one's personal aesthetic," what is this but the control and restructuring of the means by which we apprehend the world? To create such a structure, then, is to free the orientative drive from the traditions and conventions that have hitherto controlled it. And that is precisely the source of both the impersonality of Cézanne's paintings and their endless fascination, their profound emotional power. Like Mallarmé, he does not lead us to reality; he releases us from what he has released himself from. He offers us the opportunity to restructure our vision, to redeem ourselves, to seek our own sources of identity and value. As with Mallarmé, so with Cézanne: the profoundest satisfaction of the human being is to create the world, to destructure it and restructure it, to disorient ourselves and to re-orient ourselves. A painting by Cézanne is moving because it wrenches us, distorts us, and releases us. With Mallarmé, he could have said, "If I have done nothing else, I have taught people how to look at pictures."

Certainly he had that effect on Gauguin, born in 1848 and

nine years younger than Cézanne. Gauguin was lucky enough not to have received any academic training in painting. He began as an amateur, but he did not end that way. Interested in art and, for a time, well-to-do, he associated with the impressionists and through them learned to know Cézanne's work. In the early 1880's he began to buy Cézanne's paintings, and their effect on him—he was almost alone in experiencing it—was precisely what it should have been. It released his vision; he began to see what the Japanese prints had been trying to tell Western Europe. More and more fascinated, he eventually, as all the world knows, gave up his family, and in time sailed for Tahiti, a fresh and primitive world, where he could use the cleansed vision which Cézanne had given him without being continually reminded of the images and visual orientations of traditional European art.

Gauguin's development was not, like Cézanne's, parallel to Mallarmé's; he came directly under Mallarmé's influence. The poet maintained a salon, his famous Tuesday evenings, and to it were drawn virtually all the advanced artists and thinkers of Paris, all those who were feeling the difficulties of the first stage of stylism: it had established style as a mode of symbolizing the self, but the style was not functional and its presence, and therefore the self's existence, was justified only by its opposition to the horror of personality. To make the style functional was, as we have seen, the problem. An important step in Gauguin's development came when he realized that hitherto painters had found their mode of expression by selecting a subject, and that to make style functional the expression must not be found in the subject but rather in the comment the style made on the subject. The artist's feeling, as well as the self, was to be symbolized by the style.

This is the difference between the symbolism of the first stage of stylism and the symbolism of the second. That the same word should be used to designate two profoundly different conceptions of the artist's task is highly confusing; yet it is one of those semantic shifts that indicate a connection between two apparently different notions. Gustave Moreau and related artists, such as Odilon Redon, used traditional images to symbolize their orientations; Cézanne and Gauguin used the style. As we have already seen with Cézanne, this necessarily brings about a distortion of the images, a distortion even more striking with Gauguin than with the older master, who, indeed, sometimes did not quite understand what Gauguin was up to. In traditional painting the style was used to bring out the image and to reinforce its emotional significance. But if the style is non-traditional, impersonal, and individual, the image is subject to its power, and distortion necessarily results. Actually, this tendency can be seen in all European painting, but until Cézanne and Gauguin it remained only an unrealized potentiality. Indeed, only with the new vision that these two men, together with Van Gogh, gave us did it become perfectly and obviously apparent that that tendency and that possibility had always been present.

But there is a further reason for distortion, one that Mallarmé had struggled horribly with. If the choice of subject cannot be used to express the painter's feelings, if the painting itself, its use of color, line, shape, space, and so on, has to undertake this task, there are only two possibilities. One is to choose an image, a color, a line, a shape entirely at random, by a purely arbitrary act; but to do that is merely to create an absolutely private convention differing from public conventions only in its privacy. It is merely to substitute one convention for another and at the same time to open up a possibility of infinite choice with no means to control that choice. Actually, then, the other possibility is the only one, to distort and violate the conventions.

A charming moving picture, made by an unaccountable miracle in Hollywood in the late 1940's, demonstrates this principle. It was called *Yellow Sky*, and it was a Western, a horse opera. Instead of being blue, the sky was yellow; buildings, instead of being solid, were only frames; movement, instead of being naturalistic, was governed by the conventions of the ballet. The effect was to strip the naturalistic pretensions from the Western, which technically derives from objectism and emotionally from the novels of Sir Walter Scott, and to reveal it as a set of conventions. Furthermore, the movement, the camera style, the color style were charming and gay, utterly inappropriate to a typically Western narrative of murder and eroticism. Thus the Western was revealed as an emotional ritual in which the display of symbols was the only thing of real importance. The style and the distortions of traditional imagery symbolized and communicated a fresh orientation toward an established cultural tradition. *Yellow Sky* is a direct consequence of the distortion of traditional images created by Gauguin.

To say that Gauguin learned his ideas from Mallarmé is perhaps to say too much; it is probably more correct to say that the discussions in the poet's salon, especially Mallarmé's wonderful monologues, which were really why artists and thinkers came, crystallized Gauguin's ideas. Certain quotations from Gauguin and a friend of his suggest this very strongly. Charles Morice, born in 1861, a follower of Mallarmé's, was the author of a definitive statement on the symbolism of the second stage of stylism, published in 1889, *The Literature of Today*. "The book, the work of art, the musical phrase, pure thought itself are eternalizations of the '*Moi*.' Thus we create means to disengage ourselves from contingencies; the human '*Moi*' returns to the source of the absolute, to the metaphysical place of the Ideas, to God." Morice here exhibits what was fairly common in both stages of stylism, the revival of religion and Platonic and Neoplatonic metaphysics as a fiction to symbolize the separation of the self from the world of contingency, of pointless and meaningless and random and structureless accident. Probably Morice was really asserting that the work of art performs the function of religion and metaphysics. That would have been in accordance with the cultural situation.

Certainly Gauguin thought so, for as Morice himself tells us in his book about Gauguin published in 1919, Gauguin's notion of philosophy was strikingly of its times, exhibiting the anti-metaphysical metaphysics of Mallarmé's thinking. "Philosophy is heavy and stupid if it does not arise from my instincts. . . . It is not science . . . it is not a logical consequence as solemn and pompous persons would teach us; but rather a weapon which, savages that we are, we make for ourselves. It is not a reality" [that is, probably, an imitation or exhaustive description of reality] "but an image: it is like a picture, admirable if it is a masterpiece." Philosophy, like a picture, is a construct, a set of signs which appears to refer to the world but in reality symbolizes the self; a structured image which serves our profoundest necessities; a weapon, an instrument, a means of defending ourselves, of realizing the self and protecting it against any subjection to an unstructured world of randomness and horror; philosophy is a form of art.

Finally, another statement by Gauguin shows even more sharply what he was trying to do. "It was necessary . . . to think of a complete liberation, to break windows, at the risk of cutting one's fingers. . . . For this purpose one had to throw oneself into the battle body and soul, the battle against all the Schools, . . . insulting not only the officials, but also the Impressionists, the Neo-Impressionists, the ancient and the modern public. . . . As to the work, one had to have a method of contradiction . . . one had to attack the most powerful abstract ideas" [the orientations of the culture], "to do everything prohibited, to reconstruct without fear of exaggeration, even with exaggeration. One had to learn anew; then, once something was known, to learn it all over again. . . . Before his easel the painter is not a slave, neither of the past, nor of the present, nor of nature, nor of his neighbor. He, again he, always he." The task of art is to destroy our orientations, to renew our vision, to release from its profoundest levels the orientative power, and thus establish the identity in its freedom, independent of a transcendental ground, freed from the images, the patterns, the Gestalten of our cultural tradition, free to experience what is in front of us. Standing before his easel, the artist is free to symbolize his unique creation of the world.

What Cézanne and more radically, with great theoretical comprehension, Gauguin did for the eye, what Mallarmé did for poetry, Claude Debussy did for the ear; and he did it in the same way, by distortion of traditional forms: melodic structure, harmonic succession, unambiguous key relationships, rhythmic patterns. His stated aim was to express the inexpressible, and to see what he meant it is necessary to examine the whole technique of distortion somewhat more acutely than we have so far. The nature of convention is to weld a psychic bond between specific emotions and particular signs; in art these signs are particular images, words and phrases, musical patterns. Further, as the convention becomes stabilized, the signs are identified by means of words or phrases. Thus the color red, blaring trumpets, war, and anger are all connected. Baudelaire and Rimbaud and the symbolists of the first stage of stylism thought there was a necessary or "natural" connection among signs which served an equivalent function in different sign systems. Mallarmé, Cézanne, and Gauguin made the discovery that these equivalents are held together by conventions, that is, as we would say today, by psychic conditioning.

As we have seen, Gauguin and Mallarmé could not create an arbitrary sign system in lieu of the conventions because such an effort would open an infinity of choice with no basis to choose from. It would expose them to the arbitrariness and randomness of the world without any defense against it, without the philosophical weapons which, savages that we are, each of us has.

But there is a further reason why they turned to distortion rather than to arbitrary and private symbols, as their immediate predecessors had tended to do. The choice of an arbitrary sign means simply to use the color blue, for example, or a perfect circle, to express anger instead of red or a jagged line. In other words, the sign is selected to express something, and that something has already been identified by a word, in this case "anger." Such behavior, however, would not answer their purpose at all, for this reason: The effect of conventions in a cultural tradition is to limit the individual to experiencing those emotions which the conventions signify. Whether he creates a work of art or contemplates it, the range of responses is limited by the range of the emotions which the signs symbolize or evoke. The result is that the individual can experience only those emotions which his cultural tradition recognizes; or, to put it more precisely, whatever emotion he experiences he will identify by either a word or a sign. Gestures and facial expressions, for instance, are conventional signs. Thus he structures his emotional life, accepting his structure from his cultural tradition and orientation. He feels, then, only what he ought to feel; and emotions which he does feel but cannot identify he either suppresses or falsifies by assimilating them to culturally recognized emotions.

The nineteenth-century man, however, was engaged from

the beginning in a struggle to realize his identity by finding some way to discover and identify emotions other than the culturally accepted ones. He was trying to discover what he truly felt and not be limited to feeling what his culture told him he ought to feel. The original distinction between the self and the role, therefore, was the first step toward realizing the self and deriving the world from the self, because it put in one category, that of the social role, the recognized emotions and thus made possible the experiencing of the self. The result was, as we have seen, the creation of a constant flow of new symbols, such as, for example, the great symbols of cave and tower, or, earlier, the Byronic wanderer. The difficulty here, though, was that as soon as the new emotional symbol was established it began to operate precisely as the old symbols had. This is one of the reasons for the steady retreat from the personality and the identification of personality with society which culminated in the first stage of stylism.

The creative artist, then, was continually caught in an emotional and symbolic trap which his own creative imagination had set. Hence the importance of the discovery that emotional signs are conventions; that discovery made it apparent that to conventionalize the signs of emotion—even though those signs were purely arbitrary and private—was necessarily to conventionalize emotion, and that such conventionalization was to deny the area of feelings any control by the sense of identity. It meant that the feelings could not be organized by the creative imagination; for as soon as an emotion is symbolized it slips away from the imagination into the personality and thence into society.

That was the source of the determination of all three men to express the inexpressible, as it was also Debussy's determination. That is what Gauguin meant by "mystery." The emotions must be expressed and at the same time kept mysterious. Only thus could the symbols for those emotions be controlled by style, that is, by self, by the "*moi.*" In realizing that traditional symbols are conventions, they were able to perceive that the distortion of those conventions meant two things: first, it became apparent to the observer that the conventional image was not to be taken as the equivalent of the emotion the artist was expressing.

To prove his insight, in 1889 Gauguin painted a "Jesus in the Garden of Olives." A naturalistic painting of this subject, in the European tradition, with the conventional images, tells the observer precisely the pious emotion he is supposed to feel; but this painting does no such thing. Any self-respecting traditional Christian would immediately label it "irreligious," for in the face of this work he does not know what he is supposed to feel. And, of course, by the standards of conventionalized emotion, it is irreligious. It symbolizes feelings which are inexpressible precisely because it distorts the conventional image. When you contemplate it, you experience an emotion, but it is impossible to say what that emotion is, because the conventional bond between word, sign, and emotion is broken by the distortion. By introducing the technique of distortion, then, these artists expressed feelings but kept them from escaping into personality and society. The images were controlled by the style, and the feelings were kept under the organizing and structural power of the sense of identity. Thus the distortion of traditional images or patterns becomes a way of symbolizing the freedom of the self and of releasing the orientative drive from conventional and traditional controls. This also explains the difference between the meaning of "symbol" in the first stage of stylism and its meaning in the second. In the first, a symbol referred to a culturally discriminated and identifiable emotion; in the second, it symbolized a feeling which the culture had never discriminated and which, even when expressed, remained unidentifiable. Distortion, then, became the primary artistic technique of feeling what you do feel instead of what you think you ought to feel. It became an indispensable technique for solving the intolerable and paradoxical problem of becoming what you are.

The whole problem of the nineteenth century, the problem which Mallarmé, Cézanne, Gauguin, and Debussy solved, was this: As fast as the artist created new symbols for hitherto unexpressed feelings, those symbols became conventions which bound him as tightly as he had been bound before. A tower, after all, is precisely the same kind of symbol as a crucifix, and as soon as the bond is welded between "tower" and "the self in active opposition to society," it becomes as binding on the creative imagination and on the

realization of selfhood as the older but no more conventional crucifix. The artist, from this point of view, was simply transferring himself from one prison cell to another. Perhaps that is why the nineteenth-century musician tended to have a considerably longer
creative period than the visual and literary artist. His symbols
seemed less tightly, less obviously welded to identifiable feelings. As
we have seen, Beethoven, distinguishing between self and role,
broke the chains that held together musical patterns and situational
emotions. He created a way of symbolizing the activity of the self,
the psychic flow. And for that psychic flow the nineteenth century
had virtually no language, whereas we can speak of tension and relaxation, frustration and gratification, manic-depressive cycles, and
all the rest of it. Consequently, the successful introduction of distortion into music had to wait for a man born in 1862, who was
twenty-three years younger than Cézanne, twenty years younger
than Mallarmé, and fourteen years younger than Gauguin.

Debussy had the advantage of growing up in an environment in which the works of the impressionists seemed astonishingly
modern, while those of the first stage of stylism seemed almost in-
sanely non-traditional—though to us today they seem very traditional indeed. When, therefore, in the mid-1880's he began to
encounter the poetry and the ideas of Mallarmé, and when in 1887
—after his return from Rome, which he could endure for only two
years instead of the three which as a recipient of the Prix de Rome
he was supposed to spend there—he began to go to Mallarmé's
Tuesdays, he came into touch with the culturally most advanced
men of the nineteenth century. Indeed, the problem of Cézanne and
Gauguin was that even the most advanced public taste was just
beginning to accept the early impressionists, while the objectivist
*Théâtre Libre* of André Antoine was considered inconceivably advanced and daring for doing what Baudelaire and Zola had done
decades before.

Particularly, Paris was just beginning to plunge into the
Wagnerian delirium. It was impossible to be more chic than Lekeu,
who, worshiping at the Bayreuth shrine, fainted at the end of the
Prelude to *Tristan* and had to be carried out of the theater. Since

Bayreuth has no aisles, the commotion he must have been able to create could only have been enormously satisfying both to him and to his friends. Debussy, too, went on the pilgrimage to Bayreuth in 1888, a year in which *Parsifal* and *The Meistersinger* were given. Considering his intense interest in the decadents, it was probably the former he was more interested in seeing, and at that time *Parsifal* could only be seen at Bayreuth. Nevertheless, he saw both; and in 1889 he returned and heard *Tristan* as well as the other two. In 1888 he had come away awe-struck and worshiping. In 1889 he returned to Paris in disgust and began a highly articulate anti-Wagnerism which he kept up for the rest of his life, changing only toward a fiercer and more savage hatred of the Master of Bayreuth. In 1888 Wagner, particularly in *Parsifal*, was a revelation; in 1889, Wagner was blatant, over-dramatic, obvious, and coarse.

In the year between the two festivals, tendencies which we can see at work in Debussy's early music suddenly crystallized. Certainly the influence of Mallarmé and his followers was important, and probably crucial; but there were other influences as well. At the Paris World's Fair in 1889, probably both before and after the Bayreuth trip, he took a kind of musical tour of the world, hearing not only the folk music of Western Europe and of Russia, but also of the Far East—Chinese, Javanese, and Annamite orchestras. He was particularly moved by the gamelan, the Javanese orchestra of percussion instruments, the counterpoint in which, he was later to say, made Palestrina's seem like childish fumblings. And in June of that year he heard two concerts of Russian music: Cui, Balakirev, Borodin, Rimski-Korsakov, Moussorgsky, and Glazunov. Today those composers seem thoroughly conventional, but to Debussy they were a revelation, because they used scales, harmonies, and melodic contours and structures from outside the musical tradition of western Europe. Although they were a culturally delayed product of the objectist stage, their use of patterns from Russian folk and church music and Asiatic melodies and harmonies cleansed Debussy's power of hearing, just as Japanese prints had restructured Gauguin's power of vision. Indeed, Debussy's love for Japanese prints—the cover design of his tone poem "La Mer" is based on Hokusai's "Great Wave"—no doubt helped him to overcome his traditional musical orientations. The next five years, therefore, were devoted to getting Wagner out of his system, for it was not Wagner he hated so much as the Wagnerism in himself.

The key to his problem was his sudden perception of Wagner as obvious and blatant, although almost everyone else in Paris was experiencing Wagner as complex and subtle almost beyond the point of comprehension. The effect of the crystallization of his attitude was that he saw that, original as Wagner was, his musical material consisted of precisely the same patterns that had been in use in the European tradition since the early sixteenth century, patterns which had for nearly three centuries become increasingly configured, progressively more easily recognized. It is instructive that as much as he disliked Wagner, it was particularly *The Ring* he rejected. *Tristan* with its chromaticism, and certain transparent and sensuously appealing parts of *Parsifal*, he always found to a certain extent acceptable, and the continuity between these works and even the latest works of Debussy is quite apparent. That is, where Wagner most departed from the harmonic, melodic, and rhythmic patterns of the main Western musical tradition, Debussy could continue to accept him and use him. What he had perceived, however, was that as Wagner's music became familiar and as his imitators multiplied, his musical patterns became conventional. To use them meant that the composer was restricted to expressing those non-situational emotions, those aspects of the psychic flow, which, for so profoundly original a temperament as Debussy's, had become welded to particular musical patterns and aural qualities.

Debussy's revulsion against Wagner—his perception of Wagner as blatant and obvious—was a consequence of his realization that his original responses to Wagner had not come from his own feelings, from what he really was, but had been experienced because he had been culturally conditioned to experience them. He set out, then, to discover what he himself really was, what his own feelings truly were, to locate and discover his own unique individuality, that area of himself which had not come under the control of traditional and conventional cultural conditioning, that expression of his identity which could be controlled by style. He set out to do in music what Mallarmé, Gauguin, and Cézanne had already done in poetry and in painting.

In a series of songs, after settings of Baudelaire and Verlaine, and of piano pieces, the most famous of which, "Suite Bergamasque," was also inspired by Verlaine, he worked out a style; the first work which shows what he had accomplished was his quartet, but even more revealing is the "Prelude to The Afternoon of a Faun," all that he kept of what was to have been a three-part symphony on Mallarmé's famous poem. The quartet had done such peculiar things to the spirit and structure of the sonata form that many critics could not even recognize that the traditional forms were there, and most others were outraged. Yet to say that the forms were there is not exact. Debussy subjected them to a distortion which, together with the distortions of traditional rhythms, melodic patterns, harmonic sequences and modulations, and patterns of thematic development, indicated that he had solved his problem and entered on the last stage of stylism.

The "Prelude" made what he had done even more apparent, and surprisingly enough it became popular at once. Two features were immediately apparent. First, it had a unique and utterly individual aesthetic surface—a novel transparency of orchestral sound, for one thing—and that surface was characterized, if one could accept it at all, by an extraordinarily sensuous appeal. It is like the images and metaphors of Mallarmé, the landscapes of Cézanne, the Tahitian scenes of Gauguin; even if one does not understand them, even if they are mysterious, all these works have a seductive impact which, of the older composers, only Brahms, in these very years, achieved. They are novel and fresh; the color of the paintings, the imagery of the poetry, the sounds of the music, entice the aesthetic recipient by their directness and purity. A new aesthetic world is revealed.

The other feature was the use of a title derived from a poem, and in most of his subsequent works Debussy employs titles, sometimes of a fairly descriptive sort, such as the third part of "La Mer," "The Dialogue of the Wind and the Sea," or "Clouds," the first section of "Nocturnes." These titles are, however, not descriptive. The music is a symbol, or to use the more common word, an "impression" of the composer's response to some aspect of nature or some work of literature. The music is not a conventional sign nor an attempt to make a conventional sign for something in the world, in nature, or in literature. Rather, the title serves to objectify the music, to help composer and listener to understand that the conventional notion of what constitutes the psychic flow is exactly what the music is *not* about. Thus the music is no more about the sea or the sky than Cézanne's paintings are about the landscape.

The music is first of all concerned with creating an individual yet impersonal structure of sound, of innumerable relationships the possibility of which no one had ever seen before. Debussy, like Cézanne, worked very slowly. His major compositions were years in the writing, going through revision after revision; like Cézanne's paintings, they became increasingly more difficult to complete as they developed. This struggle for a unique structure is responsible for the transparency of sound, utterly opposed to the aural thickness which had been growing steadily in European music ever since the time of Beethoven, and for the clarity of the structure, so that one of his devices is exact repetition of a passage immediately after its first appearance. But second, the whole function of the musical distortions—and they became multitudinous and of increasing richness as his art developed—is to make it impossible to define in words or any other kind of sign exactly what response, what "impression," the music is symbolizing. It is instructive that attempts to use Debussy's compositions for ballets have been singularly unsuccessful, even when in later years he wrote music for a ballet, "Jeux" or "Games." When the "Prelude" was first presented, critics and some members of the public said that its effect was "to create an atmosphere," and what they meant is precisely this: the symbolization of an undefinable state of feeling, a state which could not be talked about by the conventional language for discussing emotions and which could not be assimilated into the traditional comprehension of emotions. Thus Debussy found the musical solution to the problem which tormented him and which had been the problem of music for nearly a hundred years: to express the inexpressible, and so create within the cultural tradition a pure crystalline sphere of feelings controlled by self-generated style and structure, a sphere which cultural tradition could neither penetrate nor shatter.

Mallarmé, Cézanne, Gauguin, Debussy—these are the artists who solved the problem of the nineteenth century: the creation of an aesthetic world which the Philistine could not enter without ceasing to be a Philistine. They created an aesthetic incarnation of value, a talisman which could release others from the nightmare of convention and awake them into a daylight of identity. The act of contemplating and experiencing the work of these men has the power to free the individual to redeem himself, to structure his own order, to achieve his own way of making experience meaningful, to create his own identity—out of nothingness. The problem of *Parsifal*, how the redeemer was to redeem himself, was solved. The orientative drive was, for the first time in human history, free to encounter reality, to see things as they are, and to experience freedom's terrible and dizzying dangers—and joy.

# CHAPTER XX

## *Beyond Tragedy*

O Mensch! Gib acht!
Was spricht die tiefe Mitternacht?
"Ich schlief, ich schlief—,
Aus tiefem Traum bin ich erwacht:—
Die Welt ist tief,
Und tiefer als der Tag gedacht.
Tief ist ihr Weh—,
Lust—tiefer noch als Herzeleid;
Weh spricht: Vergeh!
Doch alle Lust will Ewigkeit—,
—will tiefe, tiefe Ewigkeit!"

O man! Listen! What does the deep Midnight urge? "I slept, I slept—, from deep dreaming I am awakened:—the world is deep, and deeper than the day has thought. Deep is the world's woe—, joy—deeper still than agony; woe urges: Perish! Yet all of joy wants eternal being, wants deep, deep eternal being!"

THIS IS THE CLIMACTIC Song of the Midnight Bell in Part III of *Thus Spoke Zarathustra*, which Friedrich Nietzsche wrote in his fortieth year (he was born in 1844). It was in January, 1884, and Part III was published later that same year, Parts I and II having been published at different times in 1883. The midnight is the voice of the deepest forces in man, powers below the unconscious mind, below Schopenhauer's will, even, powers that unite man to the biological world, and beyond that to the forces of the universe.

The midnight, as Nietzsche came to realize, is the source of the human will to power, man's drive to dominate, control, and master his environment, not to adjust to it, for man cannot adjust to his environment. The effort to adjust is a will to submission, which leads to asceticism, to self-denial, to the desire to perish. The effort to adjust must always fail, for between man and his environment is an eternal disparity; man's mind is but an instrument of the midnight powers, and an instrument is necessarily other than the object it manipulates. Now the midnight is awakened from the profound slumber into which the will to submissive adjustment (what in this book is called the gratification of the orientative drive) had, throughout human history, cast it by its magic illusions.

The day, those human powers which make life fair and beautiful, had known that the world is deep, and that deep is the world's sorrow; that is why the day, the beneficent powers of Apollo, the god of the sun, had come to man's rescue. But the day had not known that the world's joy is deeper than its agony. Man's suffering says to him: Surrender, submit, give up, die, perish, vanish. But joy wants eternal being. If there were such a word, *"Ewigkeit"* would best be translated "foreverness." "Eternity," which is sometimes the word translators use, is wrong, for in the tradition of the English language it implies, as we have so often seen, something outside of the sensory world we know, something that transcends the reality before us. But by *"Ewigkeit"* Nietzsche means the power to reject the past and ignore the future—both are unrealities—and to live only in the eternal present, satisfying to its profoundest depths the drive toward reality. "Joy is deeper than sorrow"; it is what Mallarmé, Cézanne, and Gauguin were discovering in these same years. Like these artists, Nietzsche too found embodiment or incarnation of value in style, in art, and like them he found identity deeper than the level of personality, for personality is the realm of sorrow; it is also the realm of good and evil, of morality. Nietzsche, like his fellows, had to go beyond good and evil to discover moral responsibility.

Gauguin, in the passage I have quoted from, after he says

that one must insult the official, the impressionists, the neo-impressionists, the old public and the new, adds that one must also "no longer have a wife and children who disown you. Of what importance is insult? Of what importance is misery? So much for human conduct . . ." that is, morality as the Philistine knows it. And Gauguin had so perfectly expressed the heart of Nietzsche's thinking when he said that philosophy is not a reality but a weapon, that it seems almost impossible that he had not read the works of the German, who in 1888 could wish that he were writing in French, for cultural vitality, he was convinced, had left Germany—and England too—and was to be found only in France. Yet whether Gauguin had really read Nietzsche or not is of no importance; both men, born only four years apart, were the product of the same cultural forces; but Nietzsche went beyond the point the Frenchman had reached. The mind, Nietzsche realized, can only create weapons, instrumental constructs with which to come to grips with reality. His first transvaluation of all values—the evaluation of everything on a new principle—lay in precisely this realization, that "truths" are but "instruments," including "moral truths." As I suggested earlier, this is very much the position that Robert Browning was working out in the 1870's and 1880's. But then Nietzsche went beyond that position, and thus he went beyond the Frenchmen. To understand this it is useful to quote a passage near the end of Part IV of *Zarathustra*, which he wrote in 1885. It comes immediately after he has repeated the Song of the Midnight Bell.

> For all joy wants eternal being for all things; it wants honey, the dregs of wine, midnight, graves, the consolation of tears at the graveside, the gilded red of evening. What does joy not want! joy is thirstier, heartier, hungrier, more terrible, more secret than all woe, . . . joy wants love, hate; infinitely rich, joy gives, throws away, begs that someone take, thanks the taker, would like to be hated; so rich is joy that it thirsts for sorrow, for hell, for hate, for shame, for the crippled, for the *world*—and this world! oh, joy knows it well! . . . For joy wants itself; therefore it wants heart's agony. Oh happiness! Oh sorrow! Oh break, heart.

This is the reality which releases the joy that is deeper than sorrow, the world of contradictions that forces the human mind to create an instrumental construct to deal with it. The Frenchmen had seen that value arises when identity creates itself by symbolizing itself in aesthetic structure. But they remained turned away from the world of personality, society, and nature, for there lay the horror. Nietzsche, however, turned back toward the horror, for to him it was neither horror nor beauty. Since it was both hell and heaven, it was neither; it was simply there to be dealt with. And man deals with it not by one transvaluation of all values, but by a continuous transvaluation. A transvaluation creates new values, but these new values must themselves, since they are but instruments, be continually restructured. Hence, when in the 1890's and the first decade of this century, Nietzsche began to be recognized and read, he had a tremendous impact on art. For the artists, Matisse and Picasso, Schönberg and Joyce, the men of the new century, solved a problem the generation of Mallarmé and Gauguin and Debussy had bequeathed.

Once the artist has created a style which symbolizes his identity, what does he do with it? It threatens to degenerate into a mannerism; it keeps the artist active, busy, but his identity begins to fade. That happened to Gauguin and to Debussy, and would have happened to Cézanne had not his gigantic mind created an inexhaustible and almost unsolvable problem of aesthetic structure. The new artists, learning from Nietzsche, entered upon careers of continuously transforming their style, and this continuous transformation meant a continuous renewal of identity. It was an endless and ever joyful—witness Matisse in his half-crippled old age, still joyously creating—transvaluation of aesthetic values, for it was a continuously renewed encounter of the structuring mind with reality, the reality of style and the reality of sensory phenomena, (not, once a style has been created, that there is a difference). Abstract art arose to symbolize that inexhaustible, ever-renewing encounter.

Nietzsche discovered that the true dialogue of the mind is not, as Hegel had thought, a dialogue of the mind with itself, the process called the dialectic, but that the true dialectic lies in the eternally transvaluating encounter between the mind's instrumental constructs and reality in, to use the terminology of this book, a continuous restructuring of orientations. Further, in that dialectic process between reality and the mind's instruments lie identity, order, meaning, and therefore value, constantly being lost as the instruments dull and break on reality's contradictions, and constantly being renewed as the mind forges new instruments—Gauguin's weapons of savages—to renew the struggle to master the world. The world is nothingness; the midnight bell wakes us from that nothingness to struggle with nothingness, and in that struggle we forge, and continuously reforge, our identities. We cannot succeed in that struggle; nor, once the bell has sounded, can we fail. That struggle is a struggle of joy and sorrow, but the joy is deeper than the sorrow; for being, which is the result of that struggle, is, since we are human beings, better than nothingness.

Therefore, the man who has experienced the development of nineteenth-century culture—and there are very few who yet have—and has emerged where Nietzsche emerged can no longer entertain himself and the public with the tragic vision. He has gone beyond tragedy. Nietzsche found a resolution to the problem of keeping the antinomies, the contraries, the irreconcilable opposites of life, forever apart. Joy wants those opposites. To resolve them is to submit. Hence, Nietzsche created a new concept of tragedy.

> Saying Yes to life even in its strangest and hardest problems, the will to life rejoicing over its own inexhaustibility even in the very sacrifice of its highest types—that is what I call Dionysian [of the midnight] that is what I guessed to be the bridge to the psychology of the *tragic poet*. Not in order to be liberated from terror and pity, not in order to purge oneself of a dangerous affect by its vehement discharge—Aristotle understood it that way—but in order to be *oneself* the eternal joy of becoming, beyond all terror and pity—that joy which includes even joy in destroying.

But this is to use the word "tragic" in such a profoundly new way that no connection between the old meaning and the new survives. We are aware of this when we see our critics fumble with the best of modern drama, Shaw's *Heartbreak House,* for example, Samuel Beckett, or Ionesco. In truth, no truly twentieth-century man can write a tragedy. For twentieth-century man is but a continuation of nineteenth-century man, and Nietzsche's vision has been but sharpened and refined by the existentialists, the logical positivists, and the instrumentalists and operationalists, among whom is P. W. Bridgman, whose recent *The Way Things Are* is a most brilliant, scientific, and satisfying example of the stage of thinking Nietzsche reached. Nor can a truly twentieth-century man write a comedy, either.

Tragedy is supposed to be a profounder vision of human life than comedy, but from the Nietzschean point of view, they are both sentimentalities which man has outgrown. It has been said that tragedy reconciles us to life. Perfectly true. Tragedy is a dramatization of the orientation that man is inadequate to the conditions that life imposes upon us; it shows a great man failing, whether from the ill-will of the gods or from some internal weakness of which he is unaware and for which he cannot, therefore, be held responsible. And therefore tragedy says to us, "If even an Oedipus can fail, if even a Lear can fail, you can forgive yourselves if you fail. Relax!" Hence the discharge of emotional tension which Aristotle so indelicately called "catharsis." In short, tragedy reconciles us to life by persuading us to submit to it. Tragedy encourages what Nietzsche calls the slave-morality of the Philistine. It was by origin, as Nietzsche was one of the first to realize, a religious ritual, and it remains a religious ritual. It consoles us by reinforcing our orientations. Hence, after seeing a tragedy, after seeing murder and incest and the most brutal violations of personality and feeling, we leave the theater with an extraordinary sense of comfort, convinced that all is well with the world. And to tragedy, comedy is complementary. For comedy is a dramatization of the orientation that man is *adequate* to the conditions of experience, that, if he uses his wits, he can triumph over them. Thus the hero of the comedy is not a great man but a very ordinary man, a man like us. Comedy says, "Be consoled. If this very ordinary person can succeed, you can." Both

comedy and tragedy reconcile the antinomies, resolve the contradictions, expunge the contraries and the opposites of human experience, the one by saying that they do not exist, the other by saying
that it is good and right and just that they should exist.

But Nietzsche, in arriving at the the third and, it would
seem, the last stage of stylism, at least so far, the continuous renewal
of identity by continuous transformation and transvaluation of style
in art, in thought, and in individuality, realized that man is neither
adequate nor inadequate, that he has grown beyond the old tragic
vision, and the old comic vision, that to gratify the orientative drive,
man must neither reject the world in the ancient fashion, nor accept it in the Enlightenment fashion. It is neither a world which
once held value nor a world which holds value now. From the
human point of view, which is all that matters to man, it is without
value; nor is there another, transcendental world—Nietzsche was
the first to assert roundly that God is dead—from which we
descend, or to which we can ascend, or which is the ground of
being. The world is without order, without meaning, without
value. Human identity has no ground. The world is nothing, but
in emerging from that nothingness and in encountering it, we create
being. The profoundest satisfaction of the human mind, Nietzsche
concluded, is the creation of the world—out of nothingness. From
that act of creation emerges the sense of value; and the sense of
order, the sense of meaning, and the sense of identity are but our
instruments for that act. Joy is deeper than sorrow.

Thus Nietzsche solved the problem of the nineteenth century. We have seen how it arose when the Enlightenment failed to
make a consistent structure of primitive Hebrew, Greek, and Christian thinking. We have seen how the collapse of the world's structure led to pure negation, and then to turning the world inside out.
We have seen how the self was discovered, and a ground for value
was re-established by analogy between the self and the world. This
revealed the nature of the problem: What is the ground for value?
We have seen how that solution created problems which destroyed
it, and analogism was succeeded by transcendentalism, and how

that too failed. We have seen the greater and more solid success of objectism, but how that too failed to find a ground for value and was succeeded by stylism. From the last stage of stylism, we saw, Nietzsche emerged with the answer. There is no ground to value; man joyfully creates it out of suffering and nothingness, simply in order to exist; nor does he will to exist; from that nothingness flows an incomprehensible power which sounds the midnight bell and brings him into an existence which he, and he alone, unaided, and for no reason, earthly or transcendental, redeems.

One cannot resist wondering what developments have taken place since. Has Nietzsche's version of stylism been succeeded by anything that has replaced it? Has it created a problem which, in order to solve, requires us to go beyond it? Possibly not. After all, ancient thinking lasted for untold centuries, and for the over-whelmingly vast majority of mankind survives today, and a good part of the time survives in all of us; much of Nietzsche's personal-ity was, in this sense, ancient. The nineteenth century, then, may have been, in terms of high-level and advanced culture, an age of transition to the last stage of stylism, to the Nietzschean vision, which may prove serviceable far into the future.

But then, on the other hand, cultural forces are obscure; they work darkly. Man symbolizes before he conceptualizes, and only down great perspectives of time do we see the parallels in symbolizations, and the relation of symbol to concept. Perhaps today, at levels we cannot be aware of, a profound transvaluation of Nietzsche's concept of transvaluation is occurring. Sometimes one feels a difference and sometimes one does not. We must always remember, however, that even though the past begins to have struc-ture only when we look down long historical perspectives, the past is, in fact, irrecoverable.

Is the structuring of nineteenth-century culture and what led up to it that I have offered here in any sense reliable? Is it true? But that is the wrong question. As a cultural product of the twentieth century, that is, according to this book, of the last stage of nineteenth-century development, I have not pretended to offer the truth. I offer, instead, as I promised in the beginning, an instrumental construct. It was not made to explain the past; it was made to relate certain major documents and artifacts which appeared during a crucial period in human history, and in turn to relate them to others which I have not mentioned. It was made to make those artifacts and documents, which are all that truly exist, more comprehensible. The instrument I have presented here was not made to be believed; it was made to be used—to be used and to be tested. And for that testing the nineteenth century offers incalculable and infinite riches.

# Index

Antoine, André (1857?–1943), 358
Aristotle (384–322 B.C.), 369
Arnold, Matthew (1822–1888), 319-320

Bach, Johann Sebastian (1685–1750),
 152, 258, 259, 264-265, 326-327
Bacon, Francis (1561–1626), 70-71, 73,
 187, 260
Balakirev, Mili Alekseevich (1837–
 1910), 359
Balzac, Honoré de (1799–1850), 183-
 184, 186-196, 197, 198, 199, 202, 203,
 206, 211, 216, 218, 221, 230, 237, 238,
 243, 248, 250, 266, 273, 274, 287-288,
 289, 294-295, 308-309, 335
 *The Human Comedy*, 191, 195, 197,
  198, 199
 *Louis Lambert*, 189, 190
 *Père Goriot*, 190
 *Scenes of Military Life*, 194
 *Scenes of Political Life*, 194
 *Scenes of Private Life*, 194
 *Séraphita*, 189
 *Social Studies*, 194
 *The Search for the Absolute*, 187,
  190
Baudelaire, Charles (1821–1867), 206,
 215-216, 218, 219, 220, 221, 240-241,
 272, 276-279, 283, 292-293, 315, 316,
 331, 335, 348, 355, 358, 361
 *Flowers of Evil*, 276, 278-279, 292,
  316
Beaumont, Sir George (1753–1827),
 136, 139-140, 142
Beckett, Samuel (1906–    ), 369
Beethoven, Ludwig van (1770–1827),
 148, 150, 152-160, 163-167, 171, 172,
 175, 177, 178, 181, 186, 199-201, 202,
 203, 204, 208, 210, 212, 214, 216,
 266, 267, 279, 286, 358, 362
 *Fidelio*, 153-154
 Missa Solemnis, 153, 163, 208
 String Quartets Nos. 12-15, 163-167,
  208, 266
 Symphony No. 3, 156-157
 Symphony No. 5, 157-160, 163, 167
 Symphony No. 6, 167, 210
 Symphony No. 7, 154
 Symphony No. 9, 163, 208
 "Wellington's Victory," 201
Berlioz, Hector (1803–1869), 153, 198-
 208, 211, 212, 213, 214, 216, 235, 237,
 243, 264, 265, 266, 279
 "The Damnation of Faust," 201, 202,
  203, 213
 "Eight Scenes from *Faust*," 201, 203,
  216
 "Harold in Italy," 201, 202, 203, 204
 "The Infant Christ," 203
 "King Lear," 201, 202
 "Lélio," 201, 211
 "Rob Roy," 201
 "Romeo and Juliet," 201, 203, 213
 "Symphonie Fantastique," 201, 203,
  211
 "The Tempest," 201
 "Two Scenes from *Hamlet*," 201
 "Waverley," 201
Beyle, Marie Henri: see Stendhal
Bible 68, 261, 329
 Genesis, 46-51, 59
 Gospel according to St. John, 52, 122
 Job, 49, 51
 Revelation, 51, 64

Blake, William (1757–1827), 106, 220
Bonington, Richard Parkes (1802–1828), 223
Borodin, Alexander (1834–1887), 359
Bouguereau, Adolphe William (1825–1905)
Brahms, Johannes (1833–1897), 214, 272, 281, 326-331, 340, 361
  Clarinet Sonatas, Op. 120, 329
  Clarinet Quintet, Op. 115, 329
  Clarinet Trio, Op. 114, 329
  "Four Serious Songs," 329, 330
  "A German Requiem," 326
  Piano pieces, Op. 116-119, 329
  String Quintet, Op. 111, 328
  Symphony No. 4, 329
Brentano, Bettina (1785–1859), 150, 153, 154
Bridgman, Percy Williams (1882–1961), 369
Browning, Robert (1812–1889), 259, 273-276, 291-292, 293, 295, 366
  In a Balcony, 275
  Men and Women, 275
  Paracelsus, 273-274, 291
  The Ring and the Book, 259, 275-276, 293-294
  Sordello, 274, 276, 291-292, 293
Bruckner, Anton (1824–1896), 279-284, 285-286, 291, 294, 327, 328
Brunelleschi, Filippo (1377?-1446), 70
Buddha, Guatama (563?-?483 B.C.), 175, 264
Bunyan, John (1628–1688), 72
Burns, Robert (1759–1796), 89, 178
Byron, George Gordon, Lord (1788–1824), 100-107, 119, 156, 159, 166, 172, 179, 192, 201, 202, 208, 216, 235, 236, 307, 315, 356
  The Bride of Abydos, 101
  Cain, 103
  Childe Harold, 101-103, 105, 179, 191, 192, 202, 244, 307
  Don Juan, 101, 104-107, 109, 159, 166, 192, 216, 221, 307
  The Giaour, 101, 103
  Lara, 103, 108, 192
  Manfred, 101, 102, 103, 104, 105, 106, 107, 108, 124, 174, 179, 192, 236, 244, 254, 307

Calderón de la Barca, Pedro (1600–1681), 166
Carlyle, Thomas (1795–1881), 108, 176, 177-189, 191, 199, 201, 216, 218, 219, 221, 230, 235, 236, 237, 238, 241, 243, 248, 250, 274, 308-309, 336.
Cézanne, Paul (1839–1906), 299, 344-352, 355, 357, 358, 361, 362, 363, 365, 367
Charles II, King of England (1630–1685), 62
Charles X, King of France (1757–1836), 199
Chateaubriand, François René de (1768–1848), 205
Cherubini, M. L. C. Z. A. (1760–1842), 200
Chesterfield, Philip Dormer Stanhope, Earl of (1694–1773), 88
Chopin, Frédéric (1810–1849), 153, 207, 264
Christ, 45, 51, 58, 69, 130, 198, 264, 301
Coleridge, Samuel Taylor (1772–1834), 112-113, 116, 136, 140, 145, 172, 192, 197, 209, 302
  "Christabel," 209
  "The Ancient Mariner," 145, 209, 210, 246
  "Kubla Khan," 113, 209, 302
Constable, John (1776–1837), 136-145, 146, 149, 153, 157, 165, 166, 176, 204, 210, 219, 220, 221, 222, 224, 272, 297, 345
Constant, Benjamin (1767–1830), 205
Cooper, James Fenimore (1789–1851), 191
Copernicus, Nicolaus (1473–1543), 71
Courbet, Gustave (1819–1877), 296-297, 303
Cui, César (1835–1918), 359

Dante Alighieri (1265–1321), 119, 195
Danton, Georges (1759–1794), 110
Darwin, Charles (1809–1882), 295-296
David, Jacques Louis (1748–1825), 153
Debussy, Achille Claude (1862–1918) 268, 354-363, 367
  "String Quartet," 361
  "Games," 362
  "Prelude to The Afternoon of a Faun," 361, 362
  "The Sea," 361-362
  "Suite Bergamasque," 361
DeGaulle, Charles (1890–    ), 206
Defoe, Daniel (1659?-1731), 79-80, 230
  Robinson Crusoe, 79-80
Delacroix, Eugène (1799–1863), 198-199, 206, 215-221, 224-225, 241, 264, 296-297, 323, 345
  "The Abduction of Rebecca," 220

Delacroix, Eugène (*Cont.*)
"Liberty Leading the People," 219
Lithographs for *Faust*, 216-219, 225
Lithographs for *Goetz von Berlichingen*, 217
"Scenes from the Massacre at Chios," 219
De Quincey, Thomas (1785-1859), 201
deSade, Marquis (1740-1814), 81, 101
Descartes, René (1596-1650), 78
Diderot, Denis (1713-1784), 83
Disraeli, Benjamin (1804-1881), 235, 236
Donne, John (1573-1631), 291
Dostoyevsky, Fëdor (1821-1881), 272
Dryden, John (1631-1700), 312
Dvorák, Anton (1841-1904), 272

Eliot, Thomas Stearns (1888-    ), 341
Ellison, Ralph (1914-    ), 102
Emerson, Ralph Waldo (1803-1882), 179, 216, 221, 230, 236

Faulkner, William (1897-    ), 103
Feuerbach, Ludwig Andreas (1804-1872), 238, 249, 260
Fitzgerald, Edward (1809-1883), 42, 45, 48
Flaubert, Gustave (1821-1880), 206, 276-278, 286-289, 294
   *Madame Bovary*, 276-278, 286-289
   *Salammbô*, 294
   *A Sentimental Education*, 276
Fourdrinier, Henry (1766-1854) and Sealy (d. 1847), 26
Fragonard, Jean Honoré (1732-1806), 137
Franklin, Benjamin (1706-1790), 14, 61
Freud, Sigmund (1856-1939), 182, 251, 256, 272
Friedrich, Caspar David (1774-1840), 129-136, 137, 138, 141, 142, 144, 153, 155, 156, 157, 166, 172, 176, 204, 210, 220, 222, 223, 297, 345
   "The Cross in the Mountains," 130, 141
   "Monk on the Seashore," 131, 223

Gainsborough, Thomas (1727-1788), 137
Galileo, (1564-1642), 71
Gall, Franz Joseph (1758-1828), 194
Gauguin, Paul (1848-1903), 344, 350-358, 359, 361, 363, 365, 366, 367, 368

Gautier, Théophile (1811-1872), 198
Géricault, Théodore (1791-1824), 205
Gibbon, Edward (1737-1794), 178
Giorgione, Il (c. 1478-1511), 301
Glazunov, Alexander (1865-1936), 359
Gluck, Christoph Willibald (1714-1787), 154, 156
Goethe, Johann Wolfgang von (1749-1832), 87-93, 94, 98, 101, 109, 118-128, 131, 135, 155, 156, 157, 160, 166, 167, 175, 176, 178, 179, 185, 192, 193, 201, 203, 206, 208, 213, 216, 217, 222, 224, 236, 245, 255, 334
   *Faust: A Fragment*, 119, 160
   *Faust: A Tragedy*, 101, 118-128, 130, 132, 135, 157, 166, 174, 192, 201, 213, 216, 245, 248, 249, 253, 255
   *Goetz von Berlichingen*, 217
   *The Sorrows of Young Werther*, 87-93, 94, 97, 98, 101, 102, 106, 119, 130, 155, 179, 181, 191, 217, 222, 235, 254, 278, 334
   *Urfaust*, 119
   *Wilhelm Meister*, 178
Goldsmith, Oliver (1728-1774), 87-88
Grant, Ulysses S. (1822-1885), 230
Grillparzer, Franz (1791-1872), 280-281

Hals, Franz (1580?-1666), 143
Handel, George Frederick (1685-1759), 152, 156
Hanslick, Eduard (1825-1904), 279-281, 327
Haydn, Joseph (1732-1809), 152, 155, 156
Hegel, Georg Wilhelm Friedrich (1770-1831), 169-172, 176, 235, 274, 295, 367
Heine, Heinrich, (1795-1856), 198, 208, 233, 244
Herder, Johann Gottfried von (1744-1803), 35-38, 249, 288
Hitler, Adolf (1889-    ), 170, 241
Hoffmann, Ernst Theodor Amadeus (1776-1822), 209-211
Hokusai (1760-1849), 360
Hugo, Victor (1802-1885), 198, 206
Hume, David (1711-1776), 94, 96, 98, 178
Huysmans, Joris Karl (1848-1907), 324-325

Ionesco, Eugène (1912-    ), 369

Jeans, Sir James (1877–     ), 188
Jefferson, Thomas (1743–1826), 14, 61
Johnson, Samuel (1709–1784), 121
Joyce, James (1882–1941), 367
Jung, Carl Gustav (1875–     ), 264

Kant, Immanuel (1724–1804), 93-98,
    107, 115, 117, 132, 146, 148, 169, 172,
    181, 184, 185, 187, 251
  *The Critique of Judgment*, 93, 181
  *The Critique of Practical Reason*,
    169
  *The Critique of Pure Reason*, 93-98,
    169, 181
Keats, John (1795–1821), 113, 114
Kennedy, John F. (1917–     ), 63
Kerouac, Jack (1922–     ), 102
Kleist, Heinrich von (1777–1811), 131,
    222
  *Michael Kohlhaus*, 131

Lavater, Johann Kaspar (1741–1801),
    194
Lawrence, David Herbert (1885–
    1930), 101
Lee, Robert E. (1807–1870), 230
Lekeu, Guillaume (1870–1894), 358
Lesueur, Jean François (1760–1837),
    199-200
Lincoln, Abraham (1809–1865), 18,
    230
Linnaeus, Carolus (1707–1778), 35
Liszt, Franz von (1811–1886), 198, 265
Locke, John (1632–1704), 79
Lorrain, Claude (1600–1682), 222
Louis XVIII, King of France (1755–
    1824), 199
Luther, Martin (1483–1546), 64

Macaulay, Thomas Babington (1800–
    1859), 230
Mallarmé, Stéphane (1842–1898), 331-
    342, 348-350, 351, 353, 354, 355, 357,
    358, 359, 361, 363, 365, 367
Malthus, Thomas Robert (1733–1834),
    295
Manet, Édouard (1832–1883), 296-302,
    343, 345, 347
  "The Dead Christ," 301-302
  "The Execution of Maximilian," 300
  "Olympia," 300-301
  "The Picnic," 300
Mann, Thomas (1875–1955), 13-14
  *Joseph and his Brothers*, 13-14
Mantegna, Andrea (1431–1506), 324

Marx, Karl (1818–1883), 171, 176, 199,
    235
Matisse, Henri (1869–1954), 367
Medici, Catherine de (1519–1589),
    235
Melville, Herman (1819–1891), 272,
    278
  *Moby-Dick*, 278
Mendelssohn, Felix (1809–1847), 265
Michelangelo Buonarroti (1475–1564),
    70, 323, 324
Milton, John (1608–1674), 63-64, 71,
    119, 222
  *Paradise Lost*, 63-64, 119
Monet, Claude (1840–1926), 138, 323
Montesquieu, Charles, Baron de (1689–
    1755), 87
Moreau, Gustave (1826–1898), 322-325,
    340, 346, 351
  "The Apparition," 324-325
  "Jupiter and Semele," 324-325
Morice, Charles (1861–1919), 353
Morris, William (1834–1896), 312, 346
Mozart, Wolfgang Amadeus (1756–
    1791), 103-104, 152, 155, 156, 200,
    202, 216, 258
Mühlfeld, Richard (1856–1907), 329,
    331
Moussorgsky, Modest (1835–1881), 359

Napoleon I, Emperor of France (1769–
    1821), 108, 131, 153, 199
Napoleon III, Emperor of France
    (1808–1873), 321, 331
Nerval Gérard de (1808–1855), 201,
    217
Newton, Sir Isaac (1642–1727), 78
Nietzsche, Friedrich (1844–1900), 30,
    260, 364-371
  *Beyond Good and Evil*, 30
  *The Birth of Tragedy*, 30
  *Thus Spake Zarathustra* 364-368

Pater, Walter Horatio (1839–1894), 146
Phelps, William Lyon (1865–1943),
    147-148
Picasso, Pablo (1881–     ), 367
Pissarro, Camille (1830–1903), 343
Plato (427?–347 B.C.), 52-60, 68, 70,
    148, 313, 353
Poe, Edgar Allan (1809–1849), 331
Pope, Alexander (1688–1744), 28, 73-
    74, 80, 88, 312
  *The Dunciad*, 74
  *An Essay on Man*, 74, 80

Poussin, Nicolas (1594-1665), 221
Proust, Marcel (1871-1922), 315

Raphael Sanzio (1438-1520), 70, 323
Redon, Odilon (1840-1916), 351
Rembrandt van Rijn (1606-1669), 143
Renoir, Pierre Auguste (1841-1919), 298, 299, 343
Richardson, Samuel (1689-1761), 87
Richter, Jean Paul Friedrich (1763-1825), 209, 210, 211
Rimbaud, Arthur (1854-1891), 293, 296, 355
Rimski-Korsakov, Nikolai, (1844-1908), 359
Robespierre, Maximilien de (1758-1794), 76, 171
Rosa, Salvator (1615-1673), 137
Rossetti, Dante Gabriel (1828-1882), 312
Rossini, Gioacchino (1792-1868), 200
Rubens, Peter Paul (1577-1640), 139, 220
Ruskin, John (1819-1900), 139, 222, 223, 271-272, 289-290, 294, 296, 298, 299, 345, 347
Russell, Bertrand (1872-    ), 56

Sacher-Masoch, Leopold von (1836-1895), 262, 315
St. Augustine (354-430), 58-60
St. Francis (1182-1226), 175
St.-Hilaire, Etienne Geoffroy (1772-1844), 194
Sand, George (1803-1876), 198
Sappho (? 600 B.C.), 315-316
Schiller, Johann Christoph Friedrich von (1759-1805), 163
Schönberg, Arnold (1874-1951), 367
Schopenhauer, Arthur (1788-1860), 98, 100, 147-151, 159, 165, 166, 172-176, 186, 190, 202, 236, 250, 251, 255, 268, 273, 279, 295, 345, 364
Schubert, Franz (1797-1828), 152, 153, 177, 212
Schumann, Clara (1819-1896), 330
Schumann, Robert (1810-1856), 153, 205-214, 216, 218, 233, 241, 264, 266, 267, 279, 285-286
    "Butterflies," 211
    "Carnaval," 211, 212
    "A Carnival Prank from Vienna: Fantasy Images," 211
    "The Dances of the Company of David," 211

Schumann, Robert (Cont.)
    Fantasia in C Major, 211
    "Fantasy Pieces," 210-211
    Impromptu on a Theme by Clara Wieck, 212
    Intermezzi, 211
    "Kreisleriana," 210
    "Nightpiece," 210
    "A Poet's Love," 208
    Symphonic Etudes, 212, 213
    Variations on the Name Abegg, 212
Schweitzer, Albert (1875-    ), 101
Scopes, John T. (1901-    ), 62
Scott, Sir Walter (1771-1832), 191-193, 201, 202, 208, 209, 216, 220, 352
Senancour, Pivert de (1770-1846), 205
Seurat, Georges (1859-1891), 343-344
Shakespeare, William (1564-1616), 65-66, 112, 201, 203, 208, 213, 216, 265, 280
    Hamlet, 217, 337
    King Lear, 65-66, 369
    Measure for Measure, 265
    Romeo and Juliet, 202
Shaw, George Bernard, (1856-1950), 369
Shelley, Percy Bysshe (1792-1822), 106, 291
Sherman, William T. (1820-1891), 230
Sisley, Alfred (1830-1899), 299
Smith, Adam (1723-1790), 76
Smith, Alfred E. (1873-    ), 63
Southey, Robert (1774-1843), 140
Spenser, Edmund (1552?-1599), 64-65
Stael, Mme. de (1766-1817), 179, 187, 205
Stendhal (1783-1842), 107-111, 119, 156, 281, 307
    The Scarlet and the Black, 107-111
Stevens, Wallace (1879-1955), 28
Sterne, Laurence (1713-1768), 178
Swedenborg, Emanuel (1688-1772), 189
Swift, Jonathan (1667-1745), 178
Swinburne, Algernon Charles (1837-1909), 311-325, 326, 327-328, 329, 331, 340
    Atalanta in Calydon, 315, 319-321, 327
    Poems and Ballads, 315-316, 327
Symonds, John Addington (1840-1893), 315

Tchaikovsky, Peter Ilyitch (1840-1893), 328

Tennyson, Alfred (1809–1892), 196-197, 229, 245, 246, 292-293
*The Idylls of the King,* 293
*In Memoriam,* 245
"The Lady of Shalott," 196-197
*Maud,* 292-293
Titian (1477-1576), 220, 301
Tolstoy, Leo (1828-1910), 272
Toynbee, Arnold (1889–    ), 19
Turgenev, Ivan (1818-1883), 272
Turner, Joseph Mallord William (1775-1851), 222-225, 229, 297, 299, 322, 323, 345
    "Burning of the Houses of Parliament," 223
    "Interior at Petworth," 224-225
    "Rain, Steam, and Speed," 223
    "Steamer in a Snowstorm," 223-224

Van Gogh, Vincent (1853-1890), 142, 222, 352
Velásquez, Diego (1599-1660), 301
Verlaine, Paul (1844-1896), 361
Veronese, Paolo (1528-1588), 220, 221
Vinci, Leonardo da (1452-1519), 70, 323, 324
Voltaire (1694-1778), 63, 72, 81, 83
    *Candide,* 81

Wagner, Richard (1813-1883), 164, 210, 237, 240-270, 271, 273, 276, 278, 279, 280, 281, 282, 283, 285-286, 294, 310-312, 317, 319-321, 326, 327, 335, 340, 358-360
*The Fairies,* 265
*The Flying Dutchman,* 242, 243, 244-246, 250, 265, 266, 268, 285
*Lohengrin,* 242, 243, 247-248, 250, 252, 253, 258, 260, 263, 264, 267, 274, 285
*The Love Ban,* 265

Wagner, Richard (*Cont.*)
*The Meistersinger of Nürnberg,* 243, 254, 257-260, 262, 263, 265, 279, 285, 291, 294, 312, 326, 327, 359
*Parsifal,* 164, 243, 260-263, 265, 269, 270, 276, 301, 302, 310-311, 312, 314, 315, 321, 325, 330, 337, 359, 360, 363
*Rienzi,* 265
*The Ring of the Nibelung,* 242, 243, 245-255, 256, 257, 260, 265, 267, 269, 270, 272, 274, 279, 280, 285, 293, 312, 317, 327, 360
*Siegfried's Death,* 249
*Tannhäuser,* 242, 243, 246-247, 251, 267, 285
*Tristan and Isolde,* 242, 243, 254, 255-257, 260, 265-275, 280, 285, 312, 319-321, 358, 359, 360
Walpole, Horace (1717-1797), 88
Watteau, Jean Antoine (1684-1721), 137, 220
Weston, Edward (1886–    ), 298
Whistler, James McNeill (1834-1903), 344
Whitney, Eli (1765-1825), 27
Wilde, Oscar (1856-1900), 24, 318-319, 346
Wilson, Woodrow (1856-1924), 36
Wordsworth, Dorothy (1771-1855), 116, 197
Wordsworth, William (1770-1850), 111, 112-119, 122, 129, 130, 132, 133, 135, 136, 138, 139, 140, 141, 142, 144, 153, 157, 166, 169, 171, 172, 176, 192, 197, 209, 210, 274, 291, 297
*The Excursion,* 114
*Lyrical Ballads,* 140
*The Prelude,* 112-118, 133, 140, 157, 171
*The Recluse,* 113-114
"Tintern Abbey," 140, 144

Zola, Emile (1840-1902), 294-296, 299, 348, 358